A STOP TO
THE SHEDDING
OF BLOOD

BCC
PRESS

BY COMMON CONSENT PRESS is a non-profit publisher dedicated to producing affordable, high-quality books that help define and shape the Latter-day Saint experience. BCC Press publishes books that address all aspects of Mormon life. Our mission includes finding manuscripts that will contribute to the lives of thoughtful Latter-day Saints, mentoring authors and nurturing projects to completion, and distributing important books to the Mormon audience at the lowest possible cost.

Drawing critically on René Girard's theory of mimetic rivalry, Alan Goff offers a deeply theoretical examination of violence in the Book of Mormon. Goff navigates the charged intersections of divine command, human conscience, and covenantal obligation through close readings of the Book of Mormon's morally complex narratives: Nephi's execution of Laban, Abinadi's martyrdom, Captain Moroni's summary justice, and the theological puzzles of righteous warfare. Engaging phenomenology, virtue ethics, and other critical lenses, Goff demonstrates that the Nephite record is no simple morality tale but rather "saturated scripture" that demands repeated engagement.

This volume takes seriously the Book of Mormon's standing as Hebraic scripture and confronts its portrayals of divinely sanctioned violence. Goff argues that covenant requires robust ethical reflection: like Abraham bargaining for Sodom, readers must wrestle with the moral tensions embedded in sacred narrative. For scholars of Restoration scripture, students of religious ethics, and thoughtful believers seeking to deepen their engagement with difficult texts, this book models "the works of Abraham," who refused to evade the abundant, excessive, and troubling encounters with the divine that scripture records.

Erudite, theoretical, and respectful, this work gives us a Book of Mormon worthy of the most rigorous moral and theological scrutiny.

—Rosalynde Welch
Research Fellow and Associate Director, BYU Maxwell Institute
Author of *Seven Songs: Christ in the Old Testament*
and *Ether: A Brief Theological Introduction*

I always appreciate an author who can challenge my assumptions and open my heart to new ways of loving an already beloved text. Alan Goff delivers. By exploring both the remarkable possibilities and significant limitations of applying a Girardian lens to the Book of Mormon, Goff beautifully illustrates how the overflowing abundance of that inspired narrative stubbornly resists monolithic analysis and continues, as we should expect, to surprise and unsettle its readers.

—J. David Pulsipher
Professor of History, Brigham Young University–Idaho
Co-author of *Proclaim Peace: The Restoration's Answer to an Age of Conflict*, and co-editor of *War and Peace in Our Time: The Mormon Perspectives*

ALAN GOFF

A STOP TO
THE SHEDDING
OF BLOOD

THE BOOK OF MORMON, VIOLENCE, & THE SACRED

A Stop to the Shedding of Blood: Book of Mormon Narrative,
Violence, and the Sacred
Copyright © 2025 by Alan Goff

For information contact
By Common Consent Press
972 East Burnham Lane
Draper, Utah 84020

Cover design: D Christian Harrison
Book design: Andrew Heiss

www.bccpress.org

ISBN-13: 978-1-961471-25-2

10 9 8 7 6 5 4 3 2 1

To Helga, my wife, who well knows that having a spouse who has a calling as a writer accepts that the division of labor called for by such a vocation means many hours finding other work and distractions while the research and composition are advancing in the next room. But writing is commonly by necessity a solitary craft. I dedicate the results to you with love and gratitude, hoping it is some small recompense for the sheetrock repairs, painting of walls and bookcases, reading, visiting with friends, and a multitude of other deeds you performed while my writing efforts moved forward.

Therefore, it is expedient that there should be a great and last sacrifice, and then shall there be, or it is expedient there should be, a stop to the shedding of blood; then shall the law of Moses be fulfilled; yea, it shall be all fulfilled, every jot and tittle, and none shall have passed away. And behold, this is the whole meaning of the law, every whit pointing to that great and last sacrifice; and that great and last sacrifice will be the Son of God, yea, infinite and eternal.

Alma 34:13–14

For I desired mercy and not sacrifice, and the knowledge of God more than burnt offerings.

Hosea 6:6

But if ye had known what this meaneth, I will have mercy, and not sacrifice, ye would not have condemned the guiltless.

Matthew 12:7

We all exist inside some kind of religion.

René Girard[1]

1. Richard J. Golsan, *René Girard and Myth: An Introduction* (New York: Garland, 1993), 129.

Contents

On Violence and the Sacred

For my thoughts are not your thoughts, neither are your ways my ways, saith the Lord. For as the heavens are higher than the earth, so are my ways higher than your ways, and my thoughts than your thoughts.

Isaiah 55:8–9

Believe in God; believe that he is, and that he created all things, both in heaven and in earth; believe that he has all wisdom, and all power, both in heaven and in earth; believe that man doth not comprehend all the things which the Lord can comprehend.

Mosiah 4:9

René Girard (1923–2015) was a French-born theorist who spent most of his academic life in the United States. His theories have broad and increasing influence in discussions about religion, history, myth, literature, psychology, anthropology, and economics worldwide. His studies range across a broad number of fields. However, when it comes to his readings of the Bible and the western tradition, he disclaims being a theologian; rather, he sees himself as an anthropologist articulating "the distinctly anthropological perspective that he finds the Hebraic and Christian scriptural texts offering us."[1] His personal trajectory from atheism to Catholicism runs counter to the current of modern and postmodern thought among Western intellectuals with the spreading secularism in academia, media, government, and other social institutions. Girard is a careful and innovative reader, not just of the Bible but of other religious and literary texts in a variety of traditions. Girard is totally unlike the fox, with its many small truths, but is a hedgehog,[2] finding his one preoccupation with the singular origins of violence in all texts, all cultures, all historical conditions, all religions, all wars, all legal systems, and penal codes. He finds the same root of violence in all these contexts because his system posits a universal human nature. Pardon me if my disposition as a fox makes me dubious of Girard's monomaniacal approach that

---

1. Sandor Goodhart and Ann W. Astell, "Substitutive Reading: An Introduction to Girardian Thinking, Its Reception in Biblical Studies, and This Volume," in *Sacrifice, Scripture, and Substitution*, eds. Ann W. Astwell and Sandor Goodhart, 1–36 (Notre Dame, IN: University of Notre Dame Press, 2011), 9.

2. Isaiah Berlin begins his study of Tolstoy's philosophy of history with a fragment from Archilochus, an ancient Greek poet: "The fox knows many things, but the hedgehog knows one big thing." Girard is like the hedgehog "who relate[s] everything to a single central vision, one system less or more coherent or articulate, in terms of which they understand, think and feel—a single universal, organizing principle in terms of which alone all that they are and say has significance." The fox, contrary to the hedgehog's one grand truth, knows many small truths. These foxes "pursue many ends, often unrelated and even contradictory, connected, if at all, only in some *de facto* way, for some psychological or physiological cause, related by no single moral or aesthetic principle" (Isaiah Berlin, *The Hedgehog and the Fox: An Essay on Tolstoy's View of History* [New York: Touchstone, 1986], 1). These latter foxes, which I confess to being one, don't feel the need to fit every detail into that one cosmic system and are comfortable with different parts of their worldview clashing with other parts. Gary Saul Morson has elaborated on Tolstoy's view of history beyond Berlin's little parable. Morson (in *Hidden in Plain View: Narrative and Creative Potentials in "War and Peace"* [Stanford, CA: Stanford University Press, 1987]) elaborates on this Tolstoyan view that systematic thinkers do great violence to the world when they, like Procrustes, make their beds and guests fit one way or another. Tolstoy was clearly a fox, a skeptic about the possibility of historical knowledge, who believed that novelists and historians fashion out of unconnected and fragmented details a coherent and structured account that couldn't possibly be inherent in the original events but is contributed by the writer or historian rather than the world or events in themselves.

results in a monocausal explanation of variegated and diverse phenomena and historical events. Girard follows the general Christian trend of seeing in the Old Testament a prefiguration of the Christian revelation and in the New Testament a culmination of the movement toward a renunciation of violence and scapegoating in the Hebrew Bible, but with a huge difference. Beginning with Girard himself and followed up by his acolytes, Girardian biblical readings reveal new details that its readers for millennia had not noticed or had suppressed and a unifying structure that connects those details into an overarching system. These readings shine a whole new light on the biblical project. As Girard's insights are now being productively applied to the Jewish, Christian, and Muslim sacred texts, so also are they beginning to be applied to texts in the restoration tradition, particularly the Book of Mormon.

The initial and most important transformation that members of the Church of Jesus Christ of Latter-day Saints (frequently nicknamed "Mormons") will need to enact when reading the theories of René Girard is to think differently than is their custom about the sacred; adherents from all religious traditions face the same difficulty when first encountering Girard. Believers tend to think positively of the sacred as the mooring that ties them to God and a divine spirituality (equivalent to the word *holy* or something dedicated to the service of the divine), or they think in terms of a dialectic between the sacred and secular. However, to a Girardian, the word *sacred* should roll off the tongue with an edge of bitterness and guilt. The sacred is the mistaken form of religion that blames scapegoats for their own violent end: an incomplete form of belief the Christian revelation proffers to deliver us from a universal tendency to single out victims to be denounced for the social group's problems, which is present in all cultures because it is fundamental to human nature. The word (and all its etymologically related cousins: *sacrament*, *sacrifice*, *sacral*, *sacrilege*, and *sacrosanct*) should carry that odor of death when innocence is killed and burnt on the altar until the scent ascends to the heavens to be savored by the divine while being repudiated on the receiving end. The sacred is the form of worship the Bible is trying to free us from, for "it is necessary to rid ourselves of the sacred, for the sacred plays no part in the death of Jesus";[3] the death of Jesus is caused by the human propensity toward imitation and violence and has nothing to do with God's will or desires. At its best, human religion uses violence itself to disavow violence: divine religion eschews all violence.[4] For Girard, the message of the Bible is that we should shun any biblical interpretation that approves of violence, any story that sanctions sacrifice, any pronouncement that participates in violence concealed or covert, any form of the sacred that endorses the selection of a scapegoat individual or group and projects that action and selection on God or nature.

I ought to qualify at the beginning of this project my position as not being the best representative to write about Girardian perspectives on violence in the Book of Mormon. I started reading Girard when in graduate school, studying the humanities. I was particularly drawn in by his readings of biblical narratives, and, although I am a fox scurrying after a multitude of small truths, my mind is also one always drawing similarities between texts—especially between biblical and Book of Mormon narratives, textualities, and worldviews. Some people's minds immediately single out dissimilarities, but my mind zeros in on parallels and correspondences. As when I read Robert Alter's work on narrative in the Hebrew Bible, I saw in Girard's biblical readings a strong similarity to the operations of Book of Mormon narrative.[5] In reading through the criticisms of modernity by postmodern thinkers' and

---

3. René Girard, *Things Hidden since the Foundation of the World*, trans. Stephen Bann and Michael Metteer (Stanford: Stanford University Press, 1987), 231.
4. Girard, *Things*, 166.
5. Robert Alter, *The Art of Biblical Narrative* (New York: Basic, 1981). Robert Alter, *The World of Biblical Literature* (New York: Basic, 1992).

modern theorists' attempts to create grand narratives, I became dubious of metanarratives that attempt to explain all of history, culture, and human nature: metanarratives that often accompany the Enlightenment heritage. These grand narratives are easy to list: Marxist utopianism, Enlightenment emancipation, Christian millenarianism, liberal individualism, scientism, nationalism, Enlightenment notions of progress, and more. Girard's analysis of mimetic rivalry and the scapegoating mechanism is another example of a metanarrative that attempts a global explanation for a wide range of phenomena and a universal solution that purports to fix a diverse array of problems.

Although I started studying Girard thirty-five years ago and have been collecting books and articles about his work long before beginning to write this book, this study in many ways would benefit if written by a true Girardian, someone deeply committed to the notion that Girard's ideas are a universal key to understanding history, economy, religion, literature, mythology, anthropology, and politics. I find Girard to be provocative and useful, but I doubt the totalizing claims he makes, and those made by his disciples, that the unfolding biblical revelation and its prefiguration in the classical biblical prophets is and always was opposed to all violence. Such a position would make pacifism a universal rule, a categorical imperative. So, although I don't apologize for being unconvinced, I am aware that if I were, this study would have a different flavor. Years ago, I was asked by a book acquisition editor to write a study with my perspectives on Girard's ideas. This book is the result. I agree in part and disagree in part with Girard's attempts to wrench our view of the sacred by 180 degrees and from a two-dimensional axis into three dimensions. My view is that the Girardian position, although useful and insightful, needs some adjustment that goes beyond mere tweaking.

My main reservations about Girard's system emerge regarding its claim to universality. I am sufficiently postmodern that when

Girard asserts his one-key-fits-all-locks position regarding human culture (that the God of the Bible is always against violence, that when conflicts among humans emerge regardless of culture, historical position, or place, the root cause is always mimetic rivalry), I am dubious. When Girard encounters historical examples or passages of scripture that run counter to his thesis, he posits that the particular biblical writer didn't fully understand the divine message. When an Old Testament or Gospel writer's narrative supports Girard's theory, that passage gets the divine stamp of approval. My view is that history, culture, divinity, and human nature are much more pliable and variable than one overarching explanation can account for. So, I will push back on the claims to exhaustiveness when they emerge from Girard's writings and those of Girardians. I raise questions about Girard's larger conceptual scheme and his specific use of evidence in Chapter 5, "Problems with Girard's Claims."

Similarly, I am dubious about readers of the Bible or Book of Mormon who find one consistent and unified thread throughout the entire length of either scriptural text. I assert such an unfailingly uniform ideological scheme is more likely contributed by the contemporary reader. I believe the Bible's and Book of Mormon's claims to inspiration, but not all such views of revelation are of a piece. "The Lord God giveth light unto the understanding; for he speaketh unto men according to their language, unto their understanding,"[6] and that understanding includes the personal, historical, and prevailing ideological context of the reader along with the assumptions and expectations of each reader. This same assertion is given in the Doctrine and Covenants that the messages God delivers through prophets are filtered through those prophets' capacities, contexts, and understandings: "these commandments are of me, and were given unto my servants in their weakness, after

---

6. 2 Nephi 31:3.

the manner of their language, that they might come to understanding."[7] That doesn't mean there is no king in Israel, and everyone can do what is right in their own eyes,[8] interpreting sacred writ any preferred way, but it does mean that a number of valid and defensible, though contradictory, readings of a text can be produced and supported using the same textual source material, largely pivoting on the ideological preconceptions the reader brings to the text. I approach the scriptural text with the understanding that both the ancient writer and the contemporary reader bring important differences, cultural and personal assumptions, and ideological commitments that will likely contrast with other readers. I maintain that readers such as Girard, some Girardians, and Latter-day Saint scholar Eugene England take from scripture only those portions of the text that support their favored theses (and what reader doesn't cite supportive evidence favorably and downplay and neglect contrary passages?). Too many readers bowdlerize texts by ignoring portions that disagree with their favored view, make fanciful connections between different parts of the scriptural text, or expurgate some parts that attribute violence or an injunction to commit violence to divinity. I recognize that I am subject to the same limitations when reading scriptural texts—any texts. I am like Adam, cast out of paradise, handicapped with a fallen human nature that results in slanted readings in this twisted world. I also recognize that a reader can't address all relevant passages in books compiled over centuries that are as complex and varied as the Bible and Book of Mormon. I also consider the Girardian tendency to create a canon within a canon in order to exclude unfavorable excerpts and elevate favorable narratives to be a less-than-ideal way to address the issues.

---

7. Doctrine and Covenants 1:24. The revelations in the Book of Mormon are specifically mentioned just a few verses later, verse 29.
8. Judges 21:25.

I also recognize that the limits of my own language and understanding often make me mute or jabbering in a post-Babelian language before these scriptural texts, specifically the Bible and the Book of Mormon. These two inheritances of scripture are much deeper and more profound than we comprehend or have yet the capacity to absorb. Since Joseph Smith brought the Book of Mormon into the modern world and during the rise of historical criticism of the Bible, scholarly readings of the two books have tended to be reductive, to reduce (for example) the Book of Mormon to the environment in which it emerged in antebellum America, from a frontier family setting, and through a rudimentarily educated farmer. Historical criticism of the Bible also tends to fragment the Bible (both testaments) into small, incohesive parts. The Bible's historical content has been questioned in more and more sophisticated ways, especially as a historical theory called historicism has been applied to the text (historicism, in this context, is the notion that a text's meaning emerges only from the historical context of its production). Fortunately, that trend has been reversed in some important ways over the past half century, so we better understand not only the literary features of both the Bible and Book of Mormon, but also the inseparably interwoven aspects of their literary and historical elements. We ought to be committed as readers to gleaning as much as possible from these scriptural texts, and reductive readings neglect that obligation.

Much analysis of the Book of Mormon focuses on the claim that its translator asserted: the scripture is the product of the ancient world, written by descendants of an Israelite group that departed Jerusalem about 600 BCE,[9] making their way to the

---

9. The scholarly term BCE corresponds to the term BC. But to avoid using such transparently Christian-influenced chronological terminology, scholars tend to use the initialism for *Before the Common Era* instead of *Before Christ*. Similarly, scholars tend to use CE for *Common Era* instead of the Christian-centered AD, short for *Anno Domini*, which translates from Latin as "year of our Lord." I will use the scholarly designations.

Western hemisphere, and founding a millennium-long civilization divided in the first generation into two contending groups, Lamanites and Nephites, led by brothers. A high point occurs when, after his resurrection, Jesus Christ visited them, teaching the gospel established in the Old World. The Nephites kept the historical and religious records until around 421 CE, when the Lamanites killed them off. The final Nephite historian, Moroni, buried the engraved metal writings, returning as a post-mortal resurrected being—an angel—in the 1820s to deliver those records to a young man named Joseph Smith, who, by a heavenly gift, translated those writings into English and published them as the Book of Mormon. This argument presented by Joseph Smith about the origin of the Book of Mormon is a hard assertion to accept in our secular and skeptical times. Yet, many highly educated and smart people do accept it. The arguments about the book's origins go under the name of Book of Mormon historicity. I am not entering that debate in this volume. If my reader wants to see my engagement on the issue, consult my publications listed in the bibliography of this book. Here, I merely accept the explanation advanced by Joseph Smith.

One recent productive backlash to the reductive and too often simplistic historical ventures that read the Bible and Book of Mormon superficially that has emerged in the United States is the notion of "abundant events," or reading for "presence." In the European philosophical tradition, an analogous concept of "saturated phenomena" or "excess of signification" readings has emerged. Such readings acknowledge that our imaginations and concepts are insufficiently broad or flexible to encompass some events. I argue that there are more things in heaven and earth than any Horatio can bring to the discussion with an empiricist and positivist philosophy. The inheritance of modernity's presuppositions ought not to artificially and superficially limit the range of explanations we consider or deem possible. Scholar of religion Robert Orsi asserts:

> [T]he academic study of religion has been organized around a
> distinct and identifiable set of moral judgments and values that
> are most often implicit and commonly evident more in conven-
> tion and scholarly ethos than in precept. Theorizing about "reli-
> gion" has proceeded in accordance with these embedded moral
> assumptions even as religious studies has increasingly claimed
> and vehemently insisted on its "scientific" status in the secular
> university.[10]

These moral assumptions after generations are alchemized into
epistemological (assertions about how knowledge is produced)
and ontological (assertions about the nature of being or existence)
assumptions in the furnace of modernity, such that sacred or
divine events are reduced to human psychological desires. Such
reductive maneuvers ought to be conceived only after careful consideration. But the abundant rivers of the relevant scriptures overflow the teacups that secular scholars bring with them to measure
the texts and saturate the fertile ground in the watershed border-
ing the rivers of living water.

Historians of religion, sociologists of religion, religious studies
scholars, and other academic researchers have too often (under
the misapprehension that they need to operate using the approach
of the natural sciences) been reductive in explaining religious
events. Revelations, visions, miracles—all such phenomena, they
feel, need to be reduced to the psychology of the believer, the
economics of the religious community, or other sociological and
psychological factors. Such events as the appearance of the Virgin
Mary to a fourteen-year-old girl at Lourdes or directions by an
angel to find ancient writings on gold plates in a hillside in western
New York are not "real," according to this position, in the same
way that traffic accident you were involved in last week or the

---

10. Robert Orsi, *Between Heaven and Earth: The Religious Worlds People Make
and the Scholars Who Study Them* (Princeton, NJ: Princeton University Press,
2005), 178.

attacks in 2001 on the World Trade Center and Pentagon are real events. Orsi notes that scholars of religion tend to be too quick and impulsive to dismiss religious experiences as delusions or wishful thinking. They begin from the assumption that occasions when divinity interrupts common events to manifest the transcendence beyond immanent occurrences are merely this-worldly imaginary inventions. As Orsi states,

> Of all aspects of religion, the one that has been clearly most out of place in the modernizing world—the one that has proven least tolerable to modern societies—has been the radical presence of the gods to practitioners. The modern world has assiduously and systematically disciplined the senses and imagination not to experience the sacred presence; the imaginations of moderns are trained toward sacred absence.[11]

In particular, scholars of religion are conditioned to be scandalized at assertions that God or angels are real presences in people's quotidian lives and at transformative experiences that ought to be addressed with more respect than mainstream academic modernity can muster. According to "modernity's ontological singular," such claims of supernatural revelations "when the transcendent breaks into time is not what appears to be happening to the men and women to whom it is happening, nor is it what they say has happened to them. What participants say, as a matter of fact, does 'not faithfully represent actual historical occurrences.'"[12] Since many scholars are blocked by ideological and disciplinary conventions from accepting the supernatural event as narrated or experienced by the historical actor (or at least considering that narration as told by the participant a possibility), the event needs to be reduced to something else: indigestion, psychological trauma,

---

11. Orsi, *Between*, 12.
12. Robert A. Orsi, *History and Presence* (Cambridge, MA: Belknap, 2016), 59.

wish fulfillment, economic envy, or a thousand other causes more mundane but believable for an empiricist.

These reductive explanations of religious phenomena result in religious events being explained away rather than being engaged. As Orsi writes, "In its harshest formulation, which may seem to some as its most realistic and responsible formulation, if the supernatural figure has not *really* appeared, then the visionary is a psychotic; the others are dupes."[13] For the positivist or empiricist who cannot abide the possibility of a supernatural event, "it is nearly impossible to let such experiences be as they are to those involved in them without yielding to the imperative to explain them [away]. Any account of religious phenomena as social constructions runs the risk of distorting and diminishing these phenomena precisely *as* historical and cultural realities, because such phenomena are not merely this."[14] In Stephen Taysom's summary of Orsi's concept of abundant events, he notes Orsi's criticism that religion scholars refuse to actually study religion when they take up religion but use a scholarly formula to turn such religious events into something more manageable to their allegiances: "We render the religious in the language of psychology, sociology, economics, critical theory, anthropology, political science, cognitive science, and so forth. This language is not sufficient to address 'abundant events.'"[15] Regarding certain events in the Mormon tradition that qualify as abundant, such as communal visions Joseph Smith shared with other participants, Orsi notes that the categories and explanations of the academy are just inadequate to manage the explanatory task:

> Modern historiography just stops at this point; it cannot deal with such experiences historically or phenomenologically . . .

13. Orsi, *History*, 62–63.

14. Orsi, *History*, 62.

15. Stephen Taysom, "Abundant Events or Narrative Abundance: Robert Orsi and the Academic Study of Mormonism," *Dialogue: A Journal of Mormon Thought* 45, no. 2 (Winter 2012): 8.

[and ends up] either debunking such moments, claiming that the person at the center of all is a charlatan and everyone else are dupes, or translating the events into the language of the social: it's a matter of poverty, of people being on the margins of society, etcetera. But that leaves the central experiences unexamined and thus absent from history."[16]

Orsi wonders that such events as the first vision or the coming forth of the Book of Mormon cause a knee-jerk reaction among historians of religion to try to explain away the events and their meaning. Why, he marvels, can't they continue to be astounded and try to find new tools to understand these events of presence?[17]

These abundant events are too luminous and expansive to be contained by the positivistic concepts too often brought to the task by the researcher. As Orsi observes, "The abundant event is not exhausted at its source. Presence radiates out from the really real event along a network of routes, a kind of capillary of presence, filling water, relics, images, stories, and memories."[18] They are also not confined to the past the way a historian attempts to cordon off the event so it doesn't intrude on the present, living people's concerns about the heavens, and social relations contemporary and future.[19]

I find Orsi's concept of abundant events to be quite similar to what is developed under the name of "saturated phenomena" in the French phenomenological tradition. Viewing a painting is one such saturated phenomenon. The painting floods us with such excess and profusion that we can't take it all in during one visit; "we must, at regular intervals, come to re-see it."[20] As the transla-

---

16. Susanna Morrill, "Finding the Presence in Mormon History: An Interview with Susanna Morrill, Richard Lyman Bushman, and Robert Orsi," *Dialogue: A Journal of Mormon Thought* 44, no. 3 (Fall 2011): 177.
17. Morrill, "Finding," 178.
18. Orsi, *History*, 68.
19. Orsi, *History*, 70–71.
20. Jean-Luc Marion, *In Excess: Studies in Saturated Phenomena*, trans. by Robyn Horner and Vincent Berraud (New York: Fordham University Press, 2002), 70.

tors in the introduction to Jean-Luc Marion's *In Excess* note, even ordinary perception can have the impact of saturated phenomena that overflows our concepts (especially those Kantian categories of quantity, quality, relation, and modality).[21] Marion treats a revelation of God to be among the most saturated of saturated phenomena.[22] Saturated phenomena differ from "poor" or "common" phenomena in that the latter are weak in intuition but strong in concept. The abundance of intuition in saturated phenomena escapes the grasp of concepts with excess, with abundance. This bounty can be engaged by going back to revisit the painting or, if the event is mystical, repeating the encounter. As Garnet Butchart suggests,

> [T]he event saturates the category of quantity insofar as it gives itself. Showing itself (without recourse to any measure of visibility) as much as it gives itself (without recourse to any horizon of meaning or being) the event ensures for itself a quantity, the quantity of givenness as a measure of its own phenomenality. The event saturates the category of quantity by giving *too much*, more than could ever be measured, its parts infinitely exceeding their sum by continually being given.

The example Butchart gives here is a historical event that has three characteristics: (1) it is nonrepeatable; (2) it is excessive;[23] and (3) it is a possibility.[24] The event may exceed the possibility of metaphysics to encompass it or the ability of our "current modes of symbolization (ideological, scientific, artistic, and so forth)" to

---

21. Marion, *In Excess*, xiv.
22. Jean-Luc Marion, *Being Given: Toward a Phenomenology of Givenness*, trans. by Jeffrey L. Kosky (Stanford: Stanford University Press, 2002), 367n90.
23. Garnet C. Butchart, "An Excess of Signification: Or, What Is an Event?" *Semiotica* 187, no. 1–4 (2011): 294. "For example, the historic event, as epoch-making in time, overflows any instant, locale, or individual; it stands out in excess of a territory in such a way that no single gaze can seize it in its entirety. Giving too much ever to conceive the whole in terms of the sum of its parts, the event is excessive, and as such, unrepeatable" (295).
24. Butchart, "An Excess," 295.

think it through, but that doesn't cancel the possibility of phenom-
enologically experiencing it.[25]

I assert not only that the first vision and Book of Mormon
events are saturated, abundant events, but also that part of the
mystical experience of their events is repeatable in the reading and
rereading of the accounts. Girard's readings of Judeo-Christian
scripture are the most productive and insightful in his *oeuvre*, so
it is there I will focus my attention (and not, say, on his discussion
of world mythology, Shakespeare, Dostoevsky, or other such elements of the Western heritage). These issues are overwhelmingly
material for believers in the biblical tradition who assert the eternal nature and contemporary relevance of God's communications
to the world channeled through Hebraic prophets, chroniclers,
and narrative writers and their inheritors in the early phases of
Christianity. And I hereby annex the Book of Mormon to that category of Judeo-Christian scripture (belatedly, as the Nephite writers preceded me in asserting that standing themselves). I will read
that book of scripture as produced by Israelites who migrated out
of the Old World and brought with them scriptures that roughly
correspond to the Hebrew Bible we know from Genesis to parts
of Jeremiah. These Nephite writers also brought with them to
the New World the thought patterns, writing traditions, and religious and political leadership models from the old world, and
passed them on to their successors, along with a belief through
visions that the God of Abraham, Isaac, and Jacob is the God of
the New Testament writers, the God of the restoration, and a
devoted Father who loves all his children. Thus, the continuity
between Nephite historical writing and Hebraic historical writing
is bridged by those biblical covenants, revelations, compositional
styles, Hebraic culture, and divine manifestations to the children

---

25. Butchart, "An Excess," 298.

of God no matter the time, place, culture, or condition into which those children are born.

Girard proclaims that any time an endorsement of violence is ascribed to the biblical God—the command to exterminate the Canaanites, Samuel's command to slay all the Amalekites, blaming Jews for Christ's death (Matthew 27:25; Acts 3:15), anti-Jewish polemic in the epistles (1 Thessalonians 12:14–16), cosmic battles in Revelation—the plain meaning of the texts misunderstands the divine intent. He creates a canon within a canon to assert those writers who ascribe violence to the biblical God didn't understand the revolutionary nature of the Hebrew Bible and the Christian gospel, which both renounce all violence. Girard allows the misunderstood parts of the Hebrew Bible and the New Testament (except perhaps the letter to the Hebrews) in the canon but not in the canon within the canon. The passages with a complete understanding of God's will and purpose that advocate setting aside the sword, forgiving enemies, and turning the other cheek in all times and conditions are the true repositories of the divine revelation. A similar reading strategy is applied by Girardians who apply the maestro's teachings to the Book of Mormon. The biblical tradition, in a Girardian reading, evolves itself and moves its readers to evolve to a higher level, striving for and teaching complete pacifism.

Although Girard began his work in literature (the European novel) and Greek mythology, he expanded his theory to include history, philosophy, world mythology, biblical studies, and anthropology, while he always considered himself an anthropologist foremost. Girardians have expanded the scope of his ideas even further. At the center of his worldview, Girard sees a fixed core to human nature, invariant regarding different cultures, historical locations, linguistic resources, or family structures. Human society is oriented toward fixing its problems through violence, and this tendency finds release from internal or external threats by singling out an innocent victim (either an individual or a group), casting blame on that victim, achieving a catharsis by killing that victim, then raising that victim to the status of divinity for having saved the society from its dangers through the sacrifice. Then the cycle repeats.

I am a literary critic rather than a theologian, a literary theorist focusing on the scriptural canon of the Church of Jesus Christ of Latter-day Saints: the Hebrew Bible, the New Testament, and the Book of Mormon. But once anyone starts engaging in God-talk articulating the relationship between God and humanity, one has begun to theologize. So let me situate myself as a literary critic who focuses on what those parts of the canon might mean for readers in the twenty-first century. The compiler and penultimate writer of the Book of Mormon avows to his latter-day readers that they must "lay hold upon the gospel of Christ, which shall be set before you, not only in this record but also in the record which shall come unto the Gentiles from the Jews, which record shall come from the Gentiles unto you. For behold, *this* [Book of Mormon] is written for the intent that ye may believe *that* [Bible]; and if ye believe *that* [Bible] ye will believe *this* [Book of Mormon] also."[26] The Book of Mormon and the New Testament are products of the same Hebraic heritage with the same pre-Jewish and Jewish mindsets that expected the God of the Bible not only to intervene in history, but to do so repeatedly and with repetitive patterns time and again. The exodus event doesn't just return the children of Abraham to their promised land from Egypt, but the Jews from their exile in Mesopotamia and the dozens of other times in history that exodus events recur.[27] The event becomes paradigmatic for all of Abraham's progeny. The important point is to see God's mighty works of salvation reiterated time and again as

---

26. Mormon 7:8–9, emphasis mine.
27. David Daube, *The Exodus Pattern in the Bible* (London: Faber and Faber, 1963).

the pages of the Book of Mormon are interleaved with those of the Bible so that *this* witnesses *that*, and we can believe *that* and *this* as mutually reinforcing testimonies of God's mercy and grace.

From the penultimate chronicler and most prolific writer of the Nephite record to the chronologically first- and second-most prolific contributor to the record, we get a similar assertion of the mutually reinforcing nature of the biblical and Nephite records. Referring to the biblical record (specifically mentioning what we Christians call the Old Testament), Nephi sees, toward the end of his vision of the tree of life, another record, and "these last records, which thou hast seen among the Gentiles, shall establish the truth of the first, which are of the twelve apostles of the Lamb"[28] in such a way that the two scriptures will be unified in their testimony of Christ and the gospel. Nephi projects not just a correspondence between the two scriptures but a unity: "and the words of the Lamb shall be made known in the records of thy seed, as well as in the records of the twelve apostles of the Lamb; wherefore they both shall be established in one; for there is one God and one Shepherd over all the earth."[29] Any Latter-day Saint theology must recognize and acknowledge this unity in the diversity of the Hebraic/Christian and Nephite scriptures, for "they both shall be established in one."

Any restoration theology (systematic, narrative, historical, scriptural) must also account for the nature of God and humanity along with relationships between those anchor points. This accounting is especially important regarding any discussion of Girard's system, for Girard has a concept of divine nature and human nature that most readers will find novel and surprising. I will articulate those two natures (divine and human) in the first four chapters by limning the outlines of Girard's view of human

---

28. 1 Nephi 13:40.
29. 1 Nephi 13:41.

nature as naturally given to competition with a rival (the rivals can be individuals or groups) that grows more intense into a mob instinct, where the individual (but more commonly a crowd) finds some false sin or fault in the person who is scapegoated, exiled, or lynched. This violent episode relieves the tensions in society for a time until the rivalry flares up again, and this cycle repeats indefinitely. For Girard, the God of the Bible intends to mitigate that violent tendency first by establishing institutions that direct the violence toward animals (sacrifice) and institutions (e.g., judicial courts, governments, village elders who adjudicate and alleviate violence) ultimately to eliminate it altogether or at least take violent retribution out of private hands. The example of Jesus demonstrates the falsity of insisting, as all scapegoating asserts, that the victim singled out for the congregational murder is guilty. The Christian model of love without violence has taken millennia to have its effect, but in our lifetime, it has borne fruit (despite the persistence of warfare, genocide, and racism), so that we see the faces of the victims of violence in places such as Darfur, Ukraine, Myanmar, and Tigray, and no longer accept their suffering as the natural order of things.

In this book, I will summarize Girard's position and his readings of the Bible, and then I will read various Book of Mormon narratives to see how other predecessors have drawn meaning about violence out of stories such as Nephi's killing of Laban, the preaching of Alma and Amulek at Ammonihah, conflict between Nephi and his brothers, the Noachide murder of Abinadi, and other various narratives. These are foundational stories that inform the reader about the relationship between God and humanity, between family members, internal to citizens in a society, and between neighboring tribal and national groupings. General principles can be drawn from the specific workings out of conflict among individuals and groups.

Any such evaluation of God and humans in the context of violence must necessarily incorporate some value judgments. Notice that *value* is the root of the word *evaluation*. We must evaluate the morality of both human and divine acts. Our standard, post-Enlightenment approach to engaging with ethics and morality is to articulate and apply various ethical theories as they have been developed by philosophers. Such a tactic is complicated because the restoration posits a continuity between humans and God. Unlike the divinity of creedal Christianity (in the Catholic, Protestant, and to a lesser degree in the Orthodox, traditions), Joseph Smith revealed that humans and God are of the same species, developing in the same direction but at different stages of growth—children of God capable not just *to become like* divinity but *to become divine*. However, the goal is for women and men to progress along the lines of Lorenzo Snow's couplet:

> As man now is, God once was:
> As God now is, man may be.

Two consequences of this continuity—if not identity—between basic human and divine nature follow: (1) a continuity or identity exists between the divine moral code and that expected of humans, and (2) a moral sympathy binds the two together. As Terryl and Fiona Givens have pointed out (contrary to the traditional creedal God who has no passions), the restoration God is one who weeps when we weep, rejoices when we have joy, and sorrows when we sorrow.[30] The LDS tradition closes that broad chasm between the Creator and the creature. We live and grow in the same moral universe as God does, and so we expect that any framework of good and evil we share as humans is also participated in by the divine. Yet our human development of ethical

---

30. Terryl Givens and Fiona Givens, *The God Who Weeps: How Mormonism Makes Sense of Life* (Salt Lake City, UT: Ensign Peak, 2012).

discussion may ill fit a creation in which the ways of God are still puzzling and irreducible to the ways of humanity.

The following list doesn't exhaust the ethical theories over the course of such discussion, but it can be helpful to develop some differences between the ethical theories as they might apply to God and humans (I also do not explore the many permutations and subdivisions of these ethical concepts). The two most influential ethical theories are deontology and utilitarianism (the latter also called consequentialism):

1. Deontology, from the Greek *logos*, "the study of," and *deon*, "duty," focuses on what we "ought" to do. Theories in this category are often based on universal principles, or categorical imperatives, as established by Kant. For example, murder is always wrong. A clarification is that self-defense or defense of innocent life is not murder. One deontological approach separates the personal and individual circumstances from the rightness or wrongness of an action. If you could will that any person without a bicycle to get to work can steal a bike from a neighbor, you too can steal the bike. If not, you cannot steal it. Yet if you were the bike owner, you wouldn't make it permissible for anyone without a bike to steal yours. Another deontological version focuses on means and ends. If you are hungry and have no money for food, you can't treat your neighbor as a means toward the end of filling your stomach by cajoling her into spending her last twenty dollars to take you to lunch when she needs that money to buy prescription medicine. You are using your neighbor for your own selfish purposes instead of treating the person as an end in herself. Deontologists tend to advocate for universal principles: murder is *always* wrong; *never*

use another person as a means to your own end; if you could will that *all other people* can shoplift (even when, for example, you are the store owner), then you can shoplift.

2. Consequentialism, or utilitarianism, emphasizes that an action is never right or wrong itself but is measured only by the results or consequences that follow. Good actions result in good or pleasurable consequences for the largest number of people. Hence the utilitarian calculus: **g³n**, the **g**reatest **g**ood for the **g**reatest **n**umber. At times, most of us are utilitarians: if building a bridge across the Hudson River at Nyack/Tarrytown benefits more people than would a Mid-Hudson bridge at Poughkeepsie, then the ethical venue is the Tappan Zee location at Nyack. Taken to extreme, and in its simplest version is the classical argument against consequentialism: a moral action that can be reduced to mathematics might be morally objectionable to a deontologist for if we can benefit eight people with organ transplants from one healthy forced donor who can't live without a heart, lungs, liver, etc., then the ethical action is to proceed with the transplants in order to benefit the eight people.

3. Command, or divine command, means anything that God/the Pope/Donald Trump commands is right. This is often the justification used to defend Nephi's killing of Laban, a topic I'll be taking up in Chapter 7, "The Death of Laban."

4. Virtue ethics describes a system that, rather than emphasizing duty or results, emphasizes character or virtue, especially training children or youth to build moral character. One can also take a virtuous person

one admires as a model for what to do in a particular situation (WWJD?). One can refer to character training (for example, "that wasn't how I raised you"). One can attempt to instill virtue in children by reading with them from *The Book of Virtues for Young People* by William Bennett, each poem, literary story, or historical narrative selected to teach a particular virtue such as patience or kindness.

5. Moral absolutism means no circumstances or exceptions can mitigate the need to obey certain rules, such as the Ten Commandments. Cultural and historical conditions have no impact on the need for response to these rules to be invariant because right is always right and wrong is always wrong. Absolutes are absolutely inflexible. I take Girard's moral pronouncements to fall under this category when judging acts of violence: no mitigating factors can make killing another person right, but they also fall under deontology because they pronounce universal principles of conduct.

This brief survey of a few ethical theories will provide some handholds and footholds as we climb to a higher altitude to view the wider vistas of mob violence, murder, insurrection, and warfare. To demonstrate how these ethical theories might be applied to scriptural narrative, let's take the story the Bible presents of first parents. Since Latter-day Saints interpret the fall of Adam and Eve differently than creedal Christianity does, this might present a case study handy for comparing to other Book of Mormon passages that will come later in this book.

The standard Christian understanding of the fall is that Adam and Eve were in a paradise which they lost through their disobedience. God commanded them not to partake of the fruit of the tree of knowledge of good and evil. Viewing God's command as a moral absolute or through a divine command perspective, Eve and Adam committed a grave and tragic sin. If they had only obeyed the order, they and their children could have lived forever in that paradise. They disobeyed and were exiled from the garden that they otherwise would have been able to permanently inhabit, had they not eaten that fruit; they would have been able to reproduce and fill the earth with their posterity in that paradisiacal state having never pulled a weed, experienced the pain of childbirth (but somehow nevertheless have brought children into the world), prepared a meal on a stove or a fire, or died. The divine command theory condemns the pair simply because they violated a divine pronouncement. Such a reading is well within the range of plausible readings of the text. But Latter-day Saints interpret the story differently, also within the range of readings made possible by the narrative.

Adam and Eve, in an LDS cosmological view, could not reproduce as long as they were in the garden. So they were given conflicting charges: (1) they were not to eat the fruit of that tree, and if they refrained, they would remain in paradise in a state of moral innocence, not knowing good from evil, living off the land without having to contribute their own labor, and continuing in that state forever, but they would be unable to fulfill the divine mandate to reproduce. The other possibility was (2) to eat that fruit, be expelled, and have to labor in two ways and experience the consequences of mortal life: to wrest food from the ground by the sweat of their brows and to experience the labor of childbirth and the inevitability of death. God gave two conflicting commands, for to refrain from the fruit of that tree would result in remaining frozen in their current state, obstructing the fulfillment of the other divine command to multiply and fill the earth with offspring. The two decrees are in contradiction, so the humans must decide which of the mandates is more important than the other. Eve reasons through the dilemma before Adam, and they choose the wiser course to know good from evil, to raise offspring, to earn the bounty of the earth for food rather than having it merely fall off the trees and spring from the ground ready-made, and to experience the virtues and vicissitudes of mortality.

Under the divine command theory, they would have violated God's explicit instruction either way, but at least by eating of the fruit, they furthered the divine plan by triggering a fall into the lone and dreary world, having children, and experiencing death. I am going to develop in this book the argument that humans are in the image of divine parentage, and being divine is a complexity that simple formulas and definitions cannot fathom or plumb; we can hold neither God nor the human offspring of divinity to be either morally simple or easy to encapsulate. Humans (and their godly forebears) are too plentiful, too bounteous, too abundant to be boxed in by our limited and impoverished categories, conceptions, and definitions. Many of the moral decisions we make are as complex as that decision the first parents had to make. Similarly, like our first parents, the moral and ethical decisions we face often force us to decide between two or more conflicting principles, making us embrace one of the principles while violating the other. Partaking of the fruit or not partaking are both right and both wrong. The choice is layered with complexity because both prongs of the dilemma bring good and bad consequences, but one is more right than the other. That is the way of many ethical decisions: sometimes the options are comprised of only bad choices and sometimes only good choices, but more often the options are a complex amalgam of the two.

Choosing to commit violent actions in order to prevent even greater violence (say, for example, to engage in worldwide warfare to counter the fascist regimes of World War II or intervening violently to stop a massacre in Timor-Leste, an example I'll develop later in the conclusion) is a morally complex choice, fraught with moral tension and ambiguity that can't be boiled down to a strict binary opposition between pacifism or brutal violence, or one between declining the fruit of the tree in order stay in a simple idyllic world and partaking of the fruit of knowledge of good and evil. Sometimes moral choices are simple, and sometimes they are complex, and often the easy answers upon contemplation convert into multifaceted and encumbered issues.

Because the restoration Christianity view of human nature is generally more positive that that held by creedal Christianity, the Augustinian formulation of human nature is so much more dour and grim than the scriptures it emerges from. The Girardian view of natural, unchecked humanity inclined to bloodshed and aggression looks more like the creedal conception (although both do incorporate elements of redemption and grace enforced by the possibility of human reason to countervail corrupt human nature). The Latter-day Saint articulation of the problem with humanity as partakers of the divine nature highlights the positive elements in the scriptures shared with other branches of the Judeo-Christian tradition, but also with those exclusive to the restoration heritage. At the same time, those humans as partakers of the divine nature are also disfigured by a fallen nature. In other words, the Girardian configuration may fit the Augustinian inheritance better than its correspondence with the Latter-day Saint tradition, and more specifically its application to the Book of Mormon. We praise Adam and Eve (and the latter more intensively) for bringing humanity into a world where sorrow and labor are combined with childbirth and joy; whereas creedal Christianity condemns those archetypal first parents for that choice (blaming Eve more than Adam), we Latter-day Saints praise and rejoice in those elections. In any case, divine command theory configures both conceptions of that foundational choice as wrong for violating heaven's mandate. The moral world Eve and Adam entered upon expulsion was fallen and "remains perpetually divided in both good-good and good-evil tensions"[31] where Eve and Adam and their offspring were obligated to sort through the alloyed good and evil, good and less good, evil and more evil, and all sorts of combinations. We live in that world in which many choices are complex and require judgment, inspiration, and wisdom more than mere rule-following (not that rule-following is bad, and rule-following can also be complicated when various rules conflict with others, as is the situation in most of human thinking when applied to concrete, real-world circumstances).

If we were to apply a deontological theory to the choice, we would disregard consequences and focus only on the act itself. What would one do when facing conflicting commandments? Since deontology often appeals to universal principles (never tell a lie, always turn on your car's turn signal indicator before making a turn), we would face a conundrum when two principles conflict with each other: (1) don't eat the fruit and (2) do propagate. But in this case the couple can't propagate without eating the fruit, for the negative and the positive command are in contradiction, for to follow one requires violation of the other. We Latter-day Saints try to weasel (and didn't that animal get a raw deal when Adam named the creatures?) our way out of the problem by saying that Adam and Eve didn't sin by eating the fruit, but they did transgress. The slight difference in connotation doesn't solve the underlying problem that God is responsible for giving contradictory commands. One can't simultaneously be faithful to both rules. An adherent of the divine command theory would be presented with a quandary: which command to obey? One would have to import some other principle (perhaps a pragmatic one) to weigh the two options and find an approach to tip the decision one way or the other (for

---

31. Patrick Q. Mason and J. David Pulsipher, *Proclaim Peace: The Restoration's Answer to an Age of Conflict* (Provo, UT: BYU Maxwell Institute/Deseret, 2021), 71.

example, which commandment was given first? Or, which one conveys the commandment in the fewest words?).

We face choices all the time when our most cherished and fundamental principles conflict, so we have to decide which principle should take priority in a specific circumstance. If I am driving an injured person to the hospital, I may decide that impending exsanguination of the injured party demands that I do whatever can be done to save the life, but that may conflict with my imperative to obey the speed limit and other traffic regulations. We are principally committed to extending to a woman carrying a fetus diagnosed with a severe genetic defect such as Tay-Sachs disease the right to choose whether or not to continue the pregnancy. But commitment to a person's autonomy conflicts with the principle that the life of a human (or potential human) not be taken by human agency. The individual or society has to decide which principle should take precedence. Our fundamental moral allegiances frequently clash with each other and sorting out such contradictions requires attention to context, our exercise of grace, and a dose of justice.

Unlike a deontologist, the consequentialist relies only on the results of a decision. When Adam and Eve are faced with a choice, the Creator doesn't present the options deontologically but in a utilitarian way (God reacts with consequences and presents those consequences as the justification for Adam and Eve's obedience). For the Saints, God doesn't reserve unmixed punishment for the couple. They are rewarded with children and moral awareness. The mortality and labor are part of the plan—initiated from before the foundation of the world—to flow from the fall. Continued existence in a paradise without offspring is one result, and the other is hard labor, children, and knowledge of good and evil. I think our reflexive reaction when we apply ethical terminology to the Eden narrative would be to assume that God would be a deontologist or a moral absolutist when we force the decision into an ethical matrix designed by the Western heritage. But God may well present some decisions as hinging on a number of different ethical processes in various circumstances. God polices the consequences that follow from the fall, regardless of whether to maintain an immortal and laborless state or enter a fallen world. Not only might our ethical reasoning be inadequate to capture the divine purposes and actions, but these theories may be even too simplistic for human conduct because we are not only made in the (moral and physical) image of God, but our discourse about both God and humans is insufficiently complex to limn the boundaries and draw the borders with such crude tools as Kantian categorical imperatives, Benthamite calculuses, or Girardian universal mandates.

Jeremy Bentham is credited with being the founder of utilitarianism, and John Stuart Mill the most profound successor utilitarian philosopher. Mill famously responded to the objection that utilitarian thought is godless with the reply that such a question "depends upon what idea we have formed of the moral character of the Deity. If it be a true belief that God desires, above all things, the happiness of his creatures, and that this was his purpose in their creation, utility is not only not a godless doctrine, but more profoundly religious than any other."[32] Clearly, in the traditional reading of the Adam and Eve story, God is concerned with the consequences of eating or not eating the fruit of that tree, and even more intensely in the LDS rendering, God is concerned with the results of that action in order to move the divine plan for humans forward. We ought to consider several possibilities: (1) God is not only both a deontologist and a consequentialist, but our small-minded categories are not adequate to encompass the mind and will of God, or (2) God is sometimes a consequentialist, and God

---

32. John Stuart Mill, *Utilitarianism*, ed. Geraint Williams (London: Everyman, 1993 [1861]), 22.

is sometimes a deontologist (or falls into some other category) depending on the moral situation.

By adopting the quotation from Isaiah as an epigraph for this introduction, I want to express my own reticence regarding judgments we might be tempted to make about the narratives we read of Moroni's summary execution of dissenters, of Nephi's beheading of Laban, of the justness of various wars (offensive and defensive). I would also like us to think about the portrayal of the miscreants in those stories: Laman and Lemuel, King Noah, Amlici, Amalekiah, the Ammonihahite leadership, and others. Might we not be failing to consider the perspective from which the narratives were told? Might we with clean moral consciences hold that in one circumstance violent self-defense is justified and other situations not? That preemptive violence should be endorsed in some situations but not others? Might the Spirit's utilitarian argument to Nephi that it is better that one man die than an entire nation dwindle in unbelief not only be justified but also sufficient to justify the ways of God to man or the ways of man to God? None of the issues are simple, and a more nuanced answer might be required, one that not only ethical theories can justify but that human consciences can fortify.

Biblical stories about beginnings are intended to be paradigmatic, models for the use of later generations, archetypes either good or bad for the instruction of posterity. These foundational stories are prototypes of history that will be repeated in the future lives of descendants. The narrative about Cain killing Abel immediately preceding Cain's going out and founding the first city is exemplary in that it suggests that all subsequent civilizations are based on violence.[33] Saint Augustine drew that intended lesson not just from Genesis but also from the founding murder establishing Roman civilization, Romulus's murder of his brother Remus, as

---

33. Genesis 4:17.

they together were building the first walls to protect what would later become Rome, the eternal and archetypal city.[34] This archetypal viewpoint was typical of the way ancient humans thought. Foundational events were types and shadows of events that would be repeated throughout history.

The events the Bible tells of Abraham are intended to be seen as similarly typologically repeatable for his descendants and those who profess to be children of Abraham, whether genetic children or not. Jesus argues when the particular Jews he debates assert Abraham as their ancestor, a disconnect occurs: "If ye were Abraham's children, ye would do the works of Abraham."[35] That parentage is brought into question metaphorically, says the upstart rabbi, for they seek to kill Jesus. And "this did not Abraham."[36] The ancient Jewish rabbis articulated an interpretive principle that what happens to the fathers, happens to the sons, especially if those ancestors are eponymous (that is, they give their names to their descendants: children of Abraham, Israelites, Lehites, Nephites, Lamanites, etc.).[37] A fundamental question for biblical believers who engage in the type of inquiry I am pursuing is whether it is impious to do what I do in this book: questioning whether or not the acts of God related in the scriptures of Abraham (the binding/sacrifice of Isaac), of Moses (killing the Egyptian overseer, for example), of Nephi (killing Laban), of Moroni (in times of war and insurrection summarily executing mutineers) measure up the moral and ethical standards we would demand of ourselves, let alone of divinities or those called by God to announce the divine words.

---

34. St. Augustine, *The City of God*, trans. Henry Bettenson (New York: Penguin, 1984), book 15, chapter 5.

35. John 8:39.

36. John 8:40.

37. Yair Zakovitch, *"And You Shall Tell Your Son . . .": The Concept of the Exodus in the Bible* (Jerusalem: Magnes, 1991), 20. Sometimes the adage is translated "what happens to the fathers is a sign to the sons."

We Latter-day Saints should do the works of Abraham, our father. After the three angels/messengers (and, apparently the Lord) enjoy table communion with Abraham and the angels leave toward the cities of the plain, the Lord hangs around to talk with Abraham, inwardly reflecting that following their shared covenant, continuing to withhold from the patriarch what the God of heaven will do next isn't consonant with the confidential status newly established between them: "And the Lord said, Shall I hide from Abraham that thing which I do; Seeing that Abraham shall surely become a great and mighty nation, and all the nations of the earth shall be blessed in him?"[38] So the divine visitor tells Abraham about the impending destruction of Sodom and Gomorrah because of the wickedness there. Abraham has the temerity to question the justice of a God who would destroy entire cities, the righteous with the wicked.[39] What if fifty righteous people remain, will God still exercise such drastic judgment? This takes tremendous boldness to question the ethics and justice of God: "Shall not the Judge of all the earth do right?"[40] Abraham bargains the number all the way down to ten. Abraham does not back down (well, he does have some qualms, "he said unto him, Oh let not the Lord be angry, and I will speak"[41]) from questioning God's moral judgments and the actions that flow from those pronouncements. We Latter-day Saints should valorize and accept that aspect of the Jewish tradition when it comes to raising hard ethical questions about both divine and human justice.

Rabbi Irwin Kula compares two biblical stories about Abraham. The first is the one I am discussing here, about the destruction of the cities of the plain. Abraham asserts that divine justice is continuous with human morality, "that God must follow a standard

---

38. Genesis 18:17–18.
39. Genesis 18:23.
40. Genesis 18:25.
41. Genesis 18:30.

of justice comprehensible to Abraham."[42] The second is the story of the *Akedah*, the binding of Isaac, or what Christians call the sacrifice of Isaac. Abraham raises no objection to the idea of child sacrifice, even of his own son, the vessel of the promises and covenants made to Abraham and his seed. Humans can challenge the divine morality, but ultimately, such boldness must yield to God's will and a more panoramic view of the scope of history and covenants: "there is no alternative to the acceptance of God's will and that the human role in the covenant is submission."[43] Rabbi Kula notes that sometimes, questioning God is the right response when humans are faced with deep moral concerns, and other times, the proper response is submission to the divine will. God encourages us to hold the two responses in balance, searching our own divine endowment of conscience (what we Saints call the light of Christ). For Jews, Kula continues,

> The genius of the covenantal way is that these two powerful principles, autonomy and heteronomy, are yoked together and held in creative tension. Both challenging and submitting to God and the tradition are authentic covenantal responses to the dilemmas of Jewish life. The covenantal question addressed to each generation and even each person is when to act in which way.[44]

The Jewish tradition refers to this obligation we have even to argue with the God of heaven about moral concerns to be "argument for the sake of heaven,"[45] for such argumentation is for the sake of truth—not just to obtain victory or defeat an opponent but to

---

42. Irwin Kula, Obey God or Question God? Abraham's responses to the destruction of Sodom and Gemorrah and to the command to sacrifice Isaac provide two conflicting models, *My Jewish Learning*, https://www.myjewishlearning.com/article/autonomy-vs-heteronomy-in-the-covenantal-relationship/ (Accessed 9/14/2023).

43. Kula, Obey God or Question God?

44. Kula, Obey God or Question God?

45. Jonathan Sacks, Argument for the Sake of Heaven, *The Rabbi Sacks Legacy*, https://www.chabad.org/parshah/article_cdo/aid/4422484/jewish/Argument-for-the-Sake-of-Heaven.htm (Accessed 9/14/2023).

establish humans in the same moral conversation with each other and with God.

Like Abraham, Nephi initially questions the divine command when told to kill Laban, at least inwardly ("but I said in my heart: Never at any time have I shed the blood of man. And I shrunk and would that I might not slay him").[46] The reader of the full range of scripture should do the works of Abraham and of Nephi, querying commands divine and human for the sake of heaven. That is the intention of this book: to cross-examine the divine and human morality and ethics to see how they match up when overlaid.

Having summarized Abraham's questioning of the Lord's ethical decision, and following the Abrahamic model, I assert we are justified in also questioning Abraham's ethical decision-making, just as he questioned the Lord's. We refer to the *Akedah*, the binding of Isaac in Genesis 22, as Abraham's great ethical test. But it isn't the sole, or even the first, trial. The previous chapter contains some domestic tension that forces Abraham also to initiate an ordeal involving his filial obligations. Sarah has been emotionally wrought over her inability to conceive, and once her handmaiden, Hagar, has given birth to provide a potential heir for Abraham, the anxiety mounts as Hagar needles her mistress. After Sarah has finally given birth to Isaac, she demands that both Hagar and Ishmael be driven out of the household, "for the son of this bondwoman shall not be heir with my son, even with Isaac."[47] Driving his concubine and his eldest son out into the wilderness to die disturbs Abraham's conscience, as it should: "And the thing was very grievous in Abraham's sight because of his son."[48] God instructs Abraham to do as Sarah demands and provides some justification:

---

46. 1 Nephi 4:10.
47. Genesis 21:6–8.
48. Genesis 21:11.

"in Isaac shall thy seed be called," with the assurance that Ishmael will also produce a people.[49]

As Abraham arose early in the morning to travel to the mountain to sacrifice Isaac, so too he arises early to provide bread and water to Hagar and sends her out into the "wilderness of Beersheba" with their son to die. After the water supply is gone, Hagar lays the boy down under a shrub and goes a distance off so she doesn't have to hear him cry and see him die, and so she can weep. As with the child[50] endangered on Mount Moriah, God sends an angel to reassure Hagar and open her eyes to see a well for the provision of water. Philosopher Richard Kearney notes of the patriarch that "Abraham is capable of both great and terrible things. While he welcomes the three strange men (*anashim*) who announce the birth of his son, Isaac, he does not hesitate, not long afterward, to cruelly expel his foreign slave girl, Hagar, into the wilderness with their son Ishmael."[51] Like Abraham, each of us is capable of great cruelty and great kindness.

This capacity of soul and meanness of character is illustrated with the other son, for "on Mount Moriah, he has to decide between two commanding angels: one who tells him to kill his son Isaac, the other who bids him abandon the tribal ways of blood sacrifice and receive his son back as gift."[52] Kearney sees these dilemmas on the mountain and in the desert as exemplary of the choices descendants of Abraham must make through the rest of narrative in the Hebrew Bible, the Christian New Testament, and

---

49. Genesis 21:12. And one should also ask about Abraham, should it not also disturb him "because of Hagar's likely death"?

50. Midrashic traditions in the Genesis Rabbah (https://archive.org/details/RabbaGenesis/page/n543/mode/2up) place the age of Isaac sometimes as high as 37 when the events occurred. Josephus says 25. Flavius Josephus, "Antiquities of the Jews," *The Life and Works of Flavius Josephus*, trans. by William Whiston (Grand Rapids, MI: Baker, 1974 reprint), 1.13.2.

51. Richard Kearney, *Anatheism [Returning to God after God]* (New York: Columbia University Press, 2010), 19.

52. Kearney, *Anatheism*, 19.

the Islamic tradition, for "that decision for hospitality over hostility is never made once and for all; it is a wager that needs to be renewed again and again."[53] Like the children of Abraham in all ages and places, we are capable of great cruelty and violence, yet we are also able to do works of charity and kindness, such as welcoming the strangers into the tent and providing food and water.

For Girard, who also reads these ancient narratives with great insight, we are capable of hospitality in the tent and the violence of blaming victims after sacrificing them. These two "angels" prompting Abraham on his Mount Moriah journey still accompany us, even in modern times, for the biblical tradition and the Jewish heritage asserts that human nature is composite, an amalgamation of an evil inclination and a good inclination whispering the command to offer the son or the injunction not to lay a hand upon the boy: which inclination we follow is up to each person. An adherent of a divine command ethic or a morally absolutist position would merely accept the commandment and follow through. A deontologist would recognize two principles in conflict: (1) obey God and (2) do not murder. Some other principle would have to be invoked to weigh the two principles to see which should be chosen. A utilitarian would simply measure the results, perhaps even assigning numbers to the various results and adding up the sum in the positive column and then comparing to the sum in the negative column. Knowing what the result could be for a consequentialist would require more specific information.

What father would risk both his sons' lives in consecutive chapters, first, to settle a domestic dispute by exposing family members in the wilderness and, second, just on faith that the contradiction between the divine command and the call of conscience will be resolved. Abraham is willing (and believes it the divine will) to make a bloody sacrifice of the son not yet having fulfilled

---

53. Kearney, *Anatheism*, 19.

the promise of providing the seed of an immense offspring to carry the covenants God granted to Abraham outward to the world. Adam and Eve were given contradictory commandments in the garden and had to reason through which was more important to obey. Before they had even partaken of the tree of knowledge of good and evil (that is, before they had obtained moral knowledge), they still had to reason through a moral choice—which of the divine commands was more important? As with the human condition from the beginning, Abraham must reason moral choices that present themselves as contradictory or moral imperatives that yield contrasting results. We do the works of Abraham when we engage Abraham's decision (twice) to accede to the divine command, which appears to call for the murder of his son. Through life, we consistently face complex ethical and moral decisions in which the alternatives bring consequences that are all bad, are all good, or more commonly have the good and the evil so intermixed that the wheat and tares of morality will have to await a deferred judgment day, while the choices have to be made proximately. Decisions regarding actions that to human reason contradict not only other divine commands, but even our own conscience and moral code.

Part One

The Foundations
of Girardian Thought

Chapter One

The Girardian Anthropology

Questions about the past, about societies and cultures, and about religion require explicit or taken-for-granted analysis regarding fundamental questions, about epistemology (how is knowledge generated, and how do we determine what is true?), on ontology (what is fundamental reality, or what truly exists?), and on anthropology (what is human nature, or what is the basis of human society?). It is the last of these foundational questions where Girard is most original and most useful—anthropology.[1] A

---

1. I am drawing on a number of sources to summarize Girard's anthropology, including James Williams's *The Bible, Violence, and the Sacred: Liberation from the Myth of Sanctioned Violence* (San Franciso: Harper, 1991), 7–10, and the first chapter of Raymund Schwager's *Must There Be Scapegoats? Violence and Redemption in the Bible*, trans. Maria L. Assad (San Francisco: Harper & Row, 1987). Keep in mind when examining Girard's view of human nature that even though he has made the journey from atheist to Catholic, Girard's Christianity is anything but orthodox. He, in fact, labels much of orthodox Christian belief a fundamental misunderstanding of the core of the Christian gospel. When one attends the meetings of the Girard society (the Colloquium on Violence and Religion, CoV&R) one can't but be impressed by the wide array of people in attendance from Christians, Jews, and Muslims to peace activists and atheists; academics from a wide range of disciplines are drawn to this explanation of culture. Some few academics rise to almost cult-like status outside academia. So it is with Girard: "Rene Girard has been transformed into something of a sect in America, with disciples, translators, and proselytizers." J. Bottum, "Girard," http://www.firstthings.com/ftissues/ft9603/revessay.html. Committed Girardians hold widely varying political and religious positions. What makes them cohere is the acceptance of the Girardian anthropology, that humans are fundamentally mimetic, both individually and socially—we imitate other people, and such rivalry is a core human feature, is

straightforward discussion of Girard's view of human nature and society is the first order of business.

According to Girard, human desire is mimetic. It might prove useful to break down the human mimetic impulse into an individual response and a group response, even though both are driven by the same psychological force. We find ourselves in rivalry with someone else over an object: a car, a mate, or whatever. As the competition becomes more intense, the object itself pales in importance, relinquishing prominence to the need to defeat the opponent. We frequently see this behavior in children when each wants a toy simply because the other wishes it also. We witness this rivalry just as frequently in adults. Notice in people's driving habits how often one reacts just to prevent another driver from possessing a lane, merging with traffic, or accelerating faster from a traffic light. This triangular conflict becomes less about the object and more about the need to defeat the opponent. The competitors become less distinct—in Girardian terminology, they become undifferentiated from each other—until conflict eventually works its way to a violent resolution. The individual conflict often lapses over into social strife when the triangular relationship (two competitors and an object of desire) turns violent; societies feel social pressure and resolve the tension by singling out a scapegoat to purify the group from contagion.

This view of human nature understands such character to be unified, with at least some basic features as universal. Such integrated nature at the least shares some attributes across time, culture, and individual personality. Girard's concept shares the traditional Christian view of fallen human nature—it's Augustinian.

---

indeed what makes us human (although certain primates may share these tendencies also). Paisley Livingston shows how a reader might approach discarding the Christian framework of Girard's thought while retaining the view of human nature in *Models of Desire: René Girard and the Psychology of Mimesis* (Baltimore: John Hopkins University Press, 1992), xvii–xviii and 138–41.

And like the Augustinian notion of a *malum culpa*, this fall introduces humans into a world of mortality, criminality, and violence. Other concepts of human nature can be derived from the biblical story of the first parents. Jews had much the same resources as the Christian tradition when the two religions diverged, but the Christian tradition largely followed the Augustine conception of original sin corrupting inheritable human nature, constantly pushing human behavior and thought toward evil that can only be countermanded and saved by divine grace. The Jewish and later rabbinic conception of the two *yetzers*, the two impulses or inclinations, presents a very different model of human nature that emerges out of the same Hebrew Bible and rabbinic literature the New Testament writers and Christian fathers found foundational. The *yetzer hara* (evil inclination) impels humans to yield to the appetites (especially sexual) and desires resulting in wrongdoing, criminality, and ambition. But just as powerful within each human breast is the *yetzer hatov* (the good inclination) that leads them to altruism, devotion, and peace. Each human is the site of conflict between the two *yetzers*, but the individual can decide which impulse emerges dominant. One can subdue the evil inclination, but one can never amputate it. This comparison of the two frameworks of human nature emerging out of the Edenic expulsion demonstrates how thoroughly Augustinian rather than Hebraic is Girard's readings of both the Christian and Hebrew scriptures.

Modernity has largely shed that Catholic and Protestant Augustinian view of the human creature. The modern notion believes in the human capacity to use reason to make progress, to transform the human condition, and to find universal laws of nature and human improvement. Girard partakes of some of these aspects of modernity (the universality of a law-governed universe) while still maintaining a postlapsarian view of the human creature, requiring the intervention of divine grace to transform the individual, the society, and the world. For Girard, a central aspect of fallen human nature involves the human tendency to imitate the desire of adversaries and get caught up in spirals of mimetic rivalry.

Sophocles's Oedipus cycle illustrates how this mimetic reaction works. Oedipus defeats the Sphinx and is invited to become the next king of Thebes, since the position has recently been vacated, and marries the widowed queen, Jocasta. The competition between Jocasta's brother Creon and Oedipus intensifies as each becomes the other's mirror image and attributes bad faith to the other. As the rivals become less differentiated, the dilemma intensifies until resolved in violence: one of the competitors is cast into the role of the victim, and the city expiates its sin through killing or exiling the scapegoat. Oedipus is also locked into mimetic rivalry with Tiresias the prophet over who can see more clearly into the future and the past. The storyline works out until Oedipus is revealed as the unwitting killer of the previous king, his biological father. Jocasta—Oedipus's mother and later his wife—commits suicide, and Oedipus blinds himself and becomes an exile. Oedipus is made into a scapegoat by the city's inhabitants, and once he is cast out of Thebes, the city is purged of its sin and the famine accompanying that social pollution. For Girard, the city must insist that its ways are just and the scapegoat is indeed guilty of grave transgression that requires expiation; the victim, although innocent, might even agree with the victimizers about guilt. But Girard insists that the sacrificial impulse must be surrendered, and the polis needs to recognize that scapegoats are innocent. The economy of scapegoating is threatened by the revelation of the process's arbitrariness (as any random victim will do), so instead the group elevates the scapegoat to the status of deity or savior for rescuing the city by being sacrificed.

Not only are individuals caught in a spiral of rivalry that leads to violence, but societies also need to purge their social instability by singling out a scapegoat (an individual or a group) on which to impute their sin or impurity, and that victim is sacrificed to return stability to society. The scapegoat is often an ethnic minority, the poor, the rich, someone physically different (birthmarked, maimed, tall, short, liminally gendered), or any person or group easy to identify and blame. In the Rwandan genocide of 1994, the minority-but-ruling Hutus insisted the majority-but-powerless Tutsis intended to enslave their ethnic competitors. Hutu leaders planned ethnic violence by ordering and distributing over half a million machetes to ethnic Hutus and their allies. When the code phrase "Do your duty" was sent over radio and TV, the plan was implemented and more than 800,000 people died in one hundred days. Such violent episodes become ritualized and regularized, and often reverenced with a period of intentional disorder enacted (a chaotic period of misrule in which the norms and taboos of society can be disregarded) before the victim is murdered by group action. In some societies—such as priestly culture in the Old Testament—the violence is directed toward animals instead of humans. Often, after the scapegoat is killed, the group divinizes the victim as the god who saved society in its crisis. Sometime in the future, the polis might repeat the tragedy (because these violent resolutions are only temporary), and the process of sacrifice starts over again. Once again, the person or the group has a crisis of undifferentiation in which mimetic doubles spark a predicament, a scapegoat is singled out, and the group stabilizes for a time by exorcizing its violence on the victim.

Many works of scripture, literature, art, and history demonstrate the operations of this mimetic desire. Cain kills his brother Abel—whether over God's favoritism or over property—and then goes out and founds the first city. All societies are based on such primal violence, and the victimizing process is the basis of continuing social order. First events in Genesis are paradigmatic, in that they are intended to be seen as models for later generations and explanations of why the world and human society are the way they are. Girard notes in an interview that Cain's murder of Abel is a continuation of the original sin committed by their parents:

> So I say the founding murder, which is a collective murder, is like that. There is something in the first epistle of John [1 John 3:11–15] that is a reading of Cain and Abel. Satan was a murderer from the beginning. The "from the beginning" is very important because it means what I just said to you: for the Gospel, Cain and Abel are part of original sin. Cain and Abel are part of the first definition of mankind. That's very important. We are dealing with the biblical interpretation of the founding of human communities as a result of original sin, which is the law against murder in the first Cainite community.[2]

Another biblical instance of founding violence occurs when Moses leads the children of Israel to the edge of their promised land where they will found their nation. After the Israelites invade across the Jordan, they successfully attack Jericho, but the soldiers are commanded to take no booty. The village of Ai is next, but despite overwhelming numerical superiority, the Israelites are defeated.[3] This rout is inexplicable, so Joshua holds a lottery to determine who has brought this calamity upon the people. Lots are drawn until the selection process falls on Achan, who, it is discovered, violated the ban (*herem*) at Jericho by taking booty. The people gather to punish the victim, and he is stoned to death. The people must be purified of the violation by engaging in communal violence, which then enables them to continue their violent conquest of Canaan.

Dissidents, odd fellows, outcasts, the deformed, the beautiful, the outstanding, kings, even the tall—all are potential scapegoats easy to be singled out for their non-conformity. These periodic violent episodes relieve the mimetic pressures for a time, and then

---

2. Michael Hardin, ed., *Reading the Bible with René Girard: Conversations with Steven E. Berry* (Lancaster, PA: JDL, 2015), 76.
3. Joshua 7.

the procedure needs to be repeated, and it eventually becomes ritualistic. Ritual codifies the practice to make it predictable, and the reality of the situation never occurs to the participants because the scapegoating does indeed seem to relieve the pressures on society, projecting ordinary time back into sacred time by repeating episodes of foundational violence. For Girard, the Bible is full of sacrificial texts that take for granted the guilt of the victims, but there are also countervailing revelatory texts that bring out the underlying true meaning of the sacrifice and demonstrate the victim's innocence.

Ritual is one way to regularize mimetic rivalry. The two scapegoats in Leviticus 16 demonstrate this conventional cycle with the two goats (the one to be sacrificed in the temple, the other to be driven out into the wilderness, carrying the people's sins for that year). In this case, the violence of the sacrifice is deflected from humans to animals, but in many cultures and circumstances, redirection never occurs and humans become the scapegoat. Ritual sacrifice is one way humans attempt to sway divinities, bribing them to make the rains, the harvests, the battles, and all the other volatile and fickle aspects of an unforgiving world more reliable. I don't want to make God out to be a divinity of whims and caprices, but then I don't want to view humans as having such limited capacity and vision as to insist on a God of inflexible rules and procedures. One of the most inspired revelations of the restoration is that God is human, and yet metahuman, without contradiction.

The modern notion that universal laws of nature, society, economics, weather, plant growth, climate change, etc. can produce a reliable and predictable world has proven effective with studies of nature. Yet nature still has the capacity to surprise us despite our arrogance that we have understood and explained the cosmos. We need the humility to realize our understanding of the whole range of matter, from the largest to the smallest, might be wrong, or at best incomplete. Studies in the social sciences and humanities have proven much more resistant to generalization. For a short period in the 1960s, Hempelian covering laws that explain how universal laws operate in history and the social sciences were thought to be the future of historical studies, but such generalizations proved hard to come by. We no longer talk in those terms in the social sciences, despite the fact economists and psychologists still assert the scientific status of their research ("scientific" in the way science is done in the natural sciences). We have had to learn to yearn less for certainty and be satisfied with hermeneutical approaches.

In religious and theological concerns, we need also to cultivate negative capability, which poet John Keats defined as the ability to live with doubt, for the great thinker, whether philosopher, poet, or scientist, needs to be "capable of being in uncertainties, Mysteries, doubts, without any irritable reaching after fact and reason."[4] When Girardians propose universal and ineluctable laws of human and social behavior invariant across cultures, historical epochs, and differences in economic and social development, we ought to approach such explanations dubiously. That is the lot also of those who would live by faith but also those who live by fallible reason. We similarly think that we have read enough of the scripture or history to assert that we know what the divine will is and how it will unfold. We think we know how history as an impersonal force will unfold, not accounting for the patent unpredictability of events and of humans when acting in concert. We assert we have God in a box, and we can open that container a crack to find out what God has in store for the world and how the divine plan will be realized, what God's motives are when an event happens, despite being informed that "he will yet reveal many great and important things pertaining to the Kingdom of God"—great and important and surprising things.[5] Since the res-

4. John Keats, *The Letters of John Keats*, ed. by H. E. Rollins, 2 vols (Cambridge: Cambridge University Press, 1958), 1:193–94.
5. Articles of Faith, article 9.

toration commenced (we tend to date the beginning at 1820), we have experienced an unending train of restoration events, many that astonish prophets, apostles, futurists, historians, politicians, and what used to be high priest group instructors. We ought to be less confident and more humble regarding our certitudes. God is a God of wonders, and we humans partake of that divine nature. Absolute declarations such as "God is a God of peace and abhors violence universally" are the immediate context of such claims, but God may well be more pragmatic and less rule-bound than we posit, whether we approach divinity as members of the Church of Christ or as Girardians (or concurrently both).

Much myth, scripture, and drama endorse communal violence and insist on the guilt of the victim. For Girard, the difference between the Bible and myth is that the Jewish and Christian scriptures (Job, Isaiah, the Gospels) culminate in a denunciation of violence, insisting that the victims are blameless. Jesus refuses to engage in violence and, by so doing, reveals the ultimate truth about society and the world. The Christian revelation is the ultimate text that rises above sacrificial ideology to make us face the untruth of the process. Some secrets were and are still hidden from the foundation of the world, and we ought to be open to such possibilities and not foreclose the divine initiative. Biblical scholar and Girardian James Williams notes that the trajectory through the Old and New Testaments is a process of continuing revelation, as God raises human understanding through revelation first to a family (Abraham and his offspring) and then through the Christ event, bringing all people into that covenant relationship to move humans beyond their violent tendencies and cultures:

> At certain times in human history there have been disclosures that unmask the victimization mechanism that results in sacrifice and scapegoating. Such disclosures are focused and sustained in the Jewish and Christian Scriptures, though this does not exclude the possibility of other revelations. *Revelation* is a

key term, for Girard finds in the Bible the revelation or disclo-
sure of a God who does not want victims, a God who is dis-
closed in the action of those who take the side of victims.[6]

This revelation is partial, but cumulative, while evolutionary and
even sometimes misunderstood by the gospel writers. Some stories in the Old Testament—such as the one about Achan and Jericho, the conquest of Canaan, and Cain and Abel—may endorse
the cult of violence, while others—the suffering servant passages
in Isaiah, the story of Joseph and his brothers, Job, Hosea, Amos,
Micah, Jeremiah, and Ezekiel—foreshadow the Christian Gospels in refusing the comforts and dangers of violent scapegoating.
Those passages that endorse or advocate violence and singling
out a victim were composed by writers who don't understand the
sweep of God's intentions but are still enmeshed in the culture of
violence that they inherit. The Christian Old and New Testaments,
then, are in a similar relationship of fulfillment as the Christian
tradition has always posited: "In the Hebrew Bible there remains
a certain ambiguity in the relation of the God of Israel to violence.
The Gospels, however, disclose both the secret of the mythic cam-
ouflage of violence and the way of liberation through a love that
refuses violence."[7] The New Testament fulfills or completes the
central message of the Old Testament.

Girard doesn't discard all imitation. Most forms of mimesis
are bad; they lead to violence, competition, advertising, and murder. But Girard also has a notion of good mimesis. As Williams
points out, "The imitation of the divine model of the Son of Man
must replace the ancient religiocultural model of kingship, with
its tyranny and scapegoating" and substitution following Christ's
example and eschewing violence altogether.[8] In this view, mimesis
is fundamentally neutral, neither good nor bad, "a neutral capacity

6. Williams, *The Bible*, 12.
7. Williams, *The Bible*, 12.
8. Williams, *The Bible*, 223.

of the brain and of every aspect of systems that can be considered 'human.'"[9] If an accident or an act of violence occurs, if one person aids the victim, others will follow the leader. "Love is a nonviolent mimesis" capable of overcoming bad imitation and curing social ills we have despaired of solving through reason and tradition.[10] Even though the Gospels often fall back into a sacrificial under-standing of Christ's atonement (especially Mark), we the readers of the Gospels have the tools to see through the evangelists' mis-understanding of the Christian message, tools fashioned by the Christian revelation itself.[11] Following a good Christian example isn't mimesis any longer but discipleship. Having Jesus as a model means focusing on the will of the Father, not the disciple's own will or one derived from imitating others. God in heaven has no rivals in all the created order and therefore spawns no competi-tion. Serving God also means serving humans and regarding their well-being.[12] We can't be isolated individuals as liberal modernity wants to assert, finding fulfillment and joy as secluded islands standing alone; we are still defined within associations we don't freely choose (family, community, nation), but we can choose the models we emulate, for, as Mack C. Stirling notes, "imitating *some* model is an inescapable feature of human existence. It goes without saying that we unconsciously imitate some models, but we consciously choose others because we admire, respect, or love them."[13]

Girard sees Jesus as the great revelator of the human con-dition, but people and societies weren't ready for the revelation.

---

9. Williams, *The Bible*, 239.

10. Robert G. Hamerton-Kelly, *Sacred Violence: Paul's Hermeneutic of the Cross* (Minneapolis: Fortress, 1992), 46.

11. Williams, *The Bible*, 224–26.

12. Schwager, *Must There Be*, 176–77; Richard J. Golsan, *René Girard and Myth: An Introduction* (New York: Garland, 1993), 131–32.

13. Mack C. Stirling, "Violence in the Scriptures: Mormonism and the Cultural Theory of René Girard," *Dialogue: A Journal of Mormon Thought* 43, no. 1 (Spring 2010): 63–64.

The Christian revolution must spade its own ground first. Girard sees his own articulation of human and social nature as part of this gradual evolution. For his acolytes, Girard ranks with Marx, Nietzsche, and Freud as one of modernity's great masters of suspicion. Each urged that surface explanations are mere fig leaves for underlying realities: for Marx, money controls society and the individual (capital controls liberal democratic governments, for example, rather than government controlling moneyed interests); for Nietzsche, power is the underlying motivation of all action (human nature and society are driven by the will to power, the will to dominate); and for Freud, it's sex (or sexual drives developed in childhood that we aren't consciously aware of). Girard encompasses all three, asserting that violence is the primary explanation for social activity, more basic than money, power, or sex, but always operating through them.[14] Hermeneutics is the method or approach used to interpret biblical, philosophical, and literary texts, or even institutional arrangements or power structures in religious or political organizations. The word's etymology traces to the Greek god Hermes, who was the messenger god. From this view, Girard is not only a hermeneut of suspicion but the master suspicious interpreter who unveils the unseen and unsuspected fundamental motivations behind human action that have been hidden for untold human generations, were exposed in the Gospels, and are now fully and unambiguously articulated by Girard so they can be viewed systematically.

Mythological texts need to be opened with suspicion, for they recast the historical events through first, a distortion to achieve unanimous consent that the victim was guilty and through, second, a falsification to deify the deceased victim. According to Charles Mabee, "Rather than straightforwardly revealing anything of the divine or human realms, a religious text is viewed as part of a com-

---

14. Hamerton-Kelly, *Sacred Violence*, 40–41n1.

munity's covert manipulation of historical data."[15] Many modern novels, movies, stage plays, and journalistic ventures serve the same function of legitimizing and explaining violence committed against groups or individuals. We get our bearings from the stories we tell and hear. Those narratives, when handed from generation to generation, become thick with meaning and power to frame what comes next and what went before. When those stories are passed from millennium to millennium, they solidify like metamorphic rock into the landscape from here to the horizon ahead and beyond. We think that vista comprises our world until we read or view other people's stories, which causes that center of the horizon to move to other parts of the cosmos we don't call home.

Mythology, folklore, fiction, history, and tradition functioned in ancient societies to explain the structure of society and the relationship of the individual to the family. They teach us lessons about our place in society, how to rebel against a restricted view of our place in society, and how to react when crises emerge. Ancient Greek culture was largely shaped by the oral tradition and, in later written form, by a long line of poets that eventuated in what we call Homer. In many ways, Western culture has traveled a vast number of miles and kilometers from home, but in many more important ways, we still congregate in the plain between the walls of Troy and the beached Greek triremes in battle with Trojan soldiers and human nature.

The *Iliad* and the *Odyssey*, the prequel and the sequel, teach a good deal about desire, mimesis, rivalry, and violence in the Trojan War. Western culture starts with the Greeks, and Greek culture starts with Homer, as far as Western civilization is concerned.[16]

---

15. Charles Mabee, "Un/rivaling the Old Testament: Before the Law," in *Curing Violence*, eds. Mark I. Wallace and Theophus H. Smith, 100–17 (Sonoma, CA: Polebridge, 1994), 111.

16. In my summary of the *Iliad* that follows, I have incorporated some details from later Greek dramatic and written sources.

Narrowing the focus just to the *Iliad*, this paradigmatic story about honor and offense, revenge and rivalry, war and sacrifice, will provide one of two examples of Girard's anthropology before I apply that model more directly to violence in the Book of Mormon.

Paris, the Trojan prince, violates his host's hospitality by seducing Menelaus's wife, Helen, and they abscond to Troy. Paris, whose violation of his host's honor and refusal to return Helen was the trigger, which caused the killing and mayhem that followed with Trojan victimizing Greek, Greek scapegoating Trojan, and individual Greeks and individual Trojans victimizing each other. "Myths justify violence against the scapegoat, the community is never guilty."[17] Looking for a victim to persecute and sacrifice, the crowd seeks several stereotypical features, the first of which is a violent crime perpetrated against a person of authority, such as a king, the father, or "the weakest and defenseless, especially young children."[18] In the *Iliad*, the elites on both sides of the battle are scapegoated and killed. The next class of potential victims are the targets of violent sexual crimes that violate the most basic social taboos against bestiality, incest, and rape. "All these crimes seem to be fundamental. They attack the very foundation of cultural order, the family and the hierarchical differences without which there would be no social order."[19] Menelaus and Paris are the triggering mimetic rivals in a triangular competition over the object of desire, and Paris has dishonored the code of conduct by violating Menelaus's family and his honor by debasing his hospitality. Menelaus, king of Sparta and brother to Agamemnon (the latter being the leader of the Greek expeditionary force to Troy), must defend his honor and recover his wife. This one individual offense

---

17. René Girard, *When These Things Begin: Conversations with Michel Treguer*, trans. by Trevor Cribben Merrill (East Lansing: Michigan State University, 2014), 33.
18. René Girard, *The Scapegoat*, trans. Yvonne Freccero (Baltimore: Johns Hopkins University Press, 1986), 15.
19. Girard, *The Scapegoat*, 15.

will initiate a spiral of violence into a decade-long war between Greeks and Trojans.

The goddess Artemis blocks favorable winds (Agamemnon had killed one of Artemis's sacred stags, so the goddess is not going to permit the Greeks to set sail until proper redemption is made), so the Greek expeditionary force can't even leave Greece to sail to Troy. It all begins with a human sacrifice. Agamemnon's own daughter is summoned under the pretense of marrying her to Achilles, the greatest of the Greek warriors. She is sacrificed to appease Artemis: the winds of war then change direction. The violence will not only cumulate at the walls of Troy but, even upon return after ten years of war, as Aeschylus's play *Agamemnon* continues the storyline, will result in the murder of Agamemnon by his wife and her lover, still incensed after a decade about the sacrifice of her daughter. The assault on Menelaus's family spirals outward with the dissolution of Agamemnon's family in intensely personal and passionate carnage, with the personal and familial a microcosm of the chaos that results in slaughter among the Greek city-states. Such communal violence to appease the gods or murder to exact revenge emerges as a common motif in mythological narratives. Although many of the Greek leaders were reluctant to join the venture, the sacrifice of the daughter permits the Greek warriors to cohere in order to start the joint venture against Troy.

After ten years of war and another ten years of a wandering odyssey, Penelope is an object of desire (no longer just triangular but now polygonal desire) among her suitors who plot the murder of her son Telemachus so one of them can possess the "widowed" queen and the property that would come with her. When Odysseus bursts forth from his beggar's disguise and father and son kill the entourage of suitors, the spiraling violence can only be stopped by a deus ex machina. Reciprocal individual killing often triggers a vortex of mass killing. Telemachus had himself been threatened with becoming a human sacrifice before the war's beginning if Odysseus stayed at home. Agamemnon had sent Pala-medes to convince Odysseus to join the Trojan expedition. Odys-seus feigned madness to avoid being drafted. Palamedes threat-ened to kill the infant Telemachus, whereupon Odysseus dropped his maddening pretense.

The major rivalry that leads to multiple deaths is that between Agamemnon and Achilles on the battlefield in front of Troy, but the *Iliad* is populated with a large number of other rivalry epi-sodes. After Achilles's death, his armor, forged by a god, is desir-able, so the competition over who inherits the armor is keen. Shrewd Odysseus ends up winning the contest, and, furious, Ajax (he, after all, held off the Trojans while Odysseus dragged Achil-les's body off the field)—suffering from divinity-inspired delu-sions—kills the keepers of cattle, thinking they are Agamemnon and Odysseus, then kills himself. The violence is contagious and unpredictable.

That central rivalry is between Achilles and Agamemnon, the two indispensable warriors on the Greek side: Achilles represent-ing the warrior ethic and Agamemnon representing kingly honor. Achilles sulks in his tent. Agamemnon takes Chryseis (daughter of an Apollonian priest) as booty. Apollo sends a plague on the Greek camp. A plague is often a moment of crisis that activates the search for a scapegoat. Agamemnon reluctantly frees Chryseis to relieve the plague. Briseis, a Trojan captive, has been taken as booty by Achilles. Agamemnon, as recompense for his lost war slave, takes Briseis from Achilles. Achilles refuses to fight, and the Greek prospects in battle decline precipitously. Here we have the rivalry between Achilles and Agamemnon over an object of desire, not so much over a slave woman, but over the honor due each represented by the slave, and the enmity imperils the Greek war cause.

Patroclus is Achilles's tentmate and childhood friend. With Achilles out of action and the Greek boats close to being overtaken and destroyed, Patroclus in imitation and as a substitute dons Achilles's armor. Dazed by Apollo (the gods on Olympus are as divided in their favoritism as the humans are in this combat; the contagion of violence is as likely to spread from humans to gods as from humans to humans), Patroclus is wounded by a spear, then finished off by Hector. Achilles, grieving deeply, relents in his refusal to fight after Patroclus's funeral, killing Trojans as he seeks revenge for Patroclus's death. He rages over the battlefield hunting Hector down until he kills the Trojan hero. Shortly after, Achilles meets his own death by Paris's arrow, guided by Apollo, to enter his one vulnerable spot: his heel. Each violent death fails to end the cycle of violence but rather accelerates the ferocity and passion. The *Iliad* ends with Achilles's funeral, although the war goes on with other sources narrating the Trojan horse, the sack of Troy, and the deaths of most of the surviving Greeks on their way home.

These Girardian themes of contagious violence and a victim selected for sacrifice emerge in contemporary narratives. These themes Girard finds from the foundation of the world and human culture endure across all human time spans and cultures. Peter Shaffer's stage play (1979) later adapted into the movie *Amadeus* (1984) is a modern story that mimics and enacts Girard's understanding of violence, rivalry, and contagious desire. Antonio Salieri, court composer to Emperor Josef II, has heard, as has everybody, of the immense talent of the young composer and musician Wolfgang Amadeus Mozart, whom his father has paraded on continental tours playing instruments upside down and blindfolded as if in a circus sideshow. When the still youthful Mozart finally makes his way to Vienna, the court musical coterie can't quite make out what to do with this young and vulgar upstart.

The story is framed by Salieri's narration to a priest come to shrive him in a mental institution, where (many years since the rival's death and after his funeral the court composer claims to have murdered the young musician), Salieri will reside until his death.

The priest knows none of the establishment composer's music, but prompted by the inmate, the priest can finish the tune to Mozart's "A Little Night Music," demonstrating that one musician's contributions are immortal and the other's entirely forgettable, although the narrator himself has reached the height of the musical universe in the city (Vienna) and served the kingdom (Hapsburg monarchy) where conventional music is akin to worship of the heavenly.

But Mozart is vulgar and profane, writes operas about sexual and uncouth subjects and irreverent social matters, and appeals to both upper class and the low. The music the youngster composes is divine, but the musical authorities in Vienna are staid, traditional, and ossified. But Mozart's music is anything but characterized by the latter three adjectives. Emperor Josef has no musical aptitude and his judgments never go beyond describing the faults with the newcomer's compositions as "too spicy" and using "too many notes." He defers to his musical cabinet on matters musical.

Salieri recognizes Mozart's music as the work of genius, but that in itself is a cause for resentment. The establishment composer admits to jealousy because he, like Cain, just desires God's favoritism, which is wholly granted to that upstart Mozart. Salieri blames God, not Mozart, for granting such an unfathomable gift and talent to this unworthy vessel while the older man stood there, waiting his entire life for divine approval in the form of such beauty. The scapegoat often stands out because "extreme characteristics ultimately attract collective destruction at some time or other, extremes not just of wealth or poverty, but also of success and failure, beauty and ugliness, vice and virtue, the ability to please and displease. The weakness of women, children, and the elderly, as well as the strength of the most powerful, becomes a weakness in the face of the crowd. Crowds commonly turn on those who originally held exceptional power over them,"[20] and this

---

20. Girard, *The Scapegoat*, 19.

crowd is composed of the musical establishment at the court—not much given to breaking kneecaps or brandishing swords—led by Salieri. Mozart's immense talent is the reason Salieri singles him out as a scapegoat for God's misjudgment of awarding such musical endowment to such a boorish clown with such a high, giggly laugh bursting forth at inappropriate occasions.

When Mozart is first introduced to Salieri, the courtier has composed a little march in the newcomer's honor. The Emperor insists on playing the march and butchers the piece as Mozart marches in, but with that shrill and boisterous laugh, the youngster (twenty-six years old) plays the piece back perfectly following on that one botched performance on the pianoforte, and not just plays it perfectly but on the fly dramatically improves the composition. Later, at a masquerade while disguised and Mozart playing up to the common crowd, Salieri asks that Mozart play some Salieri, to which request the bold but socially unnuanced musician accedes, again improving on the court composer's music while playing from memory.

The court composer complains in his prayers that he had dedicated his life to sacred music, had risen to heights in the musical establishment, had taken a vow of chastity to spend time undistracted from wife and family, and God has given this profound talent to a "jackanape," a nobody. Salieri resents God, not Mozart so much, but he has the capacity to take that resentment out on the latter. So, Salieri begins praying violent thoughts to match his ferocious new attitude while affecting a helpful, friendly demeanor toward the younger man, even coercing the young musician's wife into infidelity in order to get revenge on his rival, which act he retreats from at the last minute (he is certain Mozart had already seduced Salieri's leading opera singer and his passion). Salieri acts out as an impotent sexual rival and not a mere musical competitor. Yet Mozart is not even aware of any competition between the two because Salieri is in a vastly different musical league.

At his moment of great despair, a miracle comes to Salieri's rescue: the Emperor yawns during a performance of Mozart's *The Marriage of Figaro*. Thus begins Mozart's decline in elite Viennese society. Even before Mozart's arrival in Vienna, the Emperor had banned any opera on the subject matter of Figaro (Mozart's opera is based on a French stage play that emphasizes class differences and the presumed entitlement of the noble class). Then Mozart's imposing and oppressive father dies. Mozart writes the costume previously worn by the father to a masquerade into the opera *Don Giovanni* and marks the young composer's descent into grief and anguish, with that same costume dressing up the avenging ghost who threatens to drag Giovanni to hell. That clothing emerges a third time as Salieri, in disguise, knocks on Mozart's door while offering a commission for Mozart to compose a funeral requiem. The requiem (which Mozart associates with his father's death) combines with alcohol to cause the composer to spiral down to his own death the more he works on that funeral mass. In this deathbed scene, Salieri becomes the dying composer's twin-but-no-longer rival as he appropriates the music Mozart dictates to finish the requiem.

Salieri has made Mozart the scapegoat and sacrificial offering, not by literally poisoning him, but by adulterating his mind. So, to the priest confessor Salieri takes credit for the murder of such unimaginable musical talent, divinizing himself as Saint Salieri by self-canonizing as the patron saint of mediocrities while the victim, Mozart, is divinized in that his music will live forever. This celestial status has been verified from generation to generation, most recently affirmed by a short put out by *The Simpsons* with Bart as Mozart on his deathbed, triumphantly declaring "But now that I am dying young, I'll be cool forever. Eat my pantaloons,"[21]

---

21. https://www.youtube.com/shorts/6yV-hJMfGBk

which is in keeping with the irreverent vibe projected by the Mozart character in *Amadeus*.

Having applied the Girardian anthropology to two narratives with which many of my readers will have some familiarity, the *Iliad* and *Amadeus*, in the rest of Part One of this book I will fill in Girard's theory with more detail. Human society, he asserts, is founded on violence, and the only cure for such a violent tendency is the Christian message of Jesus's refusal of such a pharmakon (a poison/medicine). The Gospels narrate the life of Jesus to show how humans can move beyond such violent solutions to their social problems. In important ways, Girard's readings of the Bible culminate in the Christian refusal to accept that victims of violence are guilty and deserve their own violent sacrifice. Girard's appropriation of the Christian scriptures is not entirely orthodox, so I will point out some deviations from conventional Christianity in Girard's project and some difficulties I have with both the trajectory and the specific territory the Girardian comet travels.

In Part Two of this book, I use Girardian themes to explore specific Book of Mormon themes and narratives applicable to the way and results of Girard's appropriation of the Christian Bible, both New and Old Testaments. These passages include well-known excerpts such as Nephi's killing of Laban, the confrontation between King Noah and the prophet Abinadi, generational conflict between Nephites and Lamanites, the renunciation of violence by the Anti-Nephi-Lehies, and less familiar narratives such as Nephi's almost-lynching at the hands of a mob in Zarahemla, the relentlessly conflict-ridden war chapters in Alma, and the persistent insurrections against legally constituted government also in Alma.

Chapter Two

Foundational Violence
and Human Society

Despite all the stories told by philosophers of the Enlightenment (that human origins and societies emerge from rational self-interest, from the need to protect property, from the fundamentally rational core of human nature), Girard asserts that violence, repeated and ritual violence, is the beginning of human society, humans' original sin: "Violence is precisely the key to understanding human beginnings."[1] In some ways, Girard takes his readers back to premodern thought when discussing the foundation of culture. Violence perpetrated against an innocent victim is not only the foundation of culture, but of all society's institutions (marriage, family, judiciary, kingship, religion), domestication of animals, human language, and many other features of human civilization; it is what makes human culture possible.[2] Modern thinkers place too much confidence in the assertion that humans are at core reasoning creatures,[3] and, by applying that reasoning capacity, have infinite progressive possibilities by virtue of that ratio-

---

1. James G. Williams, *The Bible, Violence, and the Sacred: Liberation from the Myth of Sanctioned Violence* (San Francisco: Harper, 1991), 25.

2. Robert North, "Violence and the Bible: The Girard Connection," *Catholic Biblical Quarterly* 47 (1985): 4.

3. These are single-name thinkers such as Voltaire, Locke, Jefferson, Rousseau, and Kant.

nality alone. Girard agrees with Freud that humans are moved by irrational drives they hardly understand or articulate. But Girard's claim is broad and encompassing:

> We propose that in *all human institutions* it is necessary to reproduce a reconciliatory murder by means of new victims. The original victim is endowed with super-human, terrifying prestige because it is seen as the source of all disorder and order. Subsequent victims inherit some of this prestige. One must look to this prestige for the source of *all political and religious sovereignty.*"[4]

At the origin of any society stands the group coalescing to blame the victim. This group is not only present at the foundation of politics but is also continuous to our day. It is the origin of all myths. Yet the Gospels are different, according to Girard, for though they depict collective violence and its injustice, "the unanimity is not emphasized in order to bow before, or submit to, its verdict as in all mythological, political, and even philosophical texts, but to denounce its total mistake, its perfect example of nontruth."[5] The Bible recognizes this foundational element of violence in any and every culture and works against such aggression to protect and absolve the victims. No matter how secular modern society rejects its biblical heritage, the sympathy for the outcast and victim that it maintains originates in the Bible. Girard doesn't view it as a genetic fallacy to think that society born in violence must repeat that violence in every generation: "the lesson of the Bible is precisely that the culture born of violence must return to violence."[6] Only a divine miracle, a redemption, can have power to intervene and stop the bloodshed. For Heidegger, to say that "only

---

4. René Girard, *Things Hidden since the Foundation of the World*, trans. Stephen Bann and Michael Metteer (Stanford: Stanford University Press, 1987), 53, emphasis added.
5. René Girard, *The Scapegoat*, trans. Yvonne Freccero (Baltimore: Johns Hopkins University Press, 1986), 115.
6. Girard, *Things*, 148.

a God can save us" is metaphorical (no political movement, such as National Socialism, nor technology offers salvation from the world's problems is what Heidegger means); for Girard, the saying is literally true.

The story of Cain and Abel is the "biblical interpretation of all founding myths" and therefore doesn't endorse the violence or the founding but begins an inquiry into the ethics of the foundational event.[7] It does appear that God is implicated in the violence because after Cain complains of being targeted as an outcast, God prevents further violence against the murderer by putting a mark on Cain to protect him from retaliation.[8] But the prohibition God articulates against murder isn't merely vengeance repeated ritually: "This difference between ritual repetition and vengeful repetition may appear fine and precarious, and it is, but is nonetheless enormously important. It bears in fact all the cultural differences to come. This first difference is the invention of human culture," for Cain bears a mark from God that protects him from others.[9] Civilization is a compact that involves the outcast, other humans, and the divine. The God of Genesis attempts to stop cycles of violence by placing a mark upon Cain to prevent revenge and cycles of revenge that can continue generationally like the feuding between Hatfields and McCoys.

The Book of Mormon is also a scriptural narrative of societies founded on violence. The Jaredites are a group who break from the Tower of Babel, the biblical story in which humans construct a building intended to be tall enough to invade heaven and displace God. Over generations, having migrated to the New World, the Jaredites get caught up in a cycle of violence and revenge until

---

7. René Girard, *I See Satan Fall Like Lightning*, trans. James G. Williams (Maryknoll, NY: Orbis, 2001), 83.

8. Genesis 4:15.

9. Girard, *I See*, 84.

they become extinct.[10] The second main group of migrants in the Book of Mormon narrative are led by Lehi, a preexilic prophet in Israel/Judah. Foreseeing the coming violence and Judah's subjugation to Babylon, the prophet Lehi and his family also journey to the Western hemisphere. Like Cain and Abel, who break away into two civilizations as pastoralists and dirt farmers, the second generation of Lehites divides into two warring factions taking the patronymics of the groups' leaders: brothers Nephi and Laman, resulting in the Nephites and Lamanites. After the patriarch Lehi's death and the attempt by dissenting brothers Laman and Lemuel to murder Nephi, the groups split, and the two civilizations continue that generative conflict for a thousand years until the Lamanites exterminate the Nephites.

All of human history has been marked by murders similar to that of Abel, according to Girard. The Gospels (especially Matthew 13 and Luke 11) connect such murders "since the foundation of the world" to the passion of Christ into one long chain that "unfolds through the same structure of mimetic escalation and the single victim mechanism."[11] The Nephites in the Book of Mormon continue this pattern of killing the prophets (as did the ancestral Jews[12]), for Samuel the Lamanite predicts that at the coming of Christ, they will lament having killed, stoned, and cast out the prophets.[13] The Nephites likewise establish a paradigmatic case of murdering God's prophets, for the Zeniffites killed Abinadi for

---

10. Even from the beginning when the Jaredites institute kingship, the Brother of Jared objects asserting that "surely this thing leadeth into captivity" (Ether 6:23). The violence is foundational from the beginning of the Jaredite compact, from the time the Jaredites graduated from being a family clan of exiles to their gathering into a socially contracted nation.

11. Girard, *I See*, 85.

12. Jacob 4:14. Jesus lays the murders of all the prophets "since the foundation of the world" at the feet of his generation of Jews, according to Luke, and predicts of the prophets and apostles that Jesus will send, "some of them they shall slay and persecute" (Luke 11:49–51).

13. Helaman 13:33; and its fulfillment in 3 Nephi 8:25.

prophesying of Christ.[14] This long chain of violence against God's prophetic messengers culminates in the murder of Jesus, and, lest one think that this violence is particular to the Jews or the Lehites, "Jesus emphasizes the violence of human culture. As always, his word signifies something universally human."[15] Just as the Gospels connect the murder of all the prophets from the foundation of the world to the impending murder of Christ ("that the blood of all the prophets, which was shed from the foundation of the world, may be required of this generation; from the blood of Abel unto the blood of Zecharias"[16]), so too does Mormon recount history from the beginning to the present as one long brutal chain from Cain to the Gadianton robbers:

> [T]hat same being who did entice our first parents to partake of the forbidden fruit—yea, that same being who did plot with Cain that if he would murder his brother Abel it should not be known unto the world. . . . Yea it is that same being who put it into the heart of Gadianton to still carry on the work of darkness, and of secret murder; and he has brought it forth from the beginning of man even down to this time.[17]

The universal character of these violent acts is emphasized in all the scriptures.

The story of Cain and Abel is archetypal for human society. Abel is a victim, clearly, but Cain is one also, according to Girard: "In one sense Abel is the beginning of human culture as the first victim, but Cain displaces him and becomes the victim-progenitor of subsequent humanity."[18] The mark placed on Cain is a sign of his victim status, a sign that marks a fratricide, but in a way protects him. We shall see more scriptural examples of victimizers

---

14. Mosiah 7:26–28.

15. Girard, *I See*, 85.

16. Luke 11:50–51.

17. Helaman 6:26–29.

18. Williams, *The Bible*, 26.

who become themselves victims in this generational propagation of violence. It is our sacrificial propensity to think of Cain solely as a murderer. Unlike the story of Romulus and Remus, another narrative in which one brother kills the other, the Bible does indeed condemn Cain for the murder, but it also sympathizes with Cain's predicament. Abel has animals to sacrifice (Cain has just the produce of the ground and therefore no blood to transfer the sacrificial tendencies to; humans aren't granted the right to kill animals for food until after the flood[19]), and therefore has a pressure valve for his mimetic tendencies. But once Cain's inadequacy before God becomes evident, Cain lashes out at Abel, who has become his mimetic double and simultaneous rival: "Cain's jealousy brings about a mimetic crisis because he does not have a real sacrificial outlet, a suitable victim to which the mimetic conflict could be transferred."[20] Because the narrative is foundational, it is important to note that it isn't like mythic texts in endorsing the violence and blaming the victim; it also sympathizes with the victim, the victims—both of them.[21]

Not just at the foundation of society do we get originary violence, but at the foundation of philosophy also; human thought—even at its historical best—engages in violence no more subtle or reasoned than human action resulting in actual violence. Andrew McKenna, correctly, sees Jacques Derrida and Girard working in conjunction to demonstrate the violence of interpretation.[22] One doesn't imagine philosophy greats out on the soccer pitch competing against each other, the Germans against the Greeks (accompanied by soccer hooligans, as might Monty Python),[23] nor on the

---

19. Genesis 9:1–7.
20. Williams, *The Bible*, 4.
21. Williams, *The Bible*, 34.
22. Andrew J. McKenna, *Violence and Difference: Girard, Derrida, and Deconstruction* (Urbana: University of Illinois Press, 1992).
23. https://www.youtube.com/watch?v=LfduUFF_i1A, the Philosophers' Football match.

battlefield, the Greeks versus the Trojans, but philosophical discourse is a ground for contestation with ideas as weapons, small and big arms that over generations have compounding influence in society, filtering down from intellectual institutions to the mundane and the common, down to machines that leverage power and control over nature and humanity. Philosophy attempts to conceal this violence. Culture is founded on points of identity and difference. "A culture develops according to principles of identity and difference as long as it succeeds in masking that resemblance."[24] Both Girard and Derrida attempt to work through the complexities of the difference and similarity we have inherited from the Enlightenment— the multitude of false dichotomies built into the modern project.[25] Add to presence and deferral, of signifier and signified, of writing and speaking such binary oppositions as persecutor and victim, the mob and the victim, the mediator and the rival.[26]

McKenna is correct that these binary oppositions (such as masculinity/femininity, First World/Third World, written word/ oral dissemination, black/white, presence/absence, right/left, genetic inheritance/cultural formation, mind/matter, mind/body, reason/emotion, historical/fictional, and many thousands more) were intensified exponentially as we transitioned from ancient to medieval and medieval to modern. We are still locked into such dualisms. At the least, such Manichaean thinking leads to violence as we other those who look, think, or act differently than we do. Such carving of the conceptual world often minimally leads to violence as we divide people, concepts, social units, and others by using a Cold War framework of us versus them or a Hot War framework of friend and enemy. Violence is not the root or branch of all concepts and conceptual schemes, but it frequently takes little genealogical work to establish the genetic connections.

24. McKenna, *Violence and Difference*, 97.
25. McKenna, *Violence and Difference*, 97–98.
26. McKenna, *Violence and Difference*, 99.

Chapter Three

Jew and Christian, the Old and the New Testaments

Girard informs us that built into human nature is a tendency to scapegoat. In Girard's view, all cultures, all religions, all historical epochs—modern, medieval, ancient—demonstrate this proclivity. Girard's universalizing tendency discomfits me, and if I fall into a similar totalizing habit of making global claims, my reader ought to call me on the hypocrisy. The proclivity toward scapegoating is, for Girard, what makes us human, impels us to create culture, and moves us to form language. Some literary texts and religions do a better job of revealing the primordial violence. Girard reads the ancient Greek playwrights (especially Sophocles), Dostoyevsky, Shakespeare, and the Bible as doing more than other cultural artifacts to reveal the truth about mimetic rivalry and the violence that flows from it.[1] The difference between the Bible and myth (Greek myth in particular, but all myth) is that the Bible takes the side of the victim while myth takes the side of the com-

---

1. René Girard, *The Scapegoat*, trans. Yvonne Freccero (Baltimore: Johns Hopkins University Press, 1986), 101. René Girard, *A Theater of Envy: William Shakespeare* (New York: Oxford University Press, 1991), 282–83, 6. René Girard, *Notes from the Underground: Feodor Dostoevski*, ed. and trans. James G. Williams (East Lansing: Michigan State University Press, 2012). Chris Fleming, *René Girard: Violence and Mimesis* (Malden, MA: Polity, 2004), 89–101.

munity of perpetrators.[2] The difference between the Joseph story from Genesis and the Oedipus story is that the Bible, says Girard, turns the tables and defends the victim, deconstructing the logic of victimage.[3] The Bible, then, demythologizes, even while many of its anthological characters and writers were still caught up in the sacrificial worldview: "Not only is the Bible not a myth; it is the source of whatever 'demythologization' has occurred in our world and will occur in the future."[4] True, the Bible contains scapegoating narratives and endorsements, but it is the only ancient source, for Girard, that critiques scapegoating so thoroughly and on a trajectory toward abolition; the Bible is a divided text with impulses that work to support mythology and others that undermine it. Greek and other myths find the victim guilty, but the Bible contains a complex process (that is, a mixture of embrace and rejection of scapegoating) of the revelation of myth for what it is.[5]

The trend in the Old Testament in portrayals of Yahweh is away from the attributions of violence and vengeance. The God of the Old Testament is never entirely free of bloodshed, but, especially in the prophetic books, the aspects of primitive violent deity are almost done away.[6] The Hebrew Bible contains elements opposed to a sacrificial ontology: psalms,[7] prophetic opposition to animal[8] and child sacrifice,[9] and the suffering servant portions

---

2. René Girard, "The Bible Is Not a Myth," *Literature and Belief* 4 (1984): 10.

3. Girard, "The Bible," 13.

4. Girard, "The Bible," 14–15.

5. Mack C. Stirling and Scott Burton, "Scandals, Scapegoats, and the Cross: An Interview with René Girard," *Dialogue: A Journal of Mormon Thought* 43, no. 1 (Spring 2010): 123.

6. René Girard, *Things Hidden Since the Foundation of the World*, trans. Stephen Bann and Michael Metteer (Stanford: Stanford University Press, 1987), 157.

7. Such as the psalms that describe the Lord as a shepherd tending with tenderness the sheep, Psalm 23. Those psalms that give a voice to those who suffer oppression. Rarely has the scapegoat been permitted to raise the cry of the victim as does Psalm 140 or have the suffering Christ on the cross afforded words and cries of anguish as Psalm 22 puts words in the mouth of Jesus.

8. Isaiah 1:15; Hosea 6:6–8.

9. Micah 6:7; Jeremiah 32:35.

of Isaiah.[10] I discuss the example just stated in greater depth later in this chapter. The story of Cain sides with Abel and notes the violence involved in founding cities: "The sign of Cain is the sign of civilization. The cross of Christ is the sign of salvation, which is revealed as the overcoming of mimetic desire and violence through the nonviolence of love and forgiveness."[11] For Girard and Girardians, Satan also is a symbolic person, the embodiment of triangular desire that leads to violence.[12] Mimetic cycles have three phases: the crisis of undifferentiation (when the two rivals—often twins or at least brothers—increasingly respond in kind and intensity until they can't be distinguished), the gathering of a crowd to observe and engage in collective violence, and the revelation that shows the victim is really innocent. The Old Testament accounts that remain sacrificial go through the first two stages but stop short of the final one: the epiphany.[13]

For example, the story of Joseph and his brothers is fully redemptive because it emphasizes the innocence of the victim. Joseph is innocent when his brothers gang up on him and expel him to Egypt. When imprisoned in Egypt and pitted against Potiphar's wife, he remains innocent.[14] When his brothers travel to Egypt for food, Joseph frankly forgives them, and despite their incredulousness, reveals that he has fully forsaken any revenge. Greek myths affirm that Oedipus should justly be exiled, but the Bible insists that Joseph is innocent at every point. The story of Joseph goes even further when his brothers, thinking him merely to be a high Egyptian official, ask for grain. Joseph manipulates them into exiling—leaving behind in a foreign country—their half-brother Benjamin, and full brother to Egypt's vizier, just as Joseph

10. Isaiah 42:1–4; 49:1–6; 50:4–11, and 52:13–53:12.
11. James G. Williams, foreword to *I See Satan Fall Like Lightning*, by René Girard, trans. James G. Williams (Maryknoll, NY: Orbis, 2001), xvii.
12. Girard, *I See*, 45.
13. Girard, *I See*, 106–107.
14. Girard, *I See*, 109.

was himself exiled and enslaved. He is testing to see if they are the
same brothers who would repeat the abandonment of a brother.
All the brothers except Judah are willing to repeat the scapegoating sin: "Only Judah resists and offers himself in the place of Benjamin. In recompense for Judah's willingness to replace Benjamin,
Joseph weeps and pardons all the brothers."[15] His forgiveness
stops cycles of violence and revenge, making this biblical narrative
very New Testament-like (or makes the New Testament narrative
very Joseph-in-Egypt-like) in refusing the temptation to answer
violence with violence. It's also very Nephi-like. After his eldest
brothers bind him and intend to leave him to die in the wilderness
or be eaten by predators, (similar to how Joseph's brothers left him
in a pit),[16] Nephi notes in his written record, "I did frankly forgive
them all that they had done."[17] Nephi does the works of Joseph, his
ancestor.

Few contemporary readers grapple with or even recognize
the massive presence of violence and deception in the Bible.
Until Girard came along, theologies did little to account for that
overwhelming feature.[18] Chapter 2 of Raymund Schwager's book
begins to document some of the violence motifs in the scripture
and the attribution of their source to God.[19] By Schwager's count,
the Old Testament contains at least a thousand cases in which
Yahweh commits violence, a hundred examples in which Yahweh
commands humans to kill, and another six hundred in which an
individual or group annihilates another group.[20] A number of bib-

15. Girard, *I See*, 111.
16. Genesis 37:21–27.
17. 1 Nephi 7:20–21.
18. Robert J. Daly, foreword to *Must There Be Scapegoats? Violence and Redemp-tion in the Bible,* by Raymund Schwager, trans. Maria L. Assad (San Francisco: Harper & Row, 1987), v–vi.
19. Raymund Schwager, *Must There Be Scapegoats? Violence and Redemption in the Bible,* trans. Maria L. Assad (San Francisco: Harper & Row), 1987.
20. S. D. Snyman, "Trends in the History of Research on the Problem of Vio-lence in the Old Testament," *Verbum et Ecclesia* 18, no. 1 (1999): 127.

lical scholars have noted the frequency of violence in the Bible and some call it the dominant theme.[21] Yet few members of the Church of Jesus Christ of Latter-day Saints, in my experience, raise objections to violence when a Sunday school or seminary lesson covers the material. Somehow the need to assert the literal, historical truth of the stories lulls our ethical responses into a deep sleep.[22] We are trained not to explore the role of Job as the victim of his people, but to rather emphasize the patience of Job (the New Testament book of James [5:11] may find patience in the text, but I see little), the faithfulness of Job, or the justice of God. We take the epilogue to the book to be the ultimate meaning of the story, as much as the narrative itself massively undermines that feel-good, Hollywood conclusion with Job's wealth and family restored (well, at least numerically).

Girard views the Old Testament as a scripture that only partially finds its way through the thicket of sacrificial ideology. It too often endorses the victimage and violence that the text in its better angelic moments renounces. "Therefore, from Girard's point of view," writes Schwager, "no clear conclusions can be drawn or expected from within this framework. The mechanisms of violence and projection remain partly hidden. The old sacred notions continue in force and, through the process of revelation, are never quite exposed in their true meaning."[23] Even at its most primitive, the Bible reveals the fundamental human problem of mimeticism better than any modern analyst has—the problem that humans tend to imitate a rival in a cycle of competition that intensifies until violence breaks out, as I have outlined in Chapter 1.[24] The biblical revelation is also nowhere close to being exhausted, but our grad-

21. Snyman, "Trends," 128.

22. Mark S. Gustavson, "Scriptural Horror and the Divine Will," *Dialogue: A Journal of Mormon Thought* 21, no. 1 (Spring 1988): 79.

23. Schwager, *Must There Be,* 43.

24. Girard, *Theater,* 282.

ual increasing awareness has been retarded by our incapacity to read the text properly.[25] Girard is extremely valuable in the task of bringing these hidden biblical themes to consciousness.

One of the most problematic elements of biblical religion for a modern person is the stories about the *herem*, or ban.[26] The Hebrew word means "to exterminate," often on a large scale. The Amalekites are to be defeated in battle, and all are to be killed.[27] Citing one example from a neighbor of Israel, John J. Collins notes that "the slaughter has a sacrificial character" because all the victims are offered as a sacrifice to the deity.[28] Every person is to be killed without exception and the judgment collective. When the Israelites invade the promised land, they are to kill all the current occupants.[29] The Bible records ambivalence about human sacrifice. Abraham is not condemned but rewarded for his willingness to sacrifice his son, and two kings of Judah—Ahaz and Manasseh—are both described as participants in the practice. But by the time the Deuteronomistic history is written, human sacrifice is criticized,[30] and the prophets living at the time also condemn it.[31] The Deuteronomist doesn't criticize the ban, but the writer does feel

---

25. Girard, *Theater*, 282–83.

26. Such as in Joshua 6:15–21, where Jericho is put under the ban. Moses also commands the Israelites upon entry to the promised land to not leave any of the inhabitants alive (Deuteronomy 7:1–2; 20:16–18).

27. 1 Samuel 15.

28. John J. Collins, "The Zeal of Phinehas: The Bible and the Legitimation of Violence," *Journal of Biblical Literature* 122, no. 1 (2003): 5.

29. Deuteronomy 7:1–2; 20:16–18.

30. Deuteronomy 12:31; 18:10. The Deuteronomistic history is comprised of those narrative books (Joshua, Judges, 1 Samuel, 2 Samuel, 1 Kings, and 2 Kings) that continue the Pentateuchal storyline through the time of the exiles of Israel and Judah (721 BCE and 587 BCE). These biblical books have a similar ideological view and writing style as the writer of Deuteronomy. Friedman even cites evidence that the book of Jeremiah and the Deuteronomistic history were written by the same author or writing school. Richard Elliott Friedman, *Who Wrote the Bible?* (New York: Summit, 1987), 126–27.

31. Micah 6:6–8; Jeremiah 19:4–6.

the need to rationalize it as necessary to combat cultural and religious assimilation.[32]

When Phinehas engages in acts of cultic purification by killing the Moabite woman and Israelite man engaging in sex, the zealous defense of religious purity is endorsed by Moses and God.[33] Other biblical stories present an inexplicable divinity whose worshippers commit irrational acts to appease their God. Under David, for example, in 2 Samuel 21, the people endure three years of famine. When David asks the cause, the Lord tells him it is the result of a blood guilt from years earlier when King Saul slaughtered the Gibeonites. David asks the residents of Gibeon how atonement can be made for the murders (one might think that since these Gibeonites were not Israelites but Amorites, and due to the ban upon the inhabitants of Canaan when Joshua led the Israelites into the promised land, Saul's massacre of the Gibeonites would be sanctioned as holy). They reply that they do not want financial reparations but revenge on Saul's descendants. David complies, turning the seven Saulide grandsons over to the Gibeonites who ritually hang them. Consequently, the rains soon fall, and the famine breaks. Mack Stirling notes of this narrative that "many instances of divine violence simply cannot be justified by any reasonable means. The story from 2 Samuel . . . is an excellent example" of the biblical God endorsing human sacrifice.[34] Explaining how the Bible can condone this kind of violence and still be a sacred work worthy of reverence, John Collins asserts that allegorizing the episodes will hardly work for moderns. Instead, we are more likely to point out the fissures within the text, the various viewpoints from which the biblical account emerges and the different views it endorses. The suffering servant material in Isaiah

---

32. Collins, "Zeal," 7.
33. See Numbers 25, especially 25:10–15; Collins, "Zeal," 12.
34. Mack C. Stirling, "Understanding the Violent Sacred," *Sunstone* 133 (July 2004): 33.

and the emphasis on the victims of history—the poor, the slaves, the aliens—can mitigate for some the difficult sayings in the text.[35] Such an approach might point out the different attitudes toward the Assyrians in books such as Nahum and Jonah. Nahum hoped to see, in the destruction of Nineveh, the hand of Yahweh in justified revenge against a wicked nation. The book of Jonah sees the possibility of redemption and conversion of Nineveh, as the Assyrians too are children of God, perhaps yet too morally ignorant to know their right from their left hands. As Leo D. Lefebre observes, "The juxtaposition of the books of Nahum and Jonah in the Bible represents both sacred violence and the renunciation of violence as part of the heritage of Israel."[36] Converts, the book of Jonah urges, don't kill: for Nahum the alliterative injunction is to be reversed.

The Hebrew prophets saw the God of the Bible as a warrior divinity who led His chosen people to victory in battle,[37] or even in victory over Israel's opponents, such as Babylon.[38] However, out of the same passages, a message emerges of yearning for a time when implements of war become tools of agriculture[39] and a text that openly condemns militarism.[40] This prophetic vision projects a millennial world absent violence where humans, as the lion and lamb, live together in peace and justice.[41] Gil Bailie makes a distinction between the God depicted in the Bible and biblical God. The depicted God endorses violence and vengeance, while the biblical God overthrows this violence: "the struggle between

35. Collins, "Zeal," 19.

36. Leo D. Lefebure, *Revelation, the Religions, and Violence* (Maryknoll, NY: Orbis, 2000), 63.

37. Isaiah 11:12–14.

38. Jeremiah 21:3–7; 34:1.

39. Isaiah 2:4.

40. Hosea 5:13; 8:9–10, 14; 10:13.

41. Isaiah 11:1–9; Lefebure, *Revelation*, 63–64.

these two religious realities is what the Bible is all about."[42] As a polyglot text, some parts of the Bible must be taken to be truer to the spirit of the scripture than others. A common approach to reconciling the contradictions in the text is to assert a scripture within a scripture, filtering out those parts of the Bible the reader finds questionable while endorsing other parts of the text that are more "authentic" or "true" to the spirit of the volume. The Christian tradition is full of this canon-within-a-canon approach that too easily and frequently becomes a process of cherry picking the parts that fit the reader's preferred interpretations. For example, (1) the New Testament finds the fulfillment of the Old in the spirit of loving God and humanity, not in the observance of the laws of Leviticus, but for observant Jews, the laws are just as much a manifestation of divine love as are stories of reconciliation and forgiveness; and (2) Luther and other Protestants deplored the emphasis on works in the epistle of James, preferring to highlight Paul's declaration of God's grace, with Luther dismissing the letter as "an epistle of straw."[43]

If it isn't clear yet, a Girardian approach to the Bible must articulate some criterion for determining that which is authentically part of the biblical telos and what is a compromise or betrayal of that goal (something beyond just which passages support or undermine one's thesis), an accommodation to the weakness of humanity intended to gradually raise biblically based cultures to a higher moral plane. For Girard, that part of the Hebrew Bible that encourages forgiveness, eschews violence, and advocates for the oppressed is part of the authentic proclamation of the Bible. Any story or passage that promotes violence or revenge undermines

---

42. Gil Bailie, *Violence Unveiled: Humanity at the Crossroads* (New York: Crossroad, 1995), 199.

43. Martin Foord, "The 'Epistle of Straw': Reflections on Luther and the Epistle of James" *Themelios* 45, no. 2 (August 2020): https://www.thegospelcoalition.org/themelios/article/the-epistle-of-straw-reflections-on-luther-and-the-epistle-of-james/.

the biblical message and is the product of human authors who understand neither the God of the Bible nor the biblical message. Latter-day Saints take up a similar position when, in the eighth article of faith, we express reticence to endorse all of scripture, for "we believe the Bible to be the word of God as far as it is translated correctly," which permits the freedom to deemphasize biblical portions that are hard to harmonize with other scripture or modern revelation as not adequately translated, even if the difference of opinion is not about translation from one language to another but from one conceptual scheme to another.

Like many forms of Christianity, Girard's version sees the Old Testament not as the Hebrew Bible—a book about God's relationship to humanity that stands on its own—but as a collection on the way to the Gospel. What is hinted at or partially revealed in the Old Testament is fully and plainly declared in the New Testament (despite most of its disciples' misunderstanding of the message). Girard's reading, to state the matter bluntly, is supersessionist, just like much of Christian readings of the Old Testament, asserting that what is partially proclaimed in the Law of Moses or by the prophets is completed or fulfilled in the Gospels. Sandor Goodhart, a prominent Jewish Girardian, has put some distance between Girard and himself by avoiding any hint of supersessionism as he asserts the Hebrew Bible itself rises to the ethical level of the New Testament on its own.[44] Supersession also has its violent episodes with blood libels as excuses for pogroms and forced conversions of Jews to Christianity, but for Girard, the Gospels are needed to show the world the way toward complete renunciation of violence, toward a way out of mythology, something the Old Testament does only partially.[45] By insisting that the full revelation of violence comes only in the New Testament,

---

44. Sandor Goodhart, "The End of Sacrifice: Reading René Girard and the Hebrew Bible," *Contagion: Journal of Violence, Mimesis, and Culture* 14 (2007): 60.
45. René Girard, "Are the Gospels Mythical?" *First Things* 62 (April 1996): 27–31.

Girard (and Gil Bailie, more especially so) opens himself up to the charge of anti-Semitism, of asserting a lesser status for the Jewish religion than the Christian revelation.[46] Sensitive to this charge that supersessionism is equivalent to anti-semitism, James Williams asserts that his position is "exceptionalist" but not "supersessionist." Exceptionalism sees continuity between the Old and New Testaments with Jews as a continuing and valid expression of God's historical covenants with his people. The supersessionist views Judaism as the "oppressive husk" that can be discarded once the Christian revelation has arrived.[47] For Williams, Jesus is thoroughly Jewish in his anti-sacrificial program.

Is the restored Gospel similarly supersessionist, viewing Judaism and the Old Testament as fulfilled in much the same way most Christians through the ages have viewed Jews as serving an outdated and completed law and revelation after the coming of Christ? Or, even more intensively, do we need to have a sense of God's saving acts for earlier generations of humanity after we claim to live in the dispensation of the fullness of time in which all past covenants and revelations are fulfilled? God forbid, as Paul would, and did, say.[48] This is how I answer the charge of supersessionism that sometimes lapses over into an accusation of anti-semitism. The cornerstone of such an answer starts with Paul who emphatically asserted that "all Israel shall be saved."[49] The apostle to the gentiles then quotes Isaiah 59:26–27: "as it is written, There shall come out of Sion the Deliverer, and shall turn away ungodliness from Jacob: For this is my covenant unto them, when I shall take away their sins." A very Jewish concept of covenant (unlike the modern notion of contract law) asserts that a covenant with God

46. Bailie, *Violence Unveiled*, 154, 199.
47. James G. Williams, "Sacrifice, Mimesis, and the Genesis of Violence: A Response to Bruce Chilton," *Bulletin for Biblical Research* 3 (1993): 39.
48. Romans 11:11.
49. Romans 11:26.

is still in place and enforceable even if the vassal breaks the promise. The royal expects the covenant to be repaired and fealty to be offered up again. The God of heaven will still send a Deliverer to renew that covenant and take away the sins of the descendants of Jacob, and not just the descendants of Israel but all the children of God.

The words "all Israel shall be saved" are emphatic. Just a few verses before that unequivocal declaration, Paul provided an allegory of the relationship between God and the Jews. The import of the allegory of hardy olive tree root stock, natural olive branches, wild branches, and the grafting of branches onto that root stock[50] is that Jews represent the natural branches that were broken off, but the gentiles should not be "highminded"[51] about that turn of fortune, for if those gentiles continue not in faith, they too can be cut off from the tree. And the Jews "if they abide not still in unbelief, shall be grafted in: for God is able to graft them in again."[52] Later divine covenants don't annul earlier ones but build upon them, sprouting new branches from the root stock while accepting the grafts of the former branches.

As Adam Miller points out, in restoration scripture, chronological time is upset and disordered when compared with the modern concept of time as empty and homogenous. Pre-Christian Nephite prophets proclaim details and teachings of Christ, writers Nephi$_1$[53] and Mormon see their audiences millennia before the birth of those readers, while writer Moroni$_2$'s[54] contemporaneous

---

50. Romans 11:17–24.
51. Romans 11:20.
52. Romans 11:23.
53. Nephi$_1$ is the son of Lehi who leads the group out of Jerusalem and is the eponymous ancestor of the Nephites. Nephi$_2$ is the son of Helaman introduced in Helaman 3:21 and disappears from the scene in 3 Nephi 1. Nephi$_3$ is the son of Nephi$_2$ and is introduced in 3 Nephi 12:1. He is one of the twelve disciples called by Jesus in his ministry to the Nephites.
54. The designation Moroni$_2$ refers to the son of Mormon, the last writer who contributed to the Book of Mormon. Moroni$_1$ is the Nephite captain who led the

audience is a null set, for all his contemporaries are dead (he writes only to an audience unseen, unknown, and yet unbirthed). Writes Miller, "It is my argument that this anachrony is neither accidental nor debilitating. Rather, this anachrony is essential because the messianic, as messianic, is what retroactively reconfigures history itself,"[55] twisting history into nonlinear knots and tangles, weaves and snarls. Covenants with God have this atemporal quality about them. They are, in other words, eternal, though the secular world may view them as anachronistic. As Miller suggests, "What is eternal—what is time-*less*—shows up in history as the *un*-timely, as anachrony."[56]

One can tell that Paul's readers in Rome were also concerned that Jews in their day had not surrendered the Mosaic covenant and law in the numbers they in their time frame had expected. Paul places himself in the line of Old Testament prophets, singling out Elijah, who in his despair lamented that he was the last true believer in Yahweh ("Lord, they have killed thy prophets, and digged down thine altars; and I am left alone, and they seek my life"). But that overly dark assessment of the state of the children of Israel was excessively pessimistic, as the Lord corrects the perception: "But what saith the answer of God unto him? I have reserved to myself seven thousand men, who have not bowed the knee to the image of Baal. Even so then at this present time also there is a remnant according to the election of grace."[57] This typological comparison for Paul's readers in Rome means in his day that "God hath not cast away his people which he foreknew."[58] Elijah, Paul,

---

Nephite armies toward the end of the book of Alma.

55. Adam S. Miller, "Messianic History: Walter Benjamin and the Book of Mormon," in *Rube Goldberg Machines: Essays in Mormon Theology*, Adam S. Miller (Salt Lake City, UT: Kofford, 2012), 21.

56. Miller, "Messianic," 22.

57. Romans 11:3-5. Citing 1 Kings 19:10–18.

58. Romans 11:2.

the Roman saints: none can encompass and fathom the election of grace and its fruits.

So, it wasn't just those we might call Jews who stood in front of Moses before they entered the Promised Land and reasserted the covenant they made at Horeb:

> Ye stand this day all of you before the Lord your God; your captains of your tribes, your elders, and your officers, with all the men of Israel, Your little ones, your wives, and thy stranger that is in thy camp, from the hewer of thy wood unto the drawer of thy water: That thou shouldest enter into covenant with the Lord thy God, and into his oath, which the Lord thy God maketh with thee this day: That he may establish thee to day for a people unto himself, and that he may be unto thee a God, as he hath said unto thee, and as he hath sworn unto thy fathers, to Abraham, to Isaac, and to Jacob. *Neither with you only do I make this covenant and this oath; But with him that standeth here with us this day before the Lord our God, and also with him that is not here with us this day.*[59]

All the children of Israel, the descendants of Abraham through Isaac and Jacob, all their camp followers, all their children, and their children's children, "him that standeth here with us this day before the Lord our God, and also with him that is not here with us this day," and those gentiles to whom Paul wrote his epistle, and all who embrace the restored gospel in the day you read this book. Their Mosaic covenant was grandfathered into the new and everlasting covenant restored in the dispensation of the fullness of times, and our covenant grandsonned and granddaughtered into their covenant at Sinai. That is the strangeness of the *un*-timely time-*less*ness of eternity. Jews are not earlier or later than Christians, and Latter-day Saint Christians not later than Former-day Christians, for we labor in the vineyard just as many hours as remain in the day when the landowner recruits us. The lord of the

---

59. Deuteronomy 29:10–15, emphasis mine.

vineyard or the olive grove decides the pay, not the laborers who were hired earliest in the morning. The landowner determines the time and the remuneration.

We inherit with grace and gratitude the Old Testament and knowledge of the covenants narrated there. We fulfill the revelations and covenants those ancestors received and recorded, for they were written also for our sake,[60] as well as for the Corinthian saints, the ancient Israelites under the Mosaic law, and Jews of all levels of adherence today. Jews don't go out of style nor to hell. They are expected to live their covenant as we are ours. We embrace them as fellow citizens in the divine commonwealth. We learn much from their walk with God and strengthen our own legs for the times when our paths diverge and farther along the way as they reconverge.

Greek dramatists and Hebrew sources, for Girard, are in partial agreement about foundational violence, and partially bring to light the scapegoating mechanism. The Bible, though, stands apart on the proper response to that violence. Such violence must be confronted and revealed for what it is: "nowhere in the Bible will we find the idea that the city of man should accommodate itself to generative violence, making room for it under the pretext that 'much wrong in the world thereby is healed.'"[61] The Gospel narratives alone see the victim as a victim without divinizing the sacrifice or scapegoating him or her.[62] The Gospels reveal the God of the Bible as being on the side of the victims, not the side of the persecutors. The Gospels show that the only way to stop cycles of violence is to reveal them as such. Portions of the Old Testament, such as the book of Job or the suffering servant songs in Isaiah, could be incorporated into the New Testament as part of the

60. 1 Corinthians 9:10.
61. René Girard, *Job: The Victim of His People*, trans. Yvonne Freccero (Stanford: Stanford University Press, 1985), 151. Girard is quoting Aeschylus' *Oresteia*.
62. Girard, *Job*, 150–51.

Christian declaration. The Gospels (and some psalms) undermine persecution and the operation of scapegoating mechanisms by proclaiming that the victim is innocent. The New Testament and the Old Testament work in conjunction in this enterprise, the former completing or fulfilling the work of the latter,[63] only because the New Testament workers are called as fresh laborers late in the heat of the day. The entire Bible has a trajectory leading away from sacrifice and toward nonviolence whose arc isn't completed until the Gospels narrate the life and death of Christ.[64] The first stage of that movement is to direct violence away from human sacrifice to animals; the second occurs during the Exodus from Egypt when the Passover ritual deemphasizes the burnt offering and highlights the community meal, and the third stage (still within the Old Testament) comes when the prophets denounce all forms of violence.[65] Every part of the renunciation of violence present in the Gospels is already there in the suffering servant songs of Isaiah, so the message of nonviolence isn't unique to the Gospels. To maintain the revelatory and exceptional status of the Gospels without falling into anti-semitism or supersessionism is a difficult balance—hence the frequent charge that Girard's ideas are anti-semitic. Parts of the Christian tradition as early as the New Testament have also been used to persecute the Jews,[66] so the risk of Girard's biblical reading is to reinforce the idea that the Hebraic/Jewish revelation is incomplete until fulfilled by the Christian epiphany—and the Jews as resistant to the completeness of their own teaching. Despite a mixed picture when it comes to reading

---

63. René Girard, *The Scapegoat*, trans. Yvonne Freccero (Baltimore: Johns Hopkins University Press), 101–103.

64. Girard, *Things Hidden*, 239.

65. Girard, *Things Hidden*, 240.

66. Sandor Goodhart, "'al lo-chamas asah' (*although he had done no violence*)': René Girard and the Innocent Victim," in *Violence Renounced: René Girard, Biblical Studies, and Peacemaking*, ed. Willard M. Swartley, 200–17 (Telford, PA: Pandora, 2000), 211.

violence in the Old Testament, Girard is a deontologist in holding that the God of the Bible forbids violence on principle and universally while attempting to mitigate its influence. Passages that show God endorsing or commanding violence are composed by writers still in the midst of a mimetic crisis and take the wrong lesson away from the biblical heritage. Such a deontological stance isn't mutually exclusive of the biblical abhorrence of the consequences of such violence. Our positions on the Russian invasion of Ukraine can both disdain Russia's arrogance in thinking it can use force to remove Ukraine's right to self-determination and deplore the resulting loss of life and injury suffered by the Ukrainian people.

The New Testament also has a mixed attitude toward violence. The Sermon on the Mount urges Christians to renounce violent retaliation; other passages depict Jesus as the humble rather than military leader in entering Jerusalem on a foal rather than on a steed with full military escort. Jesus and John and their followers accept soldiers as disciples without requiring they give up their vocation. Jesus tells his followers to put up the sword. Other parts of the New Testament, such as the book of Revelation, portray God as the divine warrior, while other portions praise God's acts of saving the Israelites from their enemies. Some of Jesus's parables invoke violence to force wedding guests to the banquet.[67] Jesus clears the temple, whip in hand (at least in the gospel of John), overturning the money changers' tables. Girard and Girardians strongly deny this is a violent act, perhaps only symbolic violence. The book of Hebrews articulates a view of sacrifice that differs very little from that of Leviticus. So, even the New Testament is a mixture of impulses when it comes to endorsing or prohibiting violence.

Williams doesn't like to use traditional fulfillment language to state that the Christian message completes or supersedes the Jew-

---

67. Lefebure, *Revelation*, 69–70.

ish ethic that came before it. Jesus does bare the scapegoat mechanism in a way no tradition did before, but Job (and the other parts of the Hebrew Bible) also teaches the futility of scapegoating. Christians, however, have misunderstood their own scripture more than they have understood that its meaning and the Gospels themselves are fundamentally Jewish.[68] It isn't God's plan or desire that the mob gathers to kill Jesus. It is the work of Satan, or the human scapegoating principle.[69] While Jesus does reveal the mimetic principle for what it is, divinity isn't implicated in the evil by which the truth is unconcealed.

The New Testament appears to continue mythological work that has been countered by the revealed parts of the Old Testament. Jesus is, after all, divine. To divinize the victim is to engage in sacrifice—mythology. So "Christianity gives the impression of falling back into mythology."[70] Jesus is guiltless, and so is the Baptist, the text insists. The difference is that something happens in the Christian story without parallel. A small group of disciples emerges that destroys the consensus that the victim is guilty. This makes Christianity unparalleled, but also goes much further to reveal the illusion of mythology to the world.[71] The Old Testament prefigures the New in this revelation, but that task of preparing the way is itself valuable and important:

> The Christian revelation in its highest sense is always aware of the biblical revelation that precedes it. It is basically of the same nature and proceeds from the same type of insight. The Christian revelation in its highest sense desires to be guided on the basis of the older, related revelation, to be enriched by its

68. James G. Williams, *The Bible, Violence, and the Sacred: Liberation from the Myth of Sanctioned Violence* (San Francisco: Harper, 1991), 175.
69. Girard, *I See*, 21.
70. Girard, *I See*, 122.
71. Girard, *I See*, 123.

treasury of knowledge and its marvelously concrete and pictur-esque forms of speech."[72]

For Girard, the Gospel writers reject all violence and attribute none to Jesus or the Father; in order to make this claim, how-ever, I don't think Girard adequately addresses Jesus's cleansing of the temple. Jesus does engage in symbolic violence (even if that symbolic violence points to the literal violence the Romans will carry out a few decades hence to the Jews and the temple, not what Jesus or God initiate) to epitomize the rejection of the temple as it functioned in his day. Andy Alexis-Baker traces the history of interpretations of the temple incident in John 2,[73] suggesting that the story was taken as an early model of what to do with heretics. Alexis-Baker makes a case for a nonviolent reading of the narrative but notes that the trajectory of interpretation has largely involved an endorsement of violence, especially notable in Augustine and Calvin.[74] So Girard's nonviolent reading is in the minority of the Christian tradition ("The Gospels speak of *sacrifices* in order to reject them and deny them any validity"[75]). Nothing in the Gos-pels, according to Girard, suggests that Jesus's atonement is sac-rificial in any of the ways (expiation, substitution, infinite offense against an infinite deity) sacrifice has been explained.[76] Jesus's death indeed saves, but not in a sacrificial way.

The epistle to the Hebrews gives the passion a sacrificial explanation, and therefore reverts to an ethic more primitive,

---

72. Girard, *I See*, 130.

73. Andy Alexis-Baker, "Violence, Nonviolence and the Temple Incident in John 2:13–15," *Biblical Interpretation* 20 (2012): 73–96. The other Gospels place the cleansing incident at the end of Jesus's ministry and omit the braiding and use of the rope, although Matthew has him overturning the tables of commerce (21:12–13), as does Mark (11:15–19). Luke merely has Jesus "drive out" those engaging in commerce (19:25).

74. Alexis-Baker, "Violence," 73–96.

75. Girard, *Things Hidden*, 180.

76. Girard, *Things Hidden*, 180.

pre-Gospels.[77] Poong-in Lee demonstrates, to the contrary, that given enough determination, a reader can interpret that same epistle anti-sacrificially.[78] Girard also later relented and eased his harsher judgments against the epistle to the Hebrews.[79] Girard's interviewer (Jean-Michel Oughourlian), in *Things Hidden since the Foundation of the World*, asks Girard if he isn't just cherry picking from the Hebrew and Christian scriptures, selecting what supports his thesis and rejecting as inadequate any passage that endorses violence or vengeance: "Are you not also compelled implicitly or explicitly to divide the gospel text into two unequal halves: the good, anti-sacrificial, humanist text, on the one hand, and the bad, sacrificial and theological one, on the other? Will you not have to expel the bad text from the Gospels, recalling in that very gesture the classic sacrificial practices?"[80] This question poses one of my own difficulties with Girard's interpretation of the Bible (not only of the Gospels) and a gesture repeated by Eugene England when he applies Girardian notions to the Book of Mormon:[81] whatever agrees in the text with the preferred thesis is accepted as inspired and divine and whatever undercuts the favored interpretation is explained away.[82] Françoise Meltzer makes a similar criticism commenting on Girard's reading of the Salomé/John the Baptist narrative, after acknowledging the "compelling and elegant" qual-

---

77. Girard, *Things Hidden*, 192; Denny Weaver also asserts that "in modern language the cleansing might be called an act of nonviolent resistance," in *The Nonviolent Atonement* (Grand Rapids, MI: Eerdmans, 2011), 40–41.

78. Poong-in Lee, "Is an Anti-sacrificial Reading of Hebrews Plausible?" In *Sacrifice, Scripture, and Substitution*, edited by Ann W. Astell and Sandor Goodhart Notre Dame, IN: University of Notre Dame Press, 2011. 424–44.

79. Kaplan, *René Girard*, 120.

80. Girard, *Things Hidden*, 185.

81. Eugene England, "A Second Witness for the Logos: The Book of Mormon and Contemporary Literary Criticism." In *By Study and Also By Faith: Nibley Festschrift*, vol. 2, ed. by John M. Lundquist and Stephen D. Ricks (Salt Lake and Provo: Deseret and FARMS, 1990), 91–125.

82. Eugene England, "Why Nephi Killed Laban: Reflections on the Truth of the Book of Mormon," *Dialogue: A Journal of Mormon Thought* 22, no. 3 (Fall 1989): 32–51. Also, Eugene England, "A Second Witness," 91–125.

ity of that reading: "As usual, however, Girard's reading depends upon a reader who, to be convinced, must overlook numerous omissions as well as swallow a series of horsepills."[83]

This approach forms a canon within the canon, with that smaller canon determining what is authentic in the larger canon while scapegoating the rest so those elements can be conveniently ignored. In the context of the Apocalypse, Girard asserts the violence of that final biblical book is a result of human hands, not God's: "Apocalyptic violence is always laid at the door of humanity in the Gospels, and never blamed on God. The commentators do not appreciate this, because they read the texts in the light of the apocalyptic passages of the Old Testament, in which God is indeed involved."[84] North notes that Girard uses the Sermon on the Mount as a canon within the canon, especially to balance the divine violence of both New and Old Testament eschatology.[85]

Girard rejects the implied violence in the parable of the wicked tenants.[86] Girard's answer is that Matthew's wording is better because it isn't the owner/lord of the vineyard who endorses the destruction of the tenants but the people generally who support that action.[87] Jesus doesn't approve the violence but lets the crowd come to their own conclusion; for Girard, Mark and Luke didn't quite understand what Matthew was up to and omit crucial details that absolve Jesus of approving violence. Jesus teaches no concept of a vengeful God, but "in order to secure the attention of his listeners, Jesus is obliged to speak their language up to a certain point and take into account illusions that cannot yet be eradicated. If his audience conceives of the deity as vengeful, then the audience can

83. Françoise Meltzer, "A Response to René Girard's Reading of Salomé," *New Literary History* 15, no. 2 (Winter 1984): 325.

84. Girard, *Things Hidden*, 187.

85. Robert North, "Violence and the Bible: The Girard Connection," *Catholic Biblical Quarterly* 47 (1985): 17.

86. Luke 20:15–16; Mark 12:9.

87. Girard, *Things Hidden*, 187.

only approach the truth if it is still partly clothed in myth."[88] When Girard's interviewer asks if Girard is selecting only those parts of the Bible that support his position and not adequately addressing those in contradiction, Girard responds, "Certainly not. I am going to show you that everything can easily be accommodated within the non-sacrificial interpretation."[89] Each gospel writer has a patchwork of understandings and misunderstandings of the gospel message, in a Girardian reading. When Mark gets Jesus right and Matthew misapprehends, then Girard endorses Mark; when Luke presents a favorable Girardian passage and John seems to disagree, then the Lukan version is preferred.

This selective use of biblical passages and narratives limits the reader's ability to accept the larger Girardian project. In chapter 2 of *Things Hidden Since the Foundation of the World*, Girard, prompted by his interviewer, addresses more generally and specifically this charge that he cherry-picks the passages that support his interpretation and finds reasons to filter out those elements that don't. In the parable of the murderous tenants of the vineyard renters, when the owner sends prophets and emissaries to collect rent, the renters beat and drive out the owner's representatives. When the lord sends his son and heir, the unruly mob kills the son.[90] Girard notes that Matthew presents the true form of the parable reflecting Jesus's ethic. When Jesus presents the parable in the Matthew version and asks his audience what will the lord of the vineyard do in response to the crowd, it is the audience who answer that God's retributive violence will result: "They say unto him, He will miserably destroy those wicked men, and will let out his vineyard unto other husbandmen."[91] In the Luke and Mark versions, the violent punishment is attributed to God and delivered out of the mouth

---

88. Girard, *Things Hidden*, 189.
89. Girard, *Things Hidden*, 185.
90. The comparable texts are Luke 20:15–16, Mark 12:9, and Matthew 21:40–41.
91. Matthew 21:41.

of Jesus: "He shall come and destroy these husbandmen, and shall give the vineyard to others."[92] The Matthew version is preferred because it supports Girard's theory.[93] When the theory drives the interpretation, that strategy undermines the strength of the theory. "The authors of Mark and Luke, or the scribes who recopied the texts, have simplified a text whose complete, meaningful form we find in Matthew."[94] Deriving source-critical conclusions based not on examination of the earliest copies of the biblical sources but based upon which gospel best supports the reader's presuppositions and conclusions is a fragile way to approach textual criticism. Blaming the texts for not saying what the theory needs to bolster the interpretation about those "minor defects [that] have managed to creep into the text, working their way sometimes into one version and sometimes into another" looks like stacking the deck.[95]

For Girard, when the Gospels espouse violence, "we must realize that the apocalyptic violence predicted by the Gospels is not divine in origin. In the Gospels, this violence is always brought home to men, and not to God."[96] When the New Testament appeals to violent imagery, it commonly (universally) dulls the edge of the violence by suggesting the violence is metaphorical: "All the references to the Old Testament are preceded with an 'as,' which suggests the metaphorical character of the mythical borrowing."[97] Girard then provides an illustration from Luke 17:26–30, indicating the signals of metaphor with italics, as I do below:

> And *as* it was in the days of Noe, so shall it be also in the days of the Son of man. They did eat, they drank, they married wives, they were given in marriage, until the day that Noe entered into the ark, and the flood came, and destroyed them all. *Likewise*

---

92. Luke 20:16.
93. Girard, *Things Hidden*, 187–88.
94. Girard, *Things Hidden*, 188.
95. Girard, *Things Hidden*, 188.
96. Girard, *Things Hidden*, 186.
97. Girard, *Things Hidden*, 186.

also *as* it was in the days of Lot; they did eat, they drank, they bought, they sold, they planted, they builded; They did eat, they drank, they married wives, they were given in marriage, until the day that Noe entered into the ark, and the flood came, and destroyed them all. But the same day that Lot went out of Sodom it rained fire and brimstone from heaven, and destroyed them all. *Even thus* shall it be in the day when the Son of man is revealed.[98]

But violent similes and metaphors sometimes translate into literal and real-life interpretations of language, resulting in actions. The book of Genesis specifically attributes the destruction in the deluge to God's anger at the sin and violence prevalent in society.[99] I don't see how the simile in Luke avoids that problem; wouldn't the destruction at the apocalypse *be like* the destruction from the flood in the causal agent in addition to the consequences? Girard argues that because the passage in Luke is not "just an explicit comparison" but metaphorical, one part of the simile can be severed from the other and the metaphorical element rescues the claim from being literal.[100] Can't some expressions be both literal and metaphorical, concurrently? Especially when using simile instead of metaphor, for a metaphor, by definition, says that something is what it literally is not (e.g., my home is a money pit). A simile calls only for a comparison and carries much less transformative freight (e.g., my home is *like* a money pit). Girard's argument seems a non sequitur to me when he blends simile and metaphor into each other.

The Christian tradition, in Girard's view, has mistakenly taken up Jesus's atonement in terms of sacrifice, not quite willing to strip away the outer mythological garment.[101] It follows the epistle to the

---

98. Girard, *Things Hidden*, 186. Girard's emphasis, quoting Luke 17:26–30.

99. Genesis 6:13.

100. Girard, *Things Hidden*, 186.

101. Girard, later in life, retracted this calumny against institutional Christianity. René Girard, *When These Things Begin: Conversations with Michel Treguer*, trans.

Hebrews in this regard. Anthropologists, theologians, and biblical critics have trod this same ancient path. But the New Testament texts radically undermine that sacrificial tendency. Girard notes that "The sacrificial reading is basically a form of regression—slight but consequential—to the notions of the Old Testament."[102] Both Christians and anti-Christians adhere to this sacrificial view, for "both groups regard the sacrificial definition as providing the final, essential meaning of the Christian text."[103] For someone like England, this observation should cause no psychological tension: the Nephites originated, after all, from Old Testament Israelites. However, England wants these Nephites to have the gospel, to come out of Jerusalem with the gospel, for Nephi hadn't even departed Jerusalem for the penultimate time when he slew Laban. When applying Girard's insights to the Book of Mormon, England wants the Nephite writers to be Girardian Christians long before Christ or Girard, for, like Girard, England is convinced that the Christian renunciation of violence is eternal and universal (rather than historical and context-bound). True enough, the Nephite prophets do reveal prophetic insight as early as Nephi's vision about the mission of Christ, but they recognize and live under the law of Moses despite that foreknowledge: "ye must keep the performances and ordinances of God until the law shall be fulfilled which was given unto Moses."[104] The Nephite situation is an amalgamation of the dispensations that is neither contradictory or supersessionist, for when Christ comes, the law won't just disap-

---

by Trevor Cribben Merrill (East Lansing: Michigan State University, 2014), 3–4. "The summary that you've given of my thesis isn't, or rather is no longer, accurate. I don't say that historical Christianity is wrong. The Church does not betray the Gospels by using the word sacrifice as it does. It uses it in a sense that comes from the depths of the past, of course, but that has been renewed by what Christ does, and I don't question its legitimacy. It is the most profound meaning, the most encompassing."

102. Girard, *Things Hidden*, 224–26.
103. Girard, *Things Hidden*, 229.
104. 2 Nephi 25:30.

pear but will be fulfilled: "And behold, this is the whole meaning of the law, every whit pointing to that great and last sacrifice; and that great and last sacrifice will be the Son of God, yea, infinite and eternal."[105] Being fulfilled is not the same as being superseded, for being fulfilled is more like preparing the custard, which when ready, is to be incorporated into the custard-based ice cream: "then shall the law of Moses be fulfilled; yea, it shall be all fulfilled, every jot and tittle, and none shall have passed away."[106] The dessert to be served is not custard but ice cream, which custard is fulfilled in the additional processes after the stovetop custarding is done.

The transformation Girard sees in the movement from the Old Testament to the New has continued with great effect for the last two millennia. For centuries, the New Testament account of Jesus's life has reshaped our perceptions and changed our understandings. As Girard writes, "It provides the interpretative grid by means of which we prevent texts of persecution from crystallizing into sacrificial mythology," and all progress we have made toward eliminating this foundational violence and its logic we owe to the gradual working through our consciousness of the gospel story.[107] The Christian revelation has been progressive and incremental in important ways. For centuries, Christianity has increased our awareness of victims and expanded our empathy. While victimization in the past was largely ignored or mythologized, in a time of the restitution of all things, we can no longer overlook the violence and refuse the pity and concern that begs intervention for victims. The increasing sensitivity wrought by Christianity prevents mythology from doing its work today.[108] Citing Girard, Philip Jenkins notes that the peaceful and pacific impulses in the

---

105. Alma 34:14. Note here that the work of atonement is designated by Amulek a "sacrifice." In the Girardian scheme, the atonement is non-sacrificial.
106. Alma 34:13.
107. Girard, *Job*, 165.
108. Bailie, *Violence Unveiled*, 24–25.

Bible have made it possible for contemporary readers to see its violent passages as repugnant: "The uglier we come to find texts such as Joshua, the more appalled we are by the slaughter of the Canaanites and Amalekites, the more evidence we have of the *success* of the biblically based religions, rather than of the primitiveness or blood lust."[109] The Gospels expand their range and squeeze out the possibility of myths being misrecognized. By revealing the mechanism by which scapegoating works, the Gospels ensure that communal violence is less effective. Philip Jenkins comments on our increased capacity to recognize the injustice of violence because the Hebrew Bible prepared the way: "That is why we have fewer and fewer myths all the time, in our universe dominated by the Gospels, and more and more texts bearing on persecution."[110]

Archaic religion worked to channel and control periodic outbreaks of violence, but the cumulative effect of Christianity for 2,000 years means it can no longer operate unseen. We also have technologies (internet, TV, ubiquitous video cameras) that decrease the efficacy of violence: we see the faces of victims from far-flung places of the Earth—in East Timor, in the former Yugoslavia, in Darfur—and the face of the Other combined with the Judeo-Christian tradition makes us empathize with the victims.[111] All the world's great religions turn the hearts to their brothers and sisters, but it is a particularly Western way (that is, influenced by the biblical tradition) to identify with the victim as a victim. Western civilization's developments (toleration, freedom, democracy) are founded on "the quintessentially biblical."[112] The difference between Judeo-Christian religion and all primitive religions is that the God of the Bible is nonviolent. The second divergence

109. Philip Jenkins, *Laying Down the Sword: Why We Can't Ignore the Bible's Violent Verses* (New York: HarperCollins, 2011), 17–18.
110. Girard, *Things Hidden*, 174.
111. Bailie, *Violence Unveiled*, 19.
112. Bailie, *Violence Unveiled*, 19.

is that nothing about Christ's death and redemption is sacrificial. Christ doesn't engage in violence to demonstrate the violence of the world. Love is the answer to mimetic rivalry.[113] This call to end violence is complete, universal, uncompromising, and unequivocal, for "God doesn't murder anyone."[114]

> Girard posits some kind of transcendence in the biblical text, something divine: At the text's origin there must have been someone outside the group, a higher intelligence that controlled the disciples and inspired their writings. As we succeed in reconstituting the mimetic theory in a kind of coming and going between the narratives and the theoretical passages, the words attributed to Jesus, we are disclosing the traces of that intelligence, not the reflections of the disciples.[115]

The Christian disciples themselves didn't understand this radically revolutionary element of the text. We see farther than do Jesus's disciples not because we are wiser or more intelligent, but because we benefit from 2,000 years of history shaped by the Gospels so we can finally grasp their meaning.[116] Essentially, we see farther because we stand on the shoulders of a moral system accumulating compound interest. Someday, just as the trend of the Old Testament was to prepare the way before the Christian message, the incorrect sacrificial account of Christianity has been, is, and will prepare the ground for a truly nonviolent acceptance of the gospel message: "many centuries must elapse before the subversive and shattering truth contained in the Gospels can be understood

---

113. Richard Beardsworth, "Logics of Violence: Religion and the Practice of Philosophy," *Cultural Values* 4, no. 2 (2000): 145.
114. Mack C. Stirling, "Violence in the Scriptures: Mormonism and the Cultural Theory of René Girard," *Dialogue: A Journal of Mormon Thought* 43, no. 1 (Spring 2010): 125; see also Mack C. Stirling and Scott Burton, "Scandals, Scapegoats, and the Cross: An Interview with René Girard," *Dialogue: A Journal of Mormon Thought* 43, no. 1 (Spring 2010): 70–71.
115. Girard, *Scapegoat*, 163.
116. Girard, *Scapegoat*, 163.

world-wide," until (perhaps) Girard comes along and prepares the way and makes the paths straight.[117]

The progressive revelation of the Christian gospel intensifies the mimetic crisis by exposing the secret of communal violence. Once we recognize the sacrificial mechanism for what it is, it can no longer work its magic to unify us as a community. "Sooner or later," writes Girard, "the ferment of the Gospels will cause the breakup of the social order it infiltrates, and the order of all similar societies, even so-called Christian societies that claim to be based on it."[118] The Christian revelation is progressive because a dialectical struggle emerges in the biblical tradition between myth and unveiling of myth, for "in biblical literature, the forces of myth and revelation contend with each other in the boldest and most explicit ways."[119] The violence in the Bible, even the endorsement of the scapegoating in the text, is troubled by the revelation of truth. The Hebrew Bible openly reveals the system of violence while dialectically challenging that system.[120]

Because we have 2,000 years of reading the biblical tradition through the Gospels, the violence of human society can no longer be hidden behind sacred masks. The violence endorsed by adherents (whether individually or corporately) of Judaism, Christianity, Islam, Hinduism, Mormonism, and Buddhism[121] has been revealed as human, and its approbation by divinity the projection of human desires upon the heavens. That makes our time a dangerous period in which the old methods of purging violence by

---

117. Girard, *Things Hidden*, 252.
118. Girard, *Scapegoat*, 191.
119. Bailie, *Violence Unveiled*, 134.
120. Bailie, *Violence Unveiled*, 134.
121. Some people assert that Buddhism's history has been one of unmixed pacifism. Violence against the Rohingya in Myanmar is only a contemporary counter-example. Michael Jerryson and Mark Juergensmeyer's collection of essays (*Buddhist Warfare*, ed. Michael Jerryson and Mark Juergensmeyer [New York: Oxford University Press, 2010]) demonstrates the simplistic nature of such a claim of nonviolence for the adherents of the religion.

selecting a scapegoat no longer work, and humans are left with few other resources to quell their violent tendencies.[122] The Bible is still the centerpiece in any attempt to overcome violence, for it revealed to humanity the origins of society in violence, unequivocally and finally.[123] Not only do the Gospels demonstrate the way beyond violence, but the rest of the Bible illuminates the struggle between myth, which approves violence, and love, which overcomes it: "while still a text in travail between myth and gospel, [it] nevertheless reveals the founding mechanism with extraordinary frankness and so speaks a clear word of criticism and hope to our time of limitless violence."[124]

122. Robert G. Hamerton-Kelly, *Sacred Violence: Paul's Hermeneutic of the Cross* (Minneapolis: Fortress, 1922), 39.
123. Hamerton-Kelly, *Sacred Violence*, 59.
124. Hamerton-Kelly, *Sacred Violence*, 59–60.

Chapter Four

Girard's Heterodoxy

While it is true that Girard converted to Catholicism very early in his academic career and is adamant that Christianity is the answer to the world's problems (although it should be possible to secularize the work of love and nonviolence, to separate them from their Christian revelation), I advise not rushing to conclude that Girard's ideas cohere with institutional Christianity. Instead, from a Girardian perspective, much of Christianity and most individual Christians cling to the sacrificial interpretation of the Bible that the better angels of our tradition lead us to abandon. Girard has waffled on the topic, arguing sometimes that he is ideologically neutral when it comes to world systems, not favoring any particular nationality, religion, or political persuasion, and without precommitments to any worldviews—religious or secular. Other times he has straightforwardly professed his favoritism: "'All of my books have been written from a Christian perspective' . . . 'Mine is a search for the anthropology of the Cross, which turns out to rehabilitate orthodox theology.'"[1] Yet Girard's program is less about "rehabilitating" or reforming "orthodox theology" and more about thoroughly transforming it. His is not a modest project. In any struggle between worldviews, Girard's theories do indeed favor

---

1. Grant Kaplan, *René Girard, Unlikely Apologist: Mimetic Theory and Fundamental Theology* (Notre Dame, IN: University of Notre Dame Press, 2016), 50.

a Christian perspective over secular and other religious systems, but slantwise in ways "orthodox" theologians might not recognize as reconcilable with Christian orthodoxy. Girard does, however, recognize biblical texts to be "divinely revealed" and Jesus as the culmination of a long process with the God of the Bible working in history, in the Jewish and pre-Jewish biblical narrative, and in the incarnation of Jesus and the New Testament writers to raise humans to a higher moral and spiritual plane to renounce sacrifice and violence and embrace the innocence of victims of violence. "As a person of faith," observes Grant Kaplan, "Girard considers the biblical texts to be divinely revealed."[2] That Christian shockwave in two thousand years has continued to reverberate to transform cultures, religious and secular. As Kaplan goes on to state, "The biblical texts and the Jesus event so shook the foundations of archaic culture and religion as to render it impotent. In its wake has arisen a 'Western' worldview, with its unique attitudes toward itself and other cultures, one manifestation of which is the field of anthropology."[3] I think it worth exploring how or if those reverberations continue through the Book of Mormon as much as Girard asserts they do through the Hebrew scriptures, the earliest of Christian writings, and through the present as manifest in Western civilization and Christendom.

The Christian revelation (and the word *revelation* isn't used metaphorically here) continues in a long continuum of revelations from the God of the Bible: from the writer(s) of the Pentateuch to the prophets, such as Isaiah and Jeremiah, and on to the Gospel writers and the New Testament epistolary compositions. That revelation has continued not just to reverberate but to expand that "revelatory power." As Kaplan notes, "in the Christian account (as in many other religious traditions), *revelation* submits itself to fur-

---

2. Kaplan, *Unlikely Apologist*, 62.
3. Kaplan, *Unlikely Apologist*, 63.

ther interpretation. This function makes it imperative for any substantial theology of revelation to at least gesture toward the process of reading these texts and recognize their ability to reshape interpretive horizons."[4] Girard believes in not just the divine and revelatory power of the Bible, but in the continuing expansion and openness of that revelation that discloses and transforms the world to bring humanity beyond violence.

Girard's theory poses a profound challenge to orthodoxy, and to the restored gospel; it requires jettisoning major portions of what Latter-day Saints share with other Christians. Let me provide some examples of LDS doctrines, structures, or beliefs that a Girardian position would reject outright or just make irrelevant.

In all of these questions, Girard claims no novelty or fresh insight. Girard's reading of the Bible sounds so new and radical to Christians, but he insists it was always there, especially in the Gospels. "If Girard's claim is correct," writes Raymund Schwager, "then his theory must lead to a new and truer understanding of the biblical writings."[5] Most Christians have just gotten scripture wrong all these centuries, but the true meaning has always been latent in the text. Girard views himself as a revealer or a restorer, not an innovator.

While liberal varieties of Christianity have recently surrendered the notion that Satan is a real being with real powers, more conservative Christian varieties insist on the literal existence of Satan. I think most members of the Church of Jesus Christ of Latter-day Saints would fall into that latter category. Girard would turn Satan into an allegory, a principle, a concept. Girard asserts that the Gospels cast Satan as not one spirit among others, nor his kingdom as one among others. Satan is the fundamental princi-

---

4. Kaplan, *Unlikely Apologist*, 70.
5. Raymund Schwager, *Must There Be Scapegoats? Violence and Redemption in the Bible*, trans. Maria L. Assad (San Francisco: Harper & Row, 1987), 42.

ple of foundational violence and sacrifice.[6] All cities, all societies, all kingdoms, all principalities and powers, all people are fundamentally divided against themselves; they are all based on original violence, and therefore they are all subsets of the kingdom of satan (reading *satan* here more like the Book of Job does, as the office or role of a prosecutor or one who tests or tries). Mimetic rivalry begins the expanding process of violence that is relieved only by the making of a sacrifice, so all societies are satanic kingdoms.[7] Viewing Satan as a satanic process rather than a literal being makes humans the offspring of Satan in that they repeat acts of bloodshed inspired by this process.[8] Similarly, Jesus is both god and man to Girard because Jesus rises above appeals to violence. Violence has no hold upon him, and he transcends humanity in that perfection.[9] The divinity of Christ is also to be taken metaphorically, his sinlessness a refusal to embrace any form of violence. In many ways Girard's version of Christianity looks a lot like the liberal modern branches of the religion.

Elements of the Christian proclamation that a Girardian would dismiss as sacrificial, have no need for, or transfigure symbolically by moving the major pieces of the Christian puzzle around, include the following:

> ▶ **an afterlife**: Girard's position attempts to address what can be done in this life to reduce and then eliminate violence. I can't recall his addressing any afterlife. One could omit it from Girard's system without loss. I wouldn't say the same if Christianity were bereft of a

6. René Girard, *The Scapegoat*, trans. Yvonne Freccero (Baltimore: Johns Hopkins University Press, 1986), 187.
7. Girard, *Scapegoat*, 188.
8. René Girard, *Things Hidden Since the Foundation of the World*, trans. Stephen Bann and Michael Metteer (Stanford: Stanford University Press, 1987), 162.
9. Girard, *Things Hidden*, 218–19.

concept of life after death. Restoration theology would be radically different with no concept of a hereafter.

▷ *eternal life*: The distinctions Latter-day Saints make about what happens after death may be part of the confessional structure of belief that grows up in denominations, but for Girard these speculations are unnecessary appendages. Living the life God lives, rewards or punishments in some future afterlife for actions in the here-and-now—these are all extraneous to a Girardian unless that Girardian's belief overlaps with some denominational framework.

▷ *exaltation*: Life spent eternally in family units, sealed relationships through marriage, adoption, birth—all these matters are incidental to Girard. Similarly, time spent discussing kingdoms of glory would be better spent on improving life in this world. Impassioned and at times contentious speculations in priesthood quorum or Sunday school about daily life in the hereafter would be put out of business by Girard.

▷ *hell*: As with positive projections of life after death, eternal suffering through torments physical or mental after death would (I presume) be dismissed by Girard as mere projections of human violence and revenge onto a next life, and upon a deity committed to peace and love. Since Latter-day Saints don't subscribe to traditional concepts of hell, institutionally, and personally, we wouldn't feel the abandonment of such a notion, but creedal Christianity would. Some Saints may still yearn for hell, for their neighbors' sake, but a fire and brimstone venue in restoration theology is mostly consigned to introducing sacrament meeting speaker jokes.

▷ *resurrection*: Like Marx, Girard would want to abandon any discussion of the next life to focus instead on improving conditions in this life. Whether resurrection is viewed as a physical, corporeal restoration as the Saints consider it or as a metaphorical or spiritual continuation of individual identity (as many liberal theologies assert) just doesn't matter to Girard. Girard does take up the resurrection assertions in the Gospels of Matthew and Mark but only to discuss a true and false resurrection—the false one being Herod's speculation that Jesus might be John the Baptist come back from the dead, the true resurrection symbolically showing the return of Jesus after execution to assert through life and death the false charge that victims are guilty.[10]

► **a pre-mortal existence**: Just as a Girardian wouldn't much care about doctrines or speculations about the afterlife, the notion of a premortal existence wouldn't matter. Exploration of a pre-Earth life might be helpful in explaining human nature or a prelapsarian state, but it wouldn't be necessary. However, consideration of a pre-creation war in heaven would add an interesting wrinkle to a Girardian framework. How do pre-corporeal beings combat, and can such bloodless warfare be considered violence? Elohim and Jehovah are integrally involved in such a conflagration (and the violence, if violence must involve physical altercation, is carried out with divine approval in LDS accounts), one embodied and the other yet-to-be embodied. Milton's *Paradise Lost* portrays one way such a conflict might be

---

10. René Girard, *I See Satan Fall Like Lightning*, trans. James G. Williams (Maryknoll, NY: Orbis, 2001), 134–36.

carried out, but that poem isn't canonical for Latter-day Saints.

▶ **priesthood**: The LDS concept of essential ordinances administered by divinely approved authority holds no sway in a Girardian system. I am extrapolating beyond what I have read by Girardians, but I posit they see most institutions as organized methods of violence used to carry out on a larger scale the tendencies of human nature (with some possibility that some institutional structures can be co-opted to reduce violence and scapegoating, for example, Quaker meetings).

▷ *laying on of hands*: Good works are to the Girardian a way to redirect the natural man (and woman). So shorn of the idea that priesthood authority must be passed on by one with authority, the idea that human touch is needed to help heal the world of its pains and vexations is a potentially good use of human compassion and empathy. Just as Jesus's healing touch is portrayed in the Gospels as part of his redemptive power, the willingness to touch the diseased, the outcast, and the dying is a major factor in the commiserating with, suffering with, and sympathizing with that characterizes Christian ministering. Since Latter-day Saints are committed to the Weeping God of Enoch,[11] a personal God who suffers and joys with us, this human touch would fit comfortably with both a Girardian system and a Girardian system bent toward the restoration.

---

11. Terryl Givens and Fiona Givens, *The God Who Weeps: How Mormonism Makes Sense of Life* (Salt Lake City, UT: Ensign Peak, 2012). Eugene England, "The Weeping God of Mormonism," *Dialogue: A Journal of Mormon Thought* 35, no. 1 (2002): 63–80.

▷ *Melchizedek and Aaronic Priesthoods*: If priesthood authority is irrelevant, so is a preparatory or apprentice priesthood leading to an exercise of that authority in its fullness.

▷ *priesthood keys*: Again, the notion that some men hold priesthood keys in an unbroken line of succession in order to supervise the work of salvation effected through the congregation is unnecessary to counteract violence, but it still might be a useful exercise of corporate authority to propagate nonviolence, forgiveness, and reconciliation. When attending the annual meetings of the Colloquium on Violence and Religion, the Girardian scholarly association, the participant can't but be impressed by the wide range of believers from diverse religious institutions and traditions who incorporate Girard's ideas into their institutional work (going way beyond just the Friends, Amish, Mennonite, Brethren, and other denominations officially calling themselves Peace Churches), and from all major world religions (I have met Christians, Sikhs, Hindus, Muslims, Jews, atheists, and more at the Colloquium on Violence and Religion [CoV&R]). Girardians work through existing institutions to try to make the world more peaceful, recognizing the shortcomings of the institutions large or small to which they belong. Girard was a committed Roman Catholic to the end of his life.

▶ **Relief Society**: As with other institutional functions, Girard doesn't have much place for organizational structures—a church. Girard does address communal features in the workings of mobs, but he rarely addresses the workings of institutions, let alone religious organizations dedicated to such work as the Quakers or Mennonites. When the Relief Society was established, the word *relief* meant something along the lines of providing charity, comfort, or aid to those less fortunate. Girard would wholeheartedly endorse such relief to the downtrodden and the outsider.

▶ **a restoration**: Girard's rediscovery of the authentic meaning of the Bible could be described similarly to a restoration of all intended since the foundation of the world. But for Girard, the true meaning was always there in the Bible. No additional revelation or scripture is needed to complete the process, just a better reading of the revelatory texts. Different parts of the scripture demonstrate understanding by those writing the parts of the anthological whole the intentions of deity better or worse than other parts, but the revelation may need to be renewed (restored) as one generation forgets, restored through a Gandhi, a Martin Luther King, a Nelson Mandela, or a Joseph Smith.

▶ **temples**: The sacred work done by Latter-day Saints in temples would combine both tendencies toward violence and work to overcome violence. Symbolic and ritual enactment of violence may lay the spiritual and intellectual foundation for literal violence in the cosmos outside the temple.

▷ *sealings and other redemptive work for the dead*: Vicarious work for the dead could focus the human mind on the other in much the same way evangelization of the living can focus our moral attention on the violence of poverty and dictatorship in much of the

world. Sacrificing our time and our talents on the
temple altar to redeem both living and dead could
cultivate empathy, causing us to abhor literal and
symbolic violence. What could be more altruistic
and charitable than performing essential ordinances
for those who have died? But absent the concept of
an afterlife, such altruistic efforts would be better
directed toward those living in need and suffering
from institutional and economic violence.

▷ *family history*: Binding the whole human family
together across all generations from Adam and Eve
until today is a huge project that extends compassion and love beyond the mere tribal and national to
global humanity. None of this is necessary or even
conceived in a Girardian system, but it could work
in tandem with such a hermeneutic to encompass all
the family of humans.

▷ *the temple*: Latter-day Saint temple worship has
already, under revealed guidance, dropped symbolic
force that since pioneer days enacted gestures of violence against those who don't keep those covenants
made in that sanctuary. Similarly, temple worship has
been updated to reflect a more equal status between
men and women. Latter-day Saint temple worship,
much as the eucharist in the Christian tradition,
could reflect an anti-sacrificial stance that in an earlier instantiation could have symbolized violence
and sacrifice in the way that Christian sacraments
"reflect a reading of reading itself as a substitute for
sacrifice and therefore as an anti-sacrificial practice"
despite appearing sacrificial to some participants in

earlier manifestations.[12] The covenant to live the law of sacrifice the Saints make in the temple constitutes not only nonviolent action but giving our time and divine gifts to serve others, and all the blessings and talents we possess are given by a graceful God.

▶ **a vicarious atonement**: However the atonement of Christ is conceived, the Girardian doesn't view it as a literal or metaphorical transfer of guilt to Jesus (that is, in fact, a sacrificial interpretation of the event). The atonement is instead an exemplary one that shows us how to renounce violence and embrace the work of love. Placing the vicarious atonement in question might also undermine other vicarious work that the Saints do. We can't have any impact by modeling good behavior on the dead. I will treat theories of atonement in Chapter 6, "The Sacrificial Soteriology of the Book of Mormon."

▶ **covenants** (such as the Abrahamic and Mosaic): In powerful ways, the restored gospel depends on covenants, binding obligations and promises tying us to the divine and each other. A Girardian position just doesn't

12. Sandor Goodhart and Ann W. Astell, "Substitutive Reading: An Introduction to Girardian Thinking, Its Reception in Biblical Studies, and This Volume," in *Sacrifice, Scripture, and Substitution*, eds. Ann W. Astell and Sandor Goodhart, 1–36 (Notre Dame, IN: University of Notre Dame Press, 2011), 31. Girard has relented on his more youthful criticism of Christian churches' use of the word *sacrifice*. In an interview published in 2014, he corrects the interviewer inquiring about his earlier position: "I don't say that historical Christianity is wrong. The Church does not betray the Gospels by using the word sacrifice as it does. It uses it in a sense that comes from the depths of the past, of course, but that has been renewed by what Christ does, and I don't question its legitimacy. It is the most profound meaning, the most encompassing." In the next paragraph, Girard sums up his change in rhetoric: "In my approach there aren't the sort of radical breaks with tradition that my language has sometimes suggested." René Girard, *When These Things Begin: Conversations with Michel Treguer*, trans. Trevor Cribben Merrill (East Lansing: Michigan State University, 2014), 4.

encounter this aspect of the dispensation of the fullness of times. Ignoring this element of the gospel would likely reduce covenant making to the status of promises, contracts, reminders (not that such promises are any less impactful than covenants necessarily are).

▶ **a Second Coming**: The way the First and Second Comings of Christ are usually thought through in confessional Christianity (coming in humility and dying in degradation the first time and with power and glory to judge the nations in the second, with judgment and condemnation for the wicked) would have to be entirely overhauled in Girard's thought. There is no need for any return, and any talk of such is too literalistic in this system. The notion of judgment, destruction, and accountability would all be questionable to Girard: too sacrificial, too violent. For Girard, the telos of social development is the overcoming of sacrifice through modifying human behavior in daily interactions and events important enough to be labeled historic.

▶ **baptism**: Not just baptism but all ordinances (what most branches of Christianity would call sacraments) are merely symbolic. They attempt to elevate the human mind by communicating transcendental realities through metaphorical transfer. Baptism, and other ordinances such as temple marriage, are figuratively important but not literally necessary in a Girardian conceptual system.

▶ **patriarchal blessings**: Like other LDS attempts to surpass the immanent and reach the transcendental realm, patriarchal blessings may be comforting and pragmatically useful, but the Girardian conception of Christianity would have no use for them except as they articulate aspirations to help people make it through life and be better people.

▶ **a church structure and administration**: Many people think institutional structures are harmful to society and individuals. Many New Testament critics assert that Jesus didn't intend to found a church, an organizational structure—the disciples did that. Girard would view a formal church with its attendant hierarchy, liturgy, and organs of coercion as potentially dangerous (think of the violence against putative witches, African slaves and their descendants, Jews during the Middle Ages, and even against the Latter-day Saints—particularly in the southern United States), but a communion of like-minded people working acts of charity through an organizational structure also holds positive potential. Latent violent potential might be offset by the sense of community and charitable structures nurtured within religious institutions.

▷ *prophetic foreknowledge*: The God of René Girard is a bit aloof from human ecology. This divinity is willing to inject a revelation about the need to eschew violence in human affairs yet allowed that radical renunciation of violence to percolate for millennia before having its intended effect. God sent prophets and Christ to correct fallible systems but, similar to the deistic view, lets the corrective work advance at its own pace rather than accelerating the timetable of change. Billions of humans had suffered from violence and death at the hands of other humans in the meantime.

▶ **the nature of God**: The most important difference between Girard's system and the restoration revolution is not obvious because Girard talks about God, celebrates God, and points to the concrete specificities of God manifest in Christ. Girard's reader may miss the extreme vagueness and generality of a God who seems more a universal principle, an amorphous concept, than a personal God. The restoration declares a God who knows our names, knows our individual circumstances, hears our daily prayers, and loves us in the way a mother or father loves a child. The *God the Father* title Latter-day Saints take literally, not figuratively. The God of the Hebrew Bible, the Book of Mormon, and the New Testament, like Alma$_1$'s[13] community in exile at the waters of Mormon, weeps with us when we weep, rejoices with us when we experience joy, reciprocates comfort when we need comforting, and stands with us when we are victims of violence and brutality, as would any divinity who has undergone the highs, lows, and golden means of mortality. The God of the Book of Mormon intervenes in history to free entire nations from slavery, leads a family halfway around the world to a promised land, and meddles in individual lives to bring a young rebel against God and his father (who had himself been an insurgent against God until he heard the words of Abinadi) back to a life of service, compassion, and grace.

Not only will I challenge the idea that LDS scripture (biblical or otherwise) leads to a pre-Girardian Girardianism, I also

---

13. Alma$_1$ is a priest of Noah turned disciple of Abinadi who leads a splinter group into the wilderness in the book of Mosiah. Alma$_2$ is the son of Alma$_1$ who enters the narrative as a rebel against his father and the church. After conversion he becomes the chief judge and high priest.

want to note that many elements of the restored gospel would be made redundant if one reads the system as in need of a Girardian swerve to correct what we have misunderstood all along. The body of the church may actually impede progress rather than cultivate it by adhering to sacrificial interpretations of the Bible when a higher law has already been revealed. The restored church of Christ incubated in the Protestant hegemonic culture of antebellum and post-bellum American culture imbibed too much of the hellfire and omni-God assumptions of the Puritan environment. We are still too Puritan in culture, if not in doctrine and scripture. One of the most helpful legacies of the Mormon Girardian Eugene England was to remind us of the God of Joseph Smith (of the Bible, of the Book of Mormon, of the early church fathers), a God who was once just like us, prone to weakness and sin along with all the frailties of corporeal and spiritual mortality. The God who before the foundation of the world saw the surrounding intelligences and provided a way to help them progress to the place and status of divinity.[14] The God who provided His Only Begotten Son to provide an exemplary pattern to show us how to return to hallowed halls where our eternal and our mortal families congregate in our true home.

---

14. Terryl Givens, *Stretching the Heavens: The Life of Eugene England and the Crisis of Modern Mormonism* (Chapel Hill, NC: University of North Carolina Press, 2021), 118–23.

Chapter Five

Problems with Girard's Claims

I, like many (post)modern readers, doubt theories that find a single key to the world's various problems. Every text Girard reads publicly yields to the Girardian insight. One reason for such similarity might be the consistency of human nature regardless of culture and history. A different explanation might be the plasticity of the explanation itself, a theory so general it always works no matter the culture, the text, or the person to which it's applied. Modernity is littered with overarching meta-theories and metanarratives that attempt to explain everything under a single heading: Marxism, Freudianism, scientism, behavioralism. These theoretical structures always work because they reduce all human behavior to what is measured by the theory and its method. Everything that doesn't fit the theory is dismissed as an anomaly or as static. Girard's theory seems too totalizing for my taste. We live in a period of petite narratives rather than grand narratives. Girardianism is a reversion to the modern project of having a social theory of everything. Girard performs brilliant readings of the Bible, Shakespeare, ancient Greek drama, Dostoyevsky, and many other works in the Western heritage. That is why I continue to read him, for the detailed analysis and the intertextual connections to other works of literature, history, and philosophy. It is the systematizing that makes a leap from narrative specifics (among writers from vastly different societies, histories, cultures, epochs, and individual proclivities and insights) to the general, especially to the moral generalizations, that cause me readerly heartburn. Intertextuality, the allusion of one text to another, comes in two main varieties: (1) a historically based intertextuality—often called synchronic—in that the alluding text is always later than the alluded to text, and (2) the postmodern variety—often called diachronic—which asserts all language is intertextual and such a historical filiation need not be demonstrated.[1] For the postmodern reader, the concept of intertextuality might have Shakespeare alluding to T. S. Eliot against the historical grain. Girard's concept of an ahistorical, acultural human nature permits him the use of a strategy similar to having Amos quoting Martin Luther King about "letting justice roll down like waters and righteousness like a mighty stream." The slightest appearance of a substitution in an account, for example, a substitution to violence, or a cluster of people, and Girard is able to connect that reference to a scapegoat, a sacrificial murder, or a mob, despite all the distance of time, geography, culture, and personality using this structural scheme. It is this ahistorical character of Girard's method that makes me skeptical.

For Girard, a single human nature exists regardless of culture and time. This tendency runs counter to so much of postmodern thought, so in many ways, Girard's theory fits into a modern intellectual framework rather than a postmodern one. If one human nature exists, then a single grand narrative provides the key to understanding the individual and society; Girard provides one of those grand narratives. While humans may believe they are thinking and acting for themselves, in actuality, for instance, the day after the 9/11 attacks, so many went down to a military recruit-

1. Benjamin D. Sommer, "Exegesis, Allusion and Intertextuality in the Hebrew Bible: A Response to Lyle Eslinger," *Vetus Testamentum* 46, no. 4 (Oct. 1996): 479–89. Russell L. Meek, "Intertextuality, Inner-Biblical Exegesis, and Inner-Biblical Allusion: The Ethics of a Methodology," *Biblica* 95, no. 2 (2014): 280–91.

ing station, such a notion of human nature as driven by irrational impulses would attribute their action to groupthink, or crowds gathering to find a scapegoat to blame and punish. My view of human nature allows more flexibility with many causal factors contributing to our behavior.

Even early in his career, Girard found the same structure, the same desire, the same human nature in novels. Referring to the invariant motive behind desire, Girard posited that we risk being confused by the excuses offered by the character for their desires rather than understanding "the metaphysical meaning of that desire" that is common to "all" protagonists in novels. As Girard wrote in *Deceit, Desire, and the Novel,*

> To grasp this metaphysical meaning we must look beyond the individual cases and see the totality. All the heroes surrender their most fundamental individual prerogative, that of choosing their own desire; we cannot attribute this unanimous abandonment to the always different qualities of the heroes. For a single phenomenon a single cause must be found. All heroes of novels hate themselves on a more essential level than that of "qualities."[2]

Of course, *Deceit, Desire, and the Novel* was one of Girard's very early works, and some might suggest a tempering of that early totalizing impulse over the course of Girard's life and corpus. For Girard, what is common "to all men" is a desire for individual autonomy; each individual comes to the conclusion at some point that he or she has lost "metaphysical autonomy."[3] This is Girardianism before Girardianism. Varieties of modernity keep promising autonomy, but every individual eventually compares that promise of freedom with the reality of the world resulting in crushing disappointment ("The more deeply it is engraved in our

---

2. René Girard, *Deceit, Desire, and the Novel: Self and Other in Literary Structure,* trans. Yvonne Freccero (Baltimore: Johns Hopkins University Press, 1965), 55.
3. Girard, *Deceit,* 56.

hearts the more violent is the contrast between this marvelous promise and the brutal disappointment inflicted by experience"). Each person mistakenly believes others have autonomy, but he or she is denied it.[4] This metaphysical desire for freedom is contagious.[5] The function of the novel is to reveal this contagious desire and its multitude of manifestations.[6] For Girard as a literary critic, Cervantes, Dostoyevsky, Flaubert, Stendhal, and Proust present a "unity in novelistic conclusion" in articulating the same message about desire and rivalry.[7] Yet to me, novelistic meaning, ritual, causes of violence, human sociality, buying and selling in financial markets, volunteering for the Marines, and so many other manifestations of human behavior seem so much more varied and complex than to be reducible to one cause.

Even this early Girard, yet to assemble a grand narrative of desire, finds in desire a universal phenomenon: "the laws of desire are universal," even if their symptoms aren't.[8] "René Girard," as Tod Swanson notes, "is one of those rare scholars who, like Freud, or Ernst Becker, is remarkably good at explaining the whole of human culture in terms of a single principle."[9] This generalizing tendency some find so attractive in Girard others find objectionable. It is a feature of Girard's early explorations of desire and the more developed discussions of scapegoats. For, Girard asserts, "all mythological heroes are fundamentally the same."[10] One suspects

4. Girard, *Deceit*, 56–57.
5. Girard, *Deceit*, 96.
6. Girard, *Deceit*, 98.
7. Jan-Melissa Schramm, "'Let Us Carve Him as a Feast Fit for the Gods': Girard and Unjust Execution in Nineteenth-Century Narrative," *Mimesis, Desire, and the Novel: Rene Girard and Literary Criticism*, eds. Pierpaolo Antonello and Heather Webb (East Lansing: Michigan State University Press, 2015), 292.
8. Girard, *Deceit*, 169.
9. Tod Swanson, "Colonial Violence and Inca Analogies to Christianity," in *Curing Violence*, ed. Mark I. Wallace and Theophus H. Smith, 121–36 (Sonoma, CA: Polebridge, 1994), 121.
10. René Girard, "Nietzsche versus the Crucified," in *The Girard Reader*, ed. James G. Williams, 243–61 (New York: Crossroad, 1996), 251.

the method that sees in Romulus the same figure as Oedipus or Laman to be too powerful and not capable of accounting for differences while catching only similarities in the net. Any evidence consonant with Girard's theory is used as proof of its truthfulness, but any contradiction is attributed to a misrecognition that (rather than undermining the interpretive key) is taken to support it. Further, Bruce Chilton points out, when Girard finds violent mimeticism, then that feeds into evidence for his scheme, but when no such evidence is found, that too supports his theory because the absence of such substantiation demonstrates how effectively the myths have concealed the reality behind mob violence.[11] Principles without exceptions make one suspect that the principle itself is inflexible rather than supple. Girard speaks of the "universal renunciation of violence" as the message of the Sermon on the Mount.[12] This goes even for what humans would often rationalize as cases of "legitimate defense."[13]

I have tried in my response to Girard and Girardianism to counter that universalizing tendency by introducing ethical language and concepts when it comes to violence. Might some violence that counters violence be ethical and necessary?[14] I have defined some ethical theories to demonstrate that flexibility in discussing violence requires that we sometimes concern ourselves with consequences instead of focusing only on the act itself. Pragmatism, even when maintaining singularly comprehensive solutions, is a necessary element when addressing concerns about the *is* and the *ought*. I attempt to open up some fissures in universalizing explanations by using various ethical theories so the reader isn't faced with a monolithic cliff face, a recognition that the sur-

11. Bruce Chilton, "Rene Girard, James Williams, and the Genesis of Violence," *Bulletin for Biblical Research* 3 (1993): 19.
12. Girard, *Things Hidden*, 197.
13. Girard, *Things Hidden*, 198.
14. A question I will take up later in this book.

face but has crevices and shelves for handholds and footholds on the climb up the cliff.

What some find so attractive (a universal theory applicable in all times and places), others find problematic. "The general accusation leveled against Girard is that of reductionism; he reduces the many causes in the socio-cultural system too quickly to the one mimetic desire."[15] Even Girard jokes about his one all-consuming tendency: "I stand revealed by these days of debate as a man of a few ideas, so simple in their principle that perhaps they amount to no more than a single idea. It would in that case qualify as an '*idée fixe.*' The suggestion has been made, and I see no reason to quarrel with it."[16] But Girard wants to redefine the ideas of his "obsession" with the scapegoat not as obsessive but as "that [which] fixes all ideas."[17] Girard anticipates my criticism of his one tool in the toolbox by teasing out the criticism often made by those who disagree with him: "Send any masterpiece you like my way . . . and it will be quite a miracle if I do not come back to you, a month or a year later, with my mimetic desire, my sacrificial crisis and above all—give the Devil his due—that bloody atrocity with which I am infatuated, the primordial, founding act of violence: the collective murder of a deity."[18] Girard's response to this criticism by joking about the tendency is an effective dodge. The researcher's *idée fixe* may be determining which examples get counted as relevant. I'll raise this possibility that confirmation bias is at work with the LDS scholar Girardian Eugene England. But anticipating a rebuttal to my own argument, England isn't Girard. The latter draws upon a vastly larger range of narrative from the ancient and modern

15. Robert G. Hamerton-Kelly, *Sacred Violence: Paul's Hermeneutic of the Cross* (Minneapolis: Fortress, 1992), 189.
16. René Girard, "The Founding Murder in the Philosophy of Nietzsche," in *Violence and Truth: On the Works of René Girard*, ed. Paul Dumouchel, 227–46 (Stanford: Stanford University Press, 1988), 227.
17. Girard, "Founding Murder," 227.
18. Girard, "Founding Murder," 229.

world, but a larger net only brings a larger pool of fish, not necessarily a representative sampling of fish. This monomania has cost
Girard some of the tremendous influence he exerted in the 1960s
and 1970s.[19] In other words, Girard's theory "explains too much
and interprets too little."[20] Seeing mimetic rivalry resulting in the
sacrificial victim in all ancient, modern, and contemporary texts
looks obsessive, according to Trevor Jordan. "His theory promotes reductive analyses of a wide range of texts. Girard's interpretations are always so confirmatory of this theory than any one
of them could nestle in comfortably beside the brilliant parodies
of other literary theorists in Frederick C. Crews classic, *The Pooh
Perplex*."[21] All humans have the tendency to fall into confirmation
bias, to favor evidence that supports positions we believe and dis-
count or reinterpret evidence which undermines our cherished
commitments. When studying texts, such an overarching precon-
ception can cause us not to see those parts of the texts that counter
our explanations. Bruce Chilton's criticisms of Girard run along
these lines, that Girard's claims that all cultures unfold with the
particular violent and imitative trends Girard focuses on, have not
been demonstrated.[22] My discomfort with Girard derives from his
ability to pull a tuna out of the ocean every time he casts, even
when fishing above continental shelves, coral reefs, and tight into
shorelines. Some would take that not as a reason for concern but
for assurance.

Thus Scubla notes it is Girard's anthropology, not the New
Testament itself, that throws this new light on Christianity. "The

19. J. Bottum, "Girard among the Girardians," *First Things* 61 (1996): 42–45.
20. Trevor L. Jordan, "Scapegoating Girard: Violence and the Future of Religion," *St. Mark's Review* 202 (2007): 31.
21. Jordan, "Scapegoating," 32.
22. Bruce Chilton, *Abraham's Curse: Child Sacrifice in the Legacies of the West*
(New York: Doubleday, 2008), 35.

Christianity of Girard is therefore not that of the gospels."[23] Williams's own advice is that the reader must deal with all parts of the biblical text, both those that agree with and support one's favored position and those that contradict it.[24] But Keim notes that Girardians (not just Girardians but all readers) often don't follow this advice, selectively appropriating the parts of the Old Testament that agree with a Girardian position while ignoring those parts that undermine the favored thesis.[25] Girardians can too easily fall into the temptation to purge from the Bible what doesn't fit their ideology. The more difficult textual task is to treat the entire text, those parts that disagree with our own preferred reading as well as those that support it. Girard's wide engagement with different parts of the biblical and other texts strives to perform the latter while too many of his followers do the former; perhaps we should treat Girard the way we treat Plato, Marx, Freud, and Strauss: the founding teacher offers profound and groundbreaking insights that his disciples apply in a mechanical way with less subtlety and skill. But perhaps we ought to approach even Girard's readings with caution. "Girard, in sum, does not provide the key to determining which scriptural texts should be accepted or dismissed; he calls for a closer reading of *all* scripture with an eye to the way that it progressively reveals human nature and its complex relationship to violence."[26] We Latter-day Saints have a text, the Book of Mormon, that Girard never took up. We might clarify and correct the

23. Lucien Scubla, "The Christianity of René Girard and the Nature of Religion," trans. Mark R. Anspach, in *Violence and Truth: On the Works of René Girard*, ed. Paul Dumouchel, 160–78 (Stanford: Stanford University Press, 1988), 170.

24. James G. Williams, *The Bible, Violence, and the Sacred: Liberation from the Myth of Sanctioned Violence* (San Francisco: Harper, 1991), 176.

25. Paul Keim, "Reading Ancient Near Eastern Literature from the Perspective of Girard's Scapegoat Theory," in *Violence Renounced: René Girard, Biblical Studies, and Peacemaking*, ed. William M. Swartley, 157–77 (Telford, PA: Pandora, 2000), 162.

26. Joseph M. Spencer, "René Girard and Mormon Scripture," *Dialogue: A Journal of Mormon Thought* 43, no. 3 (Fall 2010): 9–10.

Girardian approach by applying it to a text produced according to the same features and rules of Hebraic narrative that the biblical composers applied. Eugene England has used Girardian terminology and approaches in reading the Book of Mormon, so one of my principal objectives in this book is to apply the Girardian theory against that book of scripture and England's Girardian reading.

One of the most common criticisms of Girard's theory calls out this reductive aspect. A wide range of phenomena from a vast sampling of cultures and historical periods with consequences spanning entire continents of the social sciences and humanities, capable of explaining all religions in human history; all history in the human past; all mythology in human culture; all literature in human poetry, prose, fiction, and nonfiction—Girard's theory takes this expansive material and applies the insight about violence and the victimage mechanism to account for all of them.[27] Criticisms of Girard's approach to literary texts, according to Paisley Livingston, falls under three main headings: (1) Girard attributes the meaning he finds in texts to the texts themselves rather than allowing that his own readings, assumptions, and preunderstandings help to produce that meaning, (2) Girard attempts a too simplistic view of representation, that the text conveys an extraliterary world with little or no mediation, and (3) literature is valued only to the extent that it advances Girard's thesis about victimage and sacrifice.[28] That Girard sees the innocent victim everywhere makes one suspect that his theory is producing the effect, is reductive.[29] Even supporters of Girard note that his theory is thought by many readers to be overly broad, empirically unsupported, and reductive.[30] Some challenge his claims empirically, noting that vio-

27. Keim, "Reading Ancient Near Eastern Literature," 159.
28. Paisley Livingston, *Models of Desire: René Girard and the Psychology of Mimesis* (Baltimore: Johns Hopkins University Press, 1992).
29. Jordan, "Scapegoating Girard," 32.
30. Jordan, "Scapegoating Girard," 35.

lence seems to be more culturally oriented rather than rooted in innate human nature.[31]

A common objection to Girard is that his ideas and analyses are a reactionary defense of Christian belief; many intellectuals assert that religious belief is in decline under the assaults of modernity, and Girard is merely attempting to make Christianity reputable again. Another criticism by some feminist scholars is that Girard extends Freud's misogyny.[32] In his crowning interpretation, Girard must perform a delicate balance, showing how the New Testament rises above all other texts to reveal a final truth about the world, but to do so he must posit a truth revealed by the New Testament evangelists that they only partially understood themselves: "the true message of Jesus was pretty thoroughly missed not only by normative Christian leaders from the earliest days but also by those who formulated the NT itself, though they could not help including the key passages that make up his own 'canon within a canon.'"[33] Girard is capable of seeing through the veil that even the Gospel writers couldn't penetrate, a veil only divine intervention can rend in twain, from top to bottom.[34] Such an audacious interpretive move makes Girard into an essential fifth evangelist who sifts the obfuscation and mystification of the other four from the rough-hewn gems and pearls of great price that Girard—once finding it—sells all he has to obtain; it is a bold undertaking to correct the Bible, or the Book of Mormon for that matter. Another objection is that Girard can draw his interpretation out of any text by finding a scapegoat, sometimes where nobody else does. The most common criticism, an aspect that makes me uncomfortable as well, is the Girardian "universality" that performs the same

---

31. Jordan, "Scapegoating Girard," 37.
32. Richard J. Golsan, *René Girard and Myth: An Introduction* (New York: Garland, 1993), 111–13.
33. North, "Girard Connection," 19.
34. North, "Girard Connection," 23.

chemical reaction on a text regardless of the chemicals the experiment begins with.[35] Girard's systematic, universalizing approach poses a strong challenge to postmodernism. Postmodern thinkers react against the totalizing aspect of such ideas, preferring the local and strange, the unique and rare rather than the global and the transhistorical.[36]

Although I confront Girard's project with doubts and questions, I also want to articulate my great admiration toward his boldness and textual dexterity. I have read only a handful of readers (Robert Alter among them) who so consistently provide valuable textual insights into traditional works of literature that I care deeply about, deeply enough to challenge. I have raised my doubts and reservations in this chapter to highlight the wisdom of Girard's readings as I perceive them and engage troublesome problems. This chapter represents my major engagement with the difficulties I find in Girardian thought. I have dispersed additional scruples throughout the book in proximity to the specific readings I feel the need to engage. I view my criticism of Girard to be a way to honor his legacy and influence.

35. Golsan, *Girard and Myth*, 117–18.
36. Golsan, *Girard and Myth*, 128.

Part Two

Reading the
Book of Mormon
and Reading Girard

The Bible has influenced the Western tradition more than any other book. Yet the book is still widely misunderstood. Joseph Spencer is right to say that the very function of scripture is to be inconvenient, to unsettle its readers.[1] It isn't only Jerusalem or King Manasseh who are to be overthrown, turned upside down, and wiped clean by the God of the Bible, but each of the scripture's readers also.[2] If the Bible hasn't challenged your comfortable position as a reader, you haven't read the Bible adequately. If you think scripture aligns comfortably with any political party, philosophy, or social movement, you need to be discomfited by reading deeper. The Book of Mormon, even more than the Bible, insists on making life inconvenient for its readers.[3] Spencer insists

---

1. Joseph M. Spencer, "René Girard and Mormon Scripture," *Dialogue: A Journal of Mormon Thought* 43, no. 3 (Fall 2010): 6–20. Spencer begins his article by noting that "Scripture, as scripture, is inconvenient" (6).
2. 2 Kings 21:13.
3. Spencer, "René Girard," 6.

(correctly) that the history of biblical interpretation is a struggle between those who want to domesticate biblical narrative to make it less unsettling to conventional society and those "who stubbornly insist on the scripture's essential inconvenience." Most prominent in the latter group is Girard.[4]

We think we know the text, but it is an abundant event—a saturated phenomenon—that escapes our attempts to pin it down, to contain it. Girardian analysis of the scripture holds much promise in illuminating the text in a new way for readers. Book of Mormon narrative contains many examples of mimetic rivalry, according to Mack Stirling: Nephi and his brothers, Nephi and Laban (Spencer denies that this relationship is one of rivalry), Sherem and Jacob, Zeezrom against Alma$_2$, Ammon against Lamoni's father, Moroni$_1$ against Amalickiah, Korihor and Alma$_2$, in the Jaredite story Shiz in mortal combat with Coriantumr (representing the two factions extinguishing each other), the fight to the finish between Nephites and Lamanites.[5] I will read some of these and other narratives to see how useful Girard's theories and the Book of Mormon are in mutually informing each other. This experiment upon the word is one of testing truths, perhaps by proving contraries, perhaps by elucidating contraries, but never arriving at proofs.

4. Spencer, "René Girard," 7.
5. Mack C. Stirling, "Violence in the Scriptures: Mormonism and the Cultural Theory of René Girard," *Dialogue: A Journal of Mormon Thought* 43, no. 1 (Spring 2010): 81–83.

Chapter Six

The Sacrificial Soteriology of the Book of Mormon

Christian theology has found explaining how the Atonement works to be one of its thorniest problems. LDS theology has unique gifts, though, to contribute to the discussion of soteriology (the technical term for theological dialogue about salvation). LDS authorities have pointed out that we just don't understand how the Atonement works, yet the difficulty or impossibility of the task should not deter one from attempting to understand the mystery.[1] History has presented the following major theories to explain soteriology:

1. the ransom theory (the devil after Adam and Eve's fall holds humans captive and God must pay a ransom of his Son in order to set humans free);

2. the penal-substitution model (humans have incurred a debt in sin and Jesus steps forward as a substitute to pay our debt and free us from the prison-house of sin—a mediator is necessary because mercy cannot be

---

1. Bruce R. McConkie cited in Lorin K. Hansen, "The 'Moral' Atonement as a Mormon Interpretation," *Dialogue: A Journal of Mormon Thought* 27, no. 1 (Spring 1994): 196; James Talmage also refers to the Atonement as "incomprehensible," *Jesus the Christ: A Study of the Messiah and His Mission According to the Holy Scriptures Both Ancient and Modern* (Salt Lake City, UT: Deseret, 1976), 613.

allowed to rob justice, so God functions essentially as a bail bondsman and Jesus a vicarious inmate);

3. the satisfaction theory (this construct asserts that it isn't Satan who requires payment but God, for it is God's honor that is offended by sin and Jesus steps in to satisfy the demands of God's dignity); and

4. the moral influence theory (Jesus's life and death is the perfect example of how to live, in that it shows us a model of responding to injustice and violence; people are inspired to be better by seeing Jesus as their prototype).

Each of these theories has strengths and powerful weaknesses; each also can be supported from various passages of scripture.

The main problem with the first three views is that if extended too far, each metaphor raises difficult questions about God's nature. Why would an omnipotent God have to bargain with Satan and pay ransom? How can justice be served in the substitution theory by the injustice of having a person suffer for the sins of others? How can such vicarious suffering be efficacious anyway when transfer of guilt is explicitly denounced by Amulek?[2] How can God's honor be satisfied by the suffering and death of his own Son, which would seem to be a second offense against that honor? The moral influence theory can't answer why Jesus in particular was chosen when any example would have done, examples not requiring the torture and death of the perfect exemplar (most of liberal Christianity[3] adheres to this theory of atonement). The

---

2. Alma 34:11–12.

3. Liberal Christianity is that wing of the Christian tradition that has made its peace with modernity and with science by adapting to the tenets of the Enlightenment. Liberal Christians endorse evolutionary theory, reject inerrancy of scripture and infallibility of church officials. The Bible is often viewed by this religious branch as allegorical when it disagrees with the conclusions of modern science (that the Genesis creation account isn't literal, miracles don't happen

atonement has only the value we place on it after the fact and lacks any intrinsic quality or necessary effect. Each soteriological theory carries a debilitating burden of incompleteness in answering the questions we naturally pose about the event.[4] I see no reason to deviate from Blake Ostler's soteriological analysis, especially his criticisms of the substitution theories of atonement.[5]

Jacob Morgan and Dennis Potter have offered theories of the Atonement from within a specifically Mormon theology. For Morgan, Adam and Eve's lapse introduces a fallen nature, but the Atonement prevents a "super-fallen" state.[6] This state would have made humans much worse off, but nature is infused with a divine inoculation called the light of Christ. The fall exiles us from God's presence, but the light of Christ prevents greater depravity in humanity and destructiveness in the cosmos, permitting both justice and mercy to work out their imperatives while permitting humans moral agency.[7] Potter rejects substitution theories based on the "innocence principle" and Amulek's statement that it is wrong to punish one person for acts committed by another.[8] Lorin K. Hansen offers a variation of the moral influence theory from within LDS sources as an alternative to other possibilities. Theories of atonement reflect the cultural and social world in which they were received and propagated, so discussions of wounded

because they violate natural law but are metaphors for God's power to uplift and help people). Mainline Protestant churches (Presbyterian, Episcopal, Methodist, American Baptist, Disciples of Christ) tend to be liberal denominations. Conservative churches (Pentecostal, Holiness, Nazarene, Southern Baptist) tend to believe in literal physical resurrection, the virgin birth of Christ, and the infallibility and noncontradiction of the Bible.

4. Blake T. Ostler, "Atonement in Mormon Thought," personal website, 4; also Blake T. Ostler, *Exploring Mormon Thought: The Problems of Theism and the Love of God* (Salt Lake City: Kofford, 2006), 261–81.

5. Ostler, *Exploring Mormon Thought*, 204, 217.

6. Jacob Morgan, "The Divine-Infusion Theory: Rethinking the Atonement," *Dialogue: A Journal of Mormon Thought* 39, no. 1 (Spring 2006): 64.

7. Morgan, "The Divine-Infusion Theory," 57–81.

8. R. Dennis Potter, "Did Christ Pay for Our Sins?" *Dialogue: A Journal of Mormon Thought* 32, no. 4 (Winter 1999): 73–86.

honor or ransom manifest a medieval social and political context where maintaining the king's honor was a political imperative
and ransoming hostages kidnapped or captured in combat were
not uncommon problems. So too we would expect that a need to
explain in an LDS context the necessity for an atonement is likely
to embody modern and LDS views of nature, human nature, and
supernature.[9] Douglas Davies—like the authors I have pointed to
in this paragraph—notes that the LDS emphasis on Gethsemane
instead of Calvary has far-reaching effects on Mormon soteriology.
On the cross, Jesus suffers violence imposed on him by Jewish and
Roman authority (accepted voluntarily but still passively), but the
suffering in Gethsemane is proactive, an exercise of Jesus's moral
agency.[10] Another LDS view sees the Atonement as necessary, not
to ransom us or as a substitution, but to redeem us from a nature
where we demand sacrifice; human nature, fixed from before the
foundation of the world, demands sacrifice of man or animal, and
the Atonement shows us a more excellent way.[11] Blake Ostler also
offers what he calls the compassion theory of atonement, again,
working from within Mormon scripture and analysis: God's compassion and our gratitude work mutually on each other, on our
side to open us to the love and redemption offered by God.[12] Guilt
and shame are removed, taken by Christ to free us from its burden.
We freely and willfully separate ourselves from God and alienate
ourselves from each other.[13] This compassion theory posits that

9. Lorin K. Hansen, "The 'Moral' Atonement as a Mormon Interpretation," *Dia-logue: A Journal of Mormon Thought* 27, no. 1 (Spring 1994): 195–227.

10. Douglas Davies, "Gethsemane and Calvary in LDS Soteriology," *Dialogue: A Journal of Mormon Thought* 34, nos. 3–4 (Fall–Winter 2001): 24.

11. Mack C. Stirling, "Understanding the Violent Sacred," *Sunstone* 133 (July 2004): 35.

12. Ostler, *Exploring Mormon Thought*, 235.

13. For more, see Ostler, *Exploring Mormon Thought*, chapter 7. Let me express one reservation about Blake's view of atonement. He posits a "literal release of energy of the past that we hold onto until we repent" (Ostler, *Exploring Mormon Thought*, 259). I don't see the need to be so literal about such matters, to specify

the Atonement bridges the divide between fallen humanity and a loving God by changing us. Much of Christian history, according to Girardian thought, records the misunderstanding of the atonement and God's plan. Mormon soteriological theories (borrowed from earlier Catholic and Protestant notions) likely travel those same pathways by conceiving of the Atonement in what Girard considers sacrificial terms as requiring the divine endorsement of violence to achieve the purposes of God.

Through Christian history, the meaning of the Atonement was understood by transferring various models or metaphors: the church fathers used the ransom/conflict understanding, the medieval church the satisfaction/penal substitution metaphor, the early modern period the moral influence version, and many reformers espoused the governmental model (one can't let the laws of society go unpunished because that will result in others flouting the law; some price has to be paid for sin in order to keep good order in the universe). To this list I add Girard's "drama of salvation" model.[14] Most strands of Protestantism and Roman Catholicism have endorsed variations on the satisfaction and penal understandings of the Atonement; both theories portray a vengeful God who requires punishment and violence for sins if no substitute can be found for the sinner.[15] Boyd K. Packer has often articulated what appears to be a version of the penal substitution theory of atonement (frequently shortened to "the substitution" theory of atonement).[16] The parable is about a man who incurred a debt.

physical mechanisms by which the atonement works despite the LDS materialism that asserts all spirit is matter, just more refined.

14. Marlin E. Miller, "Girardian Perspectives and Christian Atonement," in *Violence Renounced: René Girard, Biblical Studies, and Peacemaking*, ed. Willard M. Swartley, 31–48 (Telford, PA: Pandora, 2000), 31.

15. Robin Collins, "Girard and Atonement: An Incarnational Theory of Mimetic Participation," in *Violence Renounced*, ed. Swartley, 132.

16. Boyd K. Packer, "The Mediator," *Ensign* (May 1977): 54–55. See the conference address turned into a video representation at https://www.churchofjesuschrist.org/media/video/2007-01-0005-the-mediator.

The debtor can't repay, and Jesus steps in to pay the price. Sterling McMurrin lays out the various theories of atonement (the substitution, ransom, satisfaction, and moral example theories), showing how various LDS scriptures and commentators support each theory.[17] But "the finest passage on the atonement in Mormon literature" comes from Alma 42:14–15 (according to McMurrin's assessment the excerpt typifies Anselm's satisfaction soteriology):

> And thus we see that all mankind were fallen, and they were in the grasp of justice; yea, the justice of God, which consigned them forever to be cut off from his presence. And now, the plan of mercy could not be brought about except an atonement should be made; therefore God himself atoneth for the sins of the world, to bring about the plan of mercy, to appease the demands of justice, that God might be a perfect, just God, and a merciful God also.[18]

This passage to me seems more ambiguous and could support more than just the satisfaction theory. Morgan notes that the penal-substitution theory of atonement is not only the most common one adhered by Christians but also the most common among Latter-day Saints, despite the fact that Alma 34:11–12 explicitly rebuts this view: "Now there is not any man that can sacrifice his own blood which will atone for the sins of another. Now, if a man murdereth, behold will our law, which is just, take the life of his brother? I say unto you, Nay. But the law requireth the life of him who hath murdered; therefore there can be nothing which is short of an infinite atonement which will suffice for the sins of the world."[19]

---

17. Sterling M. McMurrin, *The Theological Foundations of the Mormon Religion* (Salt Lake City, UT: University of Utah Press, 1965), 82–90.

18. McMurrin, *Theological Foundations*, 90.

19. Alma 34:11–12. Morgan, "Divine-Infusion Theory," 57; Ostler, "Atonement in Mormon Thought," 4.

The Girardian soteriology is a version of the moral influence concept of atonement first advanced by Peter Abelard (1079–1142 CE) and still advocated by liberal wings of Christianity. (Eugene England's view of atonement within the LDS tradition also falls into the moral influence category.[20]) In moral influence atonement models, Jesus is exemplary in showing us the best way to live. Collins further divides these moral influence theories, describing Girard's position as holding two narrower theories of atonement: the unmasking theory, where Jesus's death unveils the system of violence behind the victimage mechanism, and the imitation theory, where Jesus's teaching gives us good models of mimesis to replace violent ones.[21] The problem with the unmasking theory is that it only weakly intervenes to bring salvation, and it brings revelation only over many centuries of educative work performed by the Gospels (while leaving those multitudes of human generations wallowing in violence and sacrifice despite the imperative nature of the work of salvation): "Christ's atonement was supposed to save those to whom the apostles preached, not simply the beneficiaries of a nonviolent society more than two millennia later."[22] Girard provides an example from the New Testament to show how Jesus's refusal of violence provides a good model for those around him to follow: Jesus's action stops a cycle of victimage. When the woman caught in adultery is taken before Jesus, he obstructs the impulse toward violence: "he prevents the contagion from getting started. Another contagion in the reverse direction is set off, however, a contagion of nonviolence," for Jesus becomes an exemplary model as those in the crowd with stones in their hands drop them.[23] Girard mentions positive imitation but elabo-

---

20. Ostler, "Atonement in Mormon Thought," 6.
21. Collins, "Girard and Atonement," 135.
22. Collins, "Girard and Atonement," 137.
23. René Girard, *I See Satan Fall Like Lightning*, trans. James G. Williams (Maryknoll, NY: Orbis, 2001), 57.

rates little on the idea. William Swartley develops this idea based on the ubiquity in the New Testament of nonacquisitive mimesis.[24] The variegated nature of violence in the Bible calls on Girardians to assert that some who wrote the Hebrew and Christian scriptures didn't understand the full message of the writings; the same assertion would, presumably, apply to the Nephite scripture. In those passages that attribute violence to deity, notes Stirling, "the community effectively transfers its own guilt to God, sanctifying itself at God's expense."[25] God has no obligation to banish our ignorance about the Atonement. We offer explanation after interpretation. My summary of atonement theories comes nowhere near to exhausting the range of possibilities. We have no right to demand that God clear up our questions, nor does God have any obligation to do so. But remember Abraham. We could repeat the works of Abraham and request that the God of the Universe reiterate the typological and covenantal acts initiated with Abraham. "And the Lord said, Shall I hide from Abraham that thing which I do."[26] We might ask that the Lord repeat this act of unveiling; we might argue for the sake of heaven so that what is still hidden would no longer be so. For we live in the time when Abraham has become a great and mighty nation, and all the nations of the earth have been blessed in him. As Abraham questioned, "Shall not the Judge of all the earth do right?"[27] Absent an answer similar to that granted to Abraham about what the Lord was about to do to the cities of the plain, giving Abraham an opportunity to intercede on their behalf (which appeared to be an effective intervention, at least for Lot and his immediate family[28]), we have to be content with exercising negative capability and accept that we just don't

---

24. Willard M. Swartley, "Discipleship and Imitation of Jesus/Suffering Servant: The Mimeses of New Creation," in *Violence Renounced*, ed. Swartley, 219.

25. Stirling, "Violent Sacred," 34.

26. Genesis 18:17.

27. Genesis 18:35.

28. Genesis 19.

know some answers to some questions. And we must also accept that concepts of atonement, such as the ransom, penal-substitution, satisfaction, and moral influence, are merely tropes, similes that derive from some element of life we humans are familiar with to illustrate some inscrutable aspect of our relationship with God. Girard has an addition to the four theories I have articulated here as samples of attempting to make the incomprehensible comprehensible. Since Girard started engaging atonement explanations, his theory has acquired enough traction to stand on its own as a newly arrived rival to the ancient, medieval, and modern theories. Self-appointed theologian Stephen D. Morrison lists the scapegoat model as a rival to the six other theories he reviews because, puzzlingly, he considers it a nonviolent form of atonement, making it different from other theories. "Jesus is not a sacrifice," according to Morrison, "but a *victim*." [29]

I ought to invoke my earlier caveat, as we here are noting the futility of attempting to provide a satisfactory explanation of the Atonement. We ought to remember that God's ways are higher than ours, making our attempts to encompass the divine within our human rationality and moral theories inadequate (while still necessary to attempt because we humans are built to pursue knowledge of good and evil since our first parents left the garden). Blame God, if you must, for daring to plant and nurture the tree of knowledge of good and evil even before announcing to the humans the presence of that tree in their midst. Human reason alone, even combined with belief, may not be enough to solve this atonement enigma, absent further revelation, for we believe and hope God "will yet reveal many great and important things pertaining to the Kingdom of God." [30]

29. Stephen D. Morrison, Seven Theories of the Atonement Summarized, https://www.sdmorrison.org/7-theories-of-the-atonement-summarized/. Accessed 9-18-2023.
30. Articles of Faith 9.

It is worth bringing distinctively LDS resources to bear on Girard's soteriological analysis. While we must recognize the fallibility of our attempts to understand the mind of God, even if we have the mind of Christ,[31] it is in our nature to ask, as Abraham inquired about the justice of God. We bearers of the restoration message bring new concepts and associations absent from or forgotten in the creedal Christian tradition. These tools may better approximate what we hope in some other life to view more clearly when we no longer see through a glass, darkly. It is also worth emphasizing that Girard himself, and those who support his soteriology, require a repudiation of all sacrifice, of all violence. Any atonement theory that falls short of such a result would be dismissed as incomplete, a misunderstanding of the meaning of the gospel, a still blood-drenched half step toward redemption. Three Book of Mormon chapters are often cited as relevant to the discussion: 2 Nephi 9, Alma 34, and Alma 42.

Girard notes that even though he sees in the New Testament writings a repudiation of the sacrificial mentality, the Christian scriptures are not unified in the rejection of mimetic violence. The Gospels uncover collective violence for what it is. Even the Epistle to the Hebrews, which endorses a priestly view of the Atonement, portrays "the death of Christ as the perfect and definitive sacrifice, which makes all other sacrifices outmoded and any further sacrificial undertaking unacceptable,"[32] according to Girard. But even this stance isn't enough for Girard, for this would still valorize sacrifice. It is, however, for Girard, still better than alternatives, for "it does prevent a pure and simple return to the repetitive and primitive tradition of sacrifice, the kind of return we find in readings that limit martyrdom to mechanisms of violence and the sacred."[33]

---

31. 1 Corinthians 2:16.
32. René Girard, *The Scapegoat*, trans. Yvonne Freccero (Baltimore: Johns Hopkins University Press, 1986), 200.
33. Girard, *The Scapegoat*, 200.

Amulek gives his sermon on the Atonement on a missionary journey with Alma to the Zoramites. The missionaries find a receptive audience among the poor, those who have been expelled by the richer Zoramites because they are seen as coarse, filthy.[34] We have people who have been scapegoated. Alma preaches to them at Onidah, which we learn later is an armory.[35] Alma tells these Zoramites that they can worship anywhere and anytime, and he urges that they try an experiment on the word, which emphasizes not just faith but also patience. Amulek transitions from Alma's topic by mentioning both faith and patience.[36]

Here we have a society with socioeconomic stratification: richer and poorer. The poor will literally be expelled by the rich because of their poverty (not just allegorically or figuratively exiled). Sometimes the punishment meted to the scapegoat is not on the altar or in the fire but in exile. The poor classes have served their purpose by building the Zoramite houses of worship and are now disposable. Think of Oedipus exiled from Thebes or Jews from the Pale of Settlement migrating to found the nation of Israel. The consequence of being a dissident against political power can be both exile and murder.[37] Although less explicitly violent than a firing squad or a knife on an altar, exile is still violent, and a life

---

34. Alma 32:2–3.

35. Alma 47:5. A symbolic venue for a sermon on redemption, for it preaches atonement against a backdrop of warfare.

36. Alma 32:3–4.

37. Jamal Khashoggi spoke out against the policies of Mohammed bin Salman, the Crown Prince and ruler of Saudi Arabia. The consequence was exile as Khashoggi was forced out of his homeland and worked part-time as a journalist for the *Washington Post* and full-time as a critic of the Saudi government. In October 2018, that exile became even more dangerous as he was lured to the Saudi consulate in Istanbul in order to get paperwork straightened out for his upcoming wedding. "U.S. intelligence later determined that a team of 15 Saudi agents had flown to Istanbul in order to carry out a 'capture or kill' operation approved by Crown Prince Mohammed bin Salman (MBS)." Rachel Treisman states, "5 years after Khashoggi's murder, advocates say the lack of justice is dangerous," *NPR* (Oct. 2, 2023): https://www.npr.org/2023/10/02/1202937036/jamal-khashoggi-mbs-murder-saudi-arabia-human-rights, (accessed Oct. 3, 2023). Khashoggi's body was never

of poverty can also be a form of violence if the affluent in a society make structural arrangements to keep the poor permanently in that status. I will be drawing from two Spanish sociologists who have written about the 2008 Great Recession, who also use Girard's ideas to analyze the effects of structural poverty, government-sanctioned destitution.[38]

Even if the violence of poverty is "merely" symbolic violence, it is still violence. We don't know much about Nephite economic arrangements, so any analysis must necessarily be speculative and hypothetical. We do have some economic observations on the arrangements at Ammonihah, a Nephite city, about 82 BCE. The narrative sets up a confrontation between Alma and Amulek and the legal elite: the lawyers and judges. Nephite monetary denominations are laid out. The driving force behind the system is articulated:

> Now, it was for the sole purpose to get gain, because they received their wages according to their employ, therefore, they did stir up the people to riotings, and all manner of disturbances and wickedness, that they might have more employ, that they might get money according to the suits which were brought before them; therefore they did stir up the people against Alma and Amulek.[39]

Note that the violence, the riots, the disturbances, and their wickedness are specifically designed to create churn in the system, and therefore more billings. The events during the mission to the Zoramites are not much different than those among the Ammonihahites just a few years later at 74 BCE, in a city of Nephite dissent-

---

found, but Turkish surveillance recordings showed that he was murdered and his body dismembered.

38. Luis Enrique Alonso and Carlos J. Fernández Rodríguez, "Debt and Sacrifice: The Role of Scapegoats in the Economic Crises," Religions 12 (2021): https://doi.org/10.3390/rel12020128.

39. Alma 11:20.

ers, with Alma and Amulek again taking the lead.[40] The Zoramite elite secretly canvas the residents to find out who accepted the message of Alma and Amulek. Those who did were "cast out of the land."[41] These Zoramite scapegoats then sought refuge among the people of Ammon in the land of Jershon, forced out of their own city for a combination of reasons, including their poverty and acceptance of a religious ideology their governing elite contended against.

Even though the poor built the Zoramite houses of worship (the elites being more than willing to take advantage of the poor class's labor), the destitute are cast out of those synagogues.[42] These needy Zoramites "were esteemed as filthiness" and were "esteemed by their brethren as dross."[43] This deliberate exclusion of the poor was a structural barrier equivalent to contemporary lawmakers and lobbyists in a governing class who impose barriers on the poor registering to vote, obtaining higher education, accessing the tools to improve work skills and get better jobs, and organizing workers in the workplace.

Structural poverty, according to Luis Alonso and Carlos Rodríguez as they invoke Girard, as a form of sacrifice often occurs and increases in times of economic crisis. They argue, "Sacrifice takes place when some groups, often unwillingly, are forced to live with less, in order to keep the social order in balance."[44] This isn't physical violence using physical force but is rather economic violence using the force of law to maintain the status quo.

Referring to Bourdieu, Alonso and Rodríguez note that these economic crises "unleash an extraordinary degree of economic and social violence, at least in symbolic terms" in which the large-

---

40. Alma 31:8.
41. Alma 35:3–6.
42. Alma 32:5.
43. Alma 32:3.
44. Alonso and Rodríguez, "Debt," 2.

scale changes in the global economy cause middle- and low-income households to lose savings, income, and jobs, resulting in bankruptcy, increased debt, and "the loss of their livelihoods or a vicious spiral of poverty."[45] The 2008 world recession was such an event in which the "leitmotifs" of sacrifice were raised: sacrifice on welfare-state programs "to send the markets signals that might calm their speculative fury." Symbolic violence is sacrifice at the minimum but no less real or impactful than physical violence. The financial crisis was triggered by debt—financial institutions bundling high-risk investment instruments on the one hand and pushing onto consumers high-risk mortgages on the other.[46]

The increased risks on both ends of the economic spectrum are driven by mimetic behavior: consumers attempting to appear as affluent as their neighbors and financial institutions competing with each other for profit and return on investment, which leads to a conflict of financial and political interests. "This mimicry means," write Alonso and Rodríguez, "that our economic decisions that imply purchases, credits, mortgages or personal loans are a mimetic response to the behavior of others: we imitate them and, at the same time, try to compete with them."[47] In the Great Recession, scapegoats had to be found for the collapse in real estate markets, evictions, layoffs, falling wages, cuts to the social welfare net, increased taxes, and police violence against peaceful demonstrations. While some corporate executives lost their jobs and had to resort to part-time work on corporate boards (a form of corporate welfare for former CEOs, CFOs, CIOs, and other named executive officers [NEOs]), the true scapegoats were the working or middle classes who were greedy enough to demand higher wages and more access to government largesse (with correspondingly less going to corporate welfare), and who took out heavily advertised subprime

---

45. Alonso and Rodríguez, "Debt," 2.
46. Alonso and Rodríguez, "Debt," 4.
47. Alonso and Rodríguez, "Debt," 5.

loans to purchase boats and second homes that were no less heavily advertised. Following the blaming of personal victims who were evicted came the national scapegoating of the poorer countries of Southern Europe by the richer Northern countries: the Southern PIGS (Portugal, Italy, Greece, and Spain). Write Alonso and Rodríguez, "They have been forced, and their governments have agreed, to recognize their guilt, their enthusiastic adhesion to that decision which has annulled them in a script which appears taken literally from Girard."[48] No human bodies were hung from trees, dismembered torsos burned on altars, or prophets consumed on pyres; but these forms of economic violence against the poor are no less sacrificial than the poor being expelled from the Zoramites, gone over to dwell in Jershon with the Anti-Nephi-Lehies, who are exiled to be saved from the violence of sword and scimitar wielded by their brethren, the Lamanites.

Girardian readings of the Book of Mormon passages relevant to concepts of the Atonement seem to me to come up short. Amulek's Atonement discourse to the poor among the Zoramites (Alma 34) on Christ's great and last sacrifice is obviously relevant to the issue of burden-sharing obligations among the social classes, Zoramite society in particular. The listeners need to try an experiment on the word because the question they entertain is "whether the word be in the Son of God, or whether there shall be no Christ."[49] Although impoverished, the Zoramite outcasts still merit the blessings of the Atonement and can access that gift outside the sacred buildings and social leaders from which they are now disbarred. They just need to try an experiment. An atonement is expedient to redeem humans from sin.[50] Eugene England cites Alma 34:10–15 as undermining the concepts of sacrifice and scapegoating: "In addition the Book of Mormon gives perhaps the

---

48. Alonso and Rodríguez, "Debt," 8.
49. Alma 34:5.
50. Alma 34:8–9.

most direct affirmation in scripture of Girard's claim that Christ's Atonement put an end to all claims for the legitimacy of sacrifice and scapegoating."[51] This claim seems problematic to me because Amulek's discourse still asserts that Christ's Atonement is sacrificial and Amulek's argument writ large endorses the animal sacrifices that were a "type and shadow" of this ultimate sacrifice. Girard specifically denies these two claims. Mack C. Stirling asserts that Amulek's discussion of Jesus as the great and last sacrifice supports Girard's position; for in Alma 34:13–14, Amulek asserts there must be a stop to the shedding of blood. Additionally, in 3 Nephi 9:19–20, Jesus specifically commands the cessation of animal sacrifice.[52] Both England and Stirling see in Amulek's argument support for a Girardian position, but the passage seems more ambiguous to me. Support for animal sacrifice until the atoning sacrifice makes such animal offerings obsolete, but only in a future tense.

Amulek clearly calls the Atonement a sacrifice. Stirling notes that Girard has helped him understand the Mormon scriptures better but by the same method of attributing misrecognition to those parts which disagree with the thesis by the writers of scripture.[53] We humans have a fallen nature, and that condition needs to be taken personally. The writers of those scriptures are fallen as are its readers, and "as we approach difficult, violent texts, Girard asks us to read them with open eyes and realize that violent acts, projected (wrongly) onto God, were performed by humans just like us. The Bible reveals to us our own rivalry and scapegoating violence so that we might have some chance of overcoming them."[54] To endorse the work of violence presented in the text by

51. Eugene England, "Why Nephi Killed Laban: Reflections on the Truth of the Book of Mormon," *Dialogue: A Journal of Mormon Thought* 22, no. 3 (Fall 1989): 47.
52. Mack C. Stirling, "Violence in the Scriptures: Mormonism and the Cultural Theory of René Girard," *Dialogue: A Journal of Mormon Thought* 43, no. 1 (Spring 2010): 78.
53. Stirling, "Violence in," 59–105.
54. Stirling, "Violent Sacred," 34–35.

asserting God calls for sacrifice and vengeance is to slip back into the mythological framework the better angels of the biblical tradition attempt to free us from. According to Ted Grimsrud, "For Guardians, demythifying Jesus' death helps us see that Jesus did not die as such a sacrifice," but Jesus's death instead refuses the cycles of mimesis and violence. Such an interpretation asserts: "Jesus' death is *not* an act of violence *God* needs."[55] Such a position is contrary to the assertions in Alma 34. Amulek asserts the Atonement as a violent death was both necessary and in accord with God's will. In fact, the keyword "expedient" occurs five times in rapid succession in Amulek's discourse, four of the occurrences insisting on the "great and last sacrifice" and one referring to the need to end animal sacrifice once Christ has completed his Atonement. For a Girardian, Amulek may misunderstand the Atonement, and atonement more generally, but that difference of atonement theology can't be finessed so easily.

Girardians see in the Old Testament a precursor to the Christian attempt to do away with violence. It is hard to see Amulek doing Girardian work. The Amulek-text partially agrees with the Girardians in the need to do away with sacrifice, but it disagrees with them on the rationale. Job, the suffering servant passages in Isaiah, some of the minor and the major Old Testament prophets, the Gospels—the Bible is a text attempting to shed its ties to barbaric values in the cultures around it. The Epistle to the Hebrews is often seen as counter to that trend, as a return to the sacrificial commitments of all the nations—a return to Egypt when the Jordan has already been crossed. It is seen as a Christian writing embedded in the New Testament that reaffirms what Girardians assert the New Testament is trying to abolish. Michael Hardin reads Hebrews against the grain of its surface meaning, asserting that it "subverts

---

55. Ted Grimsrud, "Scapegoating No More: Christian Pacifism and New Testament Views of Jesus' Death," in *Violence Renounced*, ed. Swartley, 51.

the sacrificial process, albeit under cover of sacrificial language."[56] Perhaps such an approach might be taken to Amulek's discourse: Amulek could be seen as using sacrificial language and concepts to undermine that language and those concepts as they are commonly understood, just as Hebrews may use sacrificial language but without "accepting the victimage mechanism" such language is usually found to serve.[57] Reading Amulek against the grain of his assertions might be one approach to reconciling Girard with this Book of Mormon text, but such an approach seems convoluted to me. The standard Girardian approach to such a text that remains only partially able to escape the orbit of archaic sacrificial thought is to acknowledge that the writer (Mormon) or speaker (Amulek) sees partially, like the blind man Jesus heals a first time who still sees "men like trees, walking" and requires a second visual treatment before receiving perfect sight.[58] In this case Amulek and the writer of Hebrews would be between the two treatments.

Similar to the assertion in Alma 34, Hebrews argues Jesus completes and terminates the sacrificial system as he "dies once for all."[59] Two singular differences between Jesus's death and that of countless victims of sacrifice are that Jesus willingly offers himself without resistance or violence, and his death is never repeated. Sacrifice is built on repetition, but Jesus puts an end to such iterative systems.[60] Such a position would fit quite well with Amulek's assertion that "there should be a great and last sacrifice, and then shall there be, or it is expedient there should be, a stop to the shedding of blood."[61] The author of Hebrews walks a fine line, for the law of Moses requires sacrifice. But as the epistle explores

---

56. Michael Hardin, "Sacrificial Language in Hebrews: Reappraising René Girard," in *Violence Renounced*, ed. Swartley, 103.
57. Hardin, "Sacrificial Language in Hebrews," 106.
58. Mark 8:22–26.
59. Hebrews 9:26.
60. Hardin, "Sacrificial Language in Hebrews," 107.
61. Alma 34:13.

Psalm 40 (in Hebrews 10:8–10), it endorses revelation without appropriating the religion resulting from the revelation. The sacrificial structure of the Old Testament is the religious sediment that solidifies counter to the revelation from which it develops. "Sacrifice and violence have never been part of the divine economy."[62] Such a reading that explores Amulek's words while still retaining the Girardian soteriology might be possible for Book of Mormon readers, but that hard work has yet to be done. One can't just wish the problem away. I leave such work to more theologically oriented readers than I am. While my larger-scale overview of the issues often requires analysis of specific passages, such exegesis is not necessary for my current purposes. Sometimes critiquing others' readings is sufficient to my current purposes without supplying full-scale alternatives.

Loren Johns articulates a position (I think correctly) that asserts a text may use sacrificial language without endorsing or participating in the sacrificial mechanism.[63] Johns differs from Hardin in that he asserts Hebrews undermines sacrificial ideology by emphasizing Jesus's offering as a self-offering. Jesus reveals the scapegoating mechanism by not resisting, thereby bringing to light a misinterpretation that occurs in sacrificial activities. Jesus's Atonement is "exemplary rather than substitutionary."[64] Johns also points out that from the once-and-final argument for Christ's Atonement in Hebrews, it doesn't necessarily follow that all sacrifice is repudiated: "It is quite possible for a 'once-for-all death' to sustain and even support a sacrificial understanding of Jesus' death."[65] The same argument could easily be applied to Alma 34. As Hebrews 10:26 states, in the epistle Jesus's death isn't "better

---

62. Hardin, "Sacrificial Language in Hebrews," 113.
63. Loren L. Johns, "'A Better Sacrifice' or 'Better Than Sacrifice'? Response to Michael Hardin's 'Sacrificial Language in Hebrews,'" in *Violence Renounced*, ed. Swartley, 121.
64. Johns, "Response to Michael Hardin," 123.
65. Johns, "Response to Michael Hardin," 125.

than sacrifice" but is better than the sacrifice offered in the biblical tradition. It is still a sacrifice for the sins of the world, and as such still endorses sacrifice.[66]

Any reading such as Eugene England's that asserts that the Book of Mormon renounces sacrifice and repudiates violence must engage with passages that assert otherwise. England doesn't do sufficient tacking needed to make headway against contrary winds, even to read the text against the grain of its surface meaning. Let me cite a few examples. In 2 Nephi 2:7, Lehi explicitly states that the Messiah "offereth himself a sacrifice for sin, to answer the ends of the law." This reference to sacrifice sets the notion in a legal context. The reference to the law starts a few verses earlier, referring to Eve's gift to humanity: "And men are instructed sufficiently that they know good from evil. And the law is given unto men." But humanity isn't justified by obedience to law, "or, by the law men are cut off."[67] This legal framework makes Lehi appear to understand the Atonement within a debtor or penal substitution soteriology because they too appear in legal contexts. Here is the entire verse, which I quoted only partially earlier: "Behold, he offereth himself a sacrifice for sin, to answer the ends of the law, unto all those who have a broken heart and a contrite spirit; and unto none else can the ends of the law be answered."[68] Although the next verse mentions grace, such benevolence doesn't stand alone but is alloyed with just deserts: "there is no flesh that can dwell in the presence of God, save it be *through the merits*, and mercy, and grace of the Holy Messiah." Just as mercy and grace come through Christ's atoning work, so too do the merits. They aren't human merits. In 3 Nephi 9:19–20, Jesus commands an end to blood sacrifices, which are to be replaced by a "sacrifice" of "a broken heart and a contrite spirit." This initially appears to sup-

---

66. Johns, "Response to Michael Hardin," 126.
67. 2 Nephi 2:5.
68. 2 Nephi 2:7.

port a Girardian view of sacrifice and could be the source of a Girardian reading of the Book of Mormon, except that it endorses animal sacrifices as a preliminary step to that final sacrifice and is voiced by Jesus himself rather than by an intermediary, such as a prophet or a gospel writer. The emphasis on moving away from animal sacrifice is indeed in harmony with Girard's theory.

Mack Stirling's approach fastidiously engages with difficult passages in the Book of Mormon and uses Girard to correct the Book of Mormon (or, perhaps, to correct perceptions of it). The Book of Mormon often tells stories in which the moral voice endorses violence. In his interpretation of Nephi's endorsement of the Israelite destruction of the Canaanites in 1 Nephi 17:32, 35, Stirling argues that "from a Girardian perspective, Nephi, though a prophet, held a partially mythical view of Israel's righteousness and the Canaanites' wickedness. Influenced by his culture, he accepted the myth of divinely sanctioned violence as justification for slaughtering the Canaanites."[69] Another set of religious leaders, Alma and Amulek, preach at Ammonihah and the narrative likewise marks the violent deaths of those who oppose them, their followers are murdered, but the persecutors are also killed through divine causation when the prison walls collapse in an earthquake; God's deliverance is implied and the punishment of the persecutors divinely sanctioned.[70] Similarly, Ammon uses some violence in his missionary work among the Lamanites, against Lamoni's father (in self-defense) and against the thieves at the waters of Sebus (in self-defense and defense of property), to advance the divine project. Ammon is also protected by heavenly intervention when unconscious and one of the thieves' brothers attempts to kill him; the violator falls dead. In defending the king's flocks using violence the reader must make a distinction between good killing

69. Stirling, "Violence," 87.
70. Stirling, "Violence," 87–88.

and bad murder. But "from a Girardian perspective, a more likely interpretation is that the text reflects the incomplete understanding that Book of Mormon people had of their own violence."[71] The apocalyptic texts of the Bible and Book of Mormon pose interpretive difficulty to readers, for these end-times predictions are full of violence and destruction motivated by God's judgment against the wicked. As it is with the Bible, a Book of Mormon reading that stays within the bounds of a sacrificial hermeneutic asserts that God's justice requires a great and last sacrifice that satisfies the need for justice, and a hermeneutic that projects an apocalyptic and violent end of the world to fulfill God's judgment.[72]

Jacob's discourse in 2 Nephi 9 is one Book of Mormon passage often taken to be relevant to a Book of Mormon soteriology. While it's true that the material mentions the "infinite atonement," I take issue with that assertion. Jacob has previously referred to passages from Isaiah (chapters 49, 50, 51, and 52). For Jacob's midrashic development of Isaiah's themes, the most important passage is Isaiah 51:9–10, which in Jacob's citation says, "Awake, awake! Put on strength, O arm of the Lord; awake as in the ancient days. Art thou not he that hath cut Rahab, and wounded the dragon? Art thou not he who hath dried the sea, the waters of the great deep; that hath made the depths of the sea a way for the ransomed to pass over?"[73] Jacob is going to explicate the meaning of this passage from Isaiah. So, this discussion of the infinite atonement must fit within that Isaianic exegesis. And it all comes down not to what Isaiah means by referring to the conquest of Rahab but to what Jacob makes out of the reference to the primordial struggle between Deity and the sea creature to control the waters of chaos at creation.

---

71. Stirling, "Violence," 89.
72. James G. Williams, "'Steadfast Love and Not Sacrifice,'" in *Curing Violence: Essays on René Girard*, ed. Mark I. Wallace and Theophus H. Smith, 71–99 (Sonoma, CA: Polebridge, 1994), 73.
73. 2 Nephi 8:9–10.

Jacob keeps returning to this trope of Rahab, the dragon. Isaiah is appropriating the symbolism of Mesopotamian religion to assert that the God of the Bible is the God of creation, able to form the void into a created order. But Jacob has different uses for this symbol. Jacob wants to teach his Nephite group about death and redemption from death, so the symbol of Rahab the sea monster becomes a symbol of death, and God's conquest of Rahab symbolizes the overcoming of death through the redemption of Christ. After quoting Isaiah 51 and the first two verses of 52, Jacob notes that "our flesh must waste away and die; nevertheless, in our bodies we shall see God."[74] All humans must die. Only an "infinite atonement" can reverse this inevitability.[75] So the explicit quotation from Isaiah citing Rahab, the sea monster, becomes to Jacob a symbol of death: "O how great the goodness of our God, who prepareth a way for our escape from the grasp of this awful monster; yea, that monster, death and hell, which I call the death of the body, and also the death of the spirit."[76] I have quoted verse 10 in full, but in verses 10–12 the words *death* or *dead* are used twelve times and the word *grave* twice. There is an intense concentration on the notion of death. But for Jacob, death isn't the end of the matter. His words from the verses reduce the stock so all the flavor remains but most of the liquid evaporates. He begins these verses by stating, "O how great the goodness of our God," who prepares a way to escape death.[77] Then after that repetition of *death, dead,* and *grave,* Jacob repeats the refrain: "O how great the plan of our God," who makes a way to be resurrected and redeemed.[78]

Just in case we haven't caught the allusion to Rahab with the two previous iterations of the theme, Jacob repeats the allusion

---

74. 2 Nephi 9:4.
75. 2 Nephi 9:7.
76. 2 Nephi 9:10.
77. 2 Nephi 9:10.
78. 2 Nephi 9:13.

one more time, coupling it with the Atonement: we are delivered from death by the Atonement because Christ's work "satisfieth the demands of his justice upon all those who have not the law given to them, that they are delivered from that awful monster, death and hell, and the devil, and the lake of fire and brimstone, which is endless torment."[79] That word *satisfieth* vibrates very much like a satisfaction version of atonement. Rahab is transformed through these series of citations, from Mesopotamian mythology through the Isaiah passage and into Jacob's trope, from the symbol of chaos needing to be conquered for the world to be organized to a symbol of death to be overcome at the far end of creation as the cosmos is transformed, restored, and resurrected. As such, this chapter doesn't tell us much about soteriological views because it is about something else entirely. Even though Jacob's discourse uses the phrase "infinite atonement," the chapter does little to prefer one soteriological theory over another.

Alma 42 is often taken to be another chapter relevant to discussions of the Atonement. Alma 39 to 42 relate Alma$_2$'s counsel to his wayward son, Corianton. He advises against sexual sin. Alma$_2$ then relates that how we live in this life is restored to us in the next, evil restored if we do evil, good if we do good. When we get to chapter 42 the relationship of justice and mercy is explored in the context of the Atonement. In that context, with mercy, justice, and atonement in the mix, the best-known passage contrasts mercy and justice as if they are opposed to each other, a zero-sum relationship between the two: "do ye suppose that mercy can rob justice? I say unto you, Nay; not one whit. If so, God would cease to be God."[80] Taken in isolation, the verse implies something illicit about mercy acting as a thief against the righteous claims of justice. This pall surrounding the terms throws off the preferable

---

79. 2 Nephi 9:26.
80. Alma 42:25.

terminological positioning to favor justice in the binary opposition. A larger context is advisable. Mercy should not be viewed as
a potential robber but a necessary complement to justice on equal
terms, else we falsely dichotomize and mutually exclude the disfa-
vored term among the two concepts. The New Testament writers
don't recoil from referring to Christ's projected return by using the
simile "as a thief in the night,"[81] so this notion of mercy "robbing"
justice need not be so kleptic but perhaps more cryptic. After
all, the previous verse articulates the expansive domains of both
mercy and justice: "For behold, justice exerciseth all his demands,
and also mercy claimeth all which is her own; and thus none but
the truly penitent are saved."[82] Justice has broad demands, but
mercy also has expansive claims no less important or valuable. In
other words, if mercy can't rob justice, then justice can't rob mercy
either. Taking one verse out of context can lead to imbalancing and
overweighing the preferred half of the duality. If justice is too pre-
dominant in our lives, consider that if we all got what we deserved,
who'd escape a whipping?

If we let the artificial chapter breaks dictate our readings, we
will neglect the relevant verses at the end of Alma 41. The previous
chapter finishes up the discussion of restoration. What happens
in this life impacts a person's continuing status in the next: "the
meaning of the word restoration is to bring back again evil for evil,
or carnal for carnal, or devilish for devilish—good for that which
is good; righteous for that which is righteous; just for that which
is just; merciful for that which is merciful."[83] Alma$_2$'s emphasis on
restoration squarely throws its force on the side of justice. But
notice that both justice and mercy are mentioned, integrally connected to the discussion of restoration. If we emphasize the last
few verses of Alma 41 at the expense of Alma 42, then we might

---

81. 2 Peter 3:10; 1 Thessalonians 5:1-4; Revelation 16:15.
82. Alma 42:24.
83. Alma 41:13.

be accused of permitting justice to rob mercy. The advice to Corianton is to let both mercy and justice have their due: "see that
you are merciful unto your brethren; deal justly, judge righteously,
and do good continually; and if ye do all these things then shall
ye receive your reward; yea, ye shall have mercy restored unto
you again; ye shall have justice restored unto you again; ye shall
have a righteous judgment restored unto you again; and ye shall
have good rewarded unto you again." Implying that mercy *can rob*
justice connotes a felonious or illegitimate possibility, as if we in
this life might become criminal specialists in mercy, holding up the
bank of justice, mask concealing face and gun displaying threat-
eningly in hand. The quality of mercy is not strained to the extent
that mercy should become a public virtue and a public commodity
freely exchanged; justice extracts its price, but mercy flows freely,
abundantly, and without charge. Let those assigned to trade in
justice (judges, penal officers, police, common judges in Israel)
establish an oligopoly in justice, while the majority and residue in
society establish a free and abundant market in mercy. The only
mention of the word *atonement* in Alma 42 establishes the proper
balance between justice and mercy: "the plan of mercy could not
be brought about except an atonement should be made; therefore
God himself atoneth for the sins of the world, to bring about the
plan of mercy, to appease the demands of justice, that God might
be a perfect, just God, and a merciful God also."[84] Mercy gets top
billing when the atonement is highlighted, with justice getting its
due also. The "great plan of salvation," "the great plan of happiness," "the plan of mercy," and the "great plan of mercy" are all
mentioned in Alma 42, but reference to "the great plan of justice"

---

84. Alma 42:15. Notice here it is justice, not God, who makes the demands.
God seems to have offloaded, outsourced, the justice function. Again, the word
appease tends to favor a satisfaction theory of atonement, except Justice is the
personified principle demanding such appeasement.

is noticeably absent.[85] Both mercy and justice are anthropomor-
phized, with stern Justice making demands and generous Mercy
appeasing those demands and thus getting its way. The "great plan
of happiness,"[86] "the great plan of salvation"[87] requires an equilibrium between mercy and justice. This divine plan is called by a
number of names in this chapter, but it is never called "the great
plan of justice." It is referred to as "the great plan of mercy,"[88] and
such an emphasis on mercy doesn't in the least devalue justice but
rather balances it.

My reading deals with atonement, justice and mercy, and restoration. The message for Corianton, the message for us, is to have the
appropriate equilibrium of priorities in this life: "let the justice of
God, and his mercy, and his long-suffering have full sway in your
heart."[89] Justice and mercy are now balanced in a triangular relationship: (1) justice, (2) mercy, and (3) longsuffering. Both mercy
and justice can "have full sway" without subtracting from the
other. They, rather, work synergistically to exponentially expand
the work done by the other. The addition of a third element to justice and mercy dilutes the emphasis on justice (and on mercy, for
that matter) in words only, for in reality, each part of the triumvi-
rate is inflated and expanded by the mixture of the virtuous trinity.
If all three attributes have "full sway in your heart," the organ will
work at maximum, at the outer limit of capacity, yet that capacity
will expand.

My reading deals with atonement, justice and mercy, and restoration. The violence in the narrative comes with the judgment
of God. Alma$_2$'s admonitions to his son mix notions of resurrection and the afterlife with discussion of judgment because Corianton thinks it unjust that punishment in the next life is meted

---

85. Alma 42:5, 8, 15 (twice), and 31.
86. Alma 42:8.
87. Alma 42:5.
88. Alma 42:31.
89. Alma 42:30.

out for deeds done in this. For those given over to the devil in this life, "these shall be cast out into outer darkness; there shall be weeping, and wailing, and gnashing of teeth, and this because of their own iniquity, being led captive by the will of the devil."[90] This description of the status of some souls after death could be straight from Jonathan Edwards. "Now this is the state of the souls of the wicked, yea, in darkness, and a state of awful, fearful looking for the fiery indignation of the wrath of God upon them."[91] This state of the soul in misery imposed by God on the wicked in the interim period after death and before the final judgment is then followed when "they are cast out, and consigned to partake of the fruits of their labors or their works, which have been evil; and they drink the dregs of a bitter cup."[92] Divinely sourced violence in mortality or in the next life or violent punishment for sins in this life administered by a judge or jury may not be much of a distinction to the one being punished, especially considering Alma$_2$'s declaration that what one has done in this life will be restored in the next. The continuity between the two stages will merit just deserts, and Corianton objects to that result: "ye do try to suppose that it is injustice that the sinner should be consigned to a state of misery."[93] This seems a form of violence to me, to a similar extent that incarceration is violent treatment of offenders, except much more durable and harrowing, for this punishment is "eternal as the life of the soul should be, affixed opposite to the plan of happiness, which was as eternal also as the life of the soul."[94] The law is the instrument of that punishment, for humans need the threat of legal consequences in order to stay in line: "Now, if there was no law given—if a man murdered he should die—would he be afraid

---

90. Alma 40:13.
91. Alma 40:14.
92. Alma 40:26.
93. Alma 42:1.
94. Alma 42:16.

he would die if he should murder? And also, if there was no law given against sin men would not be afraid to sin. And if there was no law given, if men sinned what could justice do, or mercy either, for they would have no claim upon the creature?"[95] Whether in this life or the next, God's guilty verdict necessitates an eternity of violent retribution. In my view, that is, God is the causal factor in the violence following the judgment of the wicked.

Perhaps one way to avoid that conclusion is to posit that the law is the causal factor. Justice is personified in Alma$_2$'s discourse. Alma$_2$'s personification rhetoric would just need one small metaphorical step further to use apostrophe in addressing the law as more than an abstract principle and more as an agent among human agents:

> You, Justice, maintainer of universal natural law of the cosmos in earth and heaven, why do you stand so stern-faced, imposing your dictatorial rule on even deity from before not just the foundation of the world but of the cosmos, do you realize that mercy and atonement have arrived to balance your dour insistence on restoration and punishment? Rejoice in that balance and proportion. Remove that blindfold and let Mercy recalibrate those scales with abundant compassion and forgiveness.

The universe, natural law, or some force of law outside God may impose consequences that follow inexorably upon wicked acts and righteous deeds, and divinity might just be the noncausal agent of such results, having acquiesced to the law's priority. Under Aristotle's conception of causation, God would be the efficient cause, the law the material cause, the human action the formal cause, and the punishment or reward in the hereafter, the final cause. Alma$_2$ goes on to anthropomorphize justice on his own, without any need of Aristotle: "But there is a law given, and a punishment affixed, and a repentance granted; which repentance, mercy claimeth; oth-

---

erwise, justice claimeth the creature and executeth the law, and the law inflicteth the punishment; if not so, the works of justice would be destroyed, and God would cease to be God."[96] The verbs are active: mercy claims, justice claims and executes, and the law inflicts. That is a pretty austere and impersonal description of divine law that largely leaves humanity and divinity out of the process, just abstract principles at work.

Similarly, to humanize and balance the ledger, mercy is said to be an agent in this restoration in the next life for acts done in this life (and not repented for): "But God ceaseth not to be God, and mercy claimeth the penitent, and mercy cometh because of the atonement; and the atonement bringeth to pass the resurrection of the dead; and the resurrection of the dead bringeth back men into the presence of God; and thus they are restored into his presence, to be judged according to their works, according to the law and justice." This has taken the reading of Alma 42 on the atonement back to where it started: "do ye suppose that mercy can rob justice?"[97] Mercy is still personified with the suggestion that it might be a robber but is acquitted of the charge in the end. Jury foreman Alma$_2$ pronounces the verdict: "I say unto you, Nay; not one whit. If so, God would cease to be God."[98]

Any biblical or Book of Mormon reader who asserts that the God of scripture who completely abjures violence should not only feel the need to address the narratives where God countenances violence by charging humans with the duty of carrying out the dirty work here on the earth but also take up those narratives that ascribe the violence in this life and the next to God, who gets hands dirty in the details of creation and of final judgment.

As much as I have critiqued (and will address yet further) Eugene England's unsupportable claims that biblical and Book of

96. Alma 42:22.
97. Alma 42:25.
98. Alma 42:25.

Mormon texts assert certain universals regarding violence, he is also a good and sensitive reader of those texts. I want in the rest of this chapter to engage his reading of Alma 42, since I have been treating that material in this chapter. He and I are in agreement regarding that content. I defined a Girardian back in the introduction to this book as "someone deeply committed to the notion that Girard's ideas are a universal key to understanding history, economy, religion, literature, mythology, anthropology, and politics." England accurately understands that Girard's key to human nature and society is to understand the violence that emerges from mimetic rivalry. For Girard, the best guide to understanding that universal inclination toward communal violence is the Bible, and the best cure for that inclination is to accept Jesus's ethic of nonviolence articulated most fully in the Gospels. England takes that entire Girardian program and shifts it without elaboration or dissent to apply also to the Book of Mormon. Of Girard, England says,

> [Girard] has developed theoretical tools by which we can explore the powerful *content* of the Book of Mormon, content which is comparable to that of the Bible. Girard's work in anthropology led him to see similarities between various mythologies and the Bible that have led modern scholars and many others into a dogmatic religious relativism—but also helped him see crucial differences that powerfully "make manifest the uniqueness and truthfulness of biblical perspective." [99]

I doubt that England would have qualms about my calling him a Girardian, but I do so because England so fully accepts the Girard-

---

99. England, *Making Peace*, 138. England's essay about Nephi and Laban has been published three times: in *Making Peace* (1995), originally in *Dialogue* (1989), in the Nibley Festschrift ("A Second Witness for the *Logos*" [1990]). In this chapter, I will largely be drawing on the version in *Making Peace*, titled "Why Nephi Killed Laban." My real interest here is not in the Nephi/Laban narrative, to which I have dedicated a chapter (Chapter 7: The Death of Laban) already in this book, but in his reading of Alma 42 on justice and mercy.

ian anthropology (not only the theoretical framework but also the ethical and moral conclusions, as he frequently preached the latter from church pulpits, conference podiums, and seminar tables), and more importantly Girard's central contention: the universality of "Christ's demand that we reject all violence, even against those who 'deserve' it, and that never again try to justify our violence by blaming God."[100] On the next page, England expands that assertion he attributes to Nephi$_1$ that all violence resulting in death is murder, or violence more generally is forbidden. "Based on that understanding," he writes, "[Nephi] later states unequivocally the true nature of God as revealed in Christ, who was the absolute *opponent* of all imitative desire, all violence, all scapegoating, in a way that seems to contradict directly his own earlier report of what an angel had told him about God."[101] England is a Girardin because he accepts this Girardian doctrine. I am not a Girardian because, although opposed to violence as a general rule, I don't reject all violence as immoral. England is an unrepentant deontological pacifist; I am a deontologist who, when it comes to violence, asserts the need to be flexible enough to be a consequentialist occasionally.

The next Book of Mormon passage England takes up focuses on Alma 42 and the Book of Mormon concept of atonement, the

---

100. England, *Making Peace*, 146.

101. England, *Making Peace*, 147. In arraigning Nephi on the charge of murder, England then quotes 2 Nephi 26:32–33, an injunction against murder. But let me act as defendant's counsel briefly, promising to return to the subject later: "I object, your honor, to this rhetorical sleight of hand that counsel for the state uses in asserting that *killing* and *murder* mean the same thing, that they are equivalent. The prosecutor of my client Nephi should not be able to get away with implying to the jury that *murder* and *killing* are legally or morally the same. People die in car crashes all the time without the driver at fault being charged with murder. Killing in self-defense is not classified as murder under the law, and people who through negligence kill another are usually charged with manslaughter, not murder. My client straightforwardly admitted that he killed the victim. But that isn't the legal question posed in this case. The material question is, 'did he murder' the victim, Laban?" "Objection sustained. The jury will disregard the prosecutor's equivalence between killing and murder."

real subject of this chapter. My recent comments touching on Nephi and Laban are just teasers for the chapter that follows this one.

England nicely frames Alma₂'s comments on the opposition between justice and mercy as a paradox,[102] and we Latter-day Saints are a people of paradox. The biblical and Book of Mormon passages that seem to attribute violence to God might be written by authors who don't have a full understanding of God's justice and mercy, an abbreviated grasp of the precedent justice before mercy is invoked: "For instance, Alma teaches his son Corianton that God affixed laws and punishments, 'Which brought remorse of conscience unto man'; if he had not done so, 'men would not be afraid to sin . . . [and] the works of justice would be destroyed, and God would cease to be God' (Alma 42:18, 20, 22)."[103] Those laws train us to have a *quid pro quo* relationship with law and justice, expecting that "one gets what one deserves," this for that. But the law of mercy is not a law of exchange but one of grace.[104] England frames this paradox in his essay "Shakespeare and the At Onement of Jesus Christ," with justice and mercy embodied and reconciled in Jesus Christ: "It seems that the paradox of justice and mercy is ultimately resolvable only by one being, Christ, who is capable of standing in our minds as both ultimate judge and yet ultimate dispenser of mercy. He gives us our sense of justice by teaching us the law and its punishment, and he therefore is the only one able, as that same divine being, to extend mercy sufficient to appease that sense of justice."[105] The paradox containing competing demands of a stern-faced judge and kind-hearted clemency is reconciled in the Atonement but freely available to all without money and without price.

---

102. England, *Making Peace*, 149.
103. England, *Making Peace*, 150.
104. England, *Making Peace*, 151.
105. Eugene England, *Why The Church Is as True as the Gospel: Personal Essays on Mormon Experience*, (Salt Lake City, UT: Bookcraft, 1986), 47.

England then refers the reader to the two discussions of justice and mercy: the great and last sacrifice will be infinite, "And thus he shall bring salvation to all those who shall believe on his name; this being the intent of this last sacrifice, to bring about the bowels of mercy, which overpowereth justice, and bringeth about means unto men that they may have faith unto repentance."[106] Mercy intervenes, and we don't normally associate mercy with violent language such as *overpower*, but the translation does bring the notion of forcefulness, power, and influence; mercy is not weak or groveling, but enacts its role with might. Amulek specifically notes the noneconomic nature of the works of mercy: "Now there is not any man that can sacrifice his own blood which will atone for the sins of another. Now, if a man murdereth, behold will our law, which is just, take the life of his brother? I say unto you, Nay. But the law requireth the life of him who hath murdered; therefore there can be nothing which is short of an infinite atonement which will suffice for the sins of the world."[107] The next verse is included in one of my epigraphs to this book: "Therefore, it is expedient that there should be a great and last sacrifice, and then shall there be, or it is expedient there should be, a stop to the shedding of blood; then shall the law of Moses be fulfilled; yea, it shall be all fulfilled, every jot and tittle, and none shall have passed away."[108] Justice calls for a transaction (I obey the law and receive the pro- tection from the punishment of the justice, or I violate the law and justly expect to be compensated with punishment), but once the penitent reaches the mercy stage, then absolution and blessings come without strings, without price. Writes England, "Our diffi- culty with apparently contradictory scriptures may be a matter of understanding how God's justice and his mercy work *together* to bring us to self-knowledge and guilt, but also to self-acceptance

---

106. Alma 34:15.
107. Alma 34:11–12.
108. Alma 34:13.

and repentance."[109] This handoff from justice to mercy completes the relay race of atonement, with justice and mercy not always acting concurrently but always in conjunction. England frequently quotes Shakespeare's *Merchant of Venice* (Act 4, Scene 1):

> The quality of mercy is not strained;
> It droppeth as the gentle rain from heaven
> Upon the place beneath. It is twice blest;
> It blesseth him that gives and him that takes:
> 'Tis mightiest in the mightiest; it becomes
> The thronèd monarch better than his crown:
> His sceptre shows the force of temporal power,
> The attribute to awe and majesty,
> Wherein doth sit the dread and fear of kings;
> But mercy is above this sceptred sway;
> It is enthronèd in the hearts of kings,
> It is an attribute to God himself;
> And earthly power doth then show likest God's
> When mercy seasons justice.

"Mercy is not strained": today we would say "mercy is not *restrained*." It is endowed in such abundance that it refreshes all that it falls upon from the heavens and as an "attribute of God himself" in heaven and is an analogue, a type, a shadow to what can happen on earth "when mercy seasons justice."

I think England is right to depict justice and mercy as personalized moralities who not only operate together to balance the accounts of individuals but also in temporal priority. First, justice gets its due, sometimes more severely than others, and when justice is nearing the final calculations in its column in the books, the result might look austere and prospects severe. Then, mercy takes the pencil-like baton from mercy, and in the relay race, balances the accounts, always inflating the value in the merciful column with the benefit of any doubt, so that the sinner gets not that

---

109. England, *Making Peace*, 151.

deserved whipping but what mercy can judiciously supplement. Mercy is granted the final word, the final calculation, and mercy's math is generous to a fault.

That is what the Shakespeare quotation from *The Merchant of Venice* means. The merchant may get the scales out to balance the accounts, weighing good deeds against bad like Justice personified. But after Justice has finished, perfectly balancing merits against demerits, rewards against punishments, Mercy takes over the process and acknowledges that we all deserve a whipping, but that isn't what we'll get. The quality of mercy is not restrained, and, like the waters of life in Ezekiel's vision of the temple-to-be, those waters gush underneath the temple door's threshold and gently fall from heaven, flowing eastward toward the Dead Sea. At first, the waters of life and mercy flow to ankle depth, then to the knees, and soon to the loins. They are so abundant that they soon reach swimming depths. The banks of the river (more a wadi than a riverbed)—previously devoid of trees—then are thick with greenery: trees, shrubs, flowers. The land is healed and even the Dead Sea, when touched by this temple fount, is made whole with bountiful fish of all kinds drawing fishermen from everywhere to spread their nets and cast their lines.[110]

That is what the waters of life flowing from the temple cure in this broken and fallen desert of a world we inhabit whose current terrain leads to the Dead Sea. That is what happens when that quality of mercy takes over from justice and completes the great plan of mercy (with Mercy herself jotting a note at the bottom of the ledger book, "Well done thou good and faithful servant")—not robbing but supplementing with joy and greening the landscape in a way that knows no restraint in its healing and atoning power.

---

110. Ezekiel 47.

Chapter Seven

The Death of Laban

After Lehi and his group left Jerusalem, Lehi commanded Nephi and his brothers to return and acquire the brass plates from Laban, which included both genealogical and scriptural content,[1] roughly equivalent to the Old Testament up to Jeremiah's time. The first attempt by Lehi's sons has the eldest son, Laman, going solo to acquire the plates. Laban's and Laman's names differ in both Hebrew and English by that one consonant, the first indication of an identity between the two that sparks a mimetic rivalry. Laman is selected by lot to make the first attempt;[2] we have

---

1. The narrative tells the reader that Laban and Lehi were related. Both were from the Northern tribe of Manasseh. How proximately related we aren't told (1 Nephi 5:14–16; Alma 10:3). Laban's Josephite ancestors kept the record on the plates of brass: the record might have important content from Northern Israel also (as opposed to records written and collected by Judahite prophets, chroniclers, and priests from the Southern kingdom). When the Northern kingdom was destroyed by Assyria in 721 BCE and most of its elites deported to Assyria, those remaining mostly migrated and settled around Jerusalem, bringing historical and prophetic writings with them. If that is the history of the plates of brass, then Nephi and his successors may have had access to expanded records beyond what we know in the Hebrew Bible. The Book of Mormon does refer specifically to scriptural content by Zenos, Neum, Ezias, and Zenock that we don't otherwise know from the Bible. See the *Encyclopedia of Mormonism* entries for Zenock and Zenos at https://contentdm.lib.byu.edu/digital/collection/EoM/id/5938/rec/1, for Neum https://contentdm.lib.byu.edu/digital/collection/EoM/id/3995/rec/1, and for Ezias https://contentdm.lib.byu.edu/digital/collection/EoM/id/3671/rec/1.

2. 1 Nephi 3:11.

to think about lots as the ancients did, not as we moderns do. The lot is a way of letting Deity choose, not to randomize (to leave the selection to chance) the way we might think about drawing straws or playing rock/scissors/paper.[3] Laman, as the oldest brother, must attempt and fail in leadership before younger-brother Nephi can properly take the lead.

Being selected by lot can be an evil foreshadowing in the Bible. Achan is selected by lot as the violator of the ban on claiming booty at Jericho, and he ends up stoned to death.[4] Jonathan is selected by lot as the violator of Saul's proscription on his troops' eating the day of battle and is rescued from death only by the people's intervention.[5] Jonah is singled out by lot as the person on the boat guilty of bringing God's judgment on the mariners.[6] The literal scapegoat selected to cast the people's annual sins on to be driven into the wilderness is chosen by lot (as is the other scapegoat that is sacrificed on the temple's altar).[7] Saul, Israel's first and ill-fated king, is chosen by lot.[8] James G. Williams notes about these examples that "the lot is identical with the portion (*goral*) that falls upon a given individual or group by the power of deity or fate. The object of the ritual is to identify the 'odd man out,' that is, to bring about the differentiation in prevailing chaos, which entailed expelling or eliminating the one identified as threatening the community;" the one selected by lot is "the representative figure, the agent, the substitute (from the Latin *substituere*, to put under, next, or in place of) who is put in place of the group, enduring what they would otherwise have to suffer and embodying on their behalf the vic-

---

3. Proverbs 16:33.
4. Joshua 7.
5. 1 Samuel 14.
6. Jonah 1:7.
7. Leviticus 16:10.
8. 1 Samuel 10:20–24.

tory and blessings that the entire social order provides."[9] So, when Nephi and his brothers cast lots to see who will negotiate with Laban about acquiring the plates, and the lot falls on Laman, at the least the effort should be viewed as ill-fated and the venture likely to end in the death of Laman as a scapegoat.[10] I'll yet treat Laman and Lemuel as scapegoat figures, but here I ought to note that when the lot falls on Laman to go to Laban, Laman becomes the easy-to-predict scapegoat figure whom Laban will send his servants after to (unsuccessfully) kill. Laban more literally is destined to become a substitute scapegoat who must die so that an entire nation doesn't dwindle in unbelief. Nephi substitutes for Laman, shouldering the exact same role, after the latter's failure.

Laman isn't killed in his attempt to obtain the records, but the scapegoating is transferred to Laban who himself will die in the process of losing those records, which should be forecast to the reader by the similarity of names, to king-like Laban, who like Saul is "singled out by default as the difference, the scapegoat-king."[11] Laban's near-kingly status is stated by Laman and Lemuel: "How is it possible that the Lord will deliver Laban into our hands? Behold, he is a mighty man, and he can command fifty, yea, even he can slay fifty; then why not us?"[12] The biblical book of Kings (in Jewish Bibles, Kings is one book that is divided into two books in Christian Bibles) uses this term "mighty man" (*geburāh* or plural *gibborîm*) in very specific contexts referring "exclusively to royal power or might, almost always in formulaic expressions."[13] The scapegoating of Laman (whom Laban twice attempts to kill), the

---

9. James G. Williams, "History-Writing as Protest: Kingship and the Beginning of Historical Narrative," *Contagion* 1 (Spring 1994): 99.

10. 1 Nephi 3:11.

11. Williams, "History-Writing," 100.

12. 1 Nephi 3:31. Nephi poetically and hyperbolically expands that 50 into tens of thousands in the next verse, 1 Nephi 4:1.

13. Robert Polzin, *Samuel and the Deuteronomist: A Literary Study of the Deuteronomic History: 1 Samuel* (San Francisco: Harper & Row, 1989), 35.

man who would be king, is transferred to Laban, who acts king-like as the commander and mighty man. Saul also, the first Israelite king and portrayed by the biblical writer as a failed ruler, is chosen by lot. To take by lot (as the word *lakad* is translated in the RSV and NRSV) means to "'capture' or 'seize' in both its active and passive forms. It is the verb used in Joshua 7 to determine who has transgressed the rules of holy war. The use of a word like this for selecting a king must reflect a very ancient practice of determining the *pharmakos*, the sacred victim. The ritual process is a re-presentation of the situation of spontaneous violence, which is now controlled by the community with its ritual tradition."[14] So, when he is finally persuaded by the Spirit to kill Laban, Nephi "took Laban by the hair of the head, and . . . smote off his head with his own sword."[15] All forms of drawing lots touch on the operations of the sacred. Even when kings (think of the hapless Saul here) are taken by lot, the victim/king is "immediately surrounded by the ritual opposites," such as foreigner/native, scapegoat/sovereign, ruler/ruled.[16] The scapegoat is treated as if he is a transcendental signifier by the society in which he is selected.[17]

After Laman requests the plates of Laban, the two characters become undifferentiated as Laban angrily expels Laman, accusing the outcast of being a robber, and declaring his intention to slay him[18]—all actions Laman (and his posterity) will enact toward Nephi (and his posterity) before and after their migration to the promised land. Laman is first "scapegoated by Laban in classic Girardian terms," as the military commander accuses the young

---

14. James G. Williams, *The Bible, Violence, and the Sacred: Liberation from the Myth of Sanctioned Violence* (San Francisco: Harper, 1991), 133.
15. 1 Nephi 4:18.
16. René Girard, *Things Hidden Since the Foundation of the World*, trans. Stephen Bann and Michael Metteer (Stanford: Stanford University Press, 1987), 102–103.
17. Girard, *Things*, 102–103.
18. 1 Nephi 3:13.

man of theft and attempts to have him killed.[19] Then Laban himself is scapegoated when the punishment he decrees for Laman is exercised upon Laban.

The second attempt to obtain the plates has the brothers, under Nephi's leadership now, collecting their precious objects left behind at home to entice a trade with Laban. Laban becomes the thief he accuses Laman of being as he confiscates their goods and forces the brothers to flee for their lives.

After their second failure, Nephi goes alone into the city and finds Laban drunk and passed out. God then commands Nephi to kill Laban, which permits Nephi to finally acquire the plates. The pattern in this narrative is the following: Laman tries alone and fails, the brothers try together and fail, Nephi tries alone and succeeds. This trajectory points toward leadership legitimized in the Nephite record. This narrative provides the starkest test to see how compatible the Book of Mormon and Girard's theory are.

Eugene England struggles to reconcile this narrative with the nonviolence he advocates and that he asserts the Book of Mormon advocates.[20] Of the claim in 1 Nephi 4:13 that Laban must die for the preservation of a nation, England comments that the assertion is attributed in the text to the Spirit. But he is uncomfortable with the implication that Laban's scapegoating is divinely sanctioned. He first notes that in the Old Testament, such assertions are made by people yet in the grip of primitive sacrificial ideas, the expression of a people who haven't yet worked their way through myth to the true message of the gospel. Even in the New Testament, England cites Girard as the authority, suggesting that passages endorsing violence are the result of an underdeveloped idea of God and an adaptation of the surrounding culture of vio-

---

19. Eugene England, "Why Nephi Killed Laban: Reflections on the Truth of the Book of Mormon," *Dialogue: A Journal of Mormon Thought* 22, no. 3 (Fall 1989): 40.

20. England, "Why Nephi Killed Laban," 32–51.

lence that needs yet to be jettisoned to accept the larger message of the gospel.[21] Nephi's claim "directly contradicts the full revelation of God's nature as the One revealed in Christ who utterly rejects violence—and who demands we do the same."[22] England offers a number of explanations why Nephi would so directly contradict Girard (and Deity, apparently): (1) Nephi got it wrong and Nephi's psalm expresses anger, and that anger might have been directed at Laban (this assertion seems debatable because the text never directly connects the psalm with the Laban episode, but the connection must be inferred, implausibly in my view),[23] and

---

21. England, "Why Nephi Killed Laban," 41.

22. England, "Why Nephi Killed Laban," 42.

23. England associates the slaying of Laban with Nephi's psalm (2 Nephi 4) even more strongly in a way that seems too speculative when no such textual connection exists: "Certainly the experience with Laban taught Nephi something he never forgot, as is evidenced, perhaps, by his psalm of repentance—and is certainly shown in his harrowing, complex memory of the event many years later. The experience, of course, profoundly changed him and prepared him— perhaps through the softening of deep moral reflections—for additional teaching from God." See Eugene England, "A Second Witness for the *Logos*: The Book of Mormon and Contemporary Literary Criticism" in *By Study and Also By Faith: Nibley Festschrift*, ed. John M. Lundquist and Stephen D. Ricks (Salt Lake and Provo, UT: Deseret Book and FARMS, 1990), 113. This passage's curious mixture of certainty (two *certainlies*, an *as is evidenced*, and one *of course*—all about textual connections that seem so dubious offered up with only proof surrogates) and tentativeness (two *perhapses*) illustrates the ambiguity of the interpretation England seems himself to be so ambivalent about. All of this is an indication of the problematic nature of England's absolute certainty that Christ requires that his disciples renounce violence and proclaim peace, while the passage from the Book of Mormon seems to contradict this thesis. England should have provided an explanation of how Nephi became a born again Girardian sometime after killing Laban. For England, Nephi "later states unequivocally the true nature of God as revealed in Christ, the absolute opponent of all imitative desire, all violence, all scapegoating, in a way that seems to contradict his own earlier report of what an angel had told him about God" (England, "Second Witness," 114). England then cites 2 Nephi 26:32, which states in part that the "Lord God hath commanded that men should not murder" nor commit other sins. But it seems to me that one must make tremendously underdetermined connections between passages in Nephi's writing to justify these textual gymnastics. Perhaps Nephi just didn't consider his slaying of Laban to be murder; that seems to me the simpler explanation, but then the text wouldn't say what England so desperately needs it to say. *Killing* and *murder* are not equivalent. The text may consider Laban's death

(2) that God did indeed command Nephi to kill Laban but as an Abrahamic test that Nephi was (perhaps) never intended to follow through to conclusion. But Abrahamic tests should come complete with Abrahamic angels to stay the hand that wields the ritual knife or combat sword.

Nephi himself projects his own scapegoating tendencies on the Lord and carries out the slaying of Laban. As England notes, "the Bible and the Book of Mormon are at least partly limited to the perspectives of the writers, not simply to that of God himself. It is natural that those writers, though prophets, would perceive reciprocal violence and scapegoating with some of the limitations Girard has documented as occurring in all mythology and litera-ture, as well as all cultures."[24] England explains this idea further by comparing Nephi to Abraham and the "sacrifice" of Isaac: "What if it was designed to push Nephi to the limits of the human dilemma of obedience versus integrity and to teach him and all readers of the book of Mormon something very troubling but still very true about the universe and the natural requirements of establishing a saving relationship with God?"[25] The scriptural passage that Laban's death is necessary for the good of the nation and its paral-lel in the Gospel of John uttered by Caiaphas "raises the interest-ing, but rather troubling image of Laban as a type for Christ, since

---

a killing but not a murder. Val Larsen asserts that Nephi's slaying of Laban lies outside the Jewish legal umbrella because it is really an act of a sovereign. Larsen assets that Nephi was acting as an agent of another society that had already made its break with the political and social structure headquartered at Jerusalem. This idea is quite amenable to Girardian insights because it means that Nephi's killing of Laban is itself the announcement of that sovereignty and, in Girardian terms, is a founding murder just as Cain's killing of Abel is a founding murder or Romulus's slaying of Remus is the basis of Roman society. Moses also founds a new society when he kills an Egyptian and flees into the wilderness of Midian. Duane Boyce demonstrates the extreme weakness of England's reading of the Nephi/Laban story (*Even Unto Bloodshed: An LDS Perspective on War* [Salt Lake City: Greg Kofford Books, 2015], 176–79).

24. England, "Why Nephi Killed Laban," 44.
25. England, "Second Witness," 111.

the deaths of both figures are described as bringing the salvation of whole nations."[26] It is troublesome to connect Nephi's psalm with the Laban narrative on such flimsy evidence.

In the story of the madman of Gerasa and the herd of swine, it is the mob of evil spirits who plunge down the cliff, not the victim—the madman. This is a reversal of the normal pattern of collective violence.[27] The people of Gerasa are ill at ease seeing the victim now cured and whole while the porcine Legion is destroyed. This reversal threatens the entire economy of sacrifice.[28] Such a reversal is unimaginable in Greek and Roman stories; one can't consider the *Pharmakos* driving the mathematicians and philosophers over the cliff, nor the outcast in Rome forcing the consuls and Stoics over the Tarpeian precipices.[29] This about-face in a way threatens Girard's thesis, as he recognizes. Of the swine dying instead of the outcast human, he says,

> The miracle's conclusion satisfies a certain appetite for revenge, but can it be justified within the framework of my hypothesis? Does the element of revenge compromise my thesis that the spirit of revenge is absent in the Gospels? What is the force that drives the pigs into the sea of Galilee if not our desire to see them fall or the violence of Jesus himself? What can motivate a whole herd of pigs to destroy themselves without being forced by someone? The answer is obvious. It is the crowd mentality, that which makes the herd precisely a herd—in other words, the irresistible tendency to mimeticism.[30]

"The violence of Jesus himself?" Did Girard really raise that as a consideration? The reader runs into the same problem with Nephi's killing of Laban. When the reversal happens as the *Phar-*

---

26. England, "Second Witness," 106.
27. Mark 5:1–17.
28. René Girard, *The Scapegoat*, trans. Yvonne Freccero (Baltimore: Johns Hopkins University Press, 1986), 179.
29. Girard, *Scapegoat*, 182–83.
30. Girard, *Scapegoat*, 183.

makos kills the persecutor and the text endorses the killing, how do we harmonize that action with Girard's thesis? Being so unyielding about universal, exceptionless principles of interpretations causes problems in the messy, inconsistent world in which we live.

Girard grapples with the parallel text in John 11:47–53, where Caiaphas notes of Jesus "that it is better for one man to die for the people, than for the whole nation to be destroyed."[31] Nephi's narrative states a similar idea about Laban: "It is better that one man should perish than that a nation should dwindle in unbelief."[32] Caiaphas is saying what all societies say about their scapegoats: it is better to have just one person die "as a last resort to avoid an even greater violence. Caiaphas is the incarnation of politics at its best, not its worst. No one has ever been a better politician."[33] Not only does Caiaphas represent the dominant strain of politics, but "we have only just begun to understand how deeply the Caiaphas principle is embedded in all our social and psychological reflexes"; to be human is to obey the Caiaphas principle.[34] Here, the high priest is continuing one potential development from the Hebrew Bible, one that leads to animal sacrifice to deflect violence away from humans in the first place, and then later in a trajectory from the Suffering Servant portions of Isaiah and Job to the Gospels to abjure communal violence altogether.

The passage in 1 Nephi 4:13 that asserts Laban's death is better than letting a nation dwindle in destructive unbelief is part of a string of examples that go back long before Caiaphas's comments about Jesus in the Gospel of John to 2 Samuel 20 in the Bible and to Lehi's day with Jehoiakim, king of Judah, as mentioned in Jewish midrashim. The two Old Testament-period cases, the New

---

31. Girard, *Scapegoat*, 112.

32. 1 Nephi 4:13.

33. Girard, *Scapegoat*, 113.

34. Gil Bailie, *Violence Unveiled: Humanity at the Crossroads* (New York: Crossroad, 1995), 274.

Testament example, and two Book of Mormon examples (Laban and Korihor in Alma 30:47) fit the discussion about Laban into a pattern. "Over the years, the proper balance between the rights of the individual and the needs of the community was debated in Jewish law. On the one extreme, the Pharisees held that no individual was ever to be surrendered for the good of the community. On the other extreme, the Sadducees, who often cooperated with the Romans, argued that so long as the authorities named a specific victim, that was all that was necessary."[35]

Roger Aus, in the study this FARMS source is based on, notes that the entire episode of Caiaphas's statement about the one and the many is based on rabbinic sources that extended to stories in the Old Testament about King Jehoiakim and the rebel Sheba. He believes that sources with literary motifs can't be historical, so since the narrative about the high priest discussing Jesus contains these literary themes, the historicity of the John 11 passage is in question.[36] Like Laban's story, Jewish tradition has many of these stories about insurgents that end with the beheading of the rebel, sometimes with the severed head thrown over the wall of the city to the forces besieging the town.[37] The rebel is taken to be evil, and this theme influenced the portrayal of Jehoiakim.[38] Of course, in the Nephi/Laban story, the spirit specifically calls Laban wicked in the

---

35. FARMS, "Better That One Man Perish," in *Pressing Forward with the Book of Mormon: FARMS Updates of the 1990s*, eds. John W. Welch and Melvin J. Thorne (Provo: FARMS, 1999), 18.

36. I have argued against the assumption that if a text exhibits literary qualities, it can't at the same time be historical. I call this position an anti-literary positivism. The assumption that historical writing and literary writing are antithetical was common among historians half a century ago. It has gone into dramatic decline. See my treatment of the topic regarding the Book of Mormon at Alan Goff, "Types of Repetition and Shadows of History in Hebraic Narrative," *Interpreter: A Journal of Latter-day Saint Faith and Scholarship* 45 (2021): 263–318.

37. Roger David Aus, "The Death of One for All in John 11:45–54 in Light of Judaic Traditions," in *Barabbas and Esther and Other Studies in Judaic Illumination of Earliest Christianity*, Roger D. Aus (Atlanta: Scholars, 1992), 35, 42; see, for example, 2 Samuel 20:22.

38. Aus, "Death of One for All," 52–53.

same verse that discusses the surrender of the one person to save the nation.[39] An additional element of these stories with this theme of sacrificing one person for the larger good is the idea that a council is held to determine the rebel's fate. In Sheba's case it is the wise woman of Abel who consults with Joab (the besieging general) and then counsels with the people of the city before she can arrange to have Sheba's head removed and sent over the wall.[40] In the case of King Jehoiakim and the besieging Nebuchadnezzar, the rabbinic tradition uses almost the same wording from the Sheba story when Nebuchadnezzar demands of the Sanhedrin: "'Give him up to me, and I will go away,'" almost a literal borrowing from 2 Samuel 20:21. Then, in a debate about whether it is right to sacrifice one life in order to preserve others, specific mention is made of Jehoiakim's ancestress, the wise woman of Abel, who killed Sheba in such a context."[41] Aus notes that the motif emerges again in the story of Jesus and Caiaphas in John 11:50, where the high priest says before the Sanhedrin, "it is expedient for you that one man should die for the people, and that the whole nation should not perish." That same subject surfaces in the Laban story when, after having killed Laban, Nephi goes to Laban's treasury where Zoram talks about the "elders of the Jews" Laban has supposedly been consulting that night.[42] The scapegoating imagery of this cluster of stories must not be neglected either. In John 11, it is important for Caiaphas the high priest to state the expedience of letting one man die because it was Caiaphas the high priest who followed the prescription in Leviticus 16 for selecting the scapegoat by casting lots, tossing the people's annual sins on it, and driving it outside the city on the Day of Atonement and sacrificing the other scapegoat on the temple alter. "This [Caiaphas] did *in toto* approximately eighteen times, includ-

---

39. 1 Nephi 4:13.
40. See 1 Nephi 4:18.
41. Aus, "Death of One for All," 48–49.
42. 1 Nephi 4:22.

ing the year in which Jesus was put to death."[43] Part of the scapegoating process had the goat being "delivered" or "handed over"
to a priest to be "led away." Aus notes that the Hebrew word used
here means to "surrender a person to an authority": the "former
term is the same as that employed for Sheba's being 'handed over'
to Joab to be killed, and it also stands behind *paradidumi* in John
18:30, 35–36 and 19:11, 16 for Jesus being 'handed over' to Pilate
and 'the Jews' in order to be killed."[44] Just as Sheba and Christ were
handed over to the authorities, so too does the Spirit prod Nephi to
slay Laban (the phrase is repeated three times) for "the Lord hath
delivered him into thy hands."[45] Just as Caiaphas, the high priest,
presided over the altar killing of one goat and the driving out of the
second into the wilderness, so too did Caiaphas state the scapegoating rhetoric for the sacrifice of Jesus. "Jesus is thus described
here in imagery of the Day of Atonement," Aus argues, "involving
the high priest and a scapegoat, which was forced to sacrifice its life
in order to atone for the sins of all. This was imagery which was
easily discernible to the Jewish-Christian hearer of the episode, and
later to the reader of the gospel."[46]

Notice also that the scapegoating theme I have been exploring also intersects with the discussion of ethical theories I have
been applying to moral questions. The phrase "Caiaphas Principle" is usually applied in a derogatory way. Caiaphas, true enough,
cloaked his own self-interest as the high priest and a member of
the Sanhedrin in the garb of saving the nation. The Sanhedrin
faced the delicate task of balancing the potential Roman rescission
of power from the council against the people's demand for autonomy from Rome. As pastor Grant C. Richison observes,

---

43. Aus, "Death of One for All," 59.
44. Aus, "Death of One for All," 59.
45. 1 Nephi 4:11, 12, 17.
46. Aus, "Death of One for All," 60.

> Caiaphas offered an expedient alternative to their dilemma, a
> policy of escapism. He wanted to make Jesus a scapegoat for
> their problem with the Roman government. His desire was
> to maintain Sanhedrin power in Israel. This was an appeal to
> self-interest. There are those who are more concerned with cold
> expediency than truth. Fear turns to hate and hateful methods.
> They use others as scapegoats for their selfish interests.[47]

Absent the self-serving nature of Caiaphas's use of the principle
that it is better that one person die than a whole nation, this is
a rather straightforward utilitarian expression. To hear a phrase
often used by unprincipled politicians to justify an action of singling out a person for death being articulated in a narrative by
a divine messenger doesn't negate its authenticity or utility when
stated by the Spirit or when written into his record by Nephi: "It is
better that one man should perish than that a nation should dwindle and perish in unbelief."[48]

In the mode of sharing with Abraham the divine plan regarding the cities of the plain and reasoning with him about the cut-
off point for saving the cities (a discussion where the bargaining
for the life and death of humans was calculated in numbers not a
whole lot different from Caiaphas's and Nephi's calculation), the
Spirit provides Nephi additional reasons to kill Laban. Nephi then

---

47. Grant C. Richison, "John 11:49f." https://versebyversecommentary.
com/2017/11/13/john-1149f/ (Accessed 9-18-2023). The Nation online magazine
(where the nation being referred to is, apparently, Thailand) contemporizes the
Caiaphas Principle. "Earlier, some of us thought that the regime of Donald Trump
followed no principles whatsoever. Now it appears to have embraced a variation
of the Caiaphas Principle. The original Caiaphas Principle was formulated by
Joseph Caiaphas, the Jewish high priest at the time of Jesus Christ. It reads: "It is
expedient . . . that one man should die for the people, and that the whole nation
should not perish" (John 11:50). This was the rationale the Sanhedrin used in
condemning Jesus to death." The writer continues by expanding the Principle:
"The Caiaphas Principle could be extended to mean: 'Any evil can be justified if
it brings sufficient benefits to me and my people.'" The Nation, Caiaphas, Trump,
and Moral Bankruptcy, November 27, 2018, https://www.nationthailand.com/
lifestyle/30359416. Accessed 9-18-2023.
48. 1 Nephi 4:13.

produces his own to support the necessity of killing Laban: (1) "the Lord hath delivered him into thy hands"; (2) "Yea, and I also knew that he had sought to take away mine own life"; (3) "yea, and he would not hearken unto the commandments of the Lord"; and (4) "he also had taken away our property."[49] The Spirit then repeats the first and, apparently, because of the emphasis, most important justification with some elaboration: "And it came to pass that the Spirit said unto me again: Slay him, for the Lord hath delivered him into thy hands; Behold the Lord slayeth the wicked to bring forth his righteous purposes. It is better that one man should perish than that a nation should dwindle and perish in unbelief."[50] As he converses with the Spirit over the prone body of Laban, Nephi recalls an earlier divine revelation (from the Lord directly, rather than through an intermediary) written in his record just two chapters earlier:

> And now, when I, Nephi, had heard these words, I remembered the words of the Lord which he spake unto me in the wilderness, saying that: Inasmuch as thy seed shall keep my commandments, they shall prosper in the land of promise. Yea, and I also thought that they could not keep the commandments of the Lord according to the law of Moses, save they should have the law. And I also knew that the law was engraven upon the plates of brass. And again, I knew that the Lord had delivered Laban into my hands for this cause—that I might obtain the records according to his commandments.[51]

Nephi, following the Spirit's argument and adding his own justifications, efficiently relates the execution of the command: "Therefore I did obey the voice of the Spirit, and took Laban by the hair of the head, and I smote off his head with his own sword."[52]

---

49. 1 Nephi 4:11.
50. 1 Nephi 4:12–13.
51. 1 Nephi 4:14–17, referring to 1 Nephi 2:20.
52. 1 Nephi 4:18.

The Book of Mormon text asserts straightforwardly that killing Laban is God's will and Nephi's imperative. John Welch cites other instances where the biblical God "sanctioned certain slayings to promote the national existence and welfare of the righteous," including during the Israelite invasion of Canaan.[53] The Spirit tells Nephi that God has delivered Laban into his hands, using the wording of Exodus 21:13,[54] and the citation of the biblical phrasing gives more weight to the requirement, making the killing "legally justifiable and religiously excusable."[55] Of course, a Girardian would cite such after-the-fact and before-the-fact rationalizations as provided by readers and actors to maintain the correctness of sacrificial acts as further evidence of the sacrificial nature of the account.

Mack Stirling implies that Nephi is caught up in a mimetic crisis with Laban. In this story Laban "represents all of Nephi's and his family's persecutors."[56] Like Cain or Romulus, Nephi's killing of Laban makes possible the Lehite civilization and was "unconsciously mythologized by Nephi in the years before he writes his record."[57] The Girardian perspective, as Stirling rightly sees and England misunderstands, requires that we say about Nephi's killing of Laban that it can't be in accord with the "higher law" of Girard's position and God's revelation of reconciliation at the same time. Nephi would have had to misunderstand what the Spirit told him to do, if indeed Girard is right about the Christian revelation and its universal applicability: "Girardians will continue to

53. John W. Welch, "Legal Perspectives on the Slaying of Laban," *Journal of Book of Mormon Studies* 1, no. 1 (1992): 131–32.

54. "And if a man lie not in wait, but God deliver him into his hand; then I will appoint thee a place whither he shall flee." Nephi does indeed flee (not to a city of refuge but into a desert and into a new continent) and his words "And I was led by the Spirit, not knowing beforehand the things which I should do" (1 Nephi 4:6) indicate that he did not lie in wait for Laban.

55. Welch, "Legal Perspectives," 133–34.

56. Stirling, "Violence," 95.

57. Stirling, "Violence," 96.

see Nephi as a tragic illustration of the fact that even the most devoted individual may slide unconsciously into scapegoating and the violent sacred. Nephi stands as a warning against the seductive temptation to sacrifice one's rival in the name of God."[58] Of course, readers who give priority to the Book of Mormon as the more correct book "would thus reject the Girardian perspective as an absolute interpretive standard."[59] England attempts to fudge that stark choice, but Stirling straightforwardly faces up to it. England's canon within the canon is really Girard within the Bible. Both Sterling and I are committed to the Book of Mormon not just as a relic of antiquity and a sacred text, but also as a scripture one can live by, one that informs our moral and ethical actions. Speaking for myself, I don't expect the world around us to enforce or reward a foolish consistency,[60] a uniformity that can be transferred from one category of life into all others without loss. England, however, is so fully committed to pacifism as an a priori principle that he advances it as a universal moral requirement. He reads it into the actions of his scriptural heroes and texts even when other readers find such an interpretation implausible. Nephi is the actor who killed Laban and the writer who wrote it up in the small plates, yet England reads him against what he engraves into his medium. All readers are advocates for moral and ideological positions, but sometimes the texts push back on the interpretive schemes we overlay on them. Laban's death is a substitution not just for the attempted killing of Lehi's sons, but for the entire "nation" that will propagate from these four brothers and other descendants of Lehi.

Jesus's death is explicitly substitutionary, a proxy work to redeem humanity. But it lies in a long line of surrogate actions.

---

58. Stirling, "Violence," 97.
59. Stirling, "Violence," 97.
60. Emerson asserted in his essay "Self-Reliance" that a "foolish consistency is the hobgoblin of small minds." Not all consistency, mind you, but a foolish consistency.

The slaying of the firstborn of Egypt sets a certain pattern of substitutionary sacrifice for the rest of Israel's history. The first-born is dedicated to God through the rest of the Bible with various other substitutions following that first offering (the tribe of Levi, for example). This is part of the biblical narrative's concern for the preference for younger sons in founding generations. This leapfrogging of younger sons over the elder (Joseph, Jacob, Moses, David, and Nephi, for example) "shows that both the cultic sphere of sacrifice and the narrative sphere of founding stories were deeply imprinted with a substitutionary code that attempted to deal with and ameliorate the victimization mechanism that is endemic to culture. This substitutionary code took form in multiple developments and variations and could be ended only by a truly divine innocent victim who discloses the God of victims and unmasks the disguises of religion and culture."[61] In at least this one story of conflict between Nephi and Laman, we get a further substitution of violence away from the elder brother onto his doppelganger, Laban. Laban's death might symbolize the movement of covenant from Jews (soon to be taken captive into Babylon) to the Lehites, as hypothesized by Steven Olsen, where cycles of chosenness and covenant rejection start all over again. Olsen sees in Nephi's decollation of Laban a larger symbolic meaning, fully intended by Deity: "Thus God's directing Nephi to slay a Jewish religious leader by cutting off his head with his own sword symbolically indicates that Jehovah severed his covenant with the people of Israel at Jerusalem because of their wickedness. Lehi and his family were now to be the rightful heirs of the promised blessings of the covenant."[62] In this interpretation, Laban's sword becomes

---

61. James G. Williams, *The Bible, Violence, and the Sacred: Liberation from the Myth of Sanctioned Violence* (San Francisco: Harper, 1991), 120.

62. Steven L. Olsen, "The Death of Laban: A Literary Interpretation," *FARMS Review* 21, no. 1 (2009): 192–93. In the Jewish perspective, even after the Jews violate the covenant, that connection is not severed. It is still in place, and God expects the terms to continue to be carried out, after, say, returning from exile

the instrument of memory for Nephites in the future. Using a wordplay in English, Olsen asserts that Laban's dismembering is a consequence of the Israelite people's dis-remembering of the covenant and a reminder to the Nephite nation yet to be formed to keep in memory the covenants of the past.

In the biblical conflict between the brothers Jacob and Esau, Jacob is able to dupe his father into giving him the blessing through a sacrificial substitution. Jacob serves up the meat of a kid to his father instead of the wild game Esau has been sent to procure. The kid receives the violence that might otherwise be directed at Jacob, and the son must array himself in the skin of the animal (the same goat Rebekah used to prepare the meat) to fool his father about his own identity and substitute for Esau's hairy arms and neck. Two substitutions occur here simultaneously: first, an animal is sacrificed instead of a man, and second, one brother receives the blessing instead of another,[63] and they become *frères ennemis*, enemy brothers. Similarly, in the Nephi/Laban story, a double substitution is worked out. Laman is (1) originally chosen to acquire the plates from Laban, but he fails. Nephi succeeds Laman as the family representative and leader while succeeding in acquiring the records. Laban is (2) substituted for Laman as a sacrificial victim, and, like Jacob, Nephi dons the now-slain Laban's clothing to complete a deception. "Sacrificial substitution implies a degree

---

in Babylon. So let me distance my position from Olsen's view that the covenant with the Jews was "severed." For Paul, although himself a member of the tribe of Benjamin and not Judah, asserts that God's covenants with the Jews as part of Israel genetically is still in force and "all Israel shall be saved" (Romans 11:26 and 11:17–28). The apostle to the Gentiles asserts forcefully, "I say then, Hath God cast away his people? God forbid. For I also am an Israelite, of the seed of Abraham, of the tribe of Benjamin. God hath not cast away his people which he foreknew. . . . Even so then at this present time also there is a remnant according to the election of grace" (Romans 11:1–2, 5).

63. René Girard, *Violence and the Sacred*, trans. Patrick Gregory (Baltimore: Johns Hopkins University Press, 1972), 5.

of misunderstanding. Its vitality as an institution depends on its ability to conceal the displacement upon which the rite is based."[64]

Like the Esau/Jacob story, the violence in the Nephi/Laman narrative is directed away from the older brother, but the enmity remains. Esau vows to kill his brother once his grieving period for his father is ended, so Jacob must flee for his life to Haran.[65] There is good reason for the violent sacrifice to be directed away from Laman toward Laban. Girard mentions there are two substitutions: (1) one person is singled out to represent the entire society; and (2) an outsider is then substituted for that victim. If the first target ends up being sacrificed, that might not work to quell the violence but begin a new round of crisis and violence, perhaps even a cycle of revenge.[66] But if an outsider is substituted for the first person singled out by lot, that selection can end the calamity by directing the murder away from the insider to a foreigner. Often the first victim selected was the king, so redirecting the violence is certainly in the interest of the first victim, who sometimes has power to delay the consummation of the process time and again in order to ritually establish his own role as monarch. "We should not conclude, however," Girard contends, "that the surrogate victim is simply foreign to the community. Rather, he is seen as a 'monstrous double.' He partakes of all possible differences within the community, particularly the difference between within and without."[67] Laban is the near relative who is not too near, so he can substitute for a close family member.

Spencer notes the deficiencies of previous readings of the death of Laban narrative, which tend to fall into two types, "both of which take 1 Nephi as effectively uniform in portraying Nephi's character": (1) the "conservative" approach emphasizes Nephi's obedience and consistency and the command to kill Laban marks

64. Girard, *Violence and the Sacred*, 5.
65. Genesis 27:41–46.
66. Girard, *Violence and the Sacred*, 269.
67. Girard, *Violence and the Sacred*, 271.

the boundary test of his obedience, while (2) the "liberal" slant views the thought of killing Laban a temptation that Nephi ought to resist, but he gives in to through self-interested rationalization.[68] Spencer prefers to see the episode within a changing psychological and spiritual character; Nephi has several episodes that mark his conversion to God and to a divine covenantal relationship. Nephi's previous revelations from God cause him to prematurely assume prerogatives as leader and teacher over his brothers, which begins a spiral of rivalry between him and Laman that culminates in mimetic rivalry between the Nephites and Lamanites through the rest of Book of Mormon history.[69] Nephi has demonstrated obedience to God's command at every step while Laman has constantly resisted and murmured; Nephi's perfect obedience up to the point that he is told to kill Laban—when he pulls back in disgust—reveals Nephi as Laman's mimetic rival as Nephi approaches the point when he withdraws momentarily from obedience. Spencer sees Nephi as Laman's true mimetic double, not Laban. The one-letter difference between Laban's and Laman's names indicates their similar identities, so Laban is merely a substitute for Nephi's own brother. I differ here from Spencer, who insists that Nephi is so caught up in his fraternal rivalry that the command to kill Laban is intended to shock him out of his familial competition with Laman and indeed begins a process of revelation accomplishing that end gradually.[70] In my reading, Laban is more like the ram Abraham substitutes for Isaac in Nephi's drama on his own Mount Moriah. But like Spencer, I don't see the God of the Bible, the God of the Book of Mormon, as universally opposed to all violence everywhere. I think the reader has to twist the narrative to arrive at an interpretation where the narrative ultimately withdraws the divine endorsement of Laban's death.

68. Spencer, "René Girard," 11.
69. Spencer, "René Girard," 11–14.
70. Spencer, "René Girard," 14.

With this preliminary work of commenting on a Girardian approach to this passage, let me now provide a reading of the story itself:

1 Nephi 4	Commentary
2 Therefore let us go up; let us be strong like unto Moses; for he truly spake unto the waters of the Red Sea and they divided hither and thither, and our fathers came through, out of captivity, on dry ground, and the armies of Pharaoh did follow and were drowned in the waters of the Red Sea.	Nephi, as in 1 Nephi 17, portrays a conflict over building a ship; here he invokes Exodus typology to remind Laman and Lemuel of God's past saving works. This, of course, makes Nephi the parallel of Moses and Laban the equivalent of Pharaoh, leaving Laman and Lemuel out of the drama except as members of the ensemble, the undifferentiated mass who are delivered. This foreshadows the resolution of Nephi's narrative, for we all know how the Exodus story ends: with Pharaoh's/Laban's defeat and deliverance for God's chosen.

1 Nephi 4	Commentary
3 Now behold *ye know* that this is true; and *ye also know* that an angel hath spoken unto you; *wherefore can ye doubt?* Let us go up; the Lord is able to deliver us, even as our fathers, and to destroy Laban, even as the Egyptians.	Nephi reminds Laman and Lemuel of their rebellion in the previous chapter where the angel specifically mentioned that the younger brother will rule over the elder brothers and specifically commands them to return to Jerusalem where "the Lord will deliver Laban into your hands" (1 Nephi 3:31) without any specifics. As with 1 Nephi 17, this injunction is phrased epistemologically: in terms of what Laman and Lemuel know, and the opposite not of knowledge but of faith—doubt. In 1 Nephi 17 when Laman and Lemuel assert that they "know" the Jews remaining in Jerusalem are righteous (verse 22, twice) Nephi rehearses Israelite history; between verses 25 and 55, either Nephi, Laman and Lemuel, or the Lord asserts fourteen times that they know God's saving acts in the past and present. By the end of chapter 17, they are reoriented in a new epistemological direction because of the history lesson made relevant to their present circumstances. The narratives about retrieving the plates and building the ship are closely connected thematically by conflict between brothers, the invocation of the Exodus type, and

1 Nephi 4	Commentary
(v. 3, *continued*)	the temporary change of heart by Laman and Lemuel. At the end of the latter narrative, Laman and Lemuel themselves assert that *"We know of a surety* that the Lord is with you [Nephi]" (1 Nephi 17:55, emphasis mine).
4 Now when I had spoken these words, they were yet wroth, and did still continue to murmur; nevertheless they did follow me up until we came without the walls of Jerusalem.	Laman and Lemuel, complaining, nevertheless "follow" Nephi's lead, beginning already to fulfill the angel's declaration about the elder serving the younger.
5 And it was by night; and I caused that they should hide themselves without the walls. And after they had hid themselves, I, Nephi, crept into the city and went forth towards the house of Laban.	Nephi is, again, still taking the initiative. He is acting out his leadership after the angel so recently pronounced it. Nephi both comes up with a plan and at the same time leaves room for improvisation.
6 And I was led by the Spirit, not knowing beforehand the things which I should do.	Nephi doesn't plan to kill Laban; without premeditation Nephi wasn't lying in wait for Laban.[71] This is additional evidence in Nephi's mind that God was guiding the events and that he himself was not guilty of premeditated murder.

---

71. Welch, "Legal Perspectives," 124–25.

1 Nephi 4	Commentary
7 Nevertheless I went forth, and as I came near unto the house of Laban I beheld a man, and he had fallen to the earth before me, for he was drunken with wine.	I have elsewhere explored the allusive connections between Laban's death and Nabal's,[72] so let me here just invoke that analysis briefly. Like all Hebraic narrative, the Laban story works through pervasive allusion. The Book of Mormon Laban is intended to remind us of the conflict between Jacob and Laban in Genesis. Biblical scholars have already pointed out the allusive connections between Laban and one of King David's oppressors—Nabal, which is Laban spelled backward (an anadrome). The ancient rabbis pointed out that the biblical Laban and Nabal were both typological figures pointing to the Pharaoh of the Exodus. Nabal too almost lost his head when passed out from drink,[73] and he dies the next day with his prized possessions passing over to David.
8 And when I came to him I found that it was Laban.	The lack of premeditation is emphasized here, good (or perhaps divine) fortune rules rather than cunning and ambush.

72. Alan Goff, "How Then Should We Read? Reading Mormon Scripture after the Fall," *FARMS Review* 21, no. 1 (2009): 137–38.
73. 1 Samuel 25.

1 Nephi 4	Commentary
9 And I beheld his sword, and I drew it forth from the sheath thereof; and the hilt thereof was of pure gold, and the workmanship thereof was exceedingly fine, and I saw that the blade thereof was of the most precious steel.	Goliath's sword garners similar attention in the Bible, even though biblical narrative is famous for its reticence about physical description. Special attention is drawn to the sword by the deviation from biblical narrative norms. Like Goliath's sword, Laban's becomes a keepsake for later generations of Nephites, both swords used in later narratives to indicate power relationships and divine mighty acts of salvation.
10 And it came to pass that I was constrained by the Spirit that I should kill Laban; but I said in my heart: Never at any time have I shed the blood of man. And I shrunk and would that I might not slay him.	The narrative perspective shifts slightly from first person to internal dialogue. The word *constrained* indicates the divine compulsion; similarly, Nephi is going to be "constrained" to correct his brothers[74] just before he makes his final break with them. Nephi often resorts to internal dialogue to frame his revelations from God.[75]

74. 2 Nephi 4:14.
75. See 1 Nephi 2:19–24; 1 Nephi 17:7–10, 12–14, 53; 2 Nephi 5:5 is less explicit but seems to fit the same model.

1 Nephi 4	Commentary
11 And the Spirit said unto me again: Behold *the Lord hath delivered him into thy hands.* Yea, *and I also knew* that he had sought to take away mine own life; yea, and he would not hearken unto the commandments of the Lord; and he also had taken away our property.	Twice in these verses the Spirit asserts that the Lord delivered Laban into Nephi's hands, and once Nephi repeats the phrase. That triple emphasis drives home the message through repetition. This wording—"delivered into his hand"—seems to invoke the biblical law expressed about innocence and guilt when a man is killed: "He that smiteth a man, so that he die, shall be surely put to death. And if a man lie not in wait, but *God deliver him into his hand*; then I will appoint thee a place whither he shall flee."[76] Nephi does flee after killing Laban (not to a city of refuge but to another land). The same words are used by the angel when telling the brothers to return to Jerusalem: "Ye shall go up to Jerusalem again, and *the Lord will deliver Laban into your hands.*"[77]

---

76. Exodus 21:12–13.
77. 1 Nephi 3:29.

1 Nephi 4	Commentary
12 And it came to pass that the Spirit said unto me again: Slay him, for *the Lord hath delivered him into thy hands;*	The record asserts unequivocally the divine command to kill. The dual causation (sometimes called the dual causality) principle is often invoked in analyzing biblical narrative. Joseph states it unequivocally when he asserts that his brothers, in selling him into slavery in Egypt intended the act for evil, but God intended the same act for good because it results in the salvation of the entire family of Jacob.[78] A reader might blame Nephi for being convinced of the rightness of killing Laban and being the efficient cause of such a sacrificial murder, but God would, in that explanation, be the final cause.

78. Genesis 50:20–21. See generally some of the following studies: Yairah Amit, "The Dual Causality Principle and Its Effects on Biblical Literature," *Vetus Testamentum* 37, no. 4 (1987): 385–400. Michael Avioz, "Divine Intervention and Human Error in the Absalom Narrative," *Journal for the Study of the Old Testament* 37, no. 3 (2013): 339–47. Charlotte Katzoff, "Divine Causality and Moral Responsibility in the Story of Joseph and His Brothers," *IYYUN: The Jerusalem Philosophical Quarterly* 47 (Jan. 1998): 21–40. Jonathan Grossman, "The Design of the 'Dual Causality' Principle in the Narrative of Absalom's Rebellion" *Biblica* 88, n. 4 (2007): 558–66.

1 Nephi 4	Commentary
13 Behold the Lord slayeth the wicked to bring forth his righteous purposes. It is better that one man should perish than that a nation should dwindle and perish in unbelief.	The Caiaphas Principle is stated also in John 11:50. This Book of Mormon passage explicitly states, not that the Spirit commands a killing or that Nephi does the killing, but that the Lord kills the wicked "to bring forth his righteous purposes." This straightforward endorsement of violence leaves little wiggle room for someone like England. A Girardian has little choice but to attribute a misunderstanding of the divine imperative against violence. As Steven Olsen points out, this mission to obtain the plates is a personal or familial goal but now has become a national imperative, increasing the stakes for Nephi and the pressure on him.[79]

79. Olsen, "Death of Laban," 186.

1 Nephi 4	Commentary
14 And now, when I, Nephi, had heard these words, I remembered the words of the Lord which he spake unto me in the wilderness, saying that: Inasmuch as thy seed shall keep my commandments, they shall prosper in the land of promise. 15 Yea, and I also thought that they could not keep the commandments of the Lord according to the law of Moses, save they should have the law. 16 And I *also knew* that the law was engraven upon the plates of brass.	Faced with the divine requirement, Nephi devises rationalizations to support the distasteful task. Here he refers to the most common covenant that ties Book of Mormon narrative together (first stated in 1 Nephi 2:20–21). The fulfillment of the promises given to him cannot be completed unless he kills Laban to acquire the plates. Nephi thinks intertextually, applying the divine word from other occasions to apply to this situation. Nephi must act extralegally to obtain the law so his people can obey that law.
17 And again, *I knew* that *the Lord had delivered Laban into my hands* for this cause—that I might obtain the records according to his commandments.	Just as back in verse 3, Nephi asserts that Laman and Lemuel know the workings of the Lord's salvation. Three times in verses 11, 16, and 17, Nephi asserts an epistemology of action: (1) he knows Laban's guilt; (2) he knows the law is on the plates; and (3) he knows God has delivered Laban into his hands to transfer the plates to Lehi's group. Just as Laman and Lemuel must commit an act of faith based on what they know (verse 3, that is, go up to Jerusalem), so must Nephi (that is, kill Laban).

1 Nephi 4	Commentary
18 Therefore I did obey the voice of the Spirit, and took Laban by the hair of the head, and I smote off his head with his own sword.	The intertextual connections between this story and the David/Goliath narrative is not a weakness of the Book of Mormon but a strength. The reader is supposed to get the connection. Biblical narrative also operates through constant allusion to other narratives within its canon. Just as David killed Goliath and cut off his head with his own sword, Nephi does the same to Laban.

As difficult as it is to accept that the God of the Bible and Book of Mormon isn't always an orthodox Girardian, stories such as this illustrate the difficulty with being committed to both Girard's ideas and the Book of Mormon as a revealed text and "the most correct book of any book on earth." Not only does this story endorse violence, but it also attributes guilt to the victim of that violence. Both themes violate Girardian prescriptions.

Among other options, the reader can maintain the notion of the Book of Mormon as a revealed and inspired text and the event of Laban's homicide as urged by both the Lord and the Spirit, or one can advocate Girardian principles that the God of Heaven universally abhors and renounces violence, from which follows the position that the Book of Mormon writer misunderstood the divine imperative. The paradox posed by the Laban story presents a Girardian knot that is best unpuzzled by taking a sword to it rather than attempting the intricate task of unraveling with fingers. Instead of conceiving of God as a deontologist who tenaciously grasps hard and fast to categorical imperatives under all circumstances, perhaps the divine, like each human who is created in the image of God, is a sometime deontologist and sometime consequentialist because moral and ethical decision-making requires rationality, emotion, judgment, and flexibility. One must understand that Girard's rule of reading can turn any text to its use; if a character refuses violence or revels in it, if the scapegoat is the highest or the lowest in society, the theory is plastic enough to accommodate a left turn or a right turn. In a way, the principle is itself a universalizing implement, a Swiss Army knife among conceptual tools. Just as with the Shakespearian Henry V—an unpromising youth, a wastrel, a prodigal—after his father died and he accedes to the throne, he immediately turned into a genius jack-of-all-trades, a prodigy of the opposite kind, a virtuoso capable of all occupations and employments, a savant, a polymath. Say the observers,

> Hear him but reason in divinity,
> And all-admiring with an inward wish
> You would desire the king were made a prelate:
> Hear him debate of commonwealth affairs,
> You would say it hath been all in all his study:
> List his discourse of war, and you shall hear
> A fearful battle render'd you in music:
> Turn him to any cause of policy,
> The Gordian knot of it he will unloose,
> Familiar as his garter: that, when he speaks,
> The air, a charter'd libertine, is still,
> And the mute wonder lurketh in men's ears,
> To steal his sweet and honey'd sentences;
> So that the art and practic part of life
> Must be the mistress to this theoric.[80]

The Girardian reading is protean in that it can be formed to fit whatever interpretation is required by the theory. Henry, formerly Hal, emerges after his father's death a different man, Janus, having an entirely different face—the opposite of what he was when he

---

80. Shakespeare's *Henry V* (1.1.37–51).

began. He made a choice that creates an entirely new creature in the world of moral complexity, for he can no longer be a moral child while facing his responsibilities after grasping knowledge of good and evil. After all, when these problems of choice began, Eve and Adam had two contradictory laws to obey: continue in a condition of moral innocence where the only choice was whether or not to continue in a labor-free state while eating from the tree of life or launch into the unknown and unknowable future by becoming moral adults and eating of the tree of knowledge of good and evil. Eve and Adam laid aside a deontological ethic and became consequentialists by choosing the results of a fall into a lone and dreary world: propagating children, engaging in hard labor, enduring death, and moving the divine plan forward because it then came coupled with a redeemer to return their offspring to heaven, having wrestled the night through with moral unclarity and come out the morning with a limp.

The Girardian categorical imperative, like all striving for certainty and universality, exhibits a reluctance to embrace negative capability. It instead prefers ready-made mandates rather than the necessity of deliberating in every individual moral inflection point how to weigh the best against the best choice, the best against the good, the bad against the good, the good against the good, the bad against the bad, and the good against the bad while rarely offering a simple a binary choice. Note that deciding each individual moral choice doesn't entail daily, hourly, or minutely preoccupation with the morality of every choice we humans make: driving the electric car to work today or the gas-powered vehicle, driving below the speed limit or limiting the speed to ten miles over the limit, parking in the closest spot to the grocery store or far away to get some exercise walking. Ethicists break utilitarianism into varieties, including rule utilitarianism and act utilitarianism. The rule variety avoids having to make small-scale moral choices about routine decisions by establishing a rule: always drive the speed limit, take the electric car to work and save the gas-powered auto for the weekend, never park in the handicapped spots but save them for people who really need them, park in the far spots in order to get more steps in. Notice that rule utilitarians still articulate general rules, even if they feel free to break them once in a while (say, a vegetarian eating a hamburger only on Fridays). Act utilitarians continue to weigh the ethical implications of every action, even mundane ones. Moral considerations are complex and fraught with all the dangers and quandaries that come with free will.

The Grand Inquisitor in Dostoevsky's *The Brothers Karamazov* states as much to the imprisoned and suffering Jesus as the institutional agent insists that Christ completely misunderstood human nature by assuming humans want to exercise free will:

> There is for man no preoccupation more constant or more nagging than, while in a condition of freedom, quickly to find someone to bow down before. But man seeks to bow down before that which is already beyond dispute, so far beyond dispute that all human beings will instantly agree to a universal bowing-down before it. For the preoccupation of these miserable creatures consists not only in finding that before which I or another may bow down, but in finding something that everyone can come to believe in and bow down before, and that it should indeed be everyone, and that they should do it all together.
>
> It is this need for a community of bowing-down that has been the principal torment of each individual person and of mankind as a whole since the earliest ages. For the sake of a universal bowing-down they have destroyed one another with the sword. They have created gods and challenged one another: "Give up your gods and come and worship ours or else death to you and to your gods!" And so it will be until the world's end, when even gods will vanish from the world: whatever happens, they will fall down before idols.[81]

---

81. Fyodor Dostoevsky, *The Brothers Karamazov*, trans. David McDuff (New York: Penguin Books, 1993), 292.

Except, Girard wants to bury that sword along with the hatchet. Adam and Eve were exiled into a complex and difficult world of moral ambiguity. They could have remained in the garden with its clear-cut possible future of maintaining the status quo and a single moral option going forward. They instead opted for the uncertainty that would require negative capability, the obscurity that accompanies the paradox of choice, the opacity of starting off the anthropocentric age like the Assyrians of Jonah's age when humanity must learn anew to distinguish one's own moral right hand from the left, much like the cattle of Nineveh, without cutting off and casting aside either hand which might have offended.

Chapter Eight

The Death of Abinadi

The Laban narrative poses the following questions: how necessary is it that the Nephites have a record including the law of Moses? What cost is worth paying to obtain that record? The Abinadi story shows that even possessing the law doesn't ensure compliance: "If ye teach the law of Moses why do you not keep it?"[1] asks the prophet of those charged with teaching that law. The Abinadi narrative possesses classic features of scapegoating. The victim condemns the people for failing to keep divine commandments, yet he saves his harshest criticism for the king. The victim is innocent but singled out by the crowd through the travesty of a judicial process. The victim stands alone against the mob (excluding Alma₁). The king orders his arrest "that I may slay him, for he has said these things that he might stir up my people to anger one with another."[2] Then the victim is executed by immolation.

Just as Nephi compares himself to Moses, so does the record establish a typological relationship between Moses and Abinadi: "for the Spirit of the Lord was upon [Abinadi] and his face shone with exceeding luster, even as Moses' did while in the mount of Sinai."[3] The relationship between King Noah and the prophet

---

1. Mosiah 12:29.
2. Mosiah 11:28.
3. Mosiah 13:5.

Abinadi is clearly one of rivalry, for after the prophet pronounces judgment on the people, the king asks, "Who is Abinadi, that I and my people should be judged of him?"[4] Before Abinadi is executed by immolation, he announces that "what you do with me, after this, shall be as a type and shadow of things which are to come,"[5] and indeed, King Noah dies in the same way, as do the descendants of Noah's priests who participated in Abinadi's trial.[6] Abinadi and Noah are in some way mimetic doubles of each other. James G. Williams notices the same dynamic in confrontations between prophets and kings of the Old Testament:

> In the biblical tradition the prophet is, in some respects, a double of the king, assuming aspects of the monarchic role that were neglected, suppressed or given only ideological lip service once power was centralized. It is the prophets who typically stood for the victims against the king as an expression of their calling, their experience of being chosen or taken as prophets.[7]

For example, "Samuel becomes Saul's double, the antagonistic other from whom Saul can no longer distinguish himself."[8] Saul is overdependent on Samuel, unable to proceed in battle without the prophet, making the wrong decision when he proceeds without Samuel, even needing to consult Samuel after the prophet has died. This is the pattern for the two institutions of biblical social leadership after the conquest of Canaan until Babylonian exile. Abinadi and Noah are merely taking up the confrontational roles that the biblical tradition established and predicted for king and prophet.

---

4. Mosiah 11:27.

5. Mosiah 13:10; see also Mosiah 17:15, 18.

6. Mosiah 19:20; Alma 25:9–10.

7. James G. Williams, *The Bible, Violence, and the Sacred: Liberation from the Myth of Sanctioned Violence* (San Francisco: Harper, 1991), 142.

8. James G. Williams, "History-Writing as Protest: Kingship and the Begin¬ning of Historical Narrative," *Contagion* 1 (Spring 1994): 97.

The inextricable conflict and cooperation between king and prophet was also featured in the time of Jeremiah, Lehi's contemporary. Jeremiah and the revolving-door series of kings (Josiah, Jehoahaz, Jehoiakim, Jehoiachin, Zedekiah) he confronted in Judah might well be the model for the confrontation between Abinadi and Noah, with the king wielding all the state power, numerical superiority and support, and advantage of political leadership, while the prophet has only a few supporters and God's backing. "Jeremiah's understanding of his prophetic calling is a paradigm of the prophet as exception, as isolated, as one who lives in loneliness apart from his community."[9] Jeremiah, like Abinadi, confronts kings and the crowd, always treading on both sides of the line between violence and nonviolence directed at the prophet. In Jeremiah 26, the dour prophet declares the temple will become desolate and the "people gathered around about Jeremiah."[10] The coalescing mob threatens a stoning, but they aren't able to achieve unanimity because some support the prophet. The generational pattern repeats with the larger group in the crowd siding with the king and the king's henchmen against the prophet and his smaller group of supporters. According to Williams,

> The most important thing to note is that Jeremiah's chance to survive at all existed because Israelite traditions legitimated the role of the prophet in speaking out even against the most important institutions of the social order. Even though prophets were often ignored and repressed, and sometimes executed (see concerning Uriah in Jer 26:20–23), the validity of the prophet's task was too deeply embedded in the Israelite tradition not to have an important effect in reminding Israel of the God of Israel who led them out of Egypt, out of the house of slavery.[11]

---

9. Williams, *The Bible*, 144.
10. Williams, *The Bible*, 145, citing Jeremiah 26:8–9.
11. Williams, *The Bible*, 145.

Not only are Abinadi and Noah mimetic twins of each other, but Abinadi and Noah are reenacting conflicts between prophetic and monarchical institutions going back to the beginning of those institutions among the children of Israel, playing archetypal political and religious roles of longstanding tradition.

The mimetic rivalry between Noah and Abinadi follows the classic pattern of conflict between kings and prophets in the Bible.[12] Mimetic rivalry needs to be triangular: two competitors and the object of competition. In this story Noah is struggling with the Lord over to whom the people of Zeniff owe allegiance. Noah asks, "Who is Abinadi, that I and *my people* should be judged of him, or who is the Lord, that shall bring upon *my people* such great affliction?"[13] Likewise, Noah's priests assert the people are his subjects, his possession: "Now, O king, what great evil hast thou done, or what great sins have *thy people* committed, that we should be condemned of God or judged of this man?"[14] As far as Noah is concerned, the people belong to him. The Lord, on the other hand, asserts through Abinadi that the people are his: "it shall come to pass that I will smite *this my people* with sore afflictions."[15]

The Abinadi narrative intends us to see this confrontation between king and prophet as a classic repetition of that between biblical prophets and kings. Think of Elijah against Ahab, Nathan against David, Samuel against Saul, Moses versus Pharaoh, and a whole series of lesser-known prophets and kings in the historical books of the Hebrew Bible. The biblical kings occupied the very institution intended to be kept in check by the prophet.[16] Since Lehi and his family leave Jerusalem during the ministry of Jere-

---

12. I have explored the allusive connection to prophet/king type scenes in my article "Uncritical Theory and Thin Description: The Resistance to History," *Review of Books on the Book of Mormon* 7, no. 1 (1995): 170–207.
13. Mosiah 11:27.
14. Mosiah 12:13, see also verse 9.
15. Mosiah 12:4; it is the Lord who redeems "his people" in Mosiah 15:18–19.
16. Polzin, *Samuel and the Deuteronomist*, 89.

miah, it is instructive that Abinadi's ministry closely follows the pattern of prophecy modeled by Jeremiah. Jeremiah sees himself as isolated from his brethren, called in opposition to their actions. He is persecuted by their priests and kings. His "sense of being an exception is so accentuated and so imprinted with his own struggle for the revelation of God that it is difficult to conceive of the prophet as living in harmony with his community."[17] While preaching in the temple, he is taken captive by "the priests and the prophets and all the people" who declare that he must die.[18] This sounds much like Abinadi's trial. But Jeremiah was able to survive because Israelite tradition condoned the prophet's denunciation of the king: "Even though prophets were often ignored and repressed, and sometimes executed (see concerning Uriah in Jer 26:20–23), the validity of the prophet's task was too deeply embedded in Israelite traditions not to have an important effect in reminding Israel of the God of Israel who led them out of Egypt, out of the house of slavery."[19] The struggle between a philosopher or wise man and ruler is a common motif in ancient literature. The biblical type scene portraying conflict between king and prophet is also continued in the New Testament. The death of John the Baptist; Jesus's encounter with Caiaphas, Pilate, and Herod;[20] with Paul before Felix, Festus, and Agrippa[21] continue the motif.

Because modern biblical scholarship sees in the Bible the same themes about sacrifice and scapegoating, the discipline too quickly assimilates the Bible to these myths.[22] What these scholars don't see is the radical originality of the Gospels: Jesus is an incomparable victim presented as innocent who reveals the injustice of foundational murders. In this assessment, Christians hav-

17. Williams, *The Bible*, 144.
18. Jeremiah 26:8–9.
19. Williams, *The Bible*, 145.
20. Luke 22:66–23:26.
21. Acts 24–26.
22. Girard, *I See*, 70.

en't appreciated the truly revolutionary aspect of the Gospels but have tended to start from their adversary's standpoint.[23] Girard's reading of the death of John the Baptist confirms this entirely original conception of violence. Herod Antipas and his brother are truly enemy brothers, trapped in triangular desire for Herodias. John prophetically warns the tetrarch about the "evil effects of mimetic desire," to no avail.[24] John eventually must die because he reveals the mimetic principle for what it is. The tetrarch, Herodias, Salome, the "king's" guests at the banquet, the executioner: they all join into a crowd to witness and approve the decollation of the Baptist. Girard remarks, "Being alive, the prophet disturbed all their relations, and, in his death, he facilitates them by becoming this inert and docile object that is circulated on Salome's platter; the guests offer it to one another like the food or drink at Herod's banquet."[25]

Drawing upon Theodor Gaster, Williams notes the representativeness of the king in the ancient world; the king is a microcosm of the society, so disordered kingship points to a disordered society.[26] The king is a stand-in for the crowd, "the representative figure, the agent, the substitute (from the Latin *substituere*, to put under, next, or in place of) who stands in for the group, enduring what they would otherwise have to suffer and embodying on their behalf the victory and blessings that the entire social order provides."[27] This is the exact picture of kingship Mosiah articulates when he convinces the Nephites to surrender the institution of kingship. The king should no longer be an agent, a representative, but rather "the burden should come upon all the people that every

---

23. Girard, *Scapegoat*, 126.
24. René Girard, *The Scapegoat*, trans. Yvonne Freccero (Baltimore: Johns Hopkins University Press, 1986), 128.
25. Girard, *Scapegoat*, 146.
26. Williams, "History-Writing," 93.
27. Williams, "History-Writing," 93.

man might bear his part."[28] The king, either a wicked or a righteous one, is a microcosm of the social order, and following Mosiah's urgings, the people decide that "every man should have an equal chance . . . and every man expressed a willingness to answer for his own sins."[29] The righteous king is, to Mosiah, a kind of suffering servant and the wicked king is a model of iniquity whose example leads the people into sin. "The sins of many people have been caused by the iniquities of their kings; therefore their iniquities are answered upon the heads of their kings."[30] Even righteous kings vicariously suffer the burdens and sins of their people. As Mosiah related to his people, "all the trials and troubles of a righteous king, yea, all the travails of soul for their people, and also all the murmurings of the people to their king; and he explained it all unto them. And he told them that these things ought not to be."[31] This distributed responsibility that Mosiah calls for is a movement away from mobs and collectives. These individuals, presumably, wouldn't need a scapegoat to purge the group of its anxieties.

Both Alma$_1$ and Mosiah emphasize the representative nature of King Noah. When his group implores Alma$_1$ to be their king, he demurs. "Remember the iniquity of king Noah and his priests" is Alma$_1$'s refrain, for the people have been brought into sin by him and have been in slavery to him.[32] Mosiah also invokes his people's memory about the recent past, noting the equation between the king's sins and the people's: "Remember king Noah, his wickedness and his abominations, and also the wickedness and abominations of his people."[33] The king is a representative and exemplar of the people, just as the prophet is a scapegoat and redeemer of the people.

28. Mosiah 29:34.
29. Mosiah 29:38.
30. Mosiah 29:31.
31. Mosiah 29:33–34.
32. Mosiah 23:9, 12.
33. Mosiah 29:18.

Joseph Spencer has done a great service to Book of Mormon readers, explaining why the priests of Noah cite Isaiah 52:7–10 in charging Abinadi with crimes.[34] The priests take for granted the text from Isaiah that they cite means that the Zeniff colony lives in messianic times—that their colony has reclaimed the original lands of the Nephites and in these restoration, post-apocalyptic, post-prophetic times, the people no longer need prophets:

> How beautiful upon the mountains are the feet of him that bringeth good tidings; that publisheth peace; that bringeth good tidings of good; that publisheth salvation; that saith unto Zion, Thy God reigneth; thy watchmen shall lift up the voice; with the voice together shall they sing; for they shall see eye to eye when the Lord shall bring again Zion; break forth into joy; sing together ye waste places of Jerusalem; for the Lord hath comforted his people, he hath redeemed Jerusalem; The Lord hath made bare his holy arm in the eyes of all the nations, and all the ends of the earth shall see the salvation of our God?[35]

Why the priests quote this passage has always puzzled me until Spencer helped clarify; I didn't see the relevance. Zeniff and his colony asserted that "from the restoration onward, prophets were in essence no longer needed. The good tidings of the eschatological restoration of Nephi's kingdom had been definitively delivered, prophets (Isaiah, Nephi) and kings (Zeniff, Noah) had finally seen eye to eye and together lifted up the voice to sing praises."[36] Abinadi's very presence, to Noah and his priests, contradicts the eschatological moment, for prophets are no longer needed, the crowd of priests assert; Zion had been redeemed, all the promised prophetic pronouncements had been fulfilled, the God of heaven had endorsed the Zeniffite project, and all is well in Zion. The priests are likening

---

34. Mosiah 12:20–24.
35. Mosiah 12:21–24.
36. Joseph M. Spencer, *An Other Testament: On Typology* (Salem, OR: Salt, 2012), 144–45.

Isaiah to themselves. As Spencer points out, Abinadi proceeds by placing the taken-for-granted meaning of Isaiah 52 into question.

Abinadi proceeds by recontextualizing Isaiah 52 by using Isaiah 53 as the background to interpret the proper role of prophets in the biblical tradition. After referring to the law of Moses and the Ten Commandments, Abinadi notes that the law of Moses doesn't bring redemption. Instead, it points to the salvation that will come through the atonement of God, "for they understood not that there could not any man be saved except it were through the redemption of God."[37] The law of Moses and the words of the prophets were "types of things to come" and "all the prophets who have prophesied ever since the world began—have they not spoken more or less concerning these things?"[38] This redemption comes not from reclaiming the land but when "God himself should come down among the children of men" and bring salvation when "he, himself, should be oppressed and afflicted."[39]

Abinadi then substitutes the triumphalist reading of Isaiah 52 offered by the priests of Noah with his own analysis, placing Isaiah 52 against the backdrop of the following chapter, Isaiah 53. This suffering servant passage not only projects that the "God himself shall come down among the children of men, and shall redeem his people," but that the redemption will happen when that servant is "despised," "rejected," "acquainted with grief," burdened with "grief," "sorrow," and "affliction."[40] The servant is to be "wounded," "bruised," and chastised, for "with his stripes we are healed."[41] The servant will "bear their iniquities" and bear "the sins of many" as he makes "intercession for the transgressors."[42] The most important passage of Isaiah 53 for Abinadi's interpretation asserts that the

---

37. Mosiah 13:32.
38. Mosiah 13:31, 33.
39. Mosiah 13:34–35.
40. Mosiah 15:1.
41. Mosiah 14:3–5.
42. Mosiah 14:5, 11–12.

Lord will bruise the servant and make "his soul an offering for sin" when "he shall see his seed."[43] That "offering for sin" is redemptive, sacrificial. This notion of the seed of the servant is developed further in the next chapter by Abinadi: this suffering servant is Christ who shall be "led, crucified, and slain."[44] After conquering death, Christ shall "see his seed. And now what say ye? And who shall be his seed?"[45] All the holy prophets and those who follow God's prophets. Between Mosiah 15 verses 10 and 13 the phrase "his seed" is mentioned five times, asserting all who believe, but more importantly, those who declare his gospel, are his seed. Having recontextualized Isaiah 52 against Isaiah 53, Abinadi then quotes the passage the priests thought refuted Abinadi's very calling:

> Yea, and are not the prophets, every one that has opened his mouth to prophesy, that has not fallen into transgression, I mean all the holy prophets ever since the world began? I say unto you that they are his seed. And these are they who have published peace, who have brought good tidings of good, who have published salvation; and said unto Zion: Thy God reigneth! And O how beautiful upon the mountains were their feet! And again, how beautiful upon the mountains are the feet of those that are still publishing peace! And again, how beautiful upon the mountains are the feet of those who shall hereafter publish peace, yea, from this time henceforth and forever! And behold, I say unto you, this is not all. For O how beautiful upon the mountains are the feet of him that bringeth good tidings, that is the founder of peace, yea, even the Lord, who has redeemed his people; yea, him who has granted salvation unto his people.[46]

Applied to their current historical context, Abinadi and the prophets are the ones with beatific feet on the mountains, not King Noah and his priests. Abinadi then continues by declaring the prophets

---

43. Mosiah 14:10.
44. Mosiah 15:7.
45. Mosiah 15:10.
46. Mosiah 15:13–18.

and believers are the seed of this suffering servant, thus refuting the priests' assertions. Abinadi quotes the rest of the Isaiah 52 passage cited by the priests about "the watchmen" who "lift up their voice" to declare God's good works.[47] All of the law of Moses and the prophets called since the foundation of the world have declared salvation through Christ, so to the priests Abinadi demands that "if ye teach the law of Moses, also teach that it is a shadow of those things which are to come—Teach them that redemption cometh through Christ the Lord."[48] From Abinadi's perspective, the Zeniffite elite are arrogating to themselves the redemptive office that belongs to the messiah yet to come, delegated in part to prophets—not to kings and priests. These priests can't even get the law of Moses right, for if they understood they would teach that of the law "that it is a shadow of those things which are to come," and, as Abinadi enjoins them, "teach [the people] that redemption cometh through Christ the Lord, who is the very Eternal Father. Amen."[49]

Abinadi is a representative figure, a type of "all the prophets who have prophesied since the world began" about the coming of Christ.[50] The prophets are necessary because the work of salvation hasn't been done and isn't completed just because Noah's people have reclaimed their promised land from the Lamanites. Not only is the work of Christ redemptive through the substitution of the redeemer for the sinners, the prophets themselves take part in that redemptive process. Mosiah 15:14 quotes from Isaiah 52 that "these are they who have published peace, who have brought good tidings of good, who have published salvation; and said unto Zion: Thy God reigneth!" Abinadi corrects the priests' reading, asserting that these are the prophets publishing salvation to the people. To ensure that we get the point, those sinners who are redeemed

47. Mosiah 15:29–31.
48. Mosiah 16:14.
49. Mosiah 16:14–15.
50. Mosiah 12:33; 15:11.

by angelic intervention at the end of the same book of Mosiah (Alma$_2$ and the sons of Mosiah, just one generation removed from Abinadi's publishing of good tidings) turn to preaching the gospel and begin "publishing" the word to those around them. They wade through "much tribulation, being greatly persecuted by those who were unbelievers, being smitten by many of them," preaching to all who will hear, "and publishing all the things which they had seen, and explaining the prophecies and the scriptures to all who desired to hear them," so they became instruments in God's hands in the work of salvation.[51] Then the exact same scripture cited by the priests of Noah with a corrected interpretation by Abinadi is cited so we get the intertextual connection: "And how blessed are they! For they did publish peace; they did publish good tidings of good; and they did declare unto the people that the Lord reigneth."[52] Christ is a fulfillment of the suffering servant passage from Isaiah, but so were Abinadi and the sons of Mosiah, the latter two being a shadow of glorious redemption to come and the rejection of him who bore our sins, sorrows, and griefs which precede the salvation.[53] Abinadi asserts a scapegoating process by which nonviolent redemption comes by transferring the sins and sorrows of a wayward humanity not only on Jesus but also upon all his prophets from since before the world was founded who pronounce the good news. Abinadi's death by fire typifies the death and redemption of Jesus, with the victim responding nonviolently to the standard operating procedure of the world.

The confrontation between the Israelite prophet and the Zeniffite governing elite is a classic case of Girard's scapegoating pattern. It also repeats the archetypal pattern that starts with the institution of kingship in the Hebrew Bible: the king and his bureaucracy expanding the monarch's authority and the prophet upholding the

---

51. Mosiah 27:32, 35.
52. Mosiah 27:37.
53. Mosiah 16:14.

interests of God and covenant to provide a check and balance on the monarchy. A major element of that covenant comprises the king's obligation to care for the poor, the stranger, the widow, the orphan. Another major element of that covenant outlines the prophet's obligation to call the king to repentance when he neglects the interests of the disenfranchised in order to pursue his own advantage.

Jesus, in the Gospel of Matthew, notes that the people in his generation, much like the priests of Noah, believe they worship God as the law of Moses prescribes. They assert that, in Jesus's summary of their position, "If we had been in the days of our fathers, we would not have been partakers with them in the blood of the prophets. Wherefore ye be witnesses unto yourselves, that ye are the children of them which killed the prophets."[54] Yet, as with the Zeniffites, those in Jesus's audience react no differently:

> Wherefore, behold, I send unto you prophets, and wise men, and scribes: and some of them ye shall kill and crucify; and some of them shall ye scourge in your synagogues, and persecute them from city to city: That upon you may come all the righteous blood shed upon the earth, from the blood of righteous Abel unto the blood of Zacharias son of Barachias, whom ye slew between the temple and the altar. Verily I say unto you, All these things shall come upon this generation.[55]

History repeats itself: what happens to the fathers, happens to the sons, as the Hebrew Bible, New Testament, and Book Mormon testify.

The priests of Noah and King Noah misunderstand Isaiah so egregiously they can claim the millennial time prophesied by Isaiah has arrived with Noah's reign, a time of righteousness endorsed by the God of heaven, a time of peace and equity. Girard projects a future when these sacrificial victims suffer no more, and he can do so because he has read the Bible so closely. Abinadi reads the same future Girard does because the latter reads Isaiah so closely.

---

54. Matthew 23:30–31.
55. Matthew 23:34–36.

Chapter Nine

In the Way of Cain:
Nephi's Conflicts with
His Brothers

> For they have gone in the way of Cain.
> Jude 1:11

In his reading of Genesis, and particularly that of Cain and Abel, Leon Kass notes that these stories are particularly important for understanding the whole Hebrew Bible. Similarly, the stories of conflict between Nephi and Laman and Lemuel are acutely significant for understanding the Book of Mormon: "first stories are paradigmatic."[1]—they set the stage and the readers' expectations. The Cain and Abel story specifically reveals "the basic pattern of, and the unvarnished truth about, the natural relationship between brothers": that violence is how the natural man reacts to fraternal competition.[2] Laman and Lemuel go in the way of Cain.

The following tally summarizes stories of conflict between Nephi and Laman and Lemuel—usually mentioning Nephi's status as the younger brother and the struggle over who will lead the Lehite colony:

---

1. Leon R. Kass, *The Beginning of Wisdom: Reading Genesis* (New York: Free Press, 2003), 124.
2. Kass, *Beginning of Wisdom*, 124.

1. Laman and Lemuel ("being the eldest")[3] complain against their father in the valley of Lemuel while Nephi supports their father, but the older brothers "would not hearken unto [Nephi's] words."[4]

2. After twice failing to get the plates of brass from Laban, Laman and Lemuel violently castigate Nephi and Sam, "their younger brothers," until the elder brothers are reproved by an angel.[5]

3. While retrieving Ishmael and his family from Jerusalem, Laman and Lemuel rebel against Nephi, who recalls their birth order before they tie him up to leave him to die in the wilderness, whereupon Nephi is delivered by divine assistance.[6]

4. When Nephi breaks his bow, his brothers are angry with him;[7] this is the first rebellion story in which birth order isn't mentioned and only the second in which the elder brothers don't attempt to kill Nephi.

5. At Nahom after Ishmael dies, Laman and Lemuel want to return to Jerusalem and propose killing Nephi and Lehi; they also mention birth order.[8]

6. While refusing to help build the ship at Bountiful, Laman and Lemuel in anger attempt to cast Nephi into the sea[9] and Nephi mentions his status as younger brother.[10]

3. 1 Nephi 2:12.
4. 1 Nephi 2:18.
5. 1 Nephi 3:28.
6. 1 Nephi 7:8.
7. 1 Nephi 16:18.
8. 1 Nephi 16:37.
9. 1 Nephi 17:48.
10. 1 Nephi 17:55.

7. While ocean-bound, the group makes merry, and Laman and Lemuel become angry with Nephi, binding him; Laman and Lemuel mention that they won't permit their younger brother to rule.[11]

8. Lehi urges Laman and Lemuel not to rebel against Nephi, recounting the broken bow incident (apparently) when Nephi saved the party from starvation.[12]

9. As soon as the text mentions that Lehi is dead, Laman and Lemuel are angry with Nephi for preaching to them;[13] as their anger increases,[14] Laman and Lemuel propose killing their "younger brother [who] thinks to rule over us."[15] This causes the separation between the Nephites and Lamanites. Brothers Jacob and Esau also had much back and forth about murder, deception, and birthrights. Isaac's death triggers one more mimetic crisis. "The death of the patriarch in tribal society is comparable to the death of a king; it has the same effect within a clan or tribe. Hence Isaac's impending death is a mimetic crisis."[16] The same is true of Lehi's death and the separation of Nephites from Lamanites that occurs shortly after the patriarch's death. Of the biblical story, Williams notes that "the result of the mimetic crisis for Jacob is flight, which amounts to a kind of expulsion."[17] Nephi and his group also pack up their bags and move away from his eldest brothers.

---

11. 1 Nephi 18:10.
12. 2 Nephi 1:24.
13. 2 Nephi 4:13.
14. 2 Nephi 5:1.
15. 2 Nephi 5:3.
16. James G. Williams, *The Bible, Violence, and the Sacred: Liberation from the Myth of Sanctioned Violence* (San Francisco: Harper, 1991), 43.
17. Williams, *The Bible*, 45.

That is quite a list of conflicts between Lehi's sons. Most of the narratives foreground fratricidal intent and fraternal birth order. The Lamanite view of history incorporates the notion that Nephi cheated his elder brothers of their right to rule, turning familial conflict into generational and national struggle.[18]

Like Kass, Williams asserts, referring to Cain and Abel and Romulus and Remus, that narratives about enemy brothers are "master texts, paradigm cases for understanding the problems of desire and rivalry in general," and Nephi against his brothers is like these exemplary stories in being about the foundations of peoples and nations.[19]

The stories of struggle between Nephi and his older brothers are indeed paradigmatic for the length and breadth of Book of Mormon narrative. Many of these episodes I have performed readings of elsewhere, so let me single out number 6 from this list as exemplary: the story of Nephi providing leadership to convince his brothers to help build the ship (even portions of this narrative have I analyzed elsewhere, so the reading I will provide here is highly selective).[20]

Even before the Lehi group arrives at Bountiful, Nephi recounts the salvation history (a record of divine intervention to save the chosen people as the Israelites encountered miracles during their exodus through the wilderness) as the Lehi group travels through the wilderness:

18. Mosiah 10:11–18; Alma 20:10, 13; Alma 54:17, 24.

19. Williams, *The Bible*, 33.

20. Alan Goff, "Boats, Beginnings, and Repetitions," *Journal of Book of Mormon Studies* 1 (1992): 67–84.

1 Nephi 17	Commentary
2. And so great were the blessings of the Lord upon us, that while we did live upon raw meat in the wilderness, our women did give plenty of suck for their children, and were strong, yea, even like unto the men; and they began to bear their journeyings without murmurings. 3. And thus we see that the commandments of God must be fulfilled. And if it so be that the children of men keep the commandments of God he doth nourish them, and strengthen them, and *provide means whereby they can accomplish the thing which he has commanded them*; wherefore, he did provide means for us while we did sojourn in the wilderness.	Let me highlight the phrase that the Lord will "provide means whereby [his people] can accomplish the thing which he has commanded them." This phrase has come up in previous stories about impossible missions: when Nephi is given "the commandment" to retrieve the brass plates, he says, "I know that the Lord giveth no commandments unto the children of men, save he shall prepare a way for them *that they may accomplish the thing which he commandeth them*."[21] By using this key phrase, Nephi points back to that previous story of salvation. Later, in the Bountiful story, Laman and Lemuel tell Nephi "we knew that ye could not construct a ship, for we knew that ye were lacking in judgment; wherefore, *thou canst not accomplish so great a work*."[22] In response to his brothers' doubt, Nephi compares his situation to that of Moses, who led the children of Israel out of bondage ("Now ye know *that Moses was commanded of the Lord to do that great work*"[23]), thus not only comparing himself to Moses but also the journey through

21. 1 Nephi 3:7; Nephi repeats the phrase again in verse 15, and Sariah uses the same phrase when her sons have completed their mission in 1 Nephi 5:8.
22. 1 Nephi 17:19.
23. 1 Nephi 17:26.

1 Nephi 17	Commentary
(vv. 2–3, *continued*)	the wilderness and across the sea to the Israelite deliverance from Egypt, across the Red Sea, and through the wilderness to the promised land.

Laman and Lemuel attempt to kill Nephi after his extended typological comparison of the Israelites to the Lehites. The brothers attempt to murder Nephi by throwing him into the depths of the sea, an act of communal murder that seems to imply the brothers stood on cliffs above the waters :

1 Nephi 17	Commentary
48. And now it came to pass that when I had spoken these words they were angry with me, and were desirous to throw me into the depths of the sea; and as they came forth to lay their hands upon me I spake unto them, saying: In the name of the Almighty God, I command you that ye *touch me not*, for I am filled with the power of God, even unto the consuming of my flesh; and whoso shall lay his hands upon me shall wither even as a dried reed; and he shall be as naught before the power of God, for God shall smite him.	The further allusion to Moses and the children of Israel isn't obvious because it isn't explicit. The connection must be mediated by the story of Abinadi later in the Book of Mormon. The two examples show how the Nephites read the episode of Moses's shining face. When Noah commands that Abinadi be killed, the prophet responds, "*Touch me not*, for God shall smite you if ye lay your hands upon me, for I have not delivered the message which the Lord sent me to deliver." [24] Abinadi is then explicitly compared to Moses on the holy mount: "after Abinadi had spoken these words

---

24. Mosiah 13:3.

1 Nephi 17	Commentary
(v. 48, *continued*)	that the people of king Noah durst not lay their hands on him, for the Spirit of the Lord was upon him; and *his face shone with exceeding luster, even as Moses' did while in the mount of Sinai*, while speaking with the Lord."[25] The allusion is to Moses's shining face when he came down from the mountain and the people dared not approach him because the glory of God (the *kabod*) shown through him. Moses eventually veils his face to tamp down the people's fear of that manifestation of divine presence.[25]

If I am right, and Laman and Lemuel attempt to kill Nephi at Bountiful by throwing him from a cliff into the sea, then we again have a motif common to the stories of communal violence Girard takes up. High cliffs were often the scene of sacrifice. "Just like stoning, falling from a high cliff has collective, ritual, and penal connotations," and it was practiced in Rome and Greece. "The unfortunate man was made to throw himself into the sea from such a height that death was inevitable," with all the members of the community advancing on the victim to force no other alternative than plunging into the sea.[27] Just as with stoning, the whole group participates, and the entire crowd shares equal responsibility for the death.[28] Jesus, when casting out the demons from a

25. Mosiah 13:5.
26. Exodus 34:29–35.
27. René Girard, *The Scapegoat*, trans. Yvonne Freccero (Baltimore: Johns Hopkins University Press, 1986), 176.
28. Girard, *Scapegoat*, 177.

possessed man in Gadarenes, redirects the violence away from the possessed man and permits the spirits to possess swine, and the pigs "ran violently down a steep place into the sea,"—once again a scene of violence with cliffs and a sea.[29]

The Gospel of Luke tells the story of Jesus preaching in Nazareth. Scandalized, the villagers rush him up the side of a hill aiming to throw him down the cliff.[30] Girard sees in this narrative prefigurations of the passion. Luke, as in all the Gospels, "considered falling from a cliff-top and stoning as equivalents of the Crucifixion. They understood what made such an equivalence interesting. All forms of collective murder have the same significance, and that significance is revealed by Jesus in his Passion."[31] Throwing Nephi into the depths of the sea to execute the collective murder is parallel to these biblical and Roman examples.

Fraternal conflict is a common theme in the Bible and Greek mythology. The conflict that emerges with twins or rival brothers threatens to grow larger until it threatens the entire society.[32] The conflict and its resolution can serve as the foundation of a culture (as in Cain and Abel, Romulus and Remus) or it can fissure a culture for generations (Nephite versus Lamanite). In biblical stories of conflict between brothers, especially in narratives where the younger brother supersedes the elder, the conflict is not about property or inheritance (as is the case in Moses 5:33); rather "what is at stake . . . [is] the transmission of a blessing."[33] This blessing is a "theological category rather than a legal one," which marks a line of descent. These narratives "explain for the later generations how

---

29. Mark 5:13.
30. Luke 4:28–30.
31. Girard, *Scapegoat*, 178–79.
32. René Girard, *Violence and the Sacred*, trans. Patrick Gregory (Baltimore: Johns Hopkins University Press, 1972), 63–64.
33. Fredrick E. Greenspahn, *When Brothers Dwell Together: The Preeminence of Younger Siblings in the Hebrew Bible* (New York: Oxford University Press, 1994), 55.

God had determined those through whom *the* line would continue."[34] The fact that Laman and Lemuel don't kill Nephi and that the Nephites separate from the Lamanites means that the conflict will persist for generations because no sacrificial event completes the cycle. Only the extermination of the Nephites will resolve the impasse. These repeated attempts by Laman and Lemuel to kill Nephi recur whether the group succeeds in killing the victim or not. At least with the victim murdered and divinized, the cycle is complete and temporarily blocks the necessity for catharsis, but over the long term, the sacrifice doesn't resolve the conflict. According to Girard, "Once violence has penetrated a community it engages in an orgy of self-propagation. There appears to be no way of bringing the reprisals to a halt before the community has been annihilated."[35] That, in short, is the story of the millennium-long conflict between Nephites and Lamanites.

The reader can see how generational conflict could continue from that very first generation. God and these patriarchs are more pragmatic than inherited customs, such as primogeniture. We shouldn't make the mistake of believing that these biblical struggles of dominance are about property or wealth. They are about leadership or blessings. When Lehi calls his offspring together to give last blessings before he dies, he lectures Laman and Lemuel in a way that is certain to solidify longstanding conflict about their leadership status by subordinating the eldest brothers to the younger whether they are righteous or wicked.

We readers may understand that the blessing isn't about leadership or social status, but Laman and Lemuel have already demonstrated that such attempts to downplay leadership roles are futile. In fact, Lehi's phrasing is certain to trigger conflict that flares

34. Greenspahn, *When*, 56.
35. Girard, *Violence and the Sacred*, 67.

up "not many days after his death."[36] It is a hard saying when Lehi counsels his sons Laman and Lemuel in the following terms:

> Rebel no more against your brother, whose views have been glorious, and who hath kept the commandments from the time that we left Jerusalem; and who hath been an instrument in the hands of God, in bringing us forth into the land of promise; for were it not for him, we must have perished with hunger in the wilderness; nevertheless, ye sought to take away his life; yea, and he hath suffered much sorrow because of you.[37]

Cultures may be rigid about cultural and social customs such as gender roles, primogeniture, and social classes because they reliably pass from one generational cohort to the next in a stable society, but the biblical God and revolutionary prophets frequently challenge those expectations. In antique and medieval cultures, change occurred at a glacial pace. Modernity has accelerated that process in technology and generational expectation.

Note that Laman and Lemuel's rebellion against their father and brother doesn't wait until that older generation has passed on. They attempt to kill Nephi many times before their father's death and seize leadership of their family group. Some notions dominate over many generations, and it is not hard to imagine why elder brothers favor primogeniture. But the God of Israel is not bound by the traditions of the fathers. The restoration of the gospel demonstrates how God can instigate radical change. We worship a revolutionary God. Laman and Lemuel were against such innovative practices as having leadership determined by righteousness and obedience rather than birth order.

Back at Bountiful, while the ship is under construction, Laman and Lemuel are "confounded and could not contend against"

---

36. 2 Nephi 4:13.
37. 2 Nephi 1:24.

Nephi for days for fear of being destroyed by the power of God.[38] The Lord tells Nephi to demonstrate divine power and authority by touching his brothers, shocking them with the Lord's power. They then profess their knowledge of Nephi's divine authority and begin to worship him but Nephi prevents it, asserting "I am thy brother, yea, even thy younger brother; wherefore, worship the Lord thy God, and honor thy father and thy mother, that thy days may be long in the land which the Lord thy God shall give thee."[39] Nephi's brothers attempt to worship him is the textual hint of a sacralization process going on: an attempt to murder one day, and an attempt to worship on bended knee the next. The first mythification is frustrated by divine intervention and the second by Nephi himself, who refuses to permit his brothers to bow down to him, and then frankly forgives them.[40] Nephi here redirects his brothers' worship to God. The next verse demonstrates the brothers' obedience, for they "did worship the Lord, and did go forth with me" to help build the ship.[41]

The action is similar to Joseph's, Nephi's ancestor, when he tells his brothers, who have fallen down before him, offering to be his slaves, "Fear not: for am I in the place of God?"[42] In both cases, the brothers are reconciled to each other through an act of charity and forgiveness. By doing so, Joseph "attempts to nullify the deification process. He forgives his brothers," and thus ends the cycle of revenge with grace and fraternal kindness, just as Nephi ends this particular narrative by working side by side with his brothers.[43]

---

38. 1 Nephi 17:52.
39. 1 Nephi 17:55.
40. 1 Nephi 17:55.
41. 1 Nephi 18:1.
42. Genesis 50:19.
43. James G. Williams, "'Steadfast Love and Not Sacrifice,'" *Curing Violence: Essays on René Girard*, ed. Mark I. Wallace and Theophus H. Smith (Sonoma, CA: Polebridge, 1994), 82.

That this biblical theme about younger brothers obtaining the blessing and becoming the conduit of God's inheritance happens at the beginning of the Book of Mormon to an eponymous ancestor has great significance, as it does in the patriarchal stories of Genesis: "The fact that the Younger Brother motif is so fully played out precisely in the stories about the character who is himself named Israel, confirms its importance as a whole-people motif."[44] In the case of the Lehi colony, though, the cessation of violence is only temporary.

---

44. E. Fox, "Stalking the Younger Brother: Some Models for Understanding a Biblical Motif," *Journal for the Study of the Old Testament* 60 (1993): 62.

Chapter Ten

Laman and the Lamanites as Victims

My goal in this section is more complicated than just switching black hats with white ones. Here, I want to highlight a couple of reasons that might impel the reader to take a more charitable view of the Lamanites in their millennium-long conflict with the Nephites. For one, the Book of Mormon is written from the Nephite perspective. If the reader gets only one side of a conflict as longstanding and contentious as that between the Nephites and Lamanites, one is likely not to be getting the full story.[1] Even though the Lamanites eventually win the conflict, the Nephites win the story because their narrative survives. The story begins in conflict and ends with genocide. A second conundrum is caused by Lehi's last blessing to Laman, Lemuel, Sam, and the sons of Ishmael; they receive the father's first blessing only if they hearken to Nephi, but otherwise the first blessing goes to Nephi.[2] That is a lose-lose proposition in Laman and Lemuel's view. If Laman and Lemuel continue to oppose Nephi, they will be subordinate to Nephi by losing the patriarch's blessing. If they willingly submit to his leadership, they

---

1. Richard Bushman, "The Lamanite View of Book of Mormon History," in *By Study and Also By Faith*, ed. John M. Lundquist and Stephen D. Ricks (Salt Lake City and Provo, UT: Deseret Book and FARMS, 1990), 52–72.
2. 2 Nephi 1:28–29.

retain the first blessing, but Nephi is still the leader of the group. A third problem is that Nephi is, from the very start of the narrative, a killjoy. Like Moses coming down from the mount with those terrible commandments to put an end to corporeal excess, Nephi (in the exemplary story during the ocean voyage) tries to cut short the group's merriness, their singing, and their dancing.[3] It is quite natural that Nephi is perceived by his elder brothers to usurp their power and dampen all the fires of their passion and enjoyment.

In line with this natural desire that our narrative bad guys be wholly wicked, both writers and readers highlight the failings of the protagonist's adversary and find no redeeming qualities—our Benedict Arnolds, our Brutuses, our George Plantagenets, our Judas Iscariots that we see as villains impervious to good. Judas, for example, is "traditionally the great gospel scapegoat," a character who deserves reconsideration. Robert Hamerton-Kelly asserts that the Gospels show him to be no different than the other apostles. He forsakes Jesus, but so do all the others who run away at Jesus's arrest; he betrays Jesus, but so does Peter. "Judas and Peter are in fact doubles" in this regard; indeed, "Jesus refers to the fact that there is a traitor in their midst, but does not name him." Each apostle asks if he is the one, which raises the possibility that each one could be. Jesus gives a clue: the apostle who has dipped in the dish with him. But they are sharing a meal. All of them dipped in the dish with each other. Hamerton-Kelly continues, "This in effect means all of them because all share the dish with him, and that is how it turns out, because all betray him in the end."[4] Note that Judas is a scapegoat candidate because he is different, the only apostle from Judea. His name means that. The rest are Galileans, as is Jesus. Judas is different, being from the more urban part of the land, administered as a different political unit with different Roman governance.

---

3. 1 Nephi 18:9.

4. Robert G. Hamerton-Kelly, *The Gospel and the Sacred: Poetics of Violence in Mark* (Minneapolis, MN: Fortress, 1994), 44–45.

The reader and the Gospel writer may single out Judas the outsider as more culpable than the other apostles, but Jesus, Hamerton-Kelly notes, doesn't: "Judas is not marked as the scapegoat by Jesus, and the traitor is not expelled. Each disciple indicates by his questioning that he is not sure of his own loyalty. Thus Mark indicates that none of us can escape responsibility for the death of Jesus by scapegoating Judas."[5] To be a Girardian is to be able to see in Mark's narrative a distinction between the narrator's point of view and that of the character's within the narrative. Mark writes up Judas as responsible for the death of Jesus, but as Hamerton-Kelly reads the story, Jesus doesn't. In fact, immediately after each of the twelve wonder "Is it I,"[6] Jesus mentions the word *betrayal*: "It is one of the twelve, that dippeth with me in the dish. The Son of man indeed goeth, as it is written of him: but woe to that man by whom the Son of man is betrayed! Good were it for that man if he had never been born."[7] The group shares their communal meal, Jesus's last supper. Jesus then singles out not Judas but Peter as the betrayer who will abandon his master. Yet Peter declares the impossibility of such an event: "But he spake the more vehemently, If I should die with thee, I will not deny thee in any wise. Likewise also said they all."[8]

The greater betrayal among the apostles than turning Jesus over to the authorities was to urge Jesus not to do the will of the Father. After Peter testified that Jesus is the Christ, Jesus hints of his own coming rejection and death. Peter "rebukes" Jesus, who in turn "rebuked Peter, saying, Get thee behind me, Satan: for thou savourest not the things that be of God, but the things that be of men."[9] In the Gospel of Mark, "scandal" means the same as Satan.

---

5. Hamerton-Kelly, *The Gospel*, 45.
6. Mark 14:19.
7. Mark 14:20–21.
8. Mark 14:31.
9. Mark 8:33.

In 8:32–33, Peter objects to the prediction of the passion and Jesus rebukes him as Satan for thinking "as men think and not as God thinks" for urging that Jesus divert from the divine plan. According to Hamerton-Kelly, "Scandal is the inability to affirm the way of the cross or to break the relationship with Jesus altogether. It wants Jesus to use rather than to suffer sacred violence, to be a hero rather than a victim. The result of the scandal is, therefore, that the disciples wander from the way of the cross and are scattered like sheep without a shepherd (14:27)."[10] The apostles were, without distinguishing Judas from the rest, betrayers, but Peter is the model turncoat, later rehabilitated. In this Markan account, Girard asserts, the Gospel writer didn't grasp the fuller meaning of his own story: "The convergence of the content of the narratives with the theory of *skandalon*—the theory of mimetic desire—cannot be fortuitous. We are forced therefore to question whether the authors of the Gospels fully understood the scope of this desire which is revealed in their text."[11] Mark has to await Girard's arrival so the reader can fully understand what Mark (and the other evangelists) were writing.

A principle of Girardian interpretation is that the scapegoats aren't really guilty. They are pronounced guilty by the victors; to accede to that judgment is to participate in the lynching. A persistent feature of Girard's reading of myth is to demonstrate that whatever feature of the victim caused the mob to single him or her out, the choice is both random and invalid. When applied to the Book of Mormon, this interpretive principle would cause us to question the guilt of the Lamanites and their founders. The moral judgments we make as readers need to account for our own tendency to fall back into sacrificial thinking, to blame the scapegoat the way the writer of the material being read blames the victim.

---

10. Hamerton-Kelly, *The Gospel*, 48–49.
11. René Girard, *The Scapegoat*, trans. Yvonne Freccero (Baltimore: Johns Hopkins University Press, 1986), 159.

More complex moral thinking needs to recognize the tendency to single out culprits in writers and the tendency to accept without question those verdicts as readers. The mask of victimizing needs sometimes to be replaced by setting our own masks and those of others aside to see the human face beneath.

The Mark or Curse on the Lamanites

Because we live in a highly racially sensitized society, we are likely to read race into the mark or curse put on the Lamanites. That there is an ethnic component to it seems undeniable, just not the one that appears most obvious to us. The cursing resulting from their iniquity is a darker skin than that of the Nephites.[12] That seems awfully racist to us. But note that when Enos prays for the welfare of various people, he begins by supplicating for "my brethren, the Nephites" but he implores God also for "my brethren, the Lamanites," despite the fact that he sees broad cultural distinctions between them, with the Lamanites determined to destroy the Nephite records and traditions and their savagery evident to him. Still, Enos considers the Lamanites his brothers as much as the Nephites are.[13] There are broad limits to Enos's conception of the otherness of the Lamanites (as happens throughout the text, with the sons of Mosiah, for example, who also consider the Lamanites to be their brothers).[14]

When the "cursing" is first pronounced, it isn't called a mark until Mormon uses that term in Alma 3. Mormon clearly notes that the mark (and the label *Lamanite* or *Nephite*) is a consequence of which tradition or culture a person adhered to: those who believed the traditions and records originating with Nephi are

---

12. 2 Nephi 5:21.
13. Enos 1:9, 11, 14, 20.
14. Alma 26:3.

called Nephites and those who reject them are called Lamanites.[15] That distinction is more ideological than racial, and perhaps all of one and none of the other.

Some background from that earlier mark of Cain might help us understand what is going on in the Book of Mormon. Remember one principle of biblical narrative, that founding events become archetypal for the generations that follow, and Cain is of the very first generation born after the expulsion from Eden. For one thing, the mark of Cain is given to protect him from vigilante violence. Cain's sign sets him apart and prevents revenge from being taken out against him. According to Williams, "Abel is the first scapegoat, but then Cain, as the one who is 'signed' or 'marked' is the substitute for Abel."[16] The sign prevents a further cycle of victimage, for "the sign is a substitute for the victimization process that averts a new sacrificial substitution through the prohibition (i.e., 'thou shalt not murder Cain as he murdered Abel')."[17] We don't even know the physical manifestation of Cain's sign. Frazier speculates from other societies that Cain's mark might be a tattoo or some other indicator used to identify people by tribe. More likely, as a manslayer whose murder has released the victim's blood to the ground, Cain has polluted his very means of living as a farmer and must take up city life and be quarantined from his home society.[18]

Mormon, in Alma 3, refers to the mark on the Amlicites as something red on their foreheads, a signifier they themselves apply. Much of the rest of the tradition follows, as does the book of Ezekiel, the possibility that the mark is on the forehead. There, the Lord commands a mark or a sign to designate those righteous

---

15. Alma 3:11.

16. James G. Williams, *The Bible, Violence, and the Sacred: Liberation from the Myth of Sanctioned Violence*, (San Francisco: Harper), 37.

17. Williams, *The Bible*, 37.

18. James G. Frazier, *Folklore in the Old Testament* (New York: Avenel, 1988), 33–45.

to be spared punishment.[19] Histories of the interpretation of this cryptic mark of Cain have noted the possible ways the mark might be manifest: (1) a mark on the body, (2) a movement of the body (such as a tremble or quiver), or (3) some kind of blemish on the body ("leprosy, beardlessness, hairiness, blackness of skin, a horn or horns").[20] The Christian tradition later interprets the mark on the forehead to apply to the judgments of God.[21] The mark of Cain is merely a way of differentiating him from others. It is a creation of "a differential system, which serves, as always, to discourage mimetic rivalry and generalized conflict."[22] The mark God set upon the Lamanites in the Book of Mormon should be viewed in the same way: it sets the Lamanites apart—but in order to discourage violence.[23] Keep in mind that at the beginning of the mark, the dis-

---

19. Ezekiel 9:4, 6.

20. R. W. L. Moberly, "The Mark of Cain—Revealed at Last," *Harvard Theological Review* 100, no. 1 (2007): 12.

21. Revelation 7:3; 9:4; 14:9.

22. René Girard, *Things Hidden Since the Foundation of the World*, trans. Stephen Bann and Michael Metteer (Stanford: Stanford University Press, 1987), 146.

23. Some Latter-day Saints, especially in early church history, believed what many American Christians believed about the curse on Cain, that it was a black skin with the curse propagated over the universal flood through Noah's grandson Canaan. This argument was often offered as a justification for denial of the priesthood to African-Americans. "The justifications for this restriction echoed the widespread ideas about racial inferiority that had been used to argue for the legalization of black 'servitude' in the Territory of Utah. According to one view, which had been promulgated in the United States from at least the 1730s, blacks descended from the same lineage as the biblical Cain, who slew his brother Abel. Those who accepted this view believed that God's 'curse' on Cain was the mark of a dark skin. Black servitude was sometimes viewed as a second curse placed upon Noah's grandson Canaan as a result of Ham's indiscretion toward his father. Although slavery was not a significant factor in Utah's economy and was soon abolished, the restriction on priesthood ordinations remained." See the Church's Gospel Topics essay "Race and the Priesthood" under the heading The Church in an American Racial Culture, https://www.churchofjesuschrist.org/study/manual/gospel-topics-essays/race-and-the-priesthood. This was Brigham Young's position. The Church has repudiated that position, although it sometimes circulates as a folk-explanation among uninformed church members. See Joanna Brooks, "Racist Remarks By Popular BYU Religion Professor Sparks Controversy," *Religion Dispatches* (February 29, 2012), available at https://religiondispatches.org/racist-remarks-by-popular-byu-religion-professor-spark-controversy/.

tinction between the two groups is largely ethnic and tribal, but later the distinction becomes ideological. The Lamanites eventually become more righteous than the Nephites until Nephites and Lamanites unite not based on any ethnic distinction but because they were righteous and adhered to the same tradition.[24] Richard Bushman argues that the problem the mark tries to solve is not a physical or genetic mixing but one of idea mixing: "The danger was not a mixture of races or skin colors but a mixture of false traditions with true ones. Mormon said the very identity of the Nephites lay in their acceptance of the true history of origins."[25] Hugh Nibley similarly notes that the distinction between Nephites and Lamanites was a political, military, and cultural distinction rather than a racial one.[26] After the visit of Christ, there is no distinction as the people are united in faith and praxis, no "Lamanites, nor any manner of -ites."[27] But soon after, wickedness grows and the people divide into Nephites and Lamanites again, although this time there is no ethnic nor racial distinction but purely an ideological one: "there arose a people who were called the Nephites, and they were true believers in Christ." And even though the verse makes some distinction based on descent, it doesn't have to do with being a Nephite.[28] Similarly, there were those "who rejected the gospel [who] were called Lamanites, and Lemuelites, and Ishmaelites."[29]

Even the Nephite portrayal of Lamanite culture as savage has precedent in biblical narrative. Nephite writers attempt to differentiate the Lamanites: Enos (1:20–21), in particular, shows them as wild, bloodthirsty, filthy, itinerant. Most notable in the list is

---

24. Helaman 6:1–2, 34–36; 15:4–6; 3 Nephi 2:12–16, but again, with that pesky notation about skin color.
25. Bushman, "Lamanite View," 63.
26. Hugh Nibley, "Forever Tentative . . ." in Since Cumorah, Second ed., The Collected Works of Hugh Nibley: Volume 7: The Book of Mormon, Hugh Nibley (Provo and Salt Lake City, UT: Deseret Book and FARMS, 1988), 216.
27. 4 Nephi 1:17.
28. 4 Nephi 1:20, 36.
29. 4 Nephi 1:38.

that they ate beasts of prey. Also in Jarom 1:6, their drinking blood emphasizes their depravity.[30] The frequency with which Nephite writers mention that the Lamanites hunted predators or drinking the blood of animals indicates how depraved were the Lamanites—again, a cultural trait rather than an ethnic or racial one—since such practices are forbidden in the Law of Moses.[31] Similar differentiation is going on in the Jacob/Esau story. Esau sees Jacob preparing a blood broth; despite the biblical prohibitions on consuming blood, many ancient cultures thought food made with animal blood was particularly refreshing to the tired.[32] If this line of interpretation is correct, then Esau's desire for blood broth is a sign of his "wishing to violate a taboo."[33] The bloody dish then demonstrates Esau's violation of the prohibition on eating blood, which represents the life force. When Jacob offers Esau the bloody food in exchange for the birthright, the transaction is sacrificial. Esau swears an oath not to recant the deal, and Jacob engages in deception by switching from the bloody meal to a soup made with lentils. The story is less about food than about sacrifice and ritual.[34]

The preference for Nephi over Laman, the Nephites over the Lamanites, no doubt seems arbitrary in some important way; Lamanite children didn't make the choices Laman and Lemuel made: why should they suffer the consequences for it? The Cain-Abel story similarly plays upon what Ricardo Quinones calls "the arbitrariness of preference."[35] He writes,

> Difference between brothers is rendered more grievous by what
> I call the arbitrariness of preference, the fact that some arbiter,

---

30. The Bible forbids drinking blood, Leviticus 7:17, 26–27 and Genesis 9:3–4.

31. Enos 1:20; Jarom 1:6; Leviticus 7:26–27; Leviticus 11:13–20; see also John A. Tvedtnes, "The Charge of 'Racism,'" 187.

32. Genesis 9:1–7.

33. Williams, *The Bible*, 41.

34. Williams, *The Bible*, 41.

35. Ricardo J. Quinones, *The Changes of Cain* (Princeton: Princeton University Press, 1991), 12.

divine or paternal, but always fatherly—and hence authoritative and decisive—is rendering judgment vis-à-vis the difference. The tragedy of differentiation is aggravated by the arbitrariness of preference, the pathos of which is increased by the sense of earlier unity and unsuspecting innocence.[36]

Abraham, Isaac, and Jacob all have favorite sons, and each patriarch fails to learn from previous generations that fraternal rivalry results from their favoritism. Like Cain, Laman and Lemuel had experienced the downside of preferential treatment. God prefers Nephi to his older brothers, as does Lehi. In the biblical story, that election seems oddly arbitrary. We don't have the Lamanite view of history on this matter, but the reader can easily conceive how Laman and Lemuel would have viewed Nephi's elevation to ruler and teacher as arbitrary also.

Cain isn't the only brother in the Bible who was unpreferred, as both Cain and Ishmael "were alike 'unfavoured,' 'non-chosen' by YHWH in relation to their brothers."[37] But each of these brothers, though not preferred, is still given attention by Deity and angels, just as Laman and Lemuel communicate with angels and receive close attention from their father, especially in 1 Nephi 2.[38] Lehi's last blessing before he dies recognizes the implicit arbitrariness of the cursing that will soon be imposed on the Lamanites. He notes to the sons and daughters of Laman (a few verses later, he leaves the same blessing on the children of Lemuel in 2 Nephi 4:9) that he will leave them a blessing that might counterbalance any curse: "if ye are cursed, behold, I leave my blessing upon you, that the cursing may be taken from you and be answered upon the heads of your parents. Wherefore, because of my blessing the Lord God will not suffer that ye shall perish; wherefore, he will be merciful

---

36. Quinones, *Changes*, 12.
37. Moberly, "Mark of Cain," 26.
38. Moberly, "Mark of Cain," 26.

unto you and unto your seed forever."[39] Lehi recognizes that if the sons and daughters of Lemuel and Laman were taught properly, they would not depart from the right path, so any curse that falls on them will be shifted to their parents.[40]

The Mark as a Behavioral Distinction

When Nephi reluctantly becomes king,[41] he recalls the Lord's words that unless his brothers follow him, they would be cut off from the Lord.[42] After noting the fulfillment of this prophecy, Nephi says that a cursing (not a mark, that wording is Mormon's) was put on the Lamanites: because their hearts became "like unto a flint," their skin became dark also.[43] This curse is intended to keep the Lamanites and the Nephites separate, but upon conditions of repentance, the curse would be removed.[44] Here, the burden is articulated as a group event; initially, Nephi is writing about the curse as it falls on "my brethren," but then expands the impact to their descendants.[45] Both R.W.L. Moberly and Joel Lohr note the communal aspect of the mark of Cain. Both those who would avenge Abel's death by killing Cain and those who would be the victim of such revenge are plural: "all who would kill Cain" (Cain here represents a group, such as his tribe, the Kenites).[46] This Lamanite cursing, which has as much behavioral manifestation (idleness, deception, hunting) as

---

39. 2 Nephi 4:6.

40. 2 Nephi 4:5–6.

41. 2 Nephi 6:2 and Jacob 1:9 show that he initiated a line of kings; I know Joseph Spencer and Noel Reynolds assert he successfully resisted monarchy, but I disagree; however, the issue isn't germane to my discussion here.

42. 2 Nephi 5:19–20.

43. 2 Nephi 5:21.

44. 2 Nephi 5:22–23.

45. 2 Nephi 5:19, 23–24.

46. Joel N. Lohr, "'So YHWH Established a Sign for Cain': Rethinking Genesis 4,15," *Zeitschrift für die Alttestamentliche Wissenschaft* 121, no. 1 (March 2009): 101; Moberly, "Mark of Cain," 17–18.

it does physical effect, sees also conflict and warfare between the newly divided groups within decades.[47] Nephi does not attach the cursing (the skin color) to the Lamanite rebellion against him; the first iteration of this blessing and cursing just says that if Laman and Lemuel rebel against Nephi they'll be cut off from the Lord.[48] This is not phrased as the curse. Neither is the cursing a racial distinction between Nephites and Lamanites, for after the earliest period the descendants of the two groups were thoroughly intermingled.[49] In addition to rebelling against their younger brother, when they rebel against God, then they receive the curse.[50] John Tvedtnes notes that Alma 3:14–17 distinguishes between the *curse* on the Lamanites and the *mark*. In 2 Nephi 5 when Nephi writes about the curse, the mark had yet to be given. The curse was that the Lamanites are to be cut off from God; the mark was a physical skin color intended to keep the Nephites and Lamanites separate from each other so the bad ideologies of each don't corrupt the other.[51] Some Nephite prophets criticize other Nephites for their attitude of superiority, noting that the Lamanites then were more righteous than some Nephites.[52]

Let me emphasize, the cursing comes upon the Lamanites not because they rebel against Nephi and his leadership but because they turn from God and his word. As articulated through Nephi: "Inasmuch as they will not hearken unto thy words they shall be cut off from the presence of the Lord. And behold they were cut off from his presence."[53] The cursing—in both 1 Nephi 2 and 2 Nephi 5—comes from rejection of God: "And he had caused the

---

47. 2 Nephi 5:24, 34.
48. 1 Nephi 2:21.
49. Nibley, "Forever Tentative," 218.
50. 1 Nephi 2:23.
51. Tvedtnes, "Charge of 'Racism,'" 186–87.
52. Tvedtnes, "Charge of 'Racism,'" 191; see Jacob 3:5, where Jacob criticizes some Nephites for their hatred toward the Lamanites simply because of their skin color difference.
53. 2 Nephi 5:20.

cursing to come upon them, yea, even a sore cursing, because of their iniquity. For behold, they had hardened their hearts against him, that they had become like flint."[54] The curse also has other behavioral manifestations: "And because of their cursing which was upon them they did become an idle people, full of mischief and subtlety, and did seek in the wilderness for beasts of prey."[55] This hunting not just of beasts but of predators (presumably for food) seems to Nephites an indication of their lack of civilization.[56] Early in the Book of Mormon, when a struggle ensues over who will lead the descendants of Lehi, the situation is parallel to the founders of civilization in Genesis. Long have readers viewed the Cain-Abel story as the beginning of culture, of cities, and as a symbol Cain leads directly to Nimrod and the Tower at Babel: "Cain's followers are kings and philosophers."[57] The city and the sophistical reasoning it encourages cannot escape their violent origins.[58] Rodney Turner makes the connection between Cain and Laman: "Laman also descended into spiritual darkness and the spirit of murder. Both Cain and Laman came out in open rebellion against God. Both were cut off from his righteous influence. Both became marked men."[59]

A very important aspect of Girard's theory has to do with mimesis and differentiation. In the Bible, Adam and Eve have no culture, no society. They live in a state of nature even after expulsion. Culture begins when Cain kills his brother then goes out

---

54. 2 Nephi 5:21.

55. 2 Nephi 5:24.

56. See Enos 1:20 where eating predators is also a sign of wickedness and primitiveness, which is contrasted in verse 21 with Nephite occupations of pastoralism and agriculture.

57. Quinones, *Changes of Cain*, 27.

58. Quinones, *Changes of Cain*, 41.

59. Rodney Turner, "The Lamanite Mark," in *The Book of Mormon: Second Nephi, the Doctrinal Structure*, eds. Monte S. Nyman and Charles D. Tate, Jr. (Provo, UT: BYU Religious Studies Center, 1989), 134.

and founds the first city and initiates civilization.[60] Society can't be formed without dividing people into "us" and "them." Girard critiques Levi-Strauss's interpretation of the Ojibwa myth (native North Americans) and the Tikopia myth (Pacific Islanders). Each myth begins with undivided humanity, or the gods mingling with humans. They end with a sharp division between humans and deity or among humans. "The undifferentiated state corresponds to Nature, which gives way to its differentiated opposite, Culture."[61] One of the gods must be eliminated in order for the differentiation to occur. These are the scapegoats that make social units possible.

The Book of Mormon can be read as the sweeping version of this kind of differentiation. First, the Lehites must separate from the Jews at Jerusalem. From that moment, the fissures within the group are manifest and threaten to break out into open warfare or murder. As mimetic rivals, Nephi, Laman, and Lemuel struggle over leadership, which has been promised by God to the former. At the very least, Nephi is the mimetic rival of the two older brothers; Nephi seems much less inclined to treat Laman and Lemuel as *frères ennimis*. Upon arriving in the promised land, the groups are held together as long as Lehi lives, but immediately upon his death the rivalry becomes murderous again, and violence is prevented only by the physical separation of the two groups. Throughout Book of Mormon history, the two main divisions intermingle with defections, desertions, and conversions. At a certain point, the terms *Nephites* and *Lamanites* no longer serve as ethnic identifiers in the Book of Mormon and become ideological distinctions instead.

---

60. See Genesis 4:17. The "he" there refers to Cain. Culture, as in the arts and crafts, such as harp and organ, iron and brass work, come in a few generations among Cain's descendants (Genesis 4:21–22).

61. Richard J. Golsan, *René Girard and Myth: An Introduction* (New York: Garland, 1993), 71.

When a different Book of Mormon writer (Mormon) takes up the cursing, he reads the story differently than Nephi recounts it. Here is Nephi's account on the left and Mormon's on the right:

2 Nephi 5:20–25	Alma 3:14–17
20. Wherefore, the word of the Lord was fulfilled which he spake unto me, saying that: Inasmuch as they will not hearken unto thy words they shall be cut off from the presence of the Lord. And behold, they were cut off from his presence.	14. Thus the word of God is fulfilled, for these are the words which he said to Nephi: Behold, the Lamanites have I cursed, and I will set a mark on them that they and their seed may be separated from thee and thy seed, from this time henceforth and forever, except they repent of their wickedness and turn to me that I may have mercy upon them.
21. And he had caused the cursing to come upon them, yea, even a sore cursing, because of their iniquity. For behold, they had hardened their hearts against him, that they had become like unto a flint; wherefore, as they were white, and exceedingly fair and delightsome, that they might not be enticing unto my people the Lord God did cause a skin of blackness to come upon them.	15. And again: I will set a mark upon him that mingleth his seed with thy brethren, that they may be cursed also.
	16. And again: I will set a mark upon him that fighteth against thee and thy seed.
22. And thus saith the Lord God: I will cause that they shall be loathsome unto thy people, save they shall repent of their iniquities.	17. And again, I say he that departeth from thee shall no more be called thy seed; and I will bless thee, and whomsoever shall be called thy seed, henceforth and forever; and these were the promises of the Lord unto Nephi and to his seed.
23. And cursed shall be the seed of him that mixeth with their seed; for they shall be cursed even with the same cursing. And the Lord spake it, and it was done.	

2 Nephi 5:20–25	Alma 3:14–17

24. And because of their cursing which was upon them they did become an idle people, full of mischief and subtlety, and did seek in the wilderness for beasts of prey.

25. And the Lord God said unto me: They shall be a scourge unto thy seed, to stir them up in remembrance of me; and inasmuch as they will not remember me, and hearken unto my words, they shall scourge them even unto destruction.

Notice several changes in Mormon's narrative compared to Nephi's. For one, Mormon introduces the term "the mark." Nephi's version only mentions a cursing, but Mormon not only makes that into a mark, but also attaches it to rebellion against Nephi: "And the skins of the Lamanites were dark, according to the mark which was set upon their fathers. . . . And their brethren sought to destroy them, therefore they were cursed; and the Lord God set a mark upon them, yea, upon Laman and Lemuel, and also the sons of Ishmael, and Ishmaelitish women."[62] Turner notes that Nephi doesn't use the word *mark* to apply to skin color—only in Alma is that word used.[63] The mark is a result of the first cursing. That mark is removed in the period around the coming of Christ.[64] It is again imposed on the Lamanites, not on the descendants of Laman and Lemuel, but on those who adhere to the Lamanite story: "although the later mark would be similar to that which was

---

62. Alma 3:6–7.
63. Turner, "Lamanite Mark," 139.
64. Mormon 5:15.

first placed upon the Lamanite nation, the point to note is that it would not be restored only upon the posterity of Laman and his companions, but also upon the descendants of those Nephites and Mulekites who had 'taken upon them the name of Lamanites' (4 Nephi 1:20)."[65] Turner notes that some Nephites rejected the story in the records kept by the Nephites "and mixed with the Lamanites until they are no more called the Nephites, becoming wicked, and wild, and ferocious, yea, even becoming Lamanites."[66] Notice the wording here: one isn't born a Lamanite, but one *becomes* a Lamanite at this point in the Book of Mormon through behaviors, commitments, and actions. The choice to remain a Lamanite is also expressed in 3 Nephi 6:3, where some of the now-defeated Gadianton band can choose peace and were given lands, but some still "were desirous to remain Lamanites." Mormon partly attributes this marking to ethnicity (lineage) and partly to ideology (which story you adhere to—the Nephite or Lamanite narrative):

> And this was done that their seed might be distinguished from the seed of their brethren, that thereby the Lord God might preserve his people, that they might not mix and believe in incorrect traditions which would prove their destruction. And it came to pass that whosoever did mingle his seed with that of the Lamanites did bring the same curse upon his seed. Therefore, whosoever suffered himself to be led away by the Lamanites was called under that head, and there was a mark set upon him. And it came to pass that whosoever would not believe in the tradition of the Lamanites, but believed those records which were brought out of the land of Jerusalem, and also in the tradition of their fathers, which were correct, who believed in the commandments of God and kept them, were called the Nephites, or the people of Nephi, from that time forth.[67]

---

65. Turner, "Lamanite Mark," 149.
66. Helaman 3:16.
67. Alma 3:8–11.

Those who expel, those who scapegoat, those who separate always cast their actions in terms of protecting society or even the very weak who are exiled. The mark of Cain is intended to protect him from retaliation. Here, again, is the God of the Bible who protects even murderers from vendettas, but that protection function also serves to separate, to divide.[68] The mark of Cain might initially be used as a protection, but it soon expands its function to include marking off the alien, the other, the foreigner. "Cain is used to mark off and isolate that which has been unincorporated; in fact, the mark of Cain insures that no such assimilation can take place."[69] Jacob, like Mormon, connects the cursing and the skin color.[70] Not from the perspective of the writer but from the reader's view, we can see the classic elements of scapegoating going on in the text. "Proper scapegoats seem to have 'marks' that single them out for persecution: they may be members of an ethnic or religious minority; they may have some physical abnormality (bodily deformity, sickness, madness), or as marginal individuals have the physical characteristics of their age group (women, children, old men); they may have some social abnormality (they are very poor or very rich or simply don't 'fit' into the larger group). They may even be twins!"[71]

I have, from the beginning of this study, warned against our tendency to favor monolithic thinking: universal categories, categorical imperatives, uniform groupings of people. We ought to be able to embrace the different, the diverse, the unique, the dissimilar. As poet Gerard Manley Hopkins noted in his poem, "Pied Beauty," God also prefers variety:

---

68. Quinones, *Changes of Cain*, 9.
69. Quinones, *Changes of Cain*, 42.
70. Jacob 3:5.
71. Edward McMahon, "Violence-Religion-Law: A Girardian Analysis," in *Curing Violence: Essays on René Girard*, eds. Mark I. Wallace and Theophus H. Smith, 182–203 (Sonoma, CA: Polebridge, 1994), 186.

Glory be to God for dappled things—
   For skies of couple-colour as a brinded cow;
     For rose-moles all in stipple upon trout that swim;
Fresh-firecoal chestnut-falls; finches' wings;
   Landscape plotted and pieced—fold, fallow, and plough;
   And all trades, their gear and tackle and trim.
All things counter, original, spare, strange;
   Whatever is fickle, freckled (who knows how?)
     With swift, slow; sweet, sour; adazzle, dim;
He fathers-forth whose beauty is past change:
         Praise Him.

Particularly in the moral world, we have difficulty accepting a notion, a people, an action merely because it is different. Categorical thinking inspires such a reaction—again, negative capability. We are quick to judge, to dismiss, to scorn. With difficult topics and in-laws, we need to exercise some restraint, patience, and even doubt about our own judgments.

After the distinction between Nephites and Lamanites disappeared for a few generations following the appearance of Christ (during which time there was no dissension, war, economic competition), the division between Nephites and Lamanites appears again, but initially as a religious difference: "and there was still peace in the land, save it were a small part of the people who had revolted from the church and taken upon them the name of Lamanites; therefore there began to be Lamanites again in the land."[72] The newly minted Lamanites are such not by descent or ethnicity but because of differences over religious faith. A few verses later the label *Nephite* is used again after the class distinctions begin to appear and communal ownership of material goods is abandoned.[73] A competitor to the true church appears and institutes persecution and many more churches emerge.[74]

---

72. 4 Nephi 1:20.
73. 4 Nephi 1:25–26.
74. 4 Nephi 1:29, 34.

The "great division among the people" occurs and the other half of the identification of the Lehites again appears after 165 years of unity among the people: "there arose a people who were called the Nephites, and they were true believers in Christ."[75] The distinguishing feature here isn't skin color or tribal identity but ideology or religion. The same verse makes what appears to be an ethnic distinction within those who adhered to Christian doctrine and Nephite identity, for the Lamanites called them "Jacobites, and Josephites, and Zoramites." The Lamanites, more generally, were called *Lamanites* as an ideological identifier, but among the Lamanites they were further sorted out, like the Nephites, with, perhaps, some lineage factor. The conflict between Nephi and his brothers carries on through the generations and likely genetic inheritance scrambled, as cited by Ammoron as the reason for his warfare with the Nephites just six decades before the meridian of time.[76] Note too that by this time the term *Lamanite* no longer indicates descent or ethnicity.

Ammoron notes that he is a descendant of Zoram, traditionally grouped with the Nephites, both before and after Ammoron's time.[77] Despite being ethnically a Zoramite, Ammoron declares he is still "a bold Lamanite" intent on recovering the rulership rights of Laman and Lemuel and their descendants.[78] By the time 4 Nephi is recorded, the terms *Nephite* and *Lamanite* are purely ideological: those who believed in Christ were Nephites (regardless of ethnicity) and those who "rejected the gospel were called Lamanites, and Lemuelites, and Ishmaelites."[79] Both Nephites and Lamanites make ancestral distinctions, but the major form of differentiation—Nephites and Lamanites—appears most commonly

75. 4 Nephi 1:34–36.
76. Alma 54:17.
77. Jacob 1:13; 4 Nephi 1:36–37; Mormon 1:8.
78. Alma 54:24.
79. 4 Nephi 1:36–38.

to be one following political commitment, not skin color or pedigree. From the founding generation of Nephites, Jacob too knows how to sort ideological groupings as distinguished from tribal ones: "Now the people which were not Lamanites were Nephites; nevertheless, they were called Nephites, Jacobites, Josephites, Zoramites, Lamanites, Lemuelites, and Ishmaelites. But I, Jacob, shall not hereafter distinguish them by these names, but I shall call them Lamanites that seek to destroy the people of Nephi, and those who are friendly to Nephi I shall call Nephites."[80] As Mormon does in 4 Nephi, Jacob groups people by ethnic affiliation, but the major labels—Nephite and Lamanite—are an ideological distinction (which narrative about the founding generation does one adhere to).

Similarly, when Lamanites change their ideological commitment and adhere to the Nephite story, they "were numbered among the Nephites" and they were "called Nephites."[81] When the Gadianton robbers unsuccessfully laid siege to the people gathered together in one spot, their failure eventually leads to the people dispersing once the danger is past; the criminal gang is captured and taught the gospel.[82] Those who accepted the teaching were permitted to choose, astonishingly, whether to be Lamanites or Nephites: "they granted unto those robbers who had entered into a covenant to keep the peace of the land, who were desirous to remain Lamanites, lands, according to their numbers, that they might have, with their labors, wherewith to subsist upon."[83] And, Mormon asserts, a change in skin color occurred as the curse was lifted from those who were Lamanites.[84]

---

80. Jacob 1:13.
81. 3 Nephi 2:14, 16.
82. 3 Nephi 5:4–5.
83. 3 Nephi 6:3.
84. 3 Nephi 2:15.

Similarly, the lines of identification sometimes go the opposite direction, for when the Zoramites defected from the Nephite side to the Lamanite position, "the Zoramites became Lamanites."[85] Similarly, any time Nephites changed allegiances they became Lamanites "who were a compound of Laman and Lemuel, and the sons of Ishmael, and all those who had dissented from the Nephites, who were Amalekites and Zoramites, and the descendants of the priests of Noah."[86] The strife between Nephi and Laman and Lemuel shows how what began as familial conflict over generations became national because "the saga of the founding family formed the framework for the descendants of Laman and Lemuel to interpret events."[87] Eventually, the distinction becomes almost wholly ideological. The Book of Mormon interprets the darker skin not in a racial way but in a conceptual one: "The danger was not a mixture of races or skin colors, but a mixture of false traditions with true ones."[88] Mormon mentions the traditions of the Nephites and Lamanites.[89] The point is not skin color but correct tradition. The Amlicites marked themselves differently than the Lamanites were marked, but the point of the mark was to prevent adoption of ideas.[90] The initial prospect of converting the Lamanites to the truth was unlikely to succeed because "of the traditions of their fathers that caused them to remain in their state of ignorance."[91]

When missionary work succeeded in bringing some Lamanites back to the true tradition, the Lamanites expressed gratitude that the Nephites had sent teachers "to convince us of the traditions of our wicked fathers," and the Nephites recognized that the change was ideological: for the Lamanites "began to disbelieve the

85. Alma 43:40.
86. Alma 43:13.
87. Bushman, "Lamanite View," 60.
88. Bushman, "Lamanite View," 60.
89. Alma 3:11.
90. Bushman, "Lamanite View," 63.
91. Alma 9:16.

traditions of their father" and were converted to the truth.[92] Peace was at least partially restored because many Lamanites changed their minds by adopting a competing narrative: "And as many as were convinced did lay down their weapons of war, and also their hatred and the traditions of their fathers."[93] The difference between the two groups was adherence to different foundational narratives. "The moral of the Lamanite story has nothing to do with their depravity but with the terrible consequences of misunderstanding the past."[94]

Mormon's rough summary of the Lord's actions related by Nephi differs in subtle ways from Nephi's own account. Mormon's citation is in the context of the Amlicites, dissenters from the Nephites, as the Amlicites switch allegiance from the Nephite to the Lamanite side. As God's promise to Nephi anticipates, these are a people who "mixeth with their [Lamanite] seed; for they shall be cursed even with the same cursing."[95] The Amlicites mark "themselves with red on their foreheads after the manner of the Lamanites."[96] Now this marking after the manner of the Lamanites isn't the same thing as the dark skin "according to the mark which was set upon their fathers,"[97] or it has radically changed meaning in the generations since. So there appears to be two different marks so far: (1) the red mark on the Amlicites' foreheads patterned after the Lamanites' red mark on their foreheads, and (2) the mark of the dark skin in verses 6 and 7 intended to keep the Nephites from intermingling with the Lamanites.

For Mormon, the narrator, these two marks are not the same. For he states, after discussing the mark of dark skin instituted in the founding generation, "Now we will return again to the Amlic-

92. Alma 24:7; 25:6.
93. Helaman 5:51.
94. Bushman, "Lamanite View," 71.
95. 2 Nephi 5:23.
96. Alma 3:4.
97. Alma 3:6.

ites, for they also had a mark set upon them; yea, they set the mark upon themselves, yea, even a mark of red upon their foreheads."[98] We readers of the Book of Mormon, no doubt, tend to conflate the two different marks Mormon discusses. Mormon seems to have two different marks in mind, although both are used to separate and distinguish those who believe in the Nephite narrative from those who believe otherwise. The Amlicites are one example of Nephite defectors. The series of Nephite dissenters (Nehor, Korihor, Zeezrom, Amlici, the Zoramites) can be seen as history's losers, those who don't write the record of the past.

The Bible recounts similar conflicts where Moses and Joshua (and later Israelite leaders) encountered dissidents and dealt with them through eruptions of sacrificial violence (Korah, for example). "Moses and then Joshua found it necessary to augment ritual sacrifice with violent quasi-ritual purges of dissidents and holy wars against external enemies."[99] Between Alma and Korihor, a cycle of rivalry starts, concluding with Korihor's death. His story demonstrates a classic sacrificial plot: after social conflict, one person is blamed for the problem; Korihor is compelled to accept his own guilt, he is punished by being struck dumb then exiled, and the social dissension is solved by his expulsion.[100]

The Book of Mormon writers do attach the curse or the mark to skin color, but ethnic or racial identity is neither simple nor constructed the way we moderns approach race. We may deplore the way people in the past constructed racial and ideological categories, but accurate description of those differences is the first step toward understanding such cultural and historical descriptions. The Nephite record portrays the distinctions (ethnic, ideologi-

---

98. Alma 3:13.

99. Gil Bailie, *Violence Unveiled: Humanity at the Crossroads* (New York: Crossroad, 1995), 154.

100. Mack C. Stirling, "Violence in the Scriptures: Mormonism and the Cultural Theory of René Girard," *Dialogue: A Journal of Mormon Thought* 43, no. 1 (Spring 2010): 93.

cal, religious) among the various people in much more sophisticated ways than too many of its modern readers interpret. We are too quick to assimilate ideas and events from the distant past to modern templates and monolithic categories. More subtlety, more nuance, more gradation is needed, which amounts to more negative capability. We have to use categories in order to understand people, communities, and concepts, else each person would be her or his own category. We just need to be aware that such categorization can falsify as much as clarify.

Chapter Eleven

King Noah—the Victim
of His People—and the
Scapegoat Kings of the Bible

For Girard, the institution of monarchy is a response to the scapegoating impulse. Girard calls this "the starting-point of our theory" on sacrifice. The proto-king is a sacrificial victim who can delay the act by finding a substitute to replace him during (usually annual) cycles, and during the interim, he acquires political power because of his status as a revered figure of impending martyrdom before that status is made permanent. "The original victim is endowed with super-human, terrifying prestige because it is seen as the source of all disorder and order. Subsequent victims inherit some of this prestige. One must look to this prestige for the source of all political and religious sovereignty."[1] Over generations of a long line of scapegoats, the victims can acquire more power and eventually shift the burden of scapegoating onto a surrogate and become a permanent king: "Since sacrifice is always a question of substitution, it is always possible to make a new substitution and henceforth to sacrifice only a substitute of the

---

1. René Girard, *Things Hidden Since the Foundation of the World*, trans. Stephen Bann and Michael Metteer (Stanford: Stanford University Press, 1987), 53.

substitute."[2] Eventually, the memory of the connection between the sacrificial victim and the king is forgotten. But, like a Jungian archetype, the connection is always just beneath the surface. The connection between the monarchy and religion should make us always think of kings as sacred monarchs.[3]

The foundations of biblical leadership are an intricate inter-weaving of two political and religious institutions.[4] Monarchy and prophecy are integrally connected, king and prophet both repre-senting the divine in some way. Samuel the prophet chooses Isra-el's first king, Saul, who is Samuel's successor as ruler in the politi-cal transition from judges to kings, and the second, David (both of these kings were also seized by an external force to prophesy and dance with the sons of the prophets). The commissioning of kings and prophets often uses the same wording. "From this standpoint, clearly the role of the king is a *calling* that closely resembles a prophet's call," and each of the offices resembles the selection of a scapegoat.[5] Mosiah$_2$ understands this quite well in his discourse about kingship, for when he convinced his people to transition from kingship to judgeship, he laments the burden of sin and suf-fering the king must bear: "And many more things did king Mosiah write unto them, unfolding unto them all the trials and troubles of a righteous king, yea, all the travails of soul for their people."[6] Wil-liams notes that the selection of both kings and prophets is a pro-cess similar to scapegoating in which the king or prophet becomes a microcosm of the people:

> [B]oth roles stem from a "selection" that amounts to exclusion
> or expulsion from the community, whether self-imposed or not,
> and that comes to be understood by some in the Israelite con-

2. Girard, *Things Hidden*, 53.
3. Girard, *Things Hidden*, 55.
4. James G. Williams, *The Bible, Violence, and the Sacred: Liberation from the Myth of Sanctioned Violence* (San Francisco: Harper, 1991), 147.
5. Williams, *The Bible*, 130.
6. Mosiah 29:33.

text as *the call of YHWH to assume a special responsibility for those who are likewise expelled, excluded, or marginal.* Those who are thus oppressed or marginalized could be the people as a whole, individuals within the covenant community, groups or classes within the covenant people.[7]

That would make both Noah and Abinadi scapegoats and mirror images of each other, not just in the way they die but in their very roles in Nephite society. Just as Elijah and Ahab are doubles of each other, [8] Abinadi and Noah are also each others' types and opposites, so that whatever happens to Abinadi sets the pattern for what will happen to Noah. King Noah is like the first king of Israel, in that he is too easily influenced by the entreaties of his people. Saul is too much of a crowd pleaser for the Deuteronomist's tastes, doing what the people demand rather than what God requires.[9] Noah, like Saul, is too mimetically susceptible to be a good king.[10] Initially, Noah is ready to release Abinadi in the trial process because of his fear, but he is prevailed upon by his priests to execute the prophet. King Saul isn't evil, just not sufficiently principled and independent, always seeking the approbation of his people. Saul spares Agag, disobeying Samuel's orders, "because I feared the people, and obeyed their voice."[11] Saul depends too much on the prophet's advice to be a good executive official, and even after Samuel's death, Saul engages a necromancer to consult the prophet the day before the king is going to die in battle.

A survey of kingship in the biblical tradition helps set up the background for monarchy in the Book of Mormon. Both Northern Israel and Judahite kings (Ahab and Jeroboam I in the

---

7. Williams, *The Bible*, 131.

8. Williams, *The Bible*, 147.

9. 1 Samuel 13:11; 15:24.

10. James G. Williams, "King as Servant, Sacrifice as Service: Gospel Transformations," in *Violence Renounced: René Girard, Biblical Studies, and Peacemaking*, ed. Willard M. Swartley, 178–99 (Telford, PA: Pandora, 2000), 186.

11. 1 Samuel 15:24.

north and Solomon and Manasseh in the south) were blamed for bringing disaster on the people by leading them into transgression. Manasseh and Ahab are what Lasine calls "limit cases," the most extreme portrayal of evil in a king written to portray what the utmost case of monarchical evil might be.[12] The description of Manasseh's reign in 2 Kings 21:2–16 shouldn't be viewed as the way the king reigned. "The constantly increasing number of sins attributed to Manasseh by the narrator is so extreme that readers may no longer view the finished portrait as the depiction of a real villain" but rather the justification of the destruction of the southern kingdom, making Manasseh "a scapegoat whose role it is to serve as the fictional cause of Judah's real demise."[13] As the paragon of evil in Judah, Manasseh serves as a symbolic counterpoint to Josiah, the prototypical good king to the Deuteronomist.[14] Lasine mentions Girard's notion of the scapegoat when discussing Manasseh. When the Chronicler (as opposed to the Deuteronomic historian) takes up Manasseh, it has him complete the journey of the scapegoat not just by representing the people's sins but also by being expelled from the community.[15] And, much like Oedipus, Manasseh becomes a blessing to his community after his expulsion by returning from exile, engaging in building and purification projects, and serving God in a way he never did when in power.[16] Francesca Stavrakopoulou also notes the scapegoating of Manasseh, viewing the portrayal as an attempt by the biblical writers to create an ideal type of an evil king.[17]

---

12. Stuart Lasine, "Manasseh as Villain and Scapegoat," in *The New Literary Criticism and the Hebrew Bible*, eds. J. Cheryl Exum and David J. A. Clines (Valley Forge, PA: Trinity Press International, 1994), 163.

13. Lasine, "Manasseh as Villain," 163n2.

14. Lasine, "Manasseh as Villain," 177.

15. 2 Chronicles 33.

16. Lasine, "Manasseh as Villain," 179.

17. Francesca Stavrakopoulou, *King Manasseh and Child Sacrifice: Biblical Distortions of Historical Realities* (Berlin: Walter de Gruyter, 2004), 138–39.

The recurrent literary pattern of an archetypal wicked king singles out Jeroboam in the Northern Israelite tradition as the monarch most responsible for the wickedness of the people and for their eventual conquest. The biblical writers (along with the cultures surrounding them) viewed history as repetitive and paradigmatic, so the lessons of the past are exemplary for the present if what happens in the past repeats in the present and the future.[18] The "complex of motifs" surrounding Jeroboam are similar in the Mesopotamian tradition to those surrounding Naram-Sin of Akkad. Evans refers to this literary pattern as "the typology of the *Unheilsherrscher*," or the motif of the evil ruler who brings about his own and his people's destruction through his wickedness.[19] The Akkad dynasty set the pattern for later Mesopotamian cultures to view their own monarchs, and Sargon became the model of the good king, with Naram-Sin the model of the evil king for these traditions.[20] Jeroboam, the first schismatic king of the Northern Kingdom, like Naram-Sin, became the model of the *Unheilsherrscher* for the Deuteronomist, the paradigm of the evil king.[21] When Jeroboam and his wife are to suffer the death of their son, Jeroboam is being punished for sinning against God and making all of Israel to sin: "Here the main motifs of the typology appear together—the king's religious offenses bring condemnation on himself and ruin on his family and nation."[22] For the Deuteronomist, Josiah is the archetypal good king, the *Heilsherrscher*. "With the juxtaposition of both typologies, the Deuteronomist's work was a summons to his contemporaries to learn from the past, to appropriate the les-

18. Carl D. Evans, "Naram-Sin and Jeroboam: The Archetypal *Unheilscherrscher* in Mesopotamian and Biblical Historiography," in *Scripture in Context II: More Essays on the Comparative Method*, eds. William W. Hallo, James C. Moyer, and Leo G. Perdue, 97–125 (Winona Lake, IN: Eisenbrauns, 1983), 110.

19. Evans, "Naram-Sin and Jeroboam," 98–99.

20. Evans, "Naram-Sin and Jeroboam," 111.

21. Evans, "Naram-Sin and Jeroboam," 114.

22. Evans, "Naram-Sin and Jeroboam," 118; see also 1 Kings 14:1–18.

sons derived from 'good' and 'bad' rulers, and to respond with favor to the challenges offered by Josiah," and avoid the model of bad kings exemplified by Jeroboam and Manasseh.[23] The archetypal evil king must prove himself to be "worthy" of the violence and its consequences. "It is important to cultivate the future victim's supposed potential for evil, to transform him into a monster of iniquity—not for esthetic reasons, but to enable him to polarize, to literally draw to himself, all the infectious strains in the community and transform them into sources of peace and fecundity."[24]

Similarly, Benjamin is the prototypical good king in the Book of Mormon tradition. When Mosiah proposes the abolition of monarchy, he implicitly compares the model good king in the Nephite tradition—Benjamin—with the archetypal bad king—Noah: if you had kings such as Benjamin, "then it would be expedient that ye should always have kings to rule over you."[25] Just a few verses later, Mosiah warns that it isn't "expedient that ye should have a king or kings to rule over you," because it leads to the kind of wickedness inspired by Noah.[26]

The biblical politeia stretches from Judges to 2 Kings and sketches the various political experiments and structures the Israelites and God attempt in the crush of biblical practice and history. From Moses's leadership to Joshua, from judges to kings, from extreme devolution to concentration of power, the biblical politeia struggles with human weaknesses and divine aspirations in the mangle of lived political leadership. Two passages stand out, as they look forward to the shift from prophetic leadership to judgeship and then to kingship. Both are a form of legislation restraining the inevitable concentration of power that will accompany the shift to Israelite monarchy. Deuteronomy has Moses foreshadow-

23. Evans, "Naram-Sin and Jeroboam," 123–24.
24. Girard, *Violence and the Sacred*, 107.
25. Mosiah 29:13.
26. Mosiah 29:16–18.

ing what kingship will eventually be like. This passage is known as the law of the king:

> When thou art come unto the land which the Lord thy God giveth thee, and shalt possess it, and shalt dwell therein, and shalt say, I will set a king over me, like as all the nations that are about me; Thou shalt in any wise set him king over thee, whom the Lord thy God shall choose: one from among thy brethren shalt thou set king over thee: thou mayest not set a stranger over thee, which is not thy brother. But he shall not multiply horses to himself, nor cause the people to return to Egypt, to the end that he should multiply horses: forasmuch as the Lord hath said unto you, Ye shall henceforth return no more that way. Neither shall he multiply wives to himself, that his heart turn not away: neither shall he greatly multiply to himself silver and gold. And it shall be, when he sitteth upon the throne of his kingdom, that he shall write him a copy of this law in a book out of that which is before the priests the Levites.[27]

Several comments ought to be noted about this passage. For one, the desire to be "like all the nations" is the path of the fool for the biblical writers.[28] So the eventual desire for a king (with the stable and predictable generational transfer of power) is a foolish wish, for the people would be better off letting God be their king rather than trusting to some human institution. But God will grant the request, nevertheless. The king will oppress and abuse, but God acquiesces to the people's desire. The command to choose a brother restricts the people to selecting an Israelite instead of bringing in a foreigner likely to impose foreign allegiances (political and religious) on the people. In the ancient Near East, horses and chariots were the aircraft carriers of the day, so a king with horses would be able to use those weapons against foreign forces in war and dissidents in peace to concentrate power in his own

---

27. Deuteronomy 17:14–18.
28. See Ezekiel 20:32.

institutions. David followed the law of the king in this matter and hamstrung horses that fell under his control.[29] His son Solomon, however, didn't follow that commandment and benefitted from a thriving trade in horses and chariots.[30] Similarly, the king was not to have many wives; marriages were tools of politics and diplomacy, so the marriage to multiple foreign wives would soon lead to religious syncretism as those wives imported their foreign beliefs and practices.[31] The corruption that almost always accompanies power is addressed in the commandment not to multiply gold and silver. Chapter 10 of 1 Kings shows how Solomon violated the proscription against acquiring outrageous wealth. Solomon ends up being, in the second half—the foolish half—of his reign, the prototypical evil king anticipated by the Deuteronomist, in the attempt to foreclose and critique that possibility.

The other central passage regulating kingship in the Bible is 1 Samuel 8–12. Here, the people ask Samuel the prophet to give them a king "like all the nations."[32] The Lord tells Samuel to proceed after declaring the *mispat* or "manner of the king."[33] The new monarchy will abuse its power by conscripting Israelite sons, appropriating the people's land, and taking their daughters.[34] He will confiscate their property to reward his soldiers and impose a tithe on their increase: "And he will take the tenth of your seed, and of your vineyards, and give to his officers, and to his servants."[35] Yet despite Samuel's warning, the people insist on having a king

---

29. 2 Samuel 8:4.

30. 1 Kings 10:26, 28–29; 1 Kings 4:26. Chariots were not so useful in the hilly country of Judea but were much more effective on the flat plains along the Mediterranean coast and the Jordan River Valley.

31. 1 Kings 11 shows this happening to Solomon.

32. 1 Samuel 8:5; this phrase provides the strong allusive connection between the "manner of the king" and the "law of the king."

33. The passage is more like a contract, so the people know what they are getting into before the king project is launched.

34. 1 Samuel 8:11–14.

35. 1 Samuel 8:15.

so they can "be like all the nations," a king who will oppress them until they shall "cry out in that day because of your king which ye shall have chosen you; and the Lord will not hear you in that day."[36] This statement echoes the experience of slavery the children of Israel lived through in Egypt.

These two passages—the law of the king and the manner of the king—foretell the centralization of power that is described under Solomon's rule so that he becomes the archetypal evil king, which is also the function of King Noah in the Book of Mormon. Like Solomon, Noah "had many wives and concubines."[37] Samuel predicted the king would appropriate one-tenth of his people's increase; Noah doubles that, taking one-fifth—two tithes.[38] Noah replaces the priests when he came to power just as Jeroboam, the first king of Northern Israel did and as Solomon replaced the (high) priest Abiathar with Zadok.[39] Like Solomon, Noah taxed the people heavily to support his building program, as Solomon used the levy (corvée, or forced manual slave labor) as a form of taxation/temporary slavery to populate his construction program.[40]

Just as Naram-Sin in the Mesopotamian tradition, Solomon and Manasseh in the Judahite tradition, and Ahab and Jeroboam in the Northern tradition were archetypal wicked kings, Noah performs the same function in the Nephite tradition. Little trace of King Noah's victimization remains in the Book of Mormon. But, of course, Girard tells us that recognition of the victim's innocence is repressed by the oppressors, so we wouldn't expect the scripture to acknowledge the victim's status. Noah doesn't go the route of deification, so he remains the fall guy. The Zeniffite narrative

---

36. 1 Samuel 8:18, 20.
37. Mosiah 11:2.
38. Mosiah 11:3.
39. Mosiah 11:5; 1 Kings 12:31.
40. Mosiah 11:13; 1 Kings 9:13–23, where the passage asserts the Canaanite natives were forced to labor but not the Israelites; 1 Kings 5:13–15 belies that assertion.

begins with Zeniff recounting the recolonizing efforts in the first person, in his own voice.[41] This perspective ends when Zeniff notes that in his old age, he anointed his son Noah, his successor, as king.[42] The King Noah portion of the narrative is summarized in third-person narration by Mormon,[43] who had more than 550 years of intervening post-Noah history to reflect on the lessons of kingship he drew from the sources that he used to recount the history of the Zeniffite experience.

Mormon cites both Alma and Mosiah as blaming King Noah for the people's wickedness and slavery. When $Alma_1$'s[44] people try to impose the kingship on him, he notes, "it is not expedient that we should have a king," and asserts that if they could always have righteous kings, the people would have good governance. "[B]ut remember the iniquity of king Noah and his priests," $Alma_1$ reminds them.[45] The consequence is bad for the king and the people, for "ye have been oppressed by king Noah, and have been in bondage to him and his priests."[46] Similarly, Mosiah advocates a structural change in government: elected judges instead of dynastic kings. If you could always have good kings, Mosiah reminds his people in almost the same words $Alma_1$ used, "then it would be expedient that ye should always have kings to rule over you."[47] Again, Noah is the prime example of an evil king: "Yea, remem-

---

41. Mosiah 9:1.

42. Mosiah 10:22.

43. Mosiah 11:1 is that starting point that goes until the two groups of Zeniffites, led by Limhi and Alma, are reabsorbed into the main body of Nephites at Zarahemla.

44. Latter-day Saints are traditionally accustomed to hearing this Alma referred to as Alma the Elder and his son, the first elected chief judge after the institutional transformation from kingship to judgeship, called Alma the Younger. I will follow the pattern of designating these two leaders as $Alma_1$, the former priest of Noah and leader of a dissenting colony away from Noah's oppression, and the son as $Alma_2$ if there is any possibility of confusion, while not using that subscript number when quoting from the Book of Mormon.

45. Mosiah 23:7–9.

46. Mosiah 23:12.

47. Mosiah 29:13.

ber king Noah, his wickedness and his abominations, and also the wickedness and abominations of his people." God eventually hears their "cries" and "did deliver them out of bondage," but not before "the sins of many people have been caused by the iniquities of their kings."[48] The Girardian framework asks us to consider that the Nephite record is written by those who opposed Noah, and, therefore, Alma$_1$, Mosiah, and Mormon didn't understand the scapegoat status of kings. Like Oedipus in Sophocles's play cycle, Abinadi's dying words stamp the lasting image of Noah into the record: "ye shall be smitten on every hand, and shall be driven and scattered to and fro, even as a wild flock is driven by wild and ferocious beasts. And in that day ye shall be hunted, and ye shall be taken by the hand of your enemies, and then ye shall suffer, as I suffer, the pains of death by fire. Thus God executeth vengeance upon those that destroy his people."[49] And whatever Noah and his henchmen do to Abinadi "shall be as a type and shadow of things which are to come," which prophetic word is verified when the descendants of those priests are killed with fire, and even King Noah is burned to death.[50] Noah, who is killed by his own people, a mob in a crisis of conflict, is less differentiated from Abinadi than we who prefer hats to be all white or black would like. "That the king is the difference and the differentiator means that he is the *sacrificer* but also the *sacrifice* in periods of crisis."[51] Prophet and king together meet their ends in the fires of sacrifice. As "Samuel is Saul's *double*, the other from whom he cannot distinguish himself," so are Abinadi and Noah mimetic doubles and opposites seeking differentiation.[52]

King Noah can be viewed as a victim despite his portrayal as an oppressor and serial violator of biblical commandments

---

48. Mosiah 29:18, 20, 31.
49. Mosiah 17:17–19.
50. Mosiah 13:10; Alma 25:9–12; Mosiah 19:20.
51. Williams, "King as Servant," 179.
52. Williams, "King as Servant," 183.

more generally and the law of the king specifically. Girard, following James Frazier, posits that kingship emerged because societies wanted to have a designated sacrificial victim on hand in case of an emergent crisis or even to merely prevent such a crisis, and perhaps a backup also (an heir and a spare). The live example of a future sacrifice walking around the village or town might have obtained the status of deity even before the sacrifice. As a conduit of the sacred, the putative victim might have parlayed that status into power—political power enabling him to defer his own sacrifice, shifting the deed onto a substitute. Eventually, that deferral would become permanent, and the scapegoat designate would become a permanent king.[53]

Alma₁ initiates the first movement against the king's authority, defending Abinadi at his trial, then absconding when his life too is threatened, establishing a colony of former Noachide subjects in the wilderness.[54] Gideon then leads an armed rebellion against Noah that results in Noah's death by immolation.[55] Girard addresses the need to portray the king/scapegoat as a wicked character in order to justify not just the sacrifice but also the casting of the communities' sins upon the goat:

> The king must show himself "worthy" of his punishment—fully as worthy as the original outcast from whom the ceremony derives. It is important to cultivate the future victim's supposed potential for evil, to transform him into a monster of iniquity—not for esthetic reasons, but to enable him to polarize, to literally draw to himself, all the infectious strains in the community and transform them into sources of peace and fecundity. The principle of this metamorphosis has its source in the sacrifice of the monarch and subsequently pervades his entire existence on earth.[56]

---

53. George Boreas, René Girard IX: Origin of Kings, available at https://www.georgeboreas.com/blog/ren-girard-ix-origin-of-kings.

54. Mosiah 17–18.

55. Mosiah 19.

56. Girard, *Violence*, 107.

During Gideon's rebellion against King Noah, the Lamanites also invade the Zeniffite territory, posing a secondary external threat to the internal one. Noah commands his retinue to flee from the Lamanites, abandoning their families to the rebel faction and the Lamanites. Noah's Praetorian Guard soon regrets that decision, vowing to return to their families and seek revenge if their loved ones have been killed.[57] "And the king commanded them that they should not return; and they were angry with the king, and caused that he should suffer, even unto death by fire. And they were about to take the priests also and put them to death, and they fled before them."[58] The king's own soldiers become a mob and torch Noah. The priests escape the same fate only by their rapid flight. A Girardian reading would double down on the irony, that when Abinadi notes that the Messiah and the prophets vicariously carry the people's burden, the king does also—even a wicked king who gins up the people's wickedness. As Abinadi quotes the Suffering Servant passage from Isaiah 53, we could see King Noah also as one who "is despised and rejected of men; a man of sorrows, and acquainted with grief; and we hid as it were our faces from him; he was despised, and we esteemed him not. Surely he has borne our griefs, and carried our sorrows; yet we did esteem him stricken, smitten of God, and afflicted. But he was wounded for our transgressions, he was bruised for our iniquities; the chastisement of our peace was upon him; and with his stripes we are healed."[59] We readers want our Judases served straight, with no redemptive possibilities wrapped up in their narratives. But Girard encourages us to see the scapegoating tendencies in our own reading habits and the storytelling of writers such as Mormon. A character's personality and actions don't have to be unadulterated evil to be singled out by the community as a scapegoat.

---

57. Mosiah 19:9–19.
58. Mosiah 19:20–21.
59. Mosiah 14:3–5.

Chapter Twelve

So Persecuted They
All the Prophets

Paul puts Jesus in the line of prophets the Jews killed.[1] Robert Hamerton-Kelly finds (especially in the epistle to the Romans) the role of the Jews to be God's antagonists, in that they bring about the death of Jesus and therefore enable the atonement to be completed.[2] "There is a paradox in the idea of Israel's persecution of the prophets, which Paul brings out in the discussion of the role of Israel in the plan of salvation. It is that the persecutors as well as the persecuted perform an essential task for that plan. By persecution God creates the prophetic remnant and so both roles are needed."[3] The Jews are still essential in Paul's version of the plan of salvation, according to Hamerton-Kelly, for, by killing Jesus, they brought about a "wealth for the cosmos."[4] To the Jew first and then to the Gentile is not only the order of salvation but also of transgression.[5] I am uncomfortable with scaling up these claims for Jews as a category, but note that these persecutions of the prophets are a synecdoche (a figure of speech used when the

---

1. 1 Thessalonians 2:14–16.
2. Romans 9–11.
3. Robert G. Hamerton-Kelly, *Sacred Violence: Paul's Hermeneutic of the Cross* (Minneapolis: Fortress, 1992), 83.
4. Romans 11:12.
5. Hamerton-Kelly, *Sacred Violence*, 101.

part is taken to represent the whole), and the Jews are a synecdoche of all humans throughout history and their corporate reaction to the divine redemptive plan. But my narrower purpose here is to see how the Bible and the Book of Mormon frame the relationship between the covenant people and God's prophets.

The most prominent Book of Mormon prophet/martyr is Abinadi. Abinadi asks "who shall *see* his seed?" and "who shall *be* his seed?"[6] riffing on a Suffering Servant passage from Isaiah[7] to the people and groups who have suffered this persecution from the mob. Here is the Isaiah passage Abinadi is expanding on midrashically:

> He was taken from prison and from judgment; and *who shall declare his generation?* For he was cut off out of the land of the living; for the transgressions of my people was he stricken. And he made his grave with the wicked, and with the rich in his death; because he had done no evil, neither was any deceit in his mouth. Yet it pleased the Lord to bruise him; he hath put him to grief; when thou shalt make his soul an offering for sin *he shall see his seed*, he shall prolong his days, and the pleasure of the Lord shall prosper in his hand . . . because he hath poured out his soul unto death; and he was numbered with the transgressors; and he bore the sins of many, and made intercession for the transgressors.[8]

"His seed" needs to be taken to refer to generation, passing on genetic information, propagating, reproducing. Note here the phrases I have emphasized. "Who shall declare his generation?" refers to generating offspring, not merely a cohort of people whose birth dates are clustered in certain annual groupings.

Luke 11:50–51 mentions that "this generation" will have to account for the blood of every prophet, from Abel to Zechariah

---

6. Mosiah 15:10.
7. Mosiah 14:8–10 which has Abinadi quoting from Isaiah 53:8–10.
8. Mosiah 14:8–10, 12.

(that is, from A to Z), killed by the mob. The Greek translation of "generation" underlies the word *genesis*, so the foundation of culture itself is the genesis of violence from the first to the last prophet. "This 'generation' would therefore mean all cultural and religious systems for which scapegoating violence is the underlying *generative* mechanisms—in other words, to one degree or another, all conventional cultures, including our own."[9] We don't normally think of Abel (the Hebrew meaning of the root of Abel's name: a breath of air, a transitory life, that fleeting vapor of existence) as a prophet, but his death was prophetic in that it prefigured all those who die of this *generative* violence, and each presaged the murder of the Lamb slain from the foundation of the world. So the word *prophet* doesn't just mean someone who speaks for God or someone who, under mantic influence, predicts the future. Rather, it means a recipient of violence who died from sacrificial violence and through that victimization becomes "an agent of biblical revelation only in retrospect."[10] Starting with Abel, the prophets and those who believe the prophets, and Christ most of all, those who carry the burden of the community's sins are customarily singled out to be its scapegoats. Believers generally and prophets specifically have redemptively been "wounded for our transgressions," been "bruised for our iniquities," and "with [their] stripes we are healed,"[11] says Isaiah. The prophets who declare God's word and the people who accept it are the *he* referred to in that Isaiah passage (according to standard Christian readings), and *we* are the mob who persecute them, although Christ is certainly foremost among those suffering servants. Here is the Book of Mormon prophet Abinadi quoting Isaiah 53:

> He is despised and rejected of men; a man of sorrows, and acquainted with grief; and we hid as it were our faces from him;

9. Bailie, *Violence Unveiled*, 197–98.
10. Bailie, *Violence Unveiled*, 199.
11. Mosiah 14:5.

he was despised, and we esteemed him not. Surely he has borne our griefs, and carried our sorrows; yet we did esteem him stricken, smitten of God, and afflicted. But he was wounded for our transgressions, he was bruised for our iniquities; the chastisement of our peace was upon him; and with his stripes we are healed. All we, like sheep, have gone astray; we have turned every one to his own way; and the Lord hath laid on him the iniquities of us all.[12]

The servant, "his seed," and "this generation" have been scapegoated and persecuted. In answering his own question "who shall be his seed?" Abinadi will answer: those who have declared God's word and those who have received it.

I have pointed out (Chapter 8, "The Death of Abinadi"), following Joseph Spencer's exegesis, that Noah's priests pose a question of Abinadi at his trial that presupposes that King Noah has brought a period of millennial peace and righteousness in which prophets are no longer needed to confront wickedness and reprove kings for ruling through sin and violence, so why is Abinadi doing exactly that? The priests quote the following passage to Abinadi as if it is a definitive renunciation of Abinadi's message:

> How beautiful upon the mountains are the feet of him that bringeth good tidings; that publisheth peace; that bringeth good tidings of good; that publisheth salvation; that saith unto Zion, Thy God reigneth; Thy watchmen shall lift up the voice; with the voice together shall they sing; for they shall see eye to eye when the Lord shall bring again Zion; Break forth into joy; sing together ye waste places of Jerusalem; for the Lord hath comforted his people, he hath redeemed Jerusalem; The Lord hath made bare his holy arm in the eyes of all the nations, and all the ends of the earth shall see the salvation of our god?[13]

---

12. Mosiah 14:3–6
13. Mosiah 12:21–24 quoting Isaiah 52:7–10.

The priests' reading asserts that under the leadership of Noah and his priests kings have seen eye to eye with the Lord and together have brought again Zion. Abinadi, the argument goes, should be breaking into joy and singing because the Lord, under the Zeniffite elite, had comforted and redeemed the Zeniffite people and returned them to their original land of promise, the land of Nephi, the land of Nephite original possession—a repetition of an often anticipated return to Eden. So, the implicit question posed is, why is Abinadi so negative about the current generation? For the priests and Noah agree with the people, the mob, who captured Abinadi and turned him over to the authorities.

> And now, O king, what great evil hast thou done, or what great sins have thy people committed, that we should be condemned of God or judged of this man? And now, O king, behold, we are guiltless, and thou, O king, hast not sinned; therefore, this man has lied concerning you, and he has prophesied in vain. And behold, we are strong, we shall not come into bondage, or be taken captive by our enemies; yea, and thou hast prospered in the land, and thou shalt also prosper. Behold, here is the man, we deliver him into thy hands; thou mayest do with him as seemeth thee good.[14]

The wicked, persecuting crowd, egged on by their ruling class, prepare and complete a burnt sacrifice, not only of Abinadi but to persecute and exile his seed, those who accept his preaching (Alma$_1$ and those who join his community in the wilderness, for example). Not only has Isaiah's projected millennial peace been achieved—they assert—but Noah has brought about the fulfillment of God's promise to Nephi that "thou hast prospered in the land, and thou shalt also prosper."

So, to answer Abinadi's question, who are the suffering servant's seed prompted by the passage in Isaiah 53:10? The *he* here

---

14. Mosiah 12:13–16.

in "he shall see his seed" is foremost the coming Christ, for "I would that ye should understand that God himself shall come down among the children of men, and shall redeem his people." [15] The phrase "his seed" will be used five times in Mosiah 15:10–13, and they are identified as "all the holy prophets who have prophesied concerning the coming of the Lord" and "all those who have hearkened unto their words, and believed that the Lord would redeem his people." [16] Included in those two overarching categories will soon be Abinadi, his only apparent convert Alma₁, and those who accept Abinadi's message through Alma₁ at the waters of Mormon. [17]

Abinadi, after his exposition on who composes "his seed," is specifically citing Isaiah, [18] where he not only alludes again to the Isaiah passage quoted by the priests as their knock-down argument for Noah's righteous reign, but in this final verse quotes the first verse of that now-disputed passage:

> And these are they who have published peace, who have brought good tidings of good, who have published salvation; and said unto Zion: Thy God reigneth! And O how beautiful upon the mountains were their feet! And again, how beautiful upon the mountains are the feet of those that are still publishing peace! And again, how beautiful upon the mountains are the feet of those who shall hereafter publish peace, yea, from this time henceforth and forever! And behold, I say unto you, this is not all. For O how beautiful upon the mountains are the feet of him that bringeth good tidings, that is the founder of peace, yea, even the Lord, who has *redeemed* his people; yea, him who has granted *salvation* unto his people. [19]

---

15. Mosiah 15:1.
16. Mosiah 15:11.
17. Mosiah 18:1–6.
18. Mosiah 15:6.
19. Mosiah 15:14–18.

Abinadi has turned the priests' apparently favorite biblical passage against their own argument to demonstrate why prophets are still needed. And he mentions no such need for kings or priests (and neither does Isaiah). Prophets are needed to forecast the coming of the Messiah to bring human salvation and redemption. Kings and their cabinets, rulers and their advisors, are not needed in that role and often obstruct that result for their own purposes.

This salvation and redemption topic is the theme of the rest of Abinadi's sermon, "For were it not for the redemption which he hath made for his people, which was *prepared from the foundation of the world*, I say unto you, were it not for this, all mankind must have perished."[20] The reference to the foundation, in addition to the allusion to foundational generations of the world, takes us back to beginnings (or perhaps even before beginnings). Christ's atonement was prepared from *before* the foundation of the world. But the foundation of human civilization begins with the expulsion from the garden and the first murder, which leads to the first city in that primeval history portion of Genesis. In Luke, a lawyer asks why Jesus condemns Jewish leaders who assert they continue the tradition of the prophets, but Jesus emphasizes discontinuity rather than faithful connection: "ye build the sepulchres of the prophets, and your fathers killed them."[21] God's intent from the beginning was to send prophets, but the Lord knows that "I will send them prophets and apostles, and some of them they shall slay and persecute. That the blood of all the prophets, which was shed from the foundation of the world, may be required of this generation; From the blood of Abel unto the blood of Zacharias, which perished between the altar and the temple: verily I say unto you, It shall be required of this generation,"[22] this generative event.

---

20. Mosiah 15:19.

21. Luke 11:47. Jesus has previously, in verse 44, compared the scribes and Pharisees themselves to graves.

22. Luke 11:49–51. See the parallel passage in Matthew 23:27–36.

This foundational reference takes the reader explicitly back to Abel's murder. As Girard writes, "Jesus emphasizes the violence of human culture. As always, his word signifies something universally human."[23] The collective murder of Abinadi continues and extends what has been happening since the loss of paradise. Girard goes on to note,

> In the context of "the foundation of the world," is . . . a return to the theme in the story of Cain in Genesis, a deliberate adoption of the thesis that I have just set out: the first human culture has its roots in an initial collective murder, a murder similar to the Crucifixion. What shows this to be so is Luke's phrase "since the foundation of the world." What has happened since the foundation of the world, that is, since the violent foundation of the first cultures is a murder like the Crucifixion.[24]

In the context of Abinadi's trial, he too will be murdered, but he ends his discourse on the high note of a redemption and resurrection of the dead.

This redemptive and salvific action prepared from the foundation of the world will result in the resurrection of the dead, "the resurrection of all the prophets, and all those that have believed in their words,"[25] which divine intervention will be declared by these prophets "to every nation, kindred, tongue, and people."[26] Then, again, Abinadi returns to the very Isaianic passage the priests quoted as if theirs was a well-rehearsed line prepared for a televised political debate:

> Yea, Lord, thy watchmen shall lift up their voice; with the voice together shall they sing; for they shall see eye to eye, when the Lord shall bring again Zion. Break forth into joy, sing together,

23. René Girard, *I See Satan Fall Like Lightning*, trans. James G. Williams (Maryknoll, NY: Orbis, 2001), 85.
24. Girard, *I See Satan*, 85.
25. Mosiah 15:21.
26. Mosiah 15:28.

ye waste places of Jerusalem; for the Lord hath comforted his people, he hath redeemed Jerusalem. The Lord hath made bare his holy arm in the eyes of *all* the nations; and *all* the ends of the earth shall see the salvation of our God.[27]

The watchmen in this passage are not priests or kings. Those who will see eye to eye with the Lord are the prophets who declare his, not King Noah's, word.

The Book of Mormon is continuous with the Bible (both testaments) in chronicling the human resistance to the divine message delivered through the prophets. During a period of particular wickedness, Samuel notes that the Nephites reject the prophets (and their rejection of Samuel himself is the parade example):

Wo unto this people, because of this time which has arrived, that ye do cast out the prophets, and do mock them, and cast stones at them, and do slay them, and do all manner of iniquity unto them, even as they did of old time. And now when ye talk, ye say: If our days had been in the days of our fathers of old, we would not have slain the prophets; we would not have stoned them, and cast them out. Behold ye are worse than they; for as the Lord liveth, if a prophet come among you and declareth unto you the word of the Lord, which testifieth of your sins and iniquities, ye are angry with him, and cast him out and seek all manner of ways to destroy him; yea, you will say that he is a false prophet, and that he is a sinner, and of the devil, because he testifieth that your deeds are evil. But behold, if a man shall come among you and shall say: Do this, and there is no iniquity; do that and ye shall not suffer; yea, he will say: Walk after the pride of your own hearts; yea, walk after the pride of your eyes, and do whatsoever your heart desireth—and if a man shall come among you and say this, ye will receive him, and say that he is a prophet. Yea, ye will lift him up, and ye will give unto him of your substance.[28]

---

27. Mosiah 15:29–31.
28. Helaman 13:24–28. This Samuel is also known as Samuel the Lamanite, not to confuse him with the biblical prophet Samuel.

Samuel the Lamanite knows well that the prophets have always been scapegoats for the wicked, for the crowd, for the Nephite mob attempted to capture and kill him also. The Nephites of his day had reveled in wickedness, but he predicted that "your days of probation are past" because human desire outstrips the means for satisfying that desire: "ye have sought for happiness in doing iniquity, which thing is contrary to the nature of that righteousness which is in our great and Eternal Head."[29] The Nephites react to Samuel the same way the mob has always reacted to the prophets: by attempting to capture and kill him.[30]

When Christ speaks to the Nephites prior to his appearance, one of the main transgressions cited for the destruction of specific cities is to account for the blood of the prophets and saints shed by those cities, and this process is predicted as early as Nephi's record.[31] The Lehite colony begins from similar actions, as the Jews had rejected the prophets and had attempted to kill Lehi just as they had "the prophets of old," putting Lehi (and eventually Nephi) on a continuum with the biblical prophets.[32] Nephi, in confrontation with his brothers, continues that genealogy from Old Testament prophets to his own time. Just as the Jews in Jerusalem attempted to kill the prophets, Laman and Lemuel attempted to kill Lehi, and they extend that action into the very same narrative by attempting to kill Nephi again.[33] An earlier narrative dramatizes the same trajectory as Lehi's sons return to Jerusalem to retrieve Ishmael and his family; the Jews "have rejected the prophets, and Jeremiah they have cast into prison. And they have sought to take

---

29. Helaman 13:38.
30. Helaman 16:6.
31. 3 Nephi 9:5, 7, 8, 9, 11; 2 Nephi 26:3. By the way, all that death and destruction that the voice from heaven takes credit for is another instance of divine violence specifically assigned to the resurrected Christ by the risen Christ and needs to be accounted for by any commentator who asserts the Book of Mormon ultimately is a pacifist composition and the divinity most pacifist of all.
32. 1 Nephi 3:18; 1:20.
33. 1 Nephi 17:44, 48.

away the life of my father" and driven the family into exile.[34] The parallel is extended to Nephi, for the same words are used a few verses later: Laman and Lemuel were angry with Nephi and "they sought to take away my life."[35] In Third Nephi, a political connection to the killing and scapegoating of prophets is made: the same people who destroyed the government are also those who persecuted the prophets.[36] Destruction of political order is parallel to and moves in concert with murder of the prophets. It is this annihilation of the political process and devolution into the tribes that is, in fact, overshadowed by the people's regret over the killing of the prophets at the destruction that precedes the coming of Christ.[37] This tight connection between Nephite history and the coming of Christ sheds new light on the Sermon at the Temple, where Christ repeats much of the New Testament Sermon on the Mount (parallel to Matthew's version of that sermon); there, Jesus blesses those who will be persecuted and "great shall be your reward in heaven; for so persecuted they the prophets who were before you."[38] Here the ordinary persecutions experienced by the common believer are placed in that same lineage that connects the murder of all the prophets since the world began, for the mere Christian comprises his seed as much as the prophets do.

The Jaredite experience is analogous to Nephite history. Alma$_2$, speaking to his son Helaman, notes of the Jaredite records that the oaths of the wicked should be kept secret; these people too were destroyed because they murdered the prophets.[39] Moroni's summary of the Jaredite record confirms Alma$_2$'s claim, for the prophets were persecuted by the people (but protected by King

34. 1 Nephi 7:14.
35. 1 Nephi 7:16.
36. 3 Nephi 7:6, 10, 14.
37. 3 Nephi 8:25.
38. 3 Nephi 12:12.
39. Alma 37:30.

Shule) at one point.[40] Later, the Jaredites attempt to kill Ether for pronouncing judgment against them.[41] Human nature and human culture are consistent in this regard, so the persecution of God's messengers is also consistent throughout history.

The other reliability in human nature is the persecution complex. Alma$_1$ is the sole Noachide priest who believes Abinadi. He must flee for his own life after attempting to save the prophet's life. Alma$_1$ preaches in private, gathering a persecuted and exiled cluster of people to hear the word of God. Alma$_1$ resumes right where Abinadi left off as he preaches to his community in exile. He "began to teach the words of Abinadi—Yea, concerning that which was to come, and also concerning the resurrection of the dead, and the redemption of the people, which was to be brought to pass through the power, and sufferings, and death of Christ, and his resurrection and ascension into heaven."[42] Here for Alma$_1$, the founding murder of Abinadi doesn't result in a community called after Cain's son Enoch, named Babel or Babylon, Rome or Ninevah, where all the arts of oppression and violence, taxation and social stratification, are practiced and honed. Instead it is a blessed community, a Benedictine society, where Alma$_1$ teaches them, and they learn, that "there should be no contention one with another, but that they should look forward with one eye, having one faith and one baptism, having their hearts knit together in unity and in love one towards another."[43] They shared their material goods with each other and thus learned the nature of divine love as a community rather than as isolated individuals outside of social bonds living a solitary, poor, nasty, brutish, and short existence.

Having fled the lynching crowd in Noah's court, Alma$_1$ becomes not the founder of a City of Man, full of violence and

---

40. Ether 7:23–25.
41. Ether 13:22.
42. Mosiah 18:1–2.
43. Mosiah 18:21–22.

corruption,[44] but a City of God, that is, until the remnants of King Noah's city and King Noah's court (fleeing from their Lamanite attackers) stumble upon the exiles, impose their form of the city of man, and subjugate them. They once again cycle through the pattern Cain initiated. That status recurs, repeating the first such resettlement in the wilderness, because Noah's spies "discovered a movement among the people,"[45] and with their secret now known to the king, the Alma₁ group must flee farther into exile into the wilderness.[46]

When the narrative returns to the Alma₁ group, citing the model of evil kingship demonstrated by Noah, Alma₁ refuses that office.[47] The Lamanites, guided by the remainder of King Noah's priests, stumble across the Alma₁ group and oppress them until they're forced to flee farther into the wilderness, enacting an exodus to Zarahemla.[48] This group knows well what it is to be exiled. Exile is another form of violence carried out against scapegoats.

As I have previously noted, Girard compares two stories of exile, one from the Bible (Joseph's being cast in a pit then being sold into Egypt by his brothers) and one from Greek mythology (Oedipus, in Sophocles's drama). The crowd in each case gathers to select a victim. Joseph's brothers envy their father's favoritism toward their younger brother, triggering a mimetic crisis. Girard notes that "In the parallel beginnings we recognize what we expected to find, a mimetic crisis and single victim mechanism. In both instances a community gathers unanimously against one of its members and violently expels him."[49] Initially, both main characters are expelled to a new land—Joseph to Egypt and Oedipus out of Thebes (twice) after his birth parents attempt to expose

---

44. Genesis 6:11–13.
45. Mosiah 18:32.
46. Mosiah 18:34.
47. Mosiah 23.
48. Mosiah 24:16–25.
49. Girard, *I See Satan*, 107.

him in the wilderness and after his true origins are revealed. Both solve riddles (enacted in dreams in Joseph's case, the Sphinx's riddle in Oedipus's case) to pave a road toward political advancement. "Because of their initial expulsions, Oedipus and Joseph both have to become foreigners and are thus always a little suspect in the principal place where they perform their exploits."[50] The broad similarities between the biblical and Greek stories may mask a crucial difference, "an impassable gulf between the biblical story and the myth."[51] In the Greek story, the violent expulsion and cruel collective act is endorsed and justified, placing blame on the victim, who even endorses their own condemnation. In the Bible, Joseph is innocent at every instance of collective violence: his brothers are wrong to imprison and sell him into exile, Potiphar's wife is lying about her accusation.[52] Oedipus is also accused of incest and expelled again from his new/old home community.

Oedipus's tragedy ends with his expulsion from Thebes after he gouges his own eyes out. The Bible doesn't endorse such collective violence. Joseph the exile initiates reconciliation with his brothers. "It is only this pardon, this forgiveness, that is capable of stopping once and for all the spiral of reprisals."[53] This refusal to blame the victim and the refusal of the victim to accept that blame is what makes mythology so dramatically different from the Bible, according to Girard. "The biblical story condemns the general tendency of myths to justify collective violence, which is part and parcel of the accusatory, vindictive nature of foundational myths."[54]

Exiled once by King Noah, the Alma$_1$ group had already formed at the waters of Mormon a harmonious, compassionate

---

50. Girard, *I See Satan*, 108.
51. Girard, *I See Satan*, 108.
52. Girard, *I See Satan*, 109.
53. Girard, *I See Satan*, 111.
54. Girard, *I See Satan*, 112–13.

community absent all military and economic violence. Expelled again as Noah makes military preparations against this peaceful group, they trek to Helam. Discovered by the priests of Noah and the Lamanites, they are subjected to slavery. Their response was not to fashion swords or arrows. Instead, they prayed for deliverance, which the Lord provided on the divine timetable. A third exile and another exodus reunite them with the larger Nephite civilization at Zarahemla.

This group presents a Book of Mormon model to demonstrate one persistent response to collective violence. This assemblage of outcasts at the waters of Mormon forms a covenant community. Alma invites these believers to enter the waters of baptism, bear each others' burdens, and become members of God's kingdom, saying, "if this be the desire of your hearts, what have you against being baptized in the name of the Lord, as a witness before him that ye have entered into a covenant with him, that ye will serve him and keep his commandments, that he may pour out his Spirit more abundantly upon you?" Alma$_1$ (or at least Mormon's summary) uses the keyword here: covenant. Bruce Chilton notes that James Williams applies Girard's concepts to the Bible, but Williams adds an additional ingredient. He suggests that in entering into a covenant with God and each other, the Bible articulates the injection of a dramatically profound new element: "the differentiating power of the covenant, including its sacrificial instruments, is for Williams salvific."[55] The message shared by the prophets and embraced by the hearers lifts the prophetic proclamation above any violent content and becomes a means of salvation, according to Chilton. We see that happening to the community at the waters of Mormon.

A second group yet needs to be compared to the Alma$_1$ community regarding their comparable storyline. After King Noah

---

55. Bruce Chilton, "René Girard, James Williams, and the Genesis of Violence," *Bulletin for Biblical Research* 3 (1993): 24.

is killed and his son Limhi is appointed king, the Zeniffites are attacked by the Lamanites. Like the Alma$_1$ group, they too are enslaved by the Lamanites, but their response is a military venture to free themselves by force of arms.[56] After their initial defeat, the lamentation of widows and children for lost fathers moves the Limhites to pursue the same course, with the same result, and then a third time with the same outcome.[57] Having learned a harsh lesson from three military defeats, they try a different approach: "And they did humble themselves even in the depths of humility; and they did cry mightily to God; yea, even all the day long did they cry unto their God that he would deliver them out of their afflictions. And now the Lord was slow to hear their cry because of their iniquities; nevertheless the Lord did hear their cries, and began to soften the hearts of the Lamanites that they began to ease their burdens; yet the Lord did not see fit to deliver them out of bondage."[58] Eventually, like the Alma$_1$ group, the Limhi group changes tactics and makes a stealthy escape by night,[59] also making their way back to the main body of Nephites at Zarahemla.

Repetition is such a consistent feature in Hebraic narrative that when similar events are repeated, that means we readers are meant to compare the analogous stories. In this case, both Zeniffite groups are in bondage and make exoduses back to their ancestral homeland before the Zeniff project began—back to Zarahemla. The salient comparison for this study is the difference between the Alma$_1$ group and the Limhi group. When the Alma$_1$ group is conquered and enslaved by the Lamanites and former priests of Noah, they submit to their oppressors. Sandor Goodhart notes of repeated elements in the Joseph story in the Bible that, yes, "In the sense that all the Hebraic biblical narrative is structured

---

56. Mosiah 21:7–8.
57. Mosiah 21:11–12.
58. Mosiah 21:14–15.
59. Mosiah 22:3–16.

as a replaying of the same drama,"[60] history repeats itself. Such an observation ought not to be confined only to narrative in the Hebrew Bible, but to "All traditional Jewish writing . . . which is why, in a sense, we can begin anywhere."[61] So, echoing the Israelites in Egypt, the people now led by Alma₁ "cry mightily to God,"[62] as do the children of Israel in Egypt and the Limhites in the land of Nephi, and the Lord delivered each group out of bondage. The Book of Mormon text broaches no criticism of the people of Alma₁ for their pacifist approach. Likewise, the text offers no censure that the Limhites made the opposite decision to go to battle three times to try to obtain their freedom from the Lamanites.

We can draw a lesson from Mormon, the narrator of these two stories, about the different policies narrated: no universal rule applies to such concrete circumstances in the mangle and incoherence of life while we are still in the process. The Alma₁ group made an entirely valid decision (perhaps pragmatically determined, for their population then consisted of only 450 people)[63] for the circumstance they were in, while the Lamanites had armies of unnumbered strength to send after either escaping group.[64] But the Limhite decision for warfare is also a legitimate decision moved by the emotion resulting from previous losses to the Lamanites.[65] Neither alternative is condemned nor approved by the Lord, Mormon, or the text. Deriving rules of moral conduct and of human behavior are tenuous when the data cited go to particular events and personalities. Even when the events are sufficiently similar to bear comparison, the differences may be more important than the parallels.

---

60. Sandor Goodhart, "'I Am Joseph': René Girard and the Prophetic Law," In *Violence and Truth: On the Works of René Girard*, edited by Paul Dumouchel (Stanford: Stanford University Press, 1988), 71.

61. Goodhart, "I," 71.

62. Mosiah 24:10 and 21:14.

63. Mosiah 18:35.

64. Mosiah 22:15.

65. Mosiah 21:11.

Chapter Thirteen

The Anti-Nephi-Lehies
and Pacifism

The Anti-Nephi-Lehies, also known as the people of Ammon, were a Book of Mormon people—originally Lamanitish—converted to the true religion by the sons of Mosiah. Once they became righteous and friendly to the Nephites, "the curse of God did no more follow them," not because of any change in skin color, but a change in cultural habitus.[1] These people became pacifists, one acceptable model of how believers might fulfill their covenant with God when faced with collective violence. As a group they refuse to take up arms. Reading about this group should tell us a great deal about the text's orientation toward violence and about the text's readers. After the king (Lamoni's father) was converted, the bulk of the Lamanites rebel against him. This king turns the office over to his pacifist son, renamed Anti-Nephi-Lehi, and dies. None of these converts will take up arms, even to defend themselves. Having been forgiven of their many murders in the previous lives as Lamanites, this group engages in a full range of action, burying their swords deep in the earth as both a symbolic and literal renunciation of violence, even in self-defense.[2]

---

1. The name "Anti-Nephi-Lehies" is one they gave themselves when they changed their ideological allegiance "and were no more called Lamanites." Alma 23:17–18.
2. Alma 24:19.

The sons of Mosiah, who were the agents of conversion for the people of Ammon, had themselves gone through a conversion process. On a similar note, Joseph's brothers, before they went down into Egypt to save their families' lives, had been willing to sacrifice their own brother's life for their own interests. But after selling Joseph into slavery, going through an interim adulting process, and through their encounter with a yet-disguised Joseph, they come to a higher realization: "The brothers have passed from the desire to sacrifice others to a willingness to offer themselves for the other. In Girard's view, this change is the essence of Christian conversion."[3] The same statement could be made about the sons of Mosiah and Alma$_2$. Of his life before he and the sons of Mosiah experienced their conversion, Alma$_2$ says that "I had murdered many of his children, or rather led them away into destruction."[4] These royal sons begin preaching the word and being much persecuted for it, all while "zealously striving to repair all the injuries which they had done to the church."[5] The people of Ammon had a model of change before their eyes in those who had published good tidings of great joy to them despite the fact that many Nephites proposed further sacrifice of the recalcitrant Lamanites by killing them rather than preaching to them.[6]

Eugene England points to the story of the Anti-Nephi-Lehies as "the only example I can find anywhere of a group actually practicing Girard's implied unique solution to imitative violence—and with the predicted results."[7] For England, this narrative complements Girard's analysis of the biblical story of Joseph and his

3. Mack C. Stirling, "Violence in the Scriptures: Mormonism and the Cultural Theory of René Girard," *Dialogue: A Journal of Mormon Thought* 43, no. 1 (Spring 2010): 74.

4. Alma 36:14.

5. Mosiah 27:32, 35.

6. Alma 26:23–25.

7. Eugene England, "Why Nephi Killed Laban: Reflections on the Truth of the Book of Mormon," *Dialogue: A Journal of Mormon Thought* 22, no. 3 (Fall 1989): 48.

brothers, where Judah and Joseph collapse into repentance and forgiveness rather than retribution and violence as they work out the appropriate response to the original violence Joseph's brothers initiated against him. Similarly, "the dedication of the people of Anti-Nephi-Lehi stands in symmetrical opposition to the original deeds of collective violence by Laman and Lemuel and their descendants, which produced the ongoing spiral of reciprocal scapegoating central to the Book of Mormon narrative."[8] When the Lamanites attack the Anti-Nephi-Lehies and meet no resistance, more Lamanites are converted to the pacifist tradition than the number of Anti-Nephi-Lehies who are killed.

Technically, this action doesn't halt the cycle of violence. The Nephites instead shoulder the burden of violence to protect the Anti-Nephi-Lehies from Lamanite aggression: "we will set our armies between the land Jershon and the land Nephi, that we may protect our brethren in the land Jershon; and this we do for our brethren, on account of their fear to take up arms against their brethren lest they should commit sin."[9] The people of Ammon were reborn from a culture of violence. After accepting the gospel, they made a covenant of peace but had to accept Nephite protection to maintain their commitment to nonviolence.[10] But such a move is a mere outsourcing of the violence rather than a full renunciation.

The people of Ammon aren't totally innocent of violence; they were still complicit in the killing of others. They personally renounced violence but let their sons participate (note that their position isn't a principled opposition to all violence, just a commitment to fulfill the covenant they made no longer to be direct agents of bloodshed).[11] They also depended on the Nephites to protect

---

8. England, "Why Nephi Killed Laban," 49.
9. Alma 27:23.
10. Stirling, "Violence," 84–85.
11. Alma 56:3–8.

them so they could remain pacifists. This situation is similar to World War II, "the good war" as it is often called. Violence was necessary to repel fascist aggression. The results of not standing up to violence in the case of World War II would have been even greater violence and oppression from the Axis powers.

Additionally, England quotes two verses from the Book of Mormon Anti-Nephi-Lehi vignette without noting or realizing that the vocabulary used in the scripture undermines his interpretation of the Anti-Nephi-Lehi event, as it describes the pacifist refusal to defend themselves as a *sacrifice*. Ammon, rejoicing with his brothers regarding their bountiful harvest resulting from their missionary endeavors, exclaims his view of the people of Ammon's refusal to take up arms:

> For behold, they had rather *sacrifice their lives* than even to take the life of their enemy; and they have buried their weapons of war deep in the earth, because of their love towards their brethren. And now behold I say unto you, has there been so great love in all the land? Behold, I say unto you, Nay, there has not, even among the Nephites. For behold, they would take up arms against their brethren; they would not suffer themselves to be slain. But behold how many of these have laid down their lives; and we know that they have gone to their God, because of their love and of their hatred to sin.[12]

England cites this passage[13] but doesn't seem to recognize that Mormon, attributing the word *sacrifice* to the people of Ammon, describes their actions as a sacrifice, thus categorizing their peaceful response to violence as falling in the ambit of "sacrifice." Ammon and Mormon (or perhaps Joseph Smith as trans-

---

12. Alma 26:32–34. That final phrase of the excerpt may equate killing in self-defense with sinning, but that is not a necessary conclusion.

13. Eugene England, "Can Nations Love Their Enemies? An L.D.S. Theology of Peace," In *Dialogues with Myself: Personal Essays on Mormon Experience*. Eugene England, 135–52 (Midvale, UT: Orion, 1984), 136. England mistakenly attributes this passage to Alma 25:32–33. I have quoted one more verse than England does.

lator) may still be caught up in sacrificial and victimage diction and concepts in describing the people of Ammon's faithfulness, but this passage undermines England's notion that the God of the Bible and Book of Mormon has nothing to do with sacrifice. This account is the premier example of that pacific refusal of sacrifice even in self-defense.

One would think that if Ammon or Mormon thought a material moral distinction between Anti-Nephi-Lehi complete pacifism and Nephite willingness to take up arms in self-defense existed, this passage would have been the perfect place to articulate that distinction. Arguments from silence are particularly weak persuasive appeals, but both Mormon and Ammon are silent about such moral distinctions. England reads it into the text rather than reading it out of the scriptural incident.

England also commended Neville Chamberlain's appeasement policy, buying the Allies time to arm and prepare for war.[14] This seems dubious historical analysis to me. Surely Hitler would not have been so bold if the democracies of the West had confronted his imperialistic ambitions earlier. And, as Scott Cowdell notes, Girard isn't the uncompromising pacifist one might gather from England's appropriation of his ideas. Girard has suggested that World War II might have been avoided if France had only invaded the Rhineland in 1936 (a preemptive first strike can hardly be called pacifist) and that the war on terror could be called a just war. "Indeed, he argues that pacifism can be the mirror double of oppression, allowing it to flourish."[15] This position argues for the use of military force to defend victims of aggression, which "represents a wholly new and laudable historical development because

14. Eugene England, "My View: Was Chamberlain Right?" *Deseret News* (Sept. 28, 1988), https://www.deseret.com/1988/9/29/18779600/my-view-was-chamberlain-right.

15. Scott Cowdell, *René Girard and Secular Modernity* (Notre Dame, IN: University of Notre Dame Press, 2013), 177.

it is not about mimetic rivalry. This fighting for peace but without the mimetically escalating personal hatred that marks the wars that become crusades."[16] "Fighting for peace," although Cowdell's summary of Girard's position, sounds like an odd expression to describe a pacifist position.

It is too easy for political realists to dismiss pacifists as naïve, but England's biography and writings make the charge easy to demonstrate. I don't want to spend much space on England's guilelessness in his personal life (relationships of antagonism with church authorities, struggles with educational bureaucracies, publishing ventures) in order to avoid *ad hominem* positions. But some reference to the biography is historical context needed to explain how the politics and the personal are so tightly bound together, much as the cushioned cork coated with rubber comprises the pill at the center of a baseball. England's political pacifism is the cork-core of his personal, ethical nonviolence.

A consistent theme in Terryl Givens's biography of Eugene England is his naïveté in professional relationships with church leaders, educational administrators, and colleagues. England would publish provocative pieces on theological, historical, and social and political issues and then be surprised by the strong negative reaction he provoked, especially among church leaders, some of whom (Marion D. Hanks and Neal A. Maxwell) he counted as personal friends. Givens notes England's "tone deafness" to how his classroom teaching was perceived by class members and the church leaders who received complaints from those attending the classes,[17] was born not out of ill will on England's part but in an attempt to engage and provoke people to think and engage in dialogue. Kristine Haglund, England's other biographer,

---

16. Cowdell, *Secular Modernity*, 177–78.
17. Terryl Givens, *Stretching the Heavens: The Life of Eugene England and the Crisis of Modern Mormonism* (Chapel Hill, NC: University of North Carolina Press, 2021), 82. See the same term, "tone-deafness," used on page 88.

also comments on his naïveté: "In retrospect, and in the context of the authority structure of the church as it developed in the late twentieth century, England's expectation that church authorities would appreciate his efforts may seem either foolishly optimistic or shockingly naïve."[18] As Givens notes regarding the exclusion of black men from holding the priesthood, "England not only engaged this most controversial of issues at the editorial level; he also chimed in as a writer. His general strategy for dealing with difference might have been dialogue, but his intention was provocation, not common ground." Givens continues to assess England's tin ear when it came to such provocation, for in a similar difference of position a generation earlier, Lowell Bennion disagreed with church leaders, but privately. "England, in contrast, went public, and he hit hard. In a church that had experienced decades of persecution and misrepresentation, England was openly showing disloyalty; at least that was how his rhetoric struck church leaders."[19] England saw himself as a loyal church member, even an apologist for the church, a provocateur rather than a dissident.[20]

This is not to criticize England for always assuming the best of other people. And including in that "bestness" was the commitment to shared embrace of dialogue even between people who disagreed about fundamentals. When that simple, naïvely positive view of people, all people, collides with the realities of how powerful people such as Hitler, Stalin, Pol Pot, and the like exercise authority, then it is time to reassess an unquestioned and universal commitment to pacifism. In 1977, the year England was hired at BYU (likely before he discovered Girard), he wrote an article about Moroni and the war chapters in the Book of Mormon. In his conclusion he wrote a summary that could well be the thesis of

---

18. Kristine L. Haglund, *Eugene England: A Mormon Liberal* (Urbana, IL: University of Illinois Press, 2021), 57.
19. Givens, *Stretching*, 87.
20. Givens, *Stretching*, 117.

this book, in which I criticize England: the lessons to be learned from these "fighting prophets and peace-loving captains" is that "1. *War most often comes to a people because of their unrighteousness and internal dissensions. 2. No matter how it comes, there is no single morally right response to the threat of violence.*"[21] This seems a hard-headed concession to the nature and disposition of almost all men to engage in violence and create scapegoats in order to advance their own perceived interests, victims be damned. This piece shows England evolving toward pacifism but not carrying that banner yet.

In his essay "Can Nations Love Their Enemies?" England notes that the Book of Mormon contains seemingly contradictory impulses: the Anti-Nephi-Lehi model of renouncing violence altogether, even at the cost of one's own life, and the model of Mormon, a military leader who engaged in a lifetime of war. England invokes Hugh Nibley's distinction that the pacifist example illustrates a general rule and the violence of war a specific exception—not regarding the warring passages as a contradiction, but, invoking Doctrine and Covenants 98, an instance of "a distinction between what is justified and what is *best.*"[22] The best response is exemplified by "the radical example of perfect pacifism of the people of Ammon in the Book of Mormon."[23] Note that this conclusion of bestness is an inference from the Anti-Nephi-Lehi narrative, not one the scripture itself makes.

England then applies this *best* approach to his contemporary circumstances, the major frame of which was the Cold War. England's "Fasting and Food, Not Weapons" was published in 1985, a time the Soviet Union still existed. England expresses a lot

21. Eugene England, "Moroni and His Captains: Men of Peace in a Time of War," *Ensign* 7, no. 8 (Aug. 1977): available at http://churchofjesuschrist.org/study/ensign/1977/09/Moroni-and-his-captains-men-of-peace-in-a-time-of-war.
22. England, "Can Nations," 139.
23. England, "Can Nations," 142.

of confidence in what he calls "Russia" in this essay. Russia and China fear the U.S. will drop nuclear bombs on them. He traces this line of thinking back to My Lai. Considering the crooked timber of history, England is excessively simplistic when he argues that "there is a straight line from the 1969 My Lai massacre" to the Pol Pot regime, and "that kind of line goes from the blitz of London in 1940" to the carpet bombing of Berlin and related decimations of Dresden and Coventry. That "straight" line bends chronologically back to include Pearl Harbor and Hiroshima.[24] England's proposed solution to this fear the Chinese and Russians justifiably have of nuclear warfare is for the U.S. and Russia to "each give half their arms budget to meet the Third World's basic needs."[25] The fallback solution would be for the U.S. to do so unilaterally in the absence of Russia's cooperation. England then invokes guilt and spiritual manipulation as a suitable motivating factor: "All right, if we're unwilling to risk unilateral action because we really don't believe Christ and the modern prophets that loving our enemies would bring response, then let me suggest, as my first serious proposal, a perfectly safe move."[26] We could start, he says, by each superpower taking five percent of their defense budget to fund student and citizen exchanges between the two nations, allowing Russians and Americans to get to know each other personally.

That best approach, England asserts, would conform to LDS theology. He calls it "effective pacifism" that might even include "unilateral disarmament *if* accompanied by massive efforts to extend intelligent, creative, tough-minded but loving help to other nations, particularly our chief 'enemy' the Soviet Union."[27] England doesn't underestimate the difficulty of such outreach, for

---

24. Eugene England, "Fasting and Food, Not Weapons: A Mormon Response to Conflict," *BYU Studies* 25, no. 1 (Winter 1985): 13.
25. England, "Fasting," 9.
26. England, "Fasting," 12.
27. England, "Can Nations," 148.

it would require "risk, imaginative effort to overcome suspicion, hard-headed negotiation and calling to repentance at the right moment—followed by an increase of mercy and generosity."[28] That course would take much faith, and not just in God but also in Stalin/Putin types. It is safe to say that England was not much acquainted with human nature, nor the modern nation state even in its less aggressive version as representative government, and certainly not in its totalitarian instantiation.

The Nephites who protected the people of Ammon and made possible their pacifism were doing precisely what England frequently discusses as just-war violence: engaging in limited military action to protect the victims of aggression, much as the Ukrainians, assisted and supported by the Western democracies, resisted the brutal and unprovoked invasion by Russia in 2022. Paper tigers look so much more formidable, as though they are real tigers, if a line of defense isn't demarcated to show the efficacy of their violent threats and actions is illusory and counterproductive.

England refuses to read history in such a way as to give the slightest credit for successes in preventing hot wars with cold war tactics. "The recent, poignantly hopeful developments in Eastern Europe were brought about, I believe, not through President Reagan's military build-ups and threats, but by God's blessings on non-violent efforts by many people."[29] The possibility England doesn't consider is that God's blessings were obtained *through* the military buildup that bankrupted the Soviet Union and induced Gorbachev to cry uncle. England is entitled to his own interpretation of history. It is crucial to point out that this reading comes trailing clouds of ideology and assumptions about human nature and politics. Duane Boyce notes that elements of similarity exist between the people of Ammon and a pacifist orientation: the peo-

---

28. England, "Can Nations," 150.
29. Eugene England, "Healing and Making Peace—In the World and the Church," *Sunstone* 15, no. 6 (Dec. 1991): 38.

ple of Ammon sorrowed for their previous murders, they buried their weapons of warfare, they covenanted to never kill again, they died rather than violate that covenant, and they loved their enemies who killed them.[30] But this isn't enough to make them pacifists. They didn't have principled opposition to all warfare. They didn't object to Nephites engaging in war on their behalf, they didn't articulate a pacifist reason for refusing to engage in fighting, they provided material support to the Nephites protecting them, and they didn't object to their sons (who were too young to enter the covenant to surrender their weapons) volunteering to fight.[31] For the people of Ammon, their refusal to engage in violence was particular and contingent to their own condition, not some universal rule.

Boyce notes that, similar to Girard, England waffles on the notion that pacifism is a universal principle incumbent on any gospel believer. England endorsed the action of Western democracies to respond with violence to the threats from Germany, Japan, and Italy during WWII. He conceded that "absolute non-violence" is not necessarily the requirement imposed by revealed scripture. He also noted that he personally would respond with violence to protect his family. At the same time, Boyce notes seven corollaries England articulated, stating the categorical rejection of violence required of the Christian believer. "Overall, these many assertions seem to insist that pacifism—the rejection of all violence—is the only proper Christian perspective, but here and there England does carve out an exception or two."[32] England similarly reads the story of the people of Ammon's renunciation of all violence as a universal pacifist principle, and Boyce punctures such a reading,

---

30. Duane Boyce, "Were the Ammonites Pacifists?" *Journal of Book of Mormon and Other Restoration Scripture* 18, no. 1 (2009): 41.
31. Boyce, "Were the Ammonites Pacificists?" 42–43.
32. Duane Boyce, *Even Unto Bloodshed: An LDS Perspective on War* (Salt Lake City, UT: Kofford Books, 2015), 175–76.

taking up narratives about Nephi's killing of Laban, the Anti-Ne-phi-Lehies burying their weapons, and the actions of military leader Moroni₁[33] to point out counterexamples that undermine England's view.[34] "With an ordinary, though careful, reading of the text, it seems impossible to draw a pacifist message from the Book of Mormon."[35] I agree with Boyce's analysis.

England himself notes that the record of the Book of Mormon on warfare and violence is inconsistent, providing the "most impressive example of rigorous group pacifism" available in the people of Ammon and then in a few decades sending their sons off to battle with a religious leader at their head, providing paradigms of bravery and fidelity in generals who lead the people into battle and soldiers who follow their orders.[36] Citing Hugh Nibley, England finds one way through this contradiction by noting that the proscription on violence and war is the general principle God propounds in the Book of Mormon while the endorsement of violence is the specific exception to that general rule. But universal principles can't abide so many exceptions and still be comprehensive;[37] they then become mere guidelines. Yet England notes that the people of Ammon seem like an exception because theirs is the only case of such firm and steadfast refusal to resort to violence, even in self-defense.

England struggles to reconcile the endorsements of violence and the renunciation of warfare and killing in the Book of Mormon. He wants to force the scripture to conform to Girardian prescriptions (policies that are very modern in being putatively

33. Moroni₁ is the military leader who enters Book of Mormon narrative at Alma 43. Latter-day Saints sometimes call him General Moroni and sometimes demote him to Captain Moroni (which is the title given him in the scripture). Moroni₂ is the son of Mormon and the last Nephite recordkeeper.

34. Eugene England, "Hugh Nibley as Cassandra," *BYU Studies Quarterly* 30, no. 4 (1990): 112–13; Boyce, *Even Unto Bloodshed*, 109–18, 126–29.

35. Boyce, *Even Unto Bloodshed*, 109.

36. England, "Can Nations," 135–36.

37. England, "Can Nations," 136.

universally applicable), but the text seems recalcitrant. In another context, England notes that each of us must go through some Abrahamic test in which the patriarch is required "to give up his beloved son *and* his most cherished moral beliefs in order to know God."[38] To make the Book of Mormon—which England believed deeply to be both historical and divine—fit Girard's theories—which England also believes to be anthropologically universal and divinely derived—seems to me to be England's great Abrahamic trial. I don't think this task can be performed the way England goes about it. England would have to surrender his global commitment on pacifism in the Book of Mormon or on the Girardian principle; he can't have it both ways.

Regarding the more nuanced position of the Book of Mormon on warfare and pacifism, the scripture does specifically involve Deity in military activities. The standard Girardian response would be to divide the biblical prophets, the biblical chroniclers, and the Gospel writers into those who understood the divine commitment to pacifistic actions and intentions and those who misunderstood the divine commitment to peace and fell back into the sacrificial understandings of their cultures. But the Book of Mormon has three main authors: Nephi$_1$, Mormon, and Moroni$_2$—all three were soldiers defending their people with violence when required.[39] Book of Mormon composers, unlike the various Gospel writers when they record the same New Testament incident treating violence but varying in detail, can't be separated into ones with a fuller understanding of the biblical principles of nonviolence and anti-mimeticism and those more influenced by culture than by pacifist revelation. When the Lamanites, for example, destroy Ammonihah and kidnap many of its people, Zoram (the

38. England, "On Finding Truth and God," in *Why the Church Is As True As the Gospel: Personal Essays on Mormon Experience* (Salt Lake City, UT: Bookcraft, 1986), 123.
39. 2 Nephi 5:14; Mormon 2:1–3; Mormon 5:1; Mormon 6:11–12.

Nephite chief captain) inquires of Alma₂ (the high priest) who then inquires of the Lord what military strategy to use, and the Lord straightforwardly delivers the place and tactic for victory.[40] This is just one example of the narrator's endorsement of certain forms of violence in self-defense, with military victory delivered through direct revelation from God. Mormon praises Moroni₁ for accepting the burden of self-defense because the Lamanites wanted to impose hegemony over the Nephites while "the only desire of the Nephites [was] to preserve their lands, and their liberty, and their church."[41] Divine authority is even drafted to support this idea:

> [F]or the Lord had said unto them, and also unto their fathers, that: Inasmuch as ye are not guilty of the first offense, neither the second, ye shall not suffer yourselves to be slain by the hands of your enemies. And again, *the Lord has said that: Ye shall defend your families even unto bloodshed.* Therefore for this cause were the Nephites contending with the Lamanites, to defend themselves, and their families, and their lands, their country, and their rights, and their religion.[42]

When the text speaks attributing a position to God, even committed pacifist readers such as England ought not to nullify the assertion without substantial reason and textual evidence.

Even in Alma 24 where the Anti-Nephi-Lehies take their vow of pacifism, the story subtly undermines the possibility that the text is endorsing this commitment as a universal principle. Instead, the vow abjuring violence is distanced in the text as one group's religious and ethical performance. Verse 6 in chapter 24 begins the address by Anti-Nephi-Lehi, the new king of the people of Ammon. In the middle of that speech the king raises the pacifist possibility. After the group has repented and been forgiven for

---

40. Alma 16:6.
41. Alma 43:29–30.
42. Alma 43:46–47.

their murders, the king asserts they must not engage in violence again:

> [S]ince God hath taken away our stains, and our swords have become bright, then let us stain our swords no more with the blood of our brethren. Behold, I say unto you, Nay, let us retain our swords that they be not stained with the blood of our brethren; for perhaps, if we should stain our swords again they can no more be washed bright through the blood of the Son of our great God, which shall be shed for the atonement of our sins.[43]

We modern readers would view this as a dubious theology that the atonement of Christ can be applied to the sin of a perpetrator's murder just once, even when qualified by a *perhaps* (leaving aside the question of whether self-defense or killing in warfare equals murder), just as questionable as is Hamlet's theological assertion that killing his uncle/stepfather/usurper king while the latter is praying would send the stepfather to heaven (Act 3, scene 3). The Atonement is not a one-time redemption, a singularity in its application, but covers the sinner through repetitions of the same sin category. King Anti-Nephi-Lehi ends the address in verse 16. Immediately after the quote, Mormon, the narrator, distances himself from the sentiments expressed in it after summarizing the group's action of burying their swords: "this they did, *it being in their view* a testimony to God, and also to men, that they never would use weapons again for the shedding of man's blood; and *this they did*, vouching and covenanting with God, that rather than shed the blood of their brethren they would give up their own lives."[44] If this pacifist commitment were a universal principle, it would apply as much to the chronicler Mormon and those Nephites defending the people of Ammon as it would to the Anti-Nephi-Lehies. Mormon doesn't endorse the covenant of nonviolence, and he distances his own

---

43. Alma 24:12–13.
44. Alma 24:18.

position from the historical actors with his editorial intervention noting that this was the view of this particular small group, not his own. Stories carry with them a hierarchy of authority, with the narrator's authority much more presumptively reliable than that of a character within the story. Mormon is the narrator in this case, and because he undermines any universalizing of the pacifist covenant by inserting the statement "it being in their view a testimony to God," the reader has a much more difficult job asserting that the nonviolent principle should be globalized. The Anti-Nephi-Lehies don't assert that this principle is applicable to the Nephites, nor to their own sons. They don't even seem to imply that it is universal but that it is a covenant they as a group made with God. A covenant they appropriately don't want to violate, but almost do so when they see the Nephites suffer to protect them. They plan to break the covenant and symbolically dig up their buried weapons. But Helaman persuades them to maintain their covenant.[45] For the Anti-Nephi-Lehies, this is not a matter of universal principle to be asserted by their friends and protectors but of group covenant with God. As a reader of the Book of Mormon I don't in principle have anything against universal principles: always maintain fidelity to marriage covenants; treat others as you would have them treat you; worship God alone and not idols made out of stone, wood, metal, financial markets, political parties, or celebrity. I just don't think deontological categorical imperatives about violence and killing fall into those approved categories of justifiable categorical rules.

Of course, Mormon is himself a military man, so one would hardly expect him to endorse pacifism. Like other texts, especially anthological texts, the Book of Mormon speaks in multiple voices with compilers Mormon and Moroni$_2$ resorting to a host of previous records to assemble the end product. Two views on violence-

---

45. Alma 56:7–8.

in-self-defense are displayed here, but I don't think Mormon leaves any doubt as the writer/narrator of this portion of the scripture what the Book of Mormon position is. If the Anti-Nephi-Lehies desired to generalize their conduct to all humanity, they should have written their own record. If only we had any potential original writings from the people of Ammon, we might get their views on the matter. The Anti-Nephi-Lehi argument for pacifism is a local, situational, and personal commitment; England's Girardian conversion of that ethic into a universal principle leaves a large lacuna in the argument. A reader—whether Girard or England— can't merely adopt a straightforward reading of an antique textual episode and praise it for the highest of ethical and moral commitments (when it supports one's prejudices and political allegiances) but imply an authorial deficiency when the text doesn't conform to those preconceptions or principles. Such a reading principle is too easy.

Françoise Meltzer criticizes such interpretive tactics as they smooth over difficulties in the text in order to maintain a uniform reading across a multitude of texts and cultures, always producing the same result: "It is this logic which brings Girard to say, even though his tone is one of *erlebte Rede*, 'any victim will do.' It becomes increasingly clear that, with Girard, any text will do— since it always 'means' the same thing."[46] One explanation for why Girard's interpretations of wildly different texts from many genres and traditions result in such similar readings of the scapegoating mechanism might be that he has revealed a universal human phenomenon. An alternative explanation could be that "Girard's approach can seem procrustean to one who does not share his view."[47] Reading rivalry, mimesis, a contagion of violence, and

---

46. Françoise Meltzer, "A Response to René Girard's Reading of Salome," *New Literary History* 15, no. 2 (Winter 1984): 328.
47. Stuart D. Robertson, "Mimesis, Scapegoating, and Philo-Semitism: Reading Feldman and Girard," in *Sacrifice, Scripture, and Substitution*, eds. Ann W. Astell

scapegoating in virtually all texts to which Girard applies his reading talents could reveal a comprehensive and oft-repeated cultural event. But it could also demonstrate that by the dichotomous structure of the reading, these texts are being molded by the reading approach that will find a critique of such violence in scriptural, mythological, historical, or anthropological texts. And, if those texts don't yield to a critique of rivalry and imitation, then they contribute to such violence by unwittingly justifying and supporting the sacrificial point of view. Meltzer, referring to Girard's interpretation of the Salomé/John the Baptist narrative notes,

> This form of interpretive acrobatics makes Girard's reading do curious things. On the one hand, he is willing to use Josephus, "modern interpreters," and even an apocryphal story about Salome's own decapitation while ice-skating to bolster his reading. On the other hand, he rigorously disallows an entire series of other sources which might actually enrich his own interpretation. As it is, however, Girard's obsession with resolving differences and rivalry can only be accomplished by omissions and doublings.[48]

Karen Feldman offers a similar criticism, stating that Girard's readings find only what they are looking for, even if the text under examination and sources underlying that text are richer in possible meanings than Girard's approach reveals. The great texts (Bible, Shakespeare, Dostoevsky, Proust) unveil the scapegoating propensity and logic that result in violence toward scapegoats. The New Testament Gospels, more than other texts, reveal the scapegoating mechanism. But Girard's readings of those Gospels are one dimensional, drawing from the texts only those elements that support his own universalizing tendency because "here Scripture 'spells out a truth,' in an apparently unique fashion" that even the

---

and Sandor Goodhart (Notre Dame, IN: University of Notre Dame Press, 2011), 236.
48. Meltzer, "Response," 329.

greatest of other narratives don't reveal.[49] As Feldman contends, "Girard must overlook or underplay the moments that do not conform to the reading of the story of Joseph [and his brothers] that he proposes; this is theologically or anthropologically useful but literarily unsatisfying."[50] One would want a reading that accounts for all the magnificence of the biblical text rather than just those narrow elements making the reading Girardian.

Furthermore, Girard "underreads other biblical elements in order to strengthen a monolithic focus on mimeticism—which as a humanitarian project is understandable, but as a literary project is untenable."[51] Feldman's comparison of Girard's biblical readings to Robert Alter's are sophisticated in their own way, but by taking his cues from rabbinic readings of, say, the story of Joseph and his brothers, Alter makes so much more of the narrative than Girard does, incorporating what seems interruptive and irrelevant elements of the Joseph story (Judah and Tamar) to show the unity and sophistication of the story in a way Girard doesn't accomplish. Alter accounts for the indeterminacy of meaning in the narrative— shows how it can be productively interpreted in a multitude of ways. Girard focuses the meaning on only one potential possibility that omits elements that lead away from his obsessive conclusion. Feldman notes: "[Girard] reduces the Scripture to one effect: the unmasking of scapegoat logic. He thereby surrenders its literary and even theological complexity."[52] Girard's readings scapegoat a large portion not just of individual biblical narratives but the larger pattern of Hebraic textuality's constant resort to allusion and intertextuality. I assert the same is true of Book of Mormon textuality. The exiled portions of Hebraic narratives need to be

49. Karen S. Feldman, "On Girard's Biblical Realism," in *Mimesis, Desire, and the Novel: René Girard and Literary Criticism*, ed. Pierpaolo Antonello and Heather Webb (East Lansing: Michigan State University Press, 2015), 61.
50. Feldman, "On Girard's," 64.
51. Feldman, "On Girard's," 65.
52. Feldman, "On Girard's," 66.

welcomed back to Zarahemla after their generational wandering through the wilderness of Nephi, of the waters of Mormon, and the refuge of Helam.

Girard leaves so much of the harvest of biblical textuality on the ground with the stalks rather than getting a larger yield of grains into the silos. "He in my view actually loses much of the literary or aesthetic yield of Scripture, not least because the Bible contains more than what Girard states—more words, more stories, more figures, more possibilities. If Scripture is also a literary work, then there is a logic to it—to every line, to every word even, and to its flow and sequencing."[53] The aesthetic quality of the narrative is not to be dismissed as mere beauty but seen as an integral part of the content, for it is the God of the Bible who, in his very first actions in the creation, remarks at the end of each workday on the beauty of the result. And of the trees in the garden, the humans' first residence, the text declares the importance of their aesthetic qualities: "And out of the ground made the Lord God to grow every tree that is pleasant to the sight, and good for food; the tree of life also in the midst of the garden, and the tree of knowledge of good and evil."[54] Visual beauty is valued as much as practicality by the Creator.

The God of the Bible is a God of abundance, who delivers a harvest of plentitude and wastes not words nor souls. The first book of Samuel has God revealing to the youthful, soon-to-be-prophet that his mentor, Eli, and his family dynasty had grown decrepit and corrupt. Samuel was to replace the Elides. As the house of Eli dies, Samuel grows into his destiny as prophet but also as the last prophet-ruler who anoints the first king. "And the Lord was with him, and let none of his words fall to the ground."[55] Presumably it is Samuel's words that were never wasted, not the

53. Feldman, "On Girard's," 65.
54. Genesis 2:9.
55. 1 Samuel 3:19.

Lord's (the Hebrew is ambiguous on the point). All of Samuel's predictions were fulfilled.

The same ought to be true of elements of biblical narratives: none should be wasted by falling to the ground. Girard's, and England's, sieves capture and retain a whole harvestful of beautiful grains, but still leave much to be gleaned in the corners and ends of the fields. The God of the Bible and Jesus of the Gospels suffer a reduction of complexity and detail, detail that combines in the biblical text a much larger and more sophisticated whole versus the obsessive focus on just one element of the text, the scapegoating effect that is monolithic and the salvation uniform. For Alter, biblical narrative and the means used to achieve its narrative purposes is beautiful, and that beauty is a strong component of its potential truth. For Girard, such narrative is true to the extent it discloses his *idée fixe*.

Again, regarding the Salomé familiar to us from the Gospels of Mark and Matthew, Meltzer notes that "from the beginning, Girard mentions the Gospels of Matthew and Mark but drops the former with a simple 'Mark's is the richer text.' . . . The difference between the two versions of the story is erased by excluding one," the one that might complicate the Girardian expectation.[56] Similarly, England's harvest is selective, singling out those narratives that support his pacifist preferences and scapegoating the passages where divine and human initiative support and endorse the necessary resort to violence. For example, England justifiably singles out Jesus's words on the Sermon on the Mount that begin, "Resist not evil, but . . . love your enemies" and turn the other cheek.[57] A citation to the same wording but to opposite effect occurs in Pahoran's instruction to Moroni, who is urged to "let us resist evil, and whatsoever evil we cannot resist with our words, yea, such

---

56. Meltzer, "Response," 329.
57. England, Eugene, "Late Night Thoughts at the End of a War." *Dialogue: A Journal of Mormon Thought* 24, no. 2 (Summer 1991): 7.

as rebellions and dissensions, let us resist them with our swords, that we may retain our freedom, that we may rejoice in the great privilege of our church, and in the cause of our Redeemer and our God."[58] One may view the Sermon on the Mount as an expression of the general rule and Pahoran's exhortation an exception to the rule, but the exceptions need to be accounted for in any systematic or even ad hoc argument.

As I read the relevant scriptures here, violence and the production of victims come mixed together into the loaf, and they expand jointly as the yeast swells the bread. The Girardian obsession focuses on violence as the most important ingredient. The scriptures concentrate on victims rather than on violence and allow the possibility that violence is sometimes needed to reduce the number of and suffering of victims. In other words, God may be a pragmatist who at times prefers to minimize the suffering of victims and minimize the number of victims rather than rebuke all forms of violence outright. God and humans may well be called to be consequentialists when mixing, baking, and consuming the bread of life and death.

The Anti-Nephi-Lehies are without question to be considered brave, stalwart, and principled people. England asserts that "the Book of Mormon provides the only example I can find anywhere of a group actually *practicing* Girard's implied unique solution to imitative violence—and with precisely the results he predicts."[59] I have called this people *pacifists* throughout this analysis of the relevant Book of Mormon material, but Duane Boyce denies that the label is accurate because they don't act from pacific motivations.[60] England isn't alone in using the label for the group (Boyces lists, among

---

58. Alma 61:14.
59. England, "Second Witness," 119.
60. Boyce, "Were the Ammonites Pacifists?" 32–47. Boyce, *Even Unto*, chapters 4 and 5.

others, Hugh Nibley, Boyd Jay Petersen, and David Pulsipher).[61] Whether or not the term applies is not my concern. The Merriam-Webster online dictionary provides a couple of definitions of the word: (1) "someone who opposes war or violence as a means of settling disputes," and (2) a person "strongly and actively opposed to conflict and especially war."[62] If one goes by those two definitions, I don't consider the group pacifistic. The Anti-Nephi-Lehies were opposed to their involvement in war and violence and were strongly opposed to *their* own participation in explicit warfare.

The people of Ammon were right to abstain from combat with sword and scimitar not because doing so is wrong but because they had made a covenant with God not to do so. That is the word Helaman uses to persuade them not to take up arms again: "when they saw [their protectors'] tribulations for them, they were about to break the covenant which they had made and take up their weapons of war in our defence."[63] Helaman persuades them to not fight on the battlefield, not because they are pacifists, but because he didn't want them to be covenant-breakers: "But I would not suffer them that they should break this covenant which they had made."[64] The general deontological rule for the people is "do your duty." The principle was not "do not kill or engage in violence." It was "do not break covenants you have made with God." Such noble and faithful devotees are to be admired and their pacifism a model of action for those who covenant not to take up arms. These people, both corporately and individually, are not more noble or admirable than the Nephites who protected them based on their commitments regarding violence in self-defense. Different people have different duties.

61. Boyce, *Even Unto*, 49–50.
62. Merriam-Webster.com Dictionary, s.v. "pacifist," accessed October 26, 2023, https://www.merriam-webster.com/dictionary/pacifist.
63. Alma 56:7.
64. Alma 56:8.

Let me reiterate one of my main arguments in this book. Universal deontological prescriptions and proscriptions need to be tempered by local and individual conditions. Call that a universal rule, though you may think it paradoxical. But we Latter-day Saints are a people of paradox. Just ask Terryl Givens.[65]

---

65. Terryl Givens, *People of Paradox: A History of Mormon Culture* (New York: Oxford University Press, 2007).

Chapter Fourteen

Nephi$_2$ and the Mob on the Way to the Marketplace

Nephi$_2$'s lament in his garden tower is a rare story, uncommon in that we read about a mob unable to achieve the unanimity required to successfully scapegoat and attain the apotheosis that would then follow. The crowd, failing to coalesce into a lynching party, instead resorts to a judicial trial, and even then falls short of unifying around violence. Girard says that to have a successful scapegoating venture, the throng must achieve unanimity, even often the consent of the victim, to proceed to the violent stage. "If there is just one exception," he writes, "if even one single voice is raised in disagreement with the unison against the victim, then there is no guarantee of a favourable outcome. The drug loses its effect; the group's unity cracks. If the hatred appears in the least bit lukewarm, doubt may spread, [compromising] the cathartic effects on the morale of the community."[1] In various cultures and mythologies, the demand for unanimity in the sacrifice means that no individual can be blamed for the mob violence since no one can tell who delivered the final blow.[2] Girard asserts that

---

1. René Girard, *Job: The Victim of His People*, trans. Yvonne Freccero (Stanford: Stanford University Press, 1985), 111.
2. René Girard, *Violence and the Sacred*, trans. Patrick Gregory (Baltimore: Johns Hopkins University Press, 1972), 100–101, 198.

the victim's agreement is not only essential but the most important part of the community's consensus: "Oedipus is a *successful* scapegoat, because he is never recognized as such. Job is a *failed* scapegoat. He derails the mythology that is meant to envelope him, by maintaining his own point of view in the face of the formidable unanimity surrounding him."[3] Job's "comforters" are, after all, not comforting but are rather persecutors badgering him to accept the guilt they attempt to force on him. James Williams notes that "unanimity is crucially important in sacrifice and scapegoating."[4] Like Job, Nephi$_2$ resists his own censure, thus halting the victimage mechanism, grinding the sacrificial gears to a halt like a Luddite throwing a spanner into the apparatus.

Girard compares the story in John 8 of the woman taken in adultery to a Greek story in which the crowd is persuaded to stone the victim. Christ has gone to the temple, the people gather, and he teaches them. The group gathered to hear him can become a congregation or a mob. The "scribes and Pharisees" bring in the adulterous woman.[5] The bait is set in this trap, for the accusers cite the law: "Now Moses in the law commanded us, that such should be stoned: but what sayest thou?"[6] If Jesus is lenient with her, the scribes and Pharisees will condemn him for violating Moses's legal commandment. If Jesus urges that she be stoned, he adheres to the law of Moses but violates his own teachings on forgiveness and mercy.

Jesus chooses an indirect approach to this conundrum: "But Jesus stooped down, and with his finger wrote on the ground, *as though he heard them not*. So when they continued asking him, he lifted up himself, and said unto them, He that is without sin among

3. Girard, *Job*, 35.
4. James G. Williams, "Sacrifice, Mimesis, and the Genesis of Violence: A Response to Bruce Chilton," *Bulletin for Biblical Research* 3 (1993): 46.
5. John 8:4.
6. John 8:5.

you, let him first cast a stone at her."[7] Jesus then resumes his dirt work, looking down to the ground. His action is nonconfrontational, a delaying action as the accusers press him. Girard corrects the syntax. What the Greek text states is "let him cast the first stone at her." The KJV syntax doesn't specify who casts the first stone, just that he who would condemn the woman must "first cast a stone at her," along with the mob. But Deuteronomy 17:7 requires that the witnesses who testified against the accused must be the first to cast a stone. That means if the witnesses bore false witness, they must be the first to cast stones, thus making them murderers in addition to perjurers. Girard makes the following point:

> The mimetic concept of the first stone is powerfully used by Jesus, but it is not original with him. It comes from the Law which says that, in all indictments which might result in someone being stoned, there should be at least two witnesses against the accused and however convincing their case may be, it is not enough. If the victim is supposed to be stoned, the two accusers are required to cast the first stones themselves. Only afterwards, are the people invited to cast their stones as well.[8]

Jesus bends down and writes in the dirt (the only Gospel story that shows him writing). This action defuses the potentially violent situation. Rather than staring back at the accusers and getting in their faces, "Jesus' goal is to save the woman threatened with death, and he does his best to avoid even the slightest hint of visual provocation."[9]

---

7. John 8:6-7. Notice the last phrase in italics. That means the King James translators want to convey the meaning of the Greek text, but no Greek phrase is there to represent the intention meant. Sometimes the italics mark a Greek lexical unit that makes perfectly good sense in Greek, but an English word or phrase is needed to make English grammatical sense due to the original Greek lacking a corresponding word or phrase. The italics are in the KJV.

8. René Girard, "The First Stone," *Renascence* 52, no. 1 (Fall 1999): 14.

9. Girard, "First," 15.

This is a mimetic crisis that could easily go south for Jesus if he is seen as antagonistic toward the Mosaic Law. The woman is also in danger of her life. These sacrificial events when the mob gets worked up can be unpredictable and spin out of control once triggered:

> Well, they'll stone you when you walk all alone
> They'll stone you when you are walking home
> They'll stone you and then say you are brave
> They'll stone you when you are set down in your grave
>
> But I would not feel so all alone
> Everybody must get stoned.
> —Bob Dylan

The entire crowd, originally gathered to hear Jesus teach, could get caught up in a mimetic fever with volatile results. Girard notes the necessary collective action: "Everyone must throw stones. This is obviously how the mimetic hypothesis explains the existence of institutionalized stoning such as can be found codified much later in Leviticus."[10] Keep in mind that Jesus walks and teaches with the possibility of being stoned as an explicitly threatened result.[11] Jesus is attempting to prevent the first stone from being thrown because once the first one flies, the mob will imitate that action. "Why the first stone? Because it is the key. The one who throws it has nobody to imitate. There's nothing easier than imitating an example that's already been provided. Providing that example yourself is something altogether different."[12] Jesus's nonconfrontational stance and allusion to the Jewish law of witnesses "dissolve[s] the crowd. The

---

10. René Girard, *When These Things Begin: Conversations with Michel Treguer,* trans. by Trevor Cribben Merrill (East Lansing: Michigan State University, 2014), 122.
11. Girard, *When,* 122. John 10:31-42. John 8:58–59.
12. Girard, *When,* 123.

men go away one by one, according to how long it takes each of them to understand the Revelation."[13]

Recently economists and psychologists have led the way in examining the wisdom and stupidity seen in crowds. The lead example James Surowiecki cites in his *The Wisdom of Crowds* is Francis Galton's observation of those attending a Plymouth County fair who were asked to guess the butchered weight of a cow munching hay at the fair. While the estimates ranged widely, the average was quite close. The thesis is that in certain conditions crowds can be much better at making judgments than the average individual. The key problem that leads away from wisdom in crowds is that individuals in the crowd can't be too much influenced by other members' opinions. The judgments have to be tallied in a way that individual opinion is collected without the individual being aware of the other opinions being collated.[14]

One important factor often ignored by those who promote the wisdom of crowds is that the individuals who compose the group need to have good independent knowledge of the subject matter. Those attending the county fair in Plymouth and browsing the livestock section were likely to have raised their own cattle. Cass Sunsten cites Condorcet's theorem regarding the accuracy of prediction markets in which forecasts are derived for elections, movie box office results, or Oscar winners. No real betting is involved, but the "bettors" get bragging rights for correctly forecasting results by purchasing "shares." As with stock markets, individuals with the most shares in the winner's stock come out as predictive savants. High tech companies such as Microsoft and Google will set up such trading markets to let their employees buy shares on predictions for quarterly profits or success of products soon-to-be

---

13. Girard, *When*, 123.
14. James Surowiecki, *The Wisdom of Crowds: Why the Many Are Smarter Than the Few and How Collective Wisdom Shapes Business, Economies, Societies and Nations* (New York: Anchor, 2004).

released. These aggregate predictions are exceptionally accurate because the Iowa Electronic Markets, Hollywood Stock Exchange, and Google market participants have independent knowledge of the subject matter. But these aren't ordinary crowds. They are composed of insiders with specialized knowledge. Accurate information and expertise in the group are necessary elements to crowd wisdom:

> Some prediction markets fail for just this reason. They have done really badly in predicting President Bush's appointments to the Supreme Court, for example. Until roughly two hours before the official announcement, the markets were essentially ignorant of the existence of John Roberts, now the chief justice of the United States. At the close of a prominent market just one day before his nomination, "shares" in Judge Roberts were trading at $0.19—representing an estimate that Roberts had a 1.9% chance of being nominated. Why was the crowd so unwise? Because it had little accurate information to go on; these investors, even en masse, knew almost nothing about the internal deliberations in the Bush administration. For similar reasons, prediction markets were quite wrong in forecasting that weapons of mass destruction would be found in Iraq and that special prosecutor Patrick Fitzgerald would indict Deputy Chief of Staff Karl Rove in late 2005.[15]

Some commentators are less sanguine about the potential for crowds to exude wisdom. Soren Kierkegaard (1813–1855), Danish philosopher, articulated the opposite view in his posthumously published piece on the issue. The crowd, according to Kierkegaard, can embolden an individual to act rashly:

> A crowd—not this or that, one now living or long dead, a crowd of the lowly or of nobles, of rich or poor, etc., but in its very concept is untruth, since a crowd either renders the single indi-

---

15. Cass R. Sunstein, "When Crowds Aren't Wise," *Harvard Business Review* (Sept. 2006): https://hbr.org/2006/09/when-crowds-arent-wise.

vidual wholly unrepentant and irresponsible, or weakens his responsibility by making it a fraction of his decision. Observe, there was not a single soldier who dared lay a hand on Caius Marius; this was the truth. But given three or four women with the consciousness or idea of being a crowd, with a certain hope in the possibility that no one could definitely say who it was or who started it: then they had the courage for it; what untruth! The untruth is first that it is "the crowd," which does either what *only the single individual* in the crowd does, or in every case *what each single individual does*. For a crowd is an abstraction, which does not have hands; each single individual, on the other hand, normally has two hands, and when he, as a single individual, lays his two hands on Caius Marius, then it is the two hands of this single individual, not after all his neighbor's, even less—the crowd's, which has no hands.[16]

Kierkegaard continues his condemnation of mobs, for they have no respect for what a human being is and the individual parts surrender their private will to the group. Crowds, he notes, gathered often around Jesus to acclaim or murder him, but Jesus had nothing to do with crowds. Kierkegaard can sometimes sound very much like Girard: "To become a crowd, to gather a crowd around oneself, is on the contrary to distinguish life from life; even the most well-meaning one who talks about that, can easily offend a single individual. But it is the crowd which has power, influence, reputation, and domination—this is the distinction of life from life, which tyrannically overlooks the single individual as the weak and powerless one, in a temporal-worldly way overlooks the eternal truth: the single individual."[17]

When Nephi$_2$ goes to his garden tower to pray vocally, near the heavily traveled road leading to the market, his actions trigger

---

16. Soren Kierkegaard, *The Crowd Is Untruth*, trans. by Charles K. Bellinger (Grand Rapids, MI: Christian Classics Ethereal Library, [written in 1847]),. https://www.ccel.org/ccel/k/kierkegaard/untruth/cache/untruth.pdf.
17. Kierkegaard, *Crowd*.

a similar mimetic crisis: the crowd is urged on to violence, the wicked judges attempt to incite the crowd to a lynching, and eventually, the crowd dissipates because it cannot achieve unanimity. The people hear Nephi$_2$'s lament over their pervasive wickedness.[18] Seeing the crowd, Nephi$_2$ begins preaching, commanding them to repent. The root of their sin is their desire for riches, their acquisitiveness, their mimetic desire: "behold, it is to get gain, to be praised of men, yea, and that ye might get gold and silver. And ye have set your hearts upon the riches and the vain things of this world."[19] The Nephite judges, conspirators in the Gadianton gang, incite the crowd against Nephi$_2$. The rabble can't agree, for some assert Nephi$_2$ is righteous and correct.[20] Because of the divisions in the multitude, the judges fear to proceed to the lynching stage.[21] After citing a cloud of witnesses for his cause (the prophets God has called previously to declare repentance), Nephi$_2$ tells them of the secret murder of the chief judge, another Gadianton leader; the narrative is full of investigative and legal terminology, started by Nephi$_2$ when he refers to the testimony of the prophets and all the "evidences" the Nephites have "witnessed," even bearing the marks of the literary genre we today call a murder mystery.[22] When the killing is confirmed, the judges arrest Nephi$_2$ and charge him with the murder. The judges from Nephi$_2$'s garden interrogate the five messengers who ran to the chief judge to confirm Nephi$_2$'s claims and find him dead. Again, the same judges attempt to organize the throng into a lynch mob.[23]

Literary criticism about detective fiction (also called the mystery novel) often attributes the invention of the genre to Edgar

---

18. Helaman 7:10.
19. Helaman 7:21.
20. Helaman 8:7–9.
21. Helaman 8:10.
22. Helaman 8:19, 22, 24.
23. Helaman 9:16.

Allen Poe.[24] But some critics also trace precursors to Voltaire's *Zadig* or the apocryphal story of Susanna (in the Daniel cycle).[25] Some story structures are universal in that they can't be bound by genre (such as history versus literature), historical period (ancient versus modern), or mode of transmission. They are ecumenical because certain human experiences are universal, repeatable, imitable because they are archetypal. The story of Susanna and the Elders is included in the Roman Catholic version of the biblical book of Daniel and some Orthodox Churches' translations, but few other Bibles. Protestant Bibles that include the Apocrypha will provide access to the story for those who want to read the story itself instead of my summary. Susanna, a beautiful Jewish wife, sends her attendants away as she bathes inside her own walled garden. Two elders spy on her activity and are inspired by covetousness. This second story from Jewish sources of a woman facing a dire threat of stoning for adultery is even more Girardian than the story of Jesus and the woman caught in adultery because it comes with a more direct setup of triangular sexual desire. The elders intercept Susanna and demand sex, threatening to report her to authorities for having sent her attendants away because she intended to have a sexual liaison with a young man. Susanna refuses to acquiesce to this coercion, is arrested, and approaches the death sentence's execution time. The sage Daniel intervenes and does what all modern police detectives do: separates the two suspects (the two false witnessing elders) and cross-examines them individually, asking under what tree the alleged adultery occurred. When the two false witnesses name different tree species, the trial results in their deaths instead of Susanna's death. Modern detec-

24. John Gruesser, "Never Bet the Detective (or His Creator) Your Head: Character Rivalry, Authorial Sleight of Hand, and Generic Fluidity in Detective Fiction," *The Edgar Allan Poe Review* 9, no. 1 (Spring 2008): 5–23.

25. LeRoy Lad Panek, *The Origins of the American Detective Story* (Jefferson, NC: McFarland, 2006), 39. Michael Cohen, *Murder Most Fair: The Appeal of Mystery Fiction* (Teaneck, NJ: Fairleigh Dickinson University Press, 2000), 55–56.

tion narratives have learned a good deal from ancient texts about investigative techniques.

Let me propose this Book of Mormon narrative as a precursor to detective fiction also. The Nephi$_2$ narrative opens the examination with forensic language about testimony and witnesses. The judges continue in that legal trajectory, asserting that by cross-examination they will "*detect* this man, and *he shall confess his fault and make known unto us the true murderer* of this judge."[26] Reproved by the five witnesses who discovered the corpse, the judges press forward, bringing Nephi$_2$ to be interrogated before the "multitude, and *they began to question* him in divers ways that *they might cross him*, that they might accuse him to death."[27] Accusing him of murder, they demand to know who Nephi$_2$'s co-conspirators are.[28] Nephi$_2$ then tells them how to gather evidence of the real murderer by going to the house of the chief judge's brother, where if they "examine" his clothes they will find the forensic evidence of his guilt; after that, the brother will "confess" his guilt.[29] Case solved.

As does the crowd witnessing the trial of the woman taken in adultery, this crowd on the way to the marketplace simply dissipates rather than coalescing into a lynch mob, leaving Nephi$_2$ a solitary witness, standing as a congregation of one: "And it came to pass that there arose a division among the people, insomuch that they divided hither and thither and went their ways, leaving Nephi alone, as he was standing in the midst of them."[30] Similarly, as the scribes and Pharisees attempt to spawn mob violence against Jesus (with the woman used only as an object to that end), they can't

---

26. Helaman 9:17.
27. Helaman 9:19.
28. Helaman 9:20.
29. Helaman 9:31, 35.
30. Helaman 10:1.

generate the cohesion needed to finish the task. Girard notes of the story:

> The would-be lynchers came all together, as a united crowd and "they went away one by one, beginning with the elders." This last detail is fascinating. It shows that, even though the mimetic factor is still present, it is no longer paramount. There is an objective difference as well that makes certain listeners of Jesus more amenable to his teaching than others, the difference of age. The elders are more easily convinced to renounce violence, more aware that they too are sinners, just like the adulterous woman.[31]

The elders in the Susanna story, the elders in this story: Girard has a talent for making unnoticed details relevant for his larger interpretive scheme. Mobs aren't inevitable, as these examples show. The spirit can move within people to mitigate against the unanimity that pushes crowds to lynch.

Girard notes that legal institutions were important in stemming the cycles of violence that would emerge from private revenge. Think of the Hatfields and the McCoys, or the Montagues and the Capulets. Patrick Mason notes that nineteenth-century Americans (especially in the South) often resorted to private revenge when the courts didn't bring them the justice they desired, especially in cases involving wives, daughters, and sexuality.[32] When individuals, families, or tribes surrender the possibility of vigilante justice, the legal system prevents the spiraling impact of revenge killings. Legal systems are reactions to the scapegoating mechanism.[33] Communal violence tends to be more spontaneous; vigilante bru-

---

31. Girard, "First," 14.

32. Patrick Q. Mason, *The Mormon Menace: Violence and Anti-Mormonism in the Postbellum South* (New York: Oxford University Press), 5–7.

33. René Girard, *Violence and the Sacred*, trans. by Patrick Gregory (Baltimore: Johns Hopkins University Press, 1972), 21–24, 298–99. Nico Keijzer, "A Girardian View of the Criminal Justice System," https://www.girard.nl/texts_online/k/Keijzer_Nico_2.pdf.

tality tends to be unorganized but no less effective. After enough repetitions of the scapegoating, the pattern becomes more regular and organized. As Robert North points out, "This violence gradually becomes disguised as police, prison, judiciary—and eventually war and nuclear armament."[34] Legal systems sometimes default on the claim of justice and are used for private, rather than communal, interests. This is the case with the judges' use of the legal system against Nephi$_2$ and Susanna to advance their own ambitions, and those of Gadianton bands or lustful elders. In the case against Nephi$_2$, the judges couldn't stand as plaintiffs, so they kept urging the people to bring charges.[35] Under the Girardian concept of violence, police, courts, and prisons are not instituted to eliminate or ameliorate violence but to regularize it and bring it under political control. The wicked judges in Nephi$_2$'s case can't generate consensus, let alone unanimity, to incite the mob to murder. The sacrificial act is never consummated as a result, and Nephi$_2$ never becomes a scapegoat.

This lack of unanimity is explicitly mentioned at the end of the narrative. Some of the doubting Nephites were converted by their experience with Nephi$_2$, and some declared him either a prophet or a god.[36] The next verse notes the lack of consensus about Nephi$_2$: "there arose a division among the people, insomuch that they divided hither and thither and went their ways, leaving Nephi alone, as he was standing in the midst of them."[37] Lacking the unanimity needed to lynch Nephi$_2$, these Nephites never cohere into a mob, unruly or judicial.

---

34. Robert North, "Violence and the Bible: The Girard Connection," *Catholic Biblical Quarterly* 47 (1985): 6.
35. John W. Welch, *The Legal Cases in the Book of Mormon* (Provo, UT: BYU Press and Maxwell Institute, 2008), 325.
36. Helaman 9:39–41. Note that Girard points to the divinization of the sacrificial victim as the one who saved the community from its mimetic tensions.
37. Helaman 10:1.

Chapter Fifteen

Alma, Amulek, and Victimage at Ammonihah

Alma 8 continues a narrative arc that began with Alma$_2$ preaching in various Nephite cities. Just as Abinadi prophesied that Nephite prophets would be called upon to carry the people's burden of sin vicariously, Alma$_2$ preaches at Ammonihah and is reviled, spit upon, and exiled.[1] After his expulsion, he is "weighed down with sorrow, wading through much tribulation and anguish of soul, because of the wickedness of the people who were in the city of Ammonihah."[2] An angel visits him, encourages him, and redirects him back to Ammonihah. He then meets Amulek, and the two of them begin preaching to the people of the city.

Their message is rejected by the majority of the Ammonihahites, but many yet believe and "began to repent, and to search the scriptures."[3] By Alma 14:8, these believers and the scriptures will be consigned to the same fate as Abinadi and Noah: destruction by burnt offering.[4] Here the people are treated like sacred writing (obviously not written on metal plates but combustible material). Think of Paul's comparison of the Corinthian saints to writing:

---

1. Alma 8:13.
2. Alma 8:14.
3. Alma 14:1.
4. Alma 14:8.

"Ye are our epistle written in our hearts, known and read of all men."[5] Or consider 1 Peter, where Jesus is compared to writing: "because Christ also suffered for us, leaving us an example, that ye should follow his steps."[6] The Greek word translated "example" here is *hupogrammos*, a nonce word that would be invented by a child's teacher to include all the letters of the alphabet, from alpha to omega, to allow the pupil to practice writing the entire alphabet. Some people at Ammonihah believe, repent, and then immediately search the scriptures. These new converts having the scriptures newly written upon their hearts are going to be burned together with those writings. Improbably, Zeezrom (Alma$_2$ and Amulek's most vocal antagonist in Ammonihah) has also undergone the conversion process. He insists at Alma$_2$ and Amulek's trial that he is himself "guilty, and these men are spotless before God."[7]

Insisting on the innocence of the selected scapegoats, Zeezrom becomes the next victim of his people: the record says of the crowd that "they spit upon him, and cast him out from among them, and also all those who believed in the words which had been spoken by Alma$_2$ and Amulek; and they cast them out, and sent men to cast stones at them."[8] Some believers, including Zeezrom, are expelled and some become immediate martyrs. Some believers are burned to death along with the sacred writings.[9] Alma$_2$ and Amulek, being brought "to the place of martyrdom," respond with pain and anguish.[10] Amulek, recalling the power given to them at the beginning of their call to Ammonihah, insists that Alma$_2$ and he exercise that power and save the martyrs: "How can we witness this awful scene? Therefore let us stretch forth our hands,

5. 2 Corinthians 3:2.
6. 1 Peter 2:21.
7. Alma 14:7.
8. Alma 14:7.
9. Alma 14:8.
10. Alma 14:9.

and exercise the power of God which is in us, and save them from the flames."[11] But Alma₂ resists Amulek's pleading, saying,

> The Spirit constraineth me that I must not stretch forth mine hand; for behold the Lord receiveth them up unto himself, in glory; and he doth suffer that they may do this thing, or that the people may do this thing unto them, according to the hardness of their hearts, that the judgments which he shall exercise upon them in his wrath may be just; and the blood of the innocent shall stand as a witness against them, yea, and cry mightily against them at the last day.[12]

In Girardian terms, even Alma₂'s inaction is a form of sacrificial refusal to save innocent victims' lives, because these victims' deaths will bring about some larger good by bearing witness to the wicked murder of the blameless, and this refusal is attributed not to Alma₂, but to the Spirit who "constrains" him and to the Lord, who "doth suffer that they may do this thing."

Notice here that the same word from Nephi's slaying of Laban is used, with the same cluster of actors. Nephi "was *constrained by the Spirit* that [he] should kill Laban,"[13] so when Alma₂ states that "*the Spirit constraineth* me that I must not stretch forth mine hand"[14] and save the lives of the martyrs, the reader must note the parallel wording and divine involvement in the two actions. If, as readers such as England propose, *Nephi* might be mistaken that the Spirit enjoined a certain action (a proactive killing) and Alma₂ is prohibited from intervening to prevent a group murder by a wicked third party, might not that similar "constraint" by the

---

11. Alma 14:10; "And they had power given unto them, insomuch that they could not be confined in dungeons; neither was it possible that any man could slay them; nevertheless they did not exercise their power until they were bound in bands and cast into prison. Now, this was done that the Lord might show forth his power in them," Alma 8:31.
12. Alma 14:11.
13. 1 Nephi 4:10.
14. Alma 14:11.

same "Spirit" raise the possibility that Alma$_2$ too was mistaken in *his* perception of the divine will? Might Alma$_2$ similarly be justified by a deontological principle that God knows better when to save life from third-party aggressors (Abraham also argued with the Lord to save innocent life in the cities of the plain from God's first-party action: shouldn't Alma$_2$ have an obligation to do the works of Abraham? and could Amulek's reaction have been the highest ethical one? the Abrahamic one? is Amulek not right and just to argue for the lives of the innocents?)? One of Nephi's own justifications for killing Laban is to make available the word of God to future generations, but that is a consequentialist argument. The Spirit only makes two arguments for the killing: (1) "the Spirit said unto me again: Behold the Lord hath delivered him into thy hands" (which is a divine command imperative), and (2) "the Lord slayeth the wicked to bring forth his righteous purposes. It is better that one man should perish than that a nation should dwindle and perish in unbelief."[15] The priority in both cases in Jerusalem and Ammonihah is the Lord's "righteous purposes," which results in death both times. Here at Ammonihah the divine justification is not for Alma$_2$'s, Amulek's, or even the martyrs' sake—let alone for posterity: it is for God's glory and the working out of divine justice: "the Lord receiveth [the martyrs] up unto himself, in glory; and he doth *suffer* that they may do this thing, or that the people may do this thing unto them, according to the hardness of their hearts, *that the judgments which he shall exercise upon them in his wrath may be just*; and the blood of the innocent shall stand as a witness against them, yea, and cry mightily against them at the last day."[16] This instance is not a divine endorsement of the scapegoating sacrifice because the Lord doesn't sanction the violence but does acquiesce to it. Later in the same chapter that same divine power that Amu-

---

15. 1 Nephi 4:10, 13. The second argument is utilitarian. The first justification is articulated twice by the Spirit and repeated once by Nephi (1 Nephi 4:11, 12, 17).
16. Alma 14:11.

lek proposed deploying is exercised to save Alma$_2$'s and Amulek's lives.[17] Alma$_2$, in this case, doesn't use the divine power that Amulek asserts they possess to stop violence; the English word *suffer* here can mean "to permit," but it can also mean "to endure pain and anguish."[18] In Alma$_2$'s case, the former chief judge over all the land doesn't accede to Amulek's urging, for "the Spirit constraineth me that I must not stretch forth mine hand"; Alma$_2$, like Nephi in his decision about killing Laban, "was constrained by the Spirit."[19] Alma$_2$ was compelled not to intervene against violence; Nephi$_1$ was compelled to engage in it by the same source. We'll see that by the end of this very chapter, Alma$_2$ and Amulek are the recipients of intervention by that divine power to prevent their confinement in dungeons and their martyrdom.[20]

The narrative, when examined through the lenses of a Girardian hermeneutic, seems to contain a contradiction of sacrificial and anti-sacrificial impulses. Yet, it does what any Girardian reader would praise, as it vehemently insists on the innocence of the victims of sacrifice, just as the biblical Joseph story does, the Job narrative, and the Gospel accounts do.

Alma$_2$ and Amulek are then bound and brought before Ammonihah's chief judge. Having tortured and imprisoned the accused for many days, the chief judge, lawyers, and teachers perform a ritualistic scapegoating: "they all went forth and smote them, saying the same words, even until the last."[21] The divine power is then revealed after Alma$_2$ calls upon God. They break their bonds, an earthquake brings down the prison, and all die

---

17. Alma 14:26–28.
18. And let me highlight that the same word *suffer* is used later in the chapter when Alma$_2$ and Amulek are tortured but saved from murder by divine intervention; Alma 14:26, in my opinion, draws upon both meanings I have articulated of the term.
19. 1 Nephi 4:10.
20. Alma 8:31.
21. Alma 14:25.

except Alma$_2$ and Amulek, who then walk free. Yet the violence by the persecutors still occurs, but by God's agency, not the missionaries'. Curiously, and presumably anguishing to the reader of the narrative, the same divine power exercised to save Alma$_2$'s and Amulek's lives is not applied to save the lives of the twice-mentioned "women and children" and "whosoever believed or had been taught to believe in the word of God" from a fiery martyrdom.[22] This uncommented-on disparate treatment between the two preachers and their new followers shows an alarming lack of sacred intercession for the victims of mass immolation. Amulek is distressed and moved by what seems a callous disregard for the lives of the victims: "when Amulek saw the pains of the women and children who were consuming in the fire, he also was pained," and demands Alma$_2$'s forceful intrusion: "How can we witness this awful scene? Therefore let us stretch forth our hands, and exercise the power of God which is in us, and save them from the flames."[23] This isn't one of the gods of the Greeks, who are merely humans with extraordinary powers still limited by nature and the authority of other Olympians. This is the unrivaled God of the Bible and the Book of Mormon.

The Book of Mormon deity in this case has the power to perform a miracle but doesn't. Jesus had the power to provide bread from stone for his own physical needs, but he declined.[24] It is understandable that Jesus wouldn't use the gift of God for his own private interests. When Jesus, outside the territory of the Jews, is enjoined by a Canaanite woman to cast out a devil "grievously vexing" her daughter, Jesus initially declines: "I am not sent but unto the lost sheep of the house of Israel."[25] The mother persists, pleading "Lord, help me." Considering how negatively Jews view

22. Alma 14:8, 10.
23. Alma 14:10.
24. Luke 4:2–3.
25. Matthew 15:24.

dogs, Jesus's answer seems surprisingly callous: "It is not meet to take the children's bread, and cast it to the dogs." Cleverly, and in the moment, the supplicant turns Jesus's analogy back on him: "Truth, Lord: yet the dogs eat of the crumbs which fall from their masters' table."[26] Jesus then healed the daughter, and the mother, apparently, who had pleaded after the first refusal, "Lord, help me."[27]

Although not analogous in details with the immolation of the innocents at Ammonihah, both stories portray a God who could end terrible suffering but refuses, although Jesus relents after persistent and plaintive pleading. Jesus also refuses his mother's request for a miracle at the wedding in Cana, saying, "Woman, what have I to do with thee? Mine hour is not yet come."[28] One would think it would be obvious what he has to do with his own mother. Like the Syrophoenician woman, Mary shows great faith despite the initial rejection, commanding the servants to do whatever Jesus tells them to do, as if the request had not been turned down. And Jesus relents. At the garden of Gethsemane, after Peter slices off the ear of one of the arresting officers, Jesus tells Peter to put away the sword, "for all they that take the sword shall perish with the sword. Thinkest thou not that I cannot now pray to my Father, and he shall presently give me more than twelve legions of angels?"[29] Jesus also on the cross is mocked by the chief priests, scribes, and elders: "If thou be the Son of God, come down from the cross," and "He saved others; himself he cannot save. If he be the King of Israel, let him now come down from the cross, and

---

26. Matthew 15:24–28.
27. Matthew 15:25.
28. John 2:4.
29. Matthew 26:52–53. A legion of Roman soldiers is 6,000. That would total 72,000 legionnaire angels, apparently all armed for combat, whatever weapons angels arm themselves with. At least Jesus raises the possibility of the Father sending an army of angels deployed in violent defense without recoiling from the thought.

we will believe him."[30] Yet Jesus doesn't exercise divine power nor request such from his Father. His hour had not yet come, and that timing required a different demonstration of power than saving himself from the pain of the cross.

Jesus, the God of the Old Testament and the Book of Mormon, not infrequently refused miraculous intervention for himself and for others. I am not aware of any place Girard addresses these circumstances. I don't have any sources to consult about how Girard might react to this Ammonihah incident, although I can advance some inferences. Why not save the innocents at Ammonihah? Surely, the Judge of the universe had plenty of goods on the elites of Ammonihah for a tribunal at the last day: the Lord, Alma$_2$ asserts, "doth suffer that they may do this thing, or that the people may do this thing unto them, according to the hardness of their hearts, that the judgments which he shall exercise upon them in his wrath may be just; and the blood of the innocent shall stand as a witness against them, yea, and cry mightily against them at the last day."[31] Surely, the intent to commit murder and the conspiracy to do so through immolation is just as good a felony charge as actually doing it. Yet we readers cry out, like Amulek, "How can we witness this awful scene? Therefore let us stretch forth our hands, and exercise the power of God which is in us, and save them from the flames."[32] Why are the messengers through whom the proselytes are converted granted such a reprieve, but not the recipients?

Surely the God of heaven—who, when Enoch weeps for the sins of his brothers and sisters and both the heavens and the Lord follow suit causing Enoch to wonder and ask three times the question, "How is it that the heavens weep, and shed forth their tears as the rain upon the mountains?" and further, not just the heavens and

---

30. Matthew 47:41–42.
31. Alma 14:11.
32. Alma 14:10.

all creation but the Lord, "How is it that thou canst weep, seeing thou art holy, and from all eternity to all eternity?"[33]—must be tormented not just witnessing the death of these blameless victims of violence but also knowing that the power to rescue is within divine control and desire. The epigraph I included at the beginning of Part One of this book asserts that God's ways are higher than our ways and often beyond our comprehension. Intervening to save the victims of violence (especially state-sponsored violence, which is what is happening on a small-state scale at Ammonihah) is, after all, my substitute principle for a Girardian universal law that God demands the cessation and nonparticipation in all violence.

Let me trace out a hypothetical Girardian response to the instances of the divine refusing to intercede in this Ammonihah narrative and comparable examples. Surely an infinite atonement comes bundled with infinite mercy, that is, if the quality of mercy is not strained. The Doctrine and Covenants asserts what the meaning of the word *infinite* is in the restoration: "For, behold, the mystery of godliness, how great is it! For, behold, I am endless, and the punishment which is given from my hand is endless punishment, for Endless is my name. Wherefore—Eternal punishment is God's punishment. Endless punishment is God's punishment."[34] Infinite punishment, infinite atonement, infinite mercy, infinite justice: they might in these circumstances mean not "unending duration" but rather "divine _____." The nature of the universe might place limits on interventions, boundaries we humans can't appreciate. Whatever rules are at play in the Gospels, Jesus can make an exception for a non-Israelite mother whose daughter is suffering or for his own mother coming up short in her responsibilities as a wedding host; Jesus's rescue of Mary is a petite allegory of the atonement. The Cana narrative is very commonly read as a

33. Moses 7:29–31.
34. Doctrine and Covenants 19:10–12.

live-streamed commentary, a dramatic and symbolic enactment, on the relationship between the Mosaic covenant and the Christian revelation that succeeds the earlier dispensation overseen by Moses.

The wedding feast reaches a crisis stage, for, to biblical people wine symbolizes joy: "Go thy way, eat thy bread with joy, and drink thy wine with a merry heart; for God now accepteth thy works."[35] The paucity or lack of wine is a cause for mourning because wine represents rejoicing: "And joy and gladness is taken from the plentiful field, and from the land of Moab; and I have caused wine to fail from the winepresses: none shall tread with shouting; their shouting shall be no shouting."[36] Wedding feasts are occasions for rejoicing, so to run out of wine, of joy, is both bad symbolism and bad reality. The announcement that "they have no wine" is dire and a commentary on the law of Moses framing the religious life of Jews. Not only is the wine or its lack symbolic but Mary tells the servants to fill up the waterpots, which they do "to the brim." These aren't ordinary waterpots but were used "after the manner of the purifying of the Jews."[37] Moses brought water forth from the rock; Jesus is going to bring wine forth from these stone jars when only water was poured in. This side note about waterpots is an important feature because as purity requirements demanded by the law of Moses, these pots represent the emptiness and the exhaustion of the joy that once resulted from that law but is now dry. When the servants fill the pots "to the brim," this signifies that what comes anew out of the pots will renew joy to overflowing. Six waterpots are mentioned. In biblical literature, six is the number of incompleteness, even of evil. It is one less than the number of wholeness or perfection: seven days of creation, Jesus's seven miracles. The number of the beast is 666 (repeated thrice makes it tri-

---

35. Ecclesiastes 9:7.
36. Jeremiah 48:33.
37. John 2:6.

ple emphasized as a number representing ultimate evil). The new wine fermented and aged in such a short time span in old stone containers then has to be approved by the governor of the feast. He samples the wine first and makes a little joke about the quality of the wine: "Every man at the beginning doth set forth good wine; and when men have well drunk, then that which is worse: but thou hast kept the good wine until now,"[38] a joke the modern reader might not get. The good wine is usually served first and the cheap wine later when the guests are so drunk they don't know the difference (this is the clue that this was fermented wine and not just grape juice). But saving the good wine for last symbolizes the relationship between the Mosaic dispensation and the Christian dispensation, where the really good stuff has been saved for now, with ordinances and commandments of sacrifice now transformed into ordinances and communion of grace and atonement.

An LDS version of Girard might say that in the New Testament accounts, Jesus indeed suborns mercy to rob justice. After all, Mary had not made the appropriate preparations for the wedding feast and the Syrophoenician mother had the bad fortune to be born a non-Jew at a time when the rules of the Mosaic covenant established an order of priority: first the blessings go to the house of Israel and then, when the time of the gentiles has come, to the nations of the earth. Whatever the side of the borderline the incidents fall on, breaking the rules or bending them, Jesus can make an exception. But sometimes the universe is implacable and rule-insistent. Such a notion of the infinity of Deity might offend the sensibilities of those theologians apologizing for the omni-God of creedal Christianity, which conception was advanced for millennia before the restoration, but it comports with the King Follet Discourse. This Christ who suffers with us when we suffer, who suffers for us so that we might not suffer, who comforts us when

---

38. John 2:10.

we crave comfort, who bears our burdens so they are light to us but heavy in their accumulation to him, who mourns when we grieve, who rejoices when we experience joy, this Christ is our companion and friend rather than some distant and remote deistic divinity. Well, one finds it difficult for an LDS Girard to exist if that is the description of such a mythical creature. Yet such a hypothesis would address traditional problems of the omni-God conception such as the problem of evil, the unimaginability of eternity, and the supposed withdrawal of the divine when we feel the dark night of the soul and the dawn no brighter while plaintively asking "my God, my God, why hast thou forsaken me?"

I don't pretend to offer an answer, although, like Abraham, I feel justified—even provoked by Deity—to ask the question, "Shall the God of heaven do justice?" The voice out of the whirlwind brings me up short for not having an answer: "Wilt thou also disannul my judgment? wilt thou condemn me, that thou mayest be righteous? Hast thou an arm like God? or canst thou thunder with a voice like him? Deck thyself now with majesty and excellency; and array thyself with glory and beauty."[39] I have questions, but for some inquiries no answers, for I am not yet so divinely arrayed as I one day hope to be garmented, as the voice from the whirlwind points to my limited understanding.

The exiled of Ammonihah have gone to Sidom, so Alma$_2$ and Amulek follow them there to do what they can. As a new convert himself, the new king of the Anti-Nephi-Lehies leads in making a covenant of peace, and the pledge of nonviolence reminds the people of their previous murderous life and the grace they have received by being forgiven for those sins: "now behold, my brethren, since it has been all that we could do (as we were the most lost of all mankind) to repent of all our sins and the many murders which we have committed, and to get God to take them away

---

39. Job 40:8.

from our hearts, for it was all we could do to repent sufficiently before God that he would take away our stain."[40] Alma$_2$ and Amulek do what they can to heal Zeezrom and establish a church. The preachers, as well as to those they preached, share their epiphany that "Oh, how merciful is our God! And now behold, since it has been as much as we could do to get our stains taken away from us"[41] to renounce whatever sins burden our pasts so we can step into the future with the whitest garments washed clean through that infinite atonement. Amulek's status as an exiled Ammonihahite is emphasized as a parade example of victimage: Amulek, having forsaken his wealth, is "rejected by those who were once his friends and also by his father and his kindred." As an exile from home, Amulek is now taken in and nurtured by Alma to find a new home.[42]

We aren't quite finished with the people of Ammonihah. Alma and Amulek have finished preaching there, and the believers of Ammonihah have been expelled, but we have yet to deal with the destruction of the city, which is recounted once in the very next chapter. The Lamanites start a war with the Nephites, and with Ammonihah on the borderlands between the two groups, the city is at high risk: "the armies of the Lamanites had come in upon the wilderness side, into the borders of the land, even into the city of Ammonihah, and began to slay the people and destroy the city. And now it came to pass, before the Nephites could raise a sufficient army to drive them out of the land, they had destroyed the people who were in the city of Ammonihah, and also some around the borders of Noah, and taken others captive into the wilderness."[43] After defeating the Lamanites and retaking captives, the story returns to the destruction of Ammonihah:

---

40. Alma 24:11.
41. Alma 24:15.
42. Alma 15:16.
43. Alma 16:2–3.

And thus ended the eleventh year of the judges, the Lamanites having been driven out of the land, and the people of Ammonihah were destroyed; yea, *every living soul of the Ammonihahites was destroyed*, and also their great city, *which they said God could not destroy, because of its greatness*. But behold, *in one day it was left desolate*; and the carcasses were mangled by dogs and wild beasts of the wilderness. Nevertheless, after many days their dead bodies were heaped up upon the face of the earth, and they were covered with a shallow covering. And now so great was the scent thereof that the people did not go in to possess the land of Ammonihah for many years. And it was called Desolation of Nehors; for they were of the profession of Nehor, who were slain; and their lands remained desolate.[44]

We have two accounts of the destruction of Ammonihah in the book of Alma. Joseph Spencer calls this one the theological history of the event.[45] But for a theological account, it is quite secular. We need to tease out the sacred element of the historical event. All the people and the city itself were destroyed in one day, "which [city] they said God could not destroy, because of its greatness."[46] Now note that Alma had not asserted that God could destroy the city in one day. Back in Alma 9, the narrative does start with Alma speaking in the first person: "I, Alma, having been commanded of God that I should take Amulek and go forth and preach again unto this people, or the people who were in the city of Ammonihah."[47] Alma still seems to be speaking in the first person when the relevant verses come up (that is, Alma is writing his own record, and it isn't Mormon summarizing Alma at this point but quoting a source). The Ammonihahites don't understand that the earth will pass away and they assert they "will not believe thy words if thou shouldst prophesy that this great city should be destroyed in one

---

44. Alma 16:9–11.
45. Private communication.
46. Alma 16:9.
47. Alma 9:1.

day."[48] So it is the wicked of Ammonihah who voice the idea about the city being destroyed in one day, speaking predictively in denial. For "they knew not that God could do such marvelous works, for they were a hard-hearted and a stiffnecked people."[49] So when, in chapter 16, the text notes that "in one day [Ammonihah] was left desolate,"[50] it isn't to fulfill any prophecy but to show God's power to contradict even the doubts of the unbelievers and persecutors. The theological point in Alma 16 is being made implicitly by allusion to the passage in Alma 9. God can and did destroy the mighty city of Ammonihah in one day, working through the Lamanites as agents. The wicked of Ammonihah are the instruments of a negative augury, the Lamanites the instruments of death. That is Mormon's take on these "marvelous works."[51]

A second theological lesson is driven home later in the passage: "after many days [the slain of Ammonihah's] dead bodies were heaped up upon the face of the earth, and they were covered with a shallow covering. And now so great was the scent thereof that the people did not go in to possess the land of Ammonihah for many years. And it was called Desolation of Nehors; for they were of the profession of Nehor, who were slain; and their lands remained desolate."[52] Again, the theological point is being made implicitly. One has to refer back to the narrative of Alma$_2$ and Amulek in Ammonihah to see the connection. After the slaughter of the innocents, the chief judge taunts Alma$_2$ and Amulek: "ye see that ye had not power to save those who had been cast into the fire; neither has God saved them because they were of thy faith."[53] The next verse notes that this judge "was after the order and faith of Nehor." The passage is a theological reflection on the destruc-

---

48. Alma 9:4.
49. Alma 9:5.
50. Alma 16:10.
51. Alma 9:5.
52. Alma 16:11.
53. Alma 14:11, 15.

tion of Ammonihah but a nuanced one that depends on our making connections through keywords to the previous narrative element. Not only does God have the power to destroy Ammonihah in a single day; the end result of adherence to the faith of Nehor can lead to what happened to Ammonihah, so that the stench of corpses leads directly from a fiery holocaust at Ammonihah to the stench of the Desolation of Nehors. A polity with leaders who act on the faith of the Nehors results in wickedness, which leads to destruction.

Before moving on to the secular explanation of Ammonihah's destruction, let me note two important details about why we have two different accounts and why they differ. For one thing, the account from Alma 8 to Alma 12 is largely told in the first person (in Alma 13 the narration switches to third-person narration). In other words, the story is told from Alma's perspective, presumably with $Alma_2$ having recorded his account, which is later summarized with some direct quotations by the book's editor and deuteronomist—Mormon. The secular account is part of Mormon's summary, and Mormon has different narrative purposes in mind. $Alma_2$ wants to subtly show God's hand in the destruction of Ammonihah, although he leaves it up to the reader to catch the allusive connection. That is why, right at the beginning of the Ammonihah narrative, when the angel stops $Alma_2$'s departure and sends him back to meet Amulek, the angel says, "say unto them, except they repent the Lord God will destroy them."[54] $Alma_2$ wants to show that divine message delivered and the threatened destruction completed; Alma is speaking in the first person (nevertheless being quoted by Mormon) as that part of the story unfolds. Fortunately, when Mormon is summarizing the end of the narrative in chapter 16, he makes the necessary connection

---

54. Alma 8:16.

through *Leitwörter*—keywords or leading words—alluding to the previous material so the reader can see the point.

Regarding the Girardian theme of violence and the sacred, the account asserts that the angel who triggers the whole affair says, absent repentance, "the Lord God will destroy them." That is in the portion of the story told from Alma$_2$'s point of view. The sponsorship of violent punishment is attributed to God, so to maintain that God is not the author of violent retribution requires that either Alma$_2$ (or the angel) don't quite grasp the divine plan and procedure.

The second detail is that each description of Ammonihah's destruction is integrally bound into the previous storyline. The theological description fulfills the word of warning the angel told Alma$_2$ to convey to the people; the context is theological. God's word is vindicated. The secular description is bound to the story of the people of Ammon who swore off violence entirely. The Alma 25 account of the destruction of Ammonihah is ancillary to the preceding story, a mere detail, so it is weighted with theological freight, as small means frequently are.

The two versions aren't unrelated. Much has been written about the notion of "dual causation" in biblical narrative. The cause of Absalom's death and the salvation of Jacob's family from famine through Joseph's descent into Egypt are both caused by human machinations and divine will. The Book of Mormon text connects the two relevant agencies by referring to Nehor or the order of Nehors. The Nehor story takes the reader back to the first chapter of Alma. There, Nehor emerges as a new teacher of wickedness who introduces priestcraft and enforces it by killing old man Gideon. Nehor's name isn't even introduced until the verse that tells of his death. He dies "an ignominious death" on the hill Manti, but his teachings live on after him.[55] In the first narrative

---

55. Alma 1:15–16.

relating the destruction of Ammonihah, the account notes that the chief judge and the teachers were after the order of Nehor.

Here is how Mormon summarizes the episode: the Lamanites attack and kill the people of Ammon, who don't fight back. The Lamanites get frustrated after murdering so many unresisting victims and instead go off to find Nephites to kill, finding substitute victims—the people of Ammonihah—for their first victims—the people of Ammon.[56] The theological version of that narrative implies a causal connection between divine will and the destruction of Ammonihah. This version doesn't contain such a causal inference but attributes the devastation of the city to human will. The reason for this difference may not be that one is secular and one sacred (although that might underlie the difference). It may be that the narrative contexts differ. It is natural in a story about the wickedness of the Ammonihahites for God's messengers to note at the end of the story that the people were killed because of their wicked behavior. But in this later, secular story, the destruction of Ammonihah is tangential to the previous narrative about the Anti-Nephi-Lehies.

Of those who killed Anti-Nephi-Lehies, most were former Nephites, rather than Lamanite descendants. The killers were broadly represented by Nephite dissenters: they "were Amalekites and Amulonites, the greatest number of whom were after the order of the Nehors."[57] But among those moved by conscience to repudiate this act of violence, none were former Nephites: "Now, among those who joined the people of the Lord, there were none who were Amalekites or Amulonites, or who were of the order of Nehor, but they were actual descendants of Laman and Lemuel."[58] The theological point of this narrative isn't connected to Ammonihah, but to deserting the truth: "And thus we can plainly

56. Alma 25:1–2.
57. Alma 24:28.
58. Alma 24:29.

discern, that after a people have been once enlightened by the Spirit of God, and have had great knowledge of things pertaining to righteousness, and then have fallen away into sin and transgression, they become more hardened, and thus their state becomes worse than though they had never known these things."[59] Then, two verses later, the story relates the destruction of Ammonihah.[60] There is no mention of Ammonihah's sins, and no spiritual point is raised about Alma$_2$'s and Amulek's preaching. If Mormon wants the reader to make a religious connection, it is by comparing the deaths of the Ammonihahites with the deaths of the Anti-Nephi-Lehies a few verses earlier. Of the latter group, the account tells us "there was not a wicked man slain among them; but there were more than a thousand brought to the knowledge of the truth; thus we see that the Lord worketh in many ways to the salvation of his people."[61] This is odd to refer to the murders of more than a thousand peaceful nonresisters as part of the work of salvation, but both the killers who repent and the martyrs are part of the work of salvation. The account of Ammonihah's demise is not part of the work of salvation because of that people's resistance to the work. Among the remaining city residents who are killed by the Lamanites there are no innocents sent to receive a reward in the next life: contrasting the Anti-Nephi-Lehies with the Ammonihahites, those victims of the Lamanites "are blessed, for they have gone to dwell with their God." The legacy of the Nehors is the desolation of Nehors and the stench of mass graves and the unburied dead.[62]

Any assertion that the God of the Book of Mormon has a one-dimensional message whose only language is peace and pacifism has to deal with hard cases, such as the events at Ammonihah. The argument that Mormon, the major author and redactor, just

59. Alma 24:30.
60. Alma 25:2.
61. Alma 24:27.
62. Alma 24:22.

doesn't get the God of the Book of Mormon needs more clarification, elaboration, and specification. A healthy dose of negative capability would inject into the discussion of the scriptures a view of God, of humans, and of the vertical and horizontal web of connections a more complicated and nuanced landscape that includes both Ammonihah and Jershon, and with that map of the terrain, a more three-dimensional view of Deity.

Chapter Sixteen

Fourth Nephi,
Generations without Rivalry,
Economic Competition,
Disputation, or Contention:
No -Ites Nor -Isms, No Parties
Nor Schisms, No 99 Nor 1%

T he book of Fourth Nephi chronicles a period between 35 CE and 231 CE, after the visit of Christ to the Lehites, in which the people lived in harmony and equity with each other. The effects of our first parents' fall were nullified. Love, charity, is the tonic that heals the world's wounds and reconciles humanity's rifts: "there was no contention in the land, because of the love of God which did dwell in the hearts of the people."[1] This utopian era was free of warfare, economic struggle, and poverty. This peaceful time was possible because "the people were all converted unto the Lord," and "every man did deal justly one with another."[2] The notable series of genocidal wars that frames both 3 Nephi and 4 Nephi is suspended. Four times in 4 Nephi 1:2–18 the text asserts the lack

---

1. 4 Nephi 1:15.
2. 4 Nephi 1:2.

of contention in *all* the land and among *all* the people. This unity is commanded earlier among a separatist and aspiring-utopian Nephite community, which is directed that they should have "no contention one with another" but should act in unity.[3] This harmony is made possible not through the leverage of violence (that is, through the monopoly of violence asserted by the state) but through a shared ideological framework and acceptance of collective responsibility for each other's temporal condition. Alma$_1$'s people at Helam can't maintain that unity for long because they are encroached upon by outside imperialistic groups. The 4 Nephi situation can be maintained for 165 years because "there were no robbers, nor murderers, neither were there Lamanites, nor any manner of –ites, but they were in one, the children of Christ, and heirs to the kingdom of God."[4]

One would think the existence of a utopian society becoming a reality in our spatial-temporal timeline would pose a serious difficulty to the Girardian thesis. Girard's scheme requires thousands of years for the Christian message of nonviolence and anti-sacrificialism to percolate and work its effect. Girard is an anti-utopian yearning for utopia. Eugene England, on the other hand, is both openly utopian and directly hopeful that such a topos is realizable. He points to the people of Ammon and the events in 4 Nephi[5] (both in the Book of Mormon, a resource not consulted by Girard) as examples of peace and harmony from the past to model how such societies might be realized in the future.[6] England also points to Shakespeare's plays as models of forgiveness that recon-

---

3. Mosiah 18:21.
4. 4 Nephi 1:17.
5. Eugene England, "Moroni and His Captains: Men of Peace in a Time of War," *Ensign* 7, no. 8 (Aug. 1977): 28–36.
6. England Eugene, "The Tragedy of Vietnam and the Responsibility of Mormons," Eugene England Foundation. eugeneengland.org/wp-content/uploads/sbi/articles/1967_e_001.pdf. First published in *Dialogue: A Journal of Mormon Thought* 2, no. 4 (Winter 1967): 65–100 [pages 71–91 for England's contribution].

cile humans to each other.[7] One has to be amazed and touched by England's hopefulness and inexhaustible optimism in human nature and in love's capacity to change human behavior. For Girardians, human nature is alleged to function on universal principles, invariant regarding culture, time, geographic place, language, gender, or individual personality, and Girard posits that only the intervention of a God can save us[8] from the mimetic characteristic that not only emerged with the fall but traces its genealogy to Cain. How was such a fundamental human design feature overcome during that 165-year period recorded in 4 Nephi? And overcome so suddenly—not after incubating over thousands of years, as Girard describes the impact of the Gospels, but immediately upon the appearance of the resurrected Christ?

Literary critics often note the unrealized ideals of utopias in Ursula K. Le Guin's writings. In "The Ones Who Walk away from Omelas," the inhabitants have everything they need or want, immediately: food, entertainment, sexual satisfaction. But all that luxury and pleasure is premised on the suffering and torture of one scapegoat child. School children go on field trips to view that suffering child, and perhaps hurl invective or objects. Those who can't abide that one flaw in an otherwise ideal world just one day head off to the mountains, knowing nothing of what lies beyond their single-defect utopia. Le Guin's fictions "Omelas" and *The Left Hand of Darkness* focus on themes such as utopian societies not fully realized. As Rebecca Adams notes, "Both works draw on the archetype of the scapegoat, mythically representing—and critiquing—the process of the violent foundation of culture which René

---

7. Eugene England, "Healing and Making Peace—In the World and the Church," *Sunstone* 15, no. 6 (Dec. 1991): 40–42.

8. Girard mentions Heidegger's famous claim that "only a God can save us," restricted from publication by Heidegger until after his death. Girard notes that Heidegger doesn't mean the biblical God, but Dionysus, the Greek god. René Girard, *When These Things Begin: Conversations with Michel Treguer*, trans. by Trevor Cribben Merrill (East Lansing: Michigan State University, 2014), 69.

Girard terms the 'victimage mechanism.'"[9] In Girard's view, as in Le Guin's, imagining utopias is problematic because "Omelas" still has its scapegoat and *Left Hand* still has its binary-gendered alien world. Yet, like the utopia of 4 Nephi that Girard doesn't recognize but England does, they all aspire to a violence-free society. Historically, human attempts to achieve utopia have resulted in oppression and the dissolution of the equality expressly desired (Shakers, Oneida Community, Brook Farm, New Harmony), or even mass murder (Leninism, Maoism, Khmer Rouge). The 4 Nephi utopia is more durable than most because it isn't based on scarcity but on abundance and sharing. Citing the foundation of cities as articulated by Girard in the founding bloodshed of Abel and Remus, Adams notes that "Symbolically, blood is an appropriate symbol to indicate a closed economy in which the good of some depends on the denial of good to others—as if there were only a limited amount of life to go around. Because the scapegoat's regenerative power is used up with the spilling of its blood, the process of life-giving must be replicated over and over, enacting a recurrent violent regeneration of culture by means of the victimage mechanism."[10] Perhaps the 4 Nephi utopia lasted as long as it did because, for a few generations, humans can remember an end to the shedding of blood, and instead a shift in the human economy to a currency backed by love.

One could posit that since Christ had just, through the power of God, endured and overcome the sacrificial mechanism in accomplishing the atonement and resurrection just before his ministry at Bountiful, that lingering effect permitted the descendants of Lehi to experience this long period of peace. How could the delayed-release medicine that took two millennia, from the time of the Gospels until the Christian message infused modernity with a sympathy for

---

9. Rebecca Adams, "Narrative Voice and Unimaginability of the Utopian 'Feminine' in Le Guin's *The Left Hand of Darkness* and 'The Ones Who Walk away from Omelas,'" *Utopian Studies* 2, nos. 1–2 (1991): 36.
10. Adams, "Narrative," 38.

the victims, take so long to have its effect on the larger culture, but for the Nephites, the same medicine was rapidly infused throughout the body of Christ and had its curative effect immediately upon the occurrence of Christ's crucifixion, resurrection, and ministry among the Nephites but wore off after one generation? A Book of Mormon believer who is also a Girardian would need to explore why the Old-World version of the declaration was a glacially timed-release capsule and the New World variety a fast-acting pill. However long the medicine in the Gospels took to be metabolized throughout the body of Western culture, "by offering an interpretive framework to read religion non-mythically, Christianity is less a religion than a hermeneutic of religion. Christianity's powerful perspective changes the course of world history."[11]

The central characteristic of this model Christian society, no longer Nephite nor Lamanite, was their economic equality.[12] The account notes that "every man did deal justly with one another," followed immediately by an expansion of that idea: "They had all things common among them; therefore there were not rich and poor, bond and free, but they were all free, and partakers of the heavenly gift."[13] During this time free of crime or warfare, "surely there could not be a happier people among all the people who had been created by the hand of God."[14] They were all so prosperous that they no longer had to share their possessions in common, and they further lost their unity when "they began to be divided into classes."[15] The text doesn't share enough information to let us dis-

---

11. Grant Kaplan, *René Girard, Unlikely Apologist: Mimetic Theory and Fundamental Theology* (Notre Dame, IN: University of Notre Dame Press, 2016), 118.

12. The Doctrine and Covenants makes a similar assertion. See Andrew C. Skinner, "Zion Gained and Lost: Fourth Nephi as the Quintessential Model," in *The Book of Mormon: Fourth Nephi through Moroni, From Zion to Destruction*, ed. Monte S. Nyman and Charles D. Tate, Jr. (Provo, UT: Religious Studies Center, 1992) 290; see Doctrine and Covenants 78:6.

13. 4 Nephi 1:3.

14. 4 Nephi 1:16.

15. 4 Nephi 1:23, 25–26.

tinguish between social and economic stratification (almost certainly intertwined), but the context of riches and prosperity and common possession of goods clearly points toward economic class division.[16] Fourth Nephi looks very much like a critique of inequality. Let me restate that last idea: while 4 Nephi critiques economic inequality, it more importantly shows how such inequality works in tandem with violence, political division, and religious discord to bring a unified, righteous society into ruin.

Patrick Mason and J. David Pulsipher borrow language from Catholic thought on economic violence: structures of sin. They write, "Among the most common forms of structural violence that the scriptures consistently and unflinchingly denounce is the sin of economic injustice, often seen through the lens of inequality."[17] God's covenant is often framed as contracted with individuals (Abraham, Adam and Eve, Moses), but these are communal covenants, not just to Abraham but to all humans. The Nephites, the Jaredites, the Israelites: they are often judged communally, as is the latter-day church.[18] These structures of sin can implicate even those who don't directly participate in them, but our individual responsibilities are inextricably intertwined with communal obligations.[19] Zion-like communities in the Book of Mormon (Alma$_1$'s people at Helam, the 4 Nephi saints), the old world examples (Enoch, Melchizedek), and the New Testament example (the early church saints who had all their goods in common),[20] all are communities of people who "are deeply converted to the good news of Jesus and gather together in unity for both physical protection and spiritual fellowship. They establish a society in which they seek to eliminate

16. 4 Nephi 1:26.
17. Patrick Q. Mason and J. David Pulsipher, *Proclaim Peace: The Restoration's Answer to an Age of Conflict* (Provo, UT: BYU Maxwell Institute/Deseret, 2021), 200.
18. Mason and Pulsipher, *Proclaim*, 201.
19. Mason and Pulsipher, *Proclaim*, 202.
20. Acts 4:34–35.

all socioeconomic distinctions among them. They do so through a program of economic justice that goes far beyond mere sentiment, charity, or welfare."[21] These lessons from the Book of Mormon are intended as much for us modern people as for the descendants of Lehi living in Zarahemla. Lessons of utopia gained and utopia lost. Mason and Pulsipher observe, "Although the Book of Mormon narrative ultimately ends with the complete abandonment of Zion principles and a descent into genocidal warfare, these few verses in 4 Nephi, along with other scriptural accounts of other Zion communities, beckon readers to attempt similar efforts."[22]

The Book of Mormon previously made the connection between economic arrangements and violence against the poor. In the portion narrated by Mormon and just a generation before the period of peace and unity ushered in by Christ, the text notes that Nephite wickedness was the source of the people's problems: political dissension and defeat in war. Mormon summarizes:

> And it was because of the pride of their hearts, because of their exceeding riches, yea, it was because of their oppression to the poor, withholding their food from the hungry, withholding their clothing from the naked, and smiting their humble brethren upon the cheek, making a mock of that which was sacred, denying the spirit of prophecy and of revelation, murdering, plundering, lying, stealing, committing adultery, rising up in great contentions, and deserting away into the land of Nephi, among the Lamanites.[23]

King Benjamin, famously, also asserted the need to be mindful of God's grace toward us, and if so,

> [Y]e will not have a mind to injure one another, but to live peaceably, and to render to every man according to that which is his due. And ye will not suffer your children that they go hungry, or

21. Mason and Pulsipher, *Proclaim*, 207.
22. Mason and Pulsipher, *Proclaim*, 214.
23. Helaman 4:12.

naked; neither will *ye* suffer that they transgress the laws of God, and fight and quarrel one with another, and serve the devil, who is the master of sin, or who is the evil spirit which hath been spoken of by our fathers, he being an enemy to all righteousness. But *ye* will teach them to walk in the ways of truth and soberness; *ye* will teach them to love one another, and to serve one another. And also, *ye* yourselves will succor those that stand in need of your succor; *ye* will administer of your substance unto him that standeth in need; and *ye* will not suffer that the beggar putteth up his petition to you in vain, and turn him out to perish.[24]

Rendering to every man his due and seeing that children do not go hungry or naked should be viewed here not just as directed to parents ensuring the temporal support of their own children but a larger obligation to ensure the physical wellbeing of children more generally in the society in question. The opposite here of caring lovingly for children is explicitly framed as violent: the directive not to "injure" but to "live peaceably" is coupled with the injunction to parents not to let their children go hungry, be naked, disobey, quarrel, or serve the devil. I have emphasized the pronoun *ye*, which isn't common enough in contemporary English to be familiar. It is a plural pronoun, whereas *you* is a singular pronoun in early Modern, Middle, and Old English (*you* does double duty today, serving as both the singular and plural version of the second-person pronoun). When the King James version was published (1611), it was still generally used in that communal sense: "Ye are the salt of the earth," and "ye are the light of the world." Whereas the beatitudes use the third-person pronoun *they* ("blessed are *they* that mourn," "blessed are the pure in heart: for *they* shall see God") to distance and refer to a group comprised neither of the speaker nor the listeners, the more direct address of the second-person plural pronoun is more often used by Jesus in this address: "Be *ye* therefore perfect, even as your Father which

---

24. Mosiah 4:13–16. Italics added.

is in heaven is perfect." Assuming a point to Joseph Smith's use of some of these archaic linguistic forms (archaic even in 1830) in translation, we have reason to highlight Benjamin's injunction as having communal elements: "*ye* will not suffer your children that they go hungry, or naked," not only our genetic children but other children also. And our obligation to the poor isn't just to close relatives but to the larger group of humanity: "*ye* yourselves will succor those that stand in need of your succor; *ye* will administer of your substance unto him that standeth in need." Note that the *ye* as a plural pronoun is not always consistently so used in antebellum America, but it is the general rule with exceptions.

There is some textual evidence for the shift between singular second-person pronouns and plural second personal pronouns being relevant, for immediately after discussing succoring the poor, Benjamin makes a similar point using singular and plural first-person pronouns (and also, by the way, singular and plural third-person pronouns): "Perhaps *thou* shalt say: The man has brought upon himself *his* misery; therefore *I* will stay my hand, and will not give unto *him* of *my* food, nor impart unto *him* of *my* substance that *he* may not suffer, for *his* punishments are just.—"[25] This narrowing the field to a specific (hypothetical) case study focuses on the individual beggar and the individual giver: "whosoever doeth this the same hath great cause to repent; and except *he* repenteth of that which *he* hath done *he* perisheth forever, and hath no interest in the kingdom of God."[26] Benjamin then returns to the first person and plural: "For behold, are *we* not all beggars? Do *we* not all depend upon the same Being, even God, for all the substance which *we* have, for both food and raiment, and for gold, and for silver, and for all the riches which *we* have of every kind?"[27]

---

25. Mosiah 4:17. Italics added.
26. Mosiah 4:18.
27. Mosiah 4:19.

The next few verses split attention between the second-person plural and singular:

> [E]ven at this time, *ye* have been calling on his name, and begging for a remission of your sins. And has he suffered that *ye* have begged in vain? Nay; he has poured out his Spirit upon *you*, and has caused that your hearts should be filled with joy, and has caused that your mouths should be stopped that *ye* could not find utterance, so exceedingly great was your joy. And now, if God, who has created *you*, on whom *you* are dependent for your lives and for all that *ye* have and are, doth grant unto you whatsoever *ye* ask that is right, in faith, believing that *ye* shall receive, O then, how ye ought to impart of the substance that *ye* have one to another.[28]

Benjamin continues from that point, speaking in the first-person singular. Benjamin also brings attention to both an individual and communal responsibility to ensure good care for children and the stranger.

Economic divisions develop concurrently with political schisms after Christ's sojourn with the Nephites. This portion of the Book of Mormon implies rather than states the connection between economy and violence, that class division leads to social violence, that economic arrangements themselves can be a form of violence. The implication is that once the people divide into the rich and the poor, they soon distinguish themselves as rich churchgoers and poor churchgoers, rather than as Nephites and Lamanites, and then these latter two groups become mimetic rivals: "the people of Nephi began to be proud in their hearts, because of their exceeding riches, and became vain like unto their brethren, the Lamanites." Just a few years on (300 CE), Lamanites and Nephites can no longer even be differentiated: and they had "become exceedingly wicked one like unto another,"[29] a mimetic rivalry in evil.

---

28. Mosiah 4:20–21. Italics added.
29. 4 Nephi 1:43, 45.

Chapter Seventeen

Varying Attitudes toward Violence and Nonviolence in the Book of Mormon

L ike the Book of Mormon, the Bible is a fissured text: the Bible isn't uniform because it was composed by writers living centuries apart responding to local circumstances historically varied. The Book of Mormon is much more homogenous considering it has three main authors: Nephi$_1$, Mormon, and Moroni$_2$, each with his own personality, agenda, and historical context. Even so, Mormon and Moroni$_2$ are nearly a thousand years removed from Nephi$_1$. The reader would expect that divine inspiration would provide some stable latticework of consistency, tying together the different elements written by writers and assembled by redactors over such a long span.

Similarly with the Bible, expert judgment varies, but the shortest range of content production varies from 1,200 BCE to 165 CE, while the longest range estimates the beginning of that process perhaps a thousand years earlier. Keep in mind that to provide some specific dates of biblical composition, I have had to vastly oversimplify the issues. But, just to provide some concrete numbers, let me cite some biblical criticism. These dates are broadly disputed among specialists, but here is the mainstream account dating biblical books.

Biblical critics generally posit that the Pentateuch (the first five books of the Bible: Genesis, Exodus, Leviticus, Numbers, and Deuteronomy) was written in stages by different writers in different time periods. This is called the Documentary Hypothesis.[1] These four writers are designated by the first letter of the names assigned them: J (the Yahwist refers to God by the name of Yahweh, written with a J in German), the Elohist (E, for using the name Elohim or its variants for God), D (for the Deuteronomist, you guessed it—writing Deuteronomy), and P (for the Priestly writer, who presumably wrote passages about ritual, law, and genealogical lists). These writers would sometimes insert older sources bodily into their compositions (songs, quotations, proverbs, traditions) or, conversely, felt free to insert or change passages in earlier compositions. Again, though widely disputed among experts, that would put the composition starting with the writing of E between 922 and 722 BCE and J between 848 and 722 BCE.[2] D is generally viewed as responding to the two previous main bodies of work just before the Babylonian exile in 587 BCE with perhaps some edits and additions inserted after the exile. P probably came later but before 539, when R (for Redactor, or editor, who assembled the written heritage into a composite work) combined what were previously separate documents in the Torah, also called the Pen-

---

1. This hypothesis was, seventy years ago, the conventional wisdom among professional biblical critics (excepting those strongly committed to fundamentalist views of biblical inspiration and composition and those holding views adjacent to such positions). Since then, it has undergone such dramatic revision that I am not sure how much remains intact. In the absence of a consensus regarding a replacement theory, it remains the default in the profession, despite strong reservations about its defensibility. For a summary of the LDS attitude toward the biblical canon generally, see Daniel Becerra, "The Biblical Canon," in *The Bible and the Latter-day Saint Tradition*, ed. by Taylor G. Petry, Cory Crawford, and Eric A. Eliason (Salt Lake City, UT: University of Utah Press, 2023), 117–28.

2. Richard Elliott Friedman, *Who Wrote the Bible?* (New York: Summit, 1987), 87.

tateuch. A cluster of biblical critics (usually called "minimalists") moves the entire grouping of texts to centuries later than these dates, perhaps into the Persian (539–332 BCE) or Hellenistic periods (332–363 BCE).

The other portions of the Hebrew Bible followed, with Daniel the last part of the book to be composed. Making the dating process harder to be precise, these older portions of the Bible were edited and revised by successive generations to meet contemporary needs: "None of these texts have reached us in their 'original' form. Instead, all were subject to creative and repeated revision, addition, emendation and editing across a number of generations reflecting the shifting ideological interests of their curators, who regarded them as sacred writings."[3] To expect that such a literary production would speak with a single ideologically and historically unified voice and perspective would be unreasonable, especially considering all the historical, poetic, devotional, proverbial, and prophetic works that comprise the Bible. Similarly, when the Bible and the Book of Mormon discuss attitudes toward violence, one would expect different points of view. Girard sees clearly that we can't simply bowdlerize the elements of the Bible or its tradition that we find distasteful; we must account for the text as a whole.[4] In reading the Bible and the Book of Mormon, we too must deal with the book as a whole. We can't expurgate the portions we don't like. Treating the whole text, we have to recognize that there is no single meaning to be derived from it, and the parts, in tension with each other, if they are to be reconciled, must be squared using more sophisticated joinery. Just as with the Bible, the Book of Mormon advances various attitudes toward violence.

---

3. Francesca Stavrakopoulou, *God: An Anatomy* (New York: Knopf, 2022), 12.
4. Fergus Kerr, "Revealing the Scapegoat Mechanism: Christianity after Girard," in *Philosophy, Religion and the Spiritual Life*, Royal Institute of Philosophy Supplement 32 ed. Michael McGhee, 161–75. (Cambridge: Cambridge University Press, 1992), 172.

I have cited some of the passages (and will yet cite more) where the Book of Mormon seems to endorse violence, such as Nephi killing Laban to obtain the plates and the summary execution of king-men rebels and traitors by Moroni₁. The Book of Mormon contains other narratives I haven't analyzed that seem to approve of violence, or at least fail to critique it (for example, the hanging of Zemnarihah, the summary execution of king-men by Moroni₁, and Teancum's stealthy killing of Amalickiah and his brother Ammoron—all in the context of warfare).[5] There is too much going on to treat every potential reference to violence in the book. I hope I have addressed representative samples in the following material as I explore different concepts and associations attached to force.

The Logical Fallacy of Moral Equivalence

If we generate universal moral principles applicable to all relevant historical situations, cultures, and local circumstances, then we dull our moral faculties, our ability to make fine distinctions. To issue invariant universal judgments about violence requires no moral nuance. Most moral decisions don't require fine distinctions, but when those that do arise, we should have the capacity to manage them. Sometimes victims need to be defended, sometimes those in peril need to be rescued, and sometimes the perpetrators need to be punished—with violence. I say this as someone opposed in principle to capital punishment (and here is my little totalizing hypocrisy—*all* capital punishment—but on consequentialist grounds: if the state uses capital punishment as a means of enforcing the law, that establishes a pattern and a moral disposition for how less law-abiding citizens might work out their matrix of relations with other citizens). Should Vladimir Putin be charged

---

5. 3 Nephi 4:28; Alma 62:9; Alma 51:33–34; Alma 62:36.

in the International Criminal Court for war crimes his government and military have committed since the invasion of Ukraine in early 2022? (One such charge has already been made in that court about the violent abduction and removal of children from their culture and parents in a war zone, but more indictments are likely to follow.) If found guilty, should he be hung like some Nuremberg defendants were? I would oppose the last element.

One of the most common definitions of *government* political scientists offer is this: an institution that can make a plausible claim in a geographical area to a monopoly on the instruments of violence (the courts, the police, the penal institutions, the legislative and executive functions, the military, the foreign policy apparatus). The Ukrainian government (as long as its military doesn't engage in reprisals and war crimes) cannot be morally equated with the Russian government—the violence the two nations have engaged in has a totally different quality, one acting out of self-defense and the other out of invasive imperialism. The Allied governments of World War II (as long as war crimes weren't committed, or, if some were committed, the proper judicial process were invoked) cannot be morally equated with the Third Reich, the Mussolini administration, or the Tojo government. To say that an organization or an individual that engaged in violence to protect others from violence is "just as bad" as the perpetrator is a form of moral obtuseness indicating a clear lack of moral formation in the person making such an argument or the media organ publishing the assertion. Such moral equivalencies emerge from a desire to support a morally repugnant person, government, or institution without having to defend the subject's immoral actions. Such moral parity is a red herring logical fallacy attempting to distract from the relevant issues.[6] Regardless of the ethical framework that

6. See updated examples of such fallacious arguments. E. J. Dionne, Jr., "Moral Equivalence and Donald Trump," *Washington Post* (Sept. 10, 2016): https://www.washingtonpost.com/blogs/post-partisan/wp/2016/09/10/moral-equiv-

establishes the foundation of a person's examination of the issues (deontology, utilitarianism, divine command, hedonism, contractualism, egoism), to suggest the moral interchangeability of initiators of and self-defenders against wartime aggression would be a moral obscenity.

Self-defense

I can't treat all Book of Mormon passages that endorse violence in self-defense. No publisher would ever approve a single volume long enough to meet such an expectation while doing justice to the topic. Of course, it must be kept in mind that of the three main Book of Mormon writers, Mormon and Moroni$_2$ were military men. Even Nephi$_1$, the third main Nephite historian, made weapons upon the separation of the Nephites from Lamanites modeled on the sword of Laban and wielded that sword in the defense of his people.[7] To assert that Nephi$_1$ might have later in life turned pacifist, having felt guilty over making a (wrong) choice to kill Laban just lacks all textual support. We open Nephi$_1$'s own narrative with his decollation of Laban and we close it with Jacob's tribute to his brother, that same Nephi, whom Jacob describes as "a great protector for them, having wielded the sword of Laban in their defence."[8] That is how the first three books of the Book of Mormon open, and these books span the length of Nephi's life. There are two symbols that predominate and provide continuity

---

alence-and-donald-trump/. Steve Denning, "The Myth of Moral Equivalence: The Battle for the Soul of America," *Forbes* (Oct. 29, 2018): https://www.forbes.com/sites/stevedenning/2018/10/29/the-myth-of-moral-equivalence-the-battle-for-the-soul-of-america/. (Accessed 9-28-2023). Any governmental, religious, or educational institution that hasn't educated its members, citizens, or students to recognize and reject moral equivalencies such as these has failed in one of its main duties, to address the moral formation of the people it serves.

7. 2 Nephi 5:14; Jacob 1:10.

8. Jacob 1:10.

for Nephi$_1$'s vitae: (1) written records and (2) the sword of Laban. That sword emerges in the first story with Laban, is referenced after Lehi dies and the great family schism occurs, and is mentioned in Jacob's obituary for this brother. In his eulogy, Jacob calls Nephi$_1$ "a great protector" of his people who had labored "*in all his days* for their welfare."[9] Jacob explicitly mentions Nephi$_1$ wielding the sword of Laban in violent self-defense. That view of Nephi$_1$ stretches from 1 Nephi 4, to 2 Nephi 5, to Jacob 1—which is Nephi's (auto)biographical arc as portrayed in the Book of Mormon. Hypotheticals that Nephi$_1$ later repudiated his actions in his (failed) "Abrahamic test" are textually unsupported, and the notion that later in life he renounced violence to become a pacifistic psalmist must be invented whole cloth.

Another highlighted hero in the book is Moroni$_1$, who is apparently so admired by Mormon that generations later the latter names his son after him. Moroni$_1$ uses violence and the sacred concurrently to achieve his social and military aims. He advocates deadly self-defense and executes opponents; he is willing to sacrifice some for the benefit of the many when fighting insurrections, and he threatens violence in the name of God against his own rulers, whom, he later discovers, hadn't transgressed against his cause and people's interests.[10]

Mormon is the narrator in much of the Book of Mormon. His writings comprise about 206 of its 531 pages in the edition we read. That rounds up to roughly 39 percent of the text. His is the major ethical voice throughout the scripture. In that long section of Alma that recounts war after military campaign after civil conflict, it is Mormon who conveys the book's moral center of gravity. He states the goal of the Lamanites, to conquer the Nephites and

---

9. Jacob 1:10.
10. Alma 46:30–36; Mack C. Stirling, "Violence in the Scriptures: Mormonism and the Cultural Theory of René Girard," *Dialogue: A Journal of Mormon Thought* 43, no. 1 (Spring 2010): 84.

enslave them.[11] The Nephites, however, "were inspired by a better cause, for they were not fighting for monarchy nor power but they were fighting for their homes and their liberties, their wives and their children, and their all, yea, for their rites of worship and their church."[12] Twice in the next two verses Mormon puts into the mouth of God the Nephites' obligation toward their enemies:

> And they were doing that which they felt was the duty which they owed to their God; for the Lord had said unto them, and also unto their fathers, that: Inasmuch as ye are not guilty of the first offense, neither the second, ye shall not suffer yourselves to be slain by the hands of your enemies. And again, *the Lord has said that: Ye shall defend your families even unto bloodshed.* Therefore for this cause were the Nephites contending with the Lamanites, to defend themselves, and their families, and their lands, their country, and their rights, and their religion.[13]

When the text straightforwardly states "the Lord has said that: Ye shall defend your families even unto bloodshed," then it is hard to maintain that the book is universally against violence. A reader may maintain that both Mormon and Moroni₁ fell short of a complete understanding of the pre-Christian and post-Christian gospel embodied in a Girardian renunciation of evil imitation and violence, but that seems a too-facile use of a Girardian filter to sort genuinely Christian and divine elements in the text from those contaminated by fallen human nature and its mimetic inclination. It would be astonishing to attribute a pacifism to the Book of Mormon when the scripture so explicitly and repeatedly asserts the right to defend family, home, religion, and liberty through bloodshed; violence is not endorsed as a first resort nor as a preemptive measure, but the text never condemns its use in later resorts to self-defense.

---

11. Alma 43:29.
12. Alma 43:45.
13. Alma 43:46–47.

Patrick Mason and David Pulsipher offer a brief introduction to the Christian just war doctrine tradition. A just war is limited by several tests: (1) moved by a just cause (saving innocents, self-defense); (2) enacted by appropriately authorized authority (endorsed by a government, or by a supra-governmental institution such as the UN); (3) using force as a last recourse (having made good-faith diplomatic efforts); (4) in the resort to violence, making a distinction between noncombatants and combatants; and (5) using force proportionate to the offense (if a guerilla force kills two opposing regular soldiers, retaliating by killing fifty civilians is disproportionate).[14] Mason and Pulsipher note that the just war tradition is an improvement upon common human practices of wars, but calls for yet more progress. They propose several amendments and expansions based on modern revelation.[15] I use their sub-headings.

1. **Disinclination**: used as a last resort, the Doctrine and Covenants and Book of Mormon instruct to postpone any violent retaliation responses after a first, second, and third provocation.

2. **Forbearance**: be the recipient of violence before responding violently (this precludes preemptive strikes).

3. **Divine Consent**: ask for and receive divine approval before engaging in violence.

4. **Accountability**: those responding to violence with violence need to accept responsibility for that choice among the various other options available.

---

14. Patrick Q. Mason and J. David Pulsipher, *Proclaim Peace: The Restoration's Answer to an Age of Conflict* (Provo, UT: BYU Maxwell Institute/Deseret, 2021), 134–41.

15. D&C 98.

In taking the Christian just war tradition as their starting point, Mason and Pulsipher designate that doctrine as the lower law. The four points listed above begin the process of moving to a higher law, which includes the following additional elements:

a. **Restraint**: the violence should end as early as possible.

b. **Grief**: the violent reaction, though justified, should be grieved by those who cause it because of the pain and suffering it causes.

c. **Steadfast Connection**: those who receive our violent response should remain in prayer and action still spiritually bonded with us.

d. **Increased Love**: our love and charity toward the recipients of our violence should increase rather than decrease.[16] Such a higher law sets even more stringent standards for justified war than the just war tradition.

The Book of Mormon is pragmatic about these concerns. Decisions about whether to use violence are usually made by consulting God and evaluating the particular circumstances:

And this was their faith, that by so doing God would prosper them in the land, or in other words, if they were faithful in keeping the commandments of God that he would prosper them in the land; yea, warn them to flee, or to prepare for war, according to their danger; And also, that God would make it known unto them whither they should go to defend themselves against their enemies, and by so doing, the Lord would deliver them; and this was the faith of Moroni, and his heart did glory in it; not in the shedding of blood but in doing good, in preserving his people, yea, in keeping the commandments of God, yea, and resisting iniquity.[17]

---

16. Mason and Pulsipher, *Proclaim*, 141–45.
17. Alma 48:15–16.

For Mormon, violence used in self-defense is not only a viable option but sometimes the best and divinely inspired option. Self-defense isn't the first choice but can legitimately be exercised "in preserving his people, yea, in keeping the commandments of God, yea, and resisting iniquity."

Notice that the pattern Mormon just described of

1. in the case of a lethal danger,

2. "whither they should go to defend themselves against their enemies"

3. the Lord "warn[s] them"

4. "to flee," or

5. "to prepare for war, according to their danger"

6. "that God would make it known unto them," after which

7. "by so doing God would prosper them in the land, or in other words, if they were faithful in keeping the commandments of God that he would prosper them in the land."[18]

The same procedure is related in different order by Nephi₁ after Lehi's death and his brothers' threats upon his life: (1) Laman and Lemuel "did seek to take away my life,"[19] (3) so "the Lord did warn me"[20] (4) "that I, Nephi, should depart from them and flee into the wilderness, and all those who would go with me,"[21] (5) to prepare for self-defense: "And I, Nephi, did take the sword of Laban, and after the manner of it did make many swords, lest by any means the people who were now called Lamanites should come upon us and destroy us,"[22] (2) so "we did take our tents and whatsoever things

---

18. Alma 48:15–16.
19. 2 Nephi 5:4.
20. 2 Nephi 5:5.
21. 2 Nephi 5:5.
22. 2 Nephi 5:14.

were possible for us, and did journey in the wilderness for the space of many days,"[23] (6) taking a group consisting of "all those who would go with me were those who believed in the warnings and the revelations of God,"[24] and (7) God blessed Nephi's group upon their arrival in the land of Nephi, so "we began to prosper exceedingly, and to multiply in the land."[25] This pattern we see in Alma 48:15–16 is not new to Moroni$_1$, as reported by Mormon. Remember the hermeneutical principle ingrained in Hebraic, Judaic, Israelite, Nephite, and first-generation Jewish-Christian writers: what happens to the fathers happens to the sons. Nephi$_1$ set the pattern of what to do when threatened with violence: flee when warned by God to flee, reestablish the community, and prepare to defend yourself. As Mormon wrote, "Now the Nephites were taught to defend themselves against their enemies, even to the shedding of blood if it were necessary; yea, and they were also taught never to give an offense, yea, and never to raise the sword except it were against an enemy, except it were to preserve their lives."[26]

These Nephite writers, from Nephi$_1$ to Mormon—from Nephite A to Z (well, perhaps Y)—follow what generations before did, for what happens to the fathers and mothers is a lesson to the sons and daughters when it comes to issues of violence, self-defense, and self-preservation. The Book of Mormon reader of a Girardian orientation, when encountering these passages where God is reported to endorse violence committed in self-defense, can accept that the scripture is not pacifistic on a matter of principle, or can assert that the writers rely on the lesser angels of human nature, and the Nephites' stalwart defense of home, family, and religion a mistaken notion of God's expectations.

23. 2 Nephi 5:7.
24. 2 Nephi 5:6.
25. 2 Nephi 5:13, and see also verse 11.
26. Alma 48:14.

Offensive War

I have cited the passage in Alma 43:46 where the Lord tells the Nephites to abstain from violent response until the third offense. Even when the people of Limhi are in bondage to the Lamanites and launch an offensive war to liberate themselves, they have still been defeated three times (perhaps the Alma 43 passage alludes to the Zeniffite experience or the just war rule articulated in Alma 43 that is repeated there from pre-Zeniffite Nephite experience in a record not included in the Book of Mormon), after which they submit to Lamanite oppression peacefully.[27] The narrative could be read to warn against offensive warfare.

After Mormon refuses to lead the Nephites in battle, "and when they had sworn by all that had been forbidden them by our Lord and Savior Jesus Christ, that they would go up unto their enemies to battle, and avenge themselves of the blood of their brethren, behold the voice of the Lord came unto me, saying: Vengeance is mine, and I will repay; and because this people repented not after I had delivered them, behold, they shall be cut off from the face of the earth."[28] Shortly after this discussion about eschewing vengeance, Mormon notes that the Nephites suffered defeat because they engaged in offensive war: "And it was because the armies of the Nephites went up unto the Lamanites that they began to be smitten; for were it not for that, the Lamanites could have had no power over them. But, behold, the judgments of God will overtake the wicked; and it is by the wicked that the wicked are punished; for it is the wicked that stir up the hearts of the children of men unto bloodshed."[29] The Book of Mormon can reasonably be said to forbid offensive warfare.

After the sons of Mosiah reunite, having brought many Lamanites to God, having renounced their wicked ways and violence, and

---

27. Mosiah 21:10–12.
28. Mormon 3:14–15.
29. Mormon 4:4–5.

having been protected by the Nephites by moving to the land of Jershon as their inheritance (the Hebrew word *Jershon* means "to inherit"),[30] they rejoice in the success of their mission. Ammon reminds them what many Nephites said to them about the prospects of their journey: "Now do ye remember, my brethren, that we said unto our brethren in the land of Zarahemla, we go up to the land of Nephi, to preach unto our brethren, the Lamanites, and they laughed us to scorn?"[31] Mocking such aspirations of bringing the Lamanites to God, they instead propose their preferred policy toward the Lamanites:

> For they said unto us: Do ye suppose that ye can bring the Lamanites to the knowledge of the truth? Do ye suppose that ye can convince the Lamanites of the incorrectness of the traditions of their fathers, as stiffnecked a people as they are; whose hearts delight in the shedding of blood; whose days have been spent in the grossest iniquity; whose ways have been the ways of a transgressor from the beginning? Now my brethren, ye remember that this was their language. And moreover they did say: Let us take up arms against them, that we destroy them and their iniquity out of the land, lest they overrun us and destroy us.[32]

That latter policy would have been an offensive, preemptive war and would have been immoral and contrary to divine injunctions. These converted Lamanites have not only embraced the preachers' message of peace but have also exhibited their love toward God with concrete action: "For behold, they had rather sacrifice their lives than even to take the life of their enemy; and they have buried their weapons of war deep in the earth, because of their love towards their brethren. And now behold I say unto you, has there been so great love in all the land? Behold, I say unto you, Nay, there has not, even among the Nephites."[33] I have, in my discussion of the people of Ammon, noted

---

30. "Jershon," Book of Mormon Onomasticon, https://onoma.lib.byu.edu/index.php/JERSHON). (Accessed 10-9-2023).
31. Alma 26:23.
32. Alma 26:24–25.
33. Alma 26:32–33.

that Ammon in this passage characterizes their dying by not resisting as a form of "sacrifice," an offering with a positive connotation.

The Book of Mormon's War Chapters

Moroni₁ is introduced in Alma 43:16. From that chapter to the end of the book of Alma (more precisely, to the penultimate chapter 62), these war chapters relentlessly relate the conflicts between the Nephites and Lamanites, only pausing for breath to summarize conflict internal to the Nephite polity. Mormon does occasionally extol the greatness of Moroni₁, but always in the context of Moroni₁'s leadership. In chapter 50, the onrushing warfare narrative points to cities rebuilt and prosperity obtained, despite the Nephites' inability to stay unified internally to make themselves stronger in their struggles with the Lamanites: "for it has been their quarrelings and their contentions, yea, their murderings, and their plunderings, their idolatry, their whoredoms, and their abominations, which were among themselves, which brought upon them their wars and their destructions."[34] In other parts of the Book of Mormon these vices are usually attributed to the Lamanites, not the Nephites. Oddly, this period of prosperity without peace is credited not to the chief judge but to the military leader (in the U.S., we don't attribute prosperity during a conflict or otherwise to the Chairman of the Joint Chief of Staff but to the civilian leader—the President—and the exchange between Moroni₁ and Pahoran demonstrates something similar to civilian command of the military), with an allusion to Nephi: "But behold there never was a happier time among the people of Nephi, since the days of Nephi, than in the days of Moroni, yea, even at this time, in the twenty and first year of the reign of the judges."[35] Moroni₁ is compared to

---

34. Alma 50:21.
35. Alma 50:23. This alludes to what we know as 2 Nephi 5:27.

the first Nephi who came out of Jerusalem—high praise from Mormon to write up $Moroni_1$ as a recapitulation of $Nephi_1$.

Not only is $Moroni_1$ compared to $Nephi_1$, he is also contrasted with Amalickiah (one of the Nephite dissenters), defector to the Lamanite side, and eventually, Lamanite king. Mormon demonstrates the motivational difference between the Nephite and Lamanite military leaders. After Amalickiah became king by hook, crook, and murder, he prepared the Lamanites for war with anti-Nephite propaganda[36] and indoctrinated his people with the hatred they needed to accomplish the new king's goal: "to overpower the Nephites and to bring them into bondage."[37] But $Moroni_1$ was driven by entirely different desires.

The central theme of these war years (74 BCE–57 BCE) until $Moroni_1$ retires as military commander[38] is first broached in chapter 50—that the promises of prosperity were delivered because the people kept the commandments, more or less:

> And we see that these promises have been verified to the people of Nephi; for it has been their quarrelings and their contentions, yea, their murderings, and their plunderings, their idolatry, their whoredoms, and their abominations, which were among themselves, which brought upon them their wars and their destructions. And those who were faithful in keeping the commandments of the Lord were delivered at all times, whilst thousands of their wicked brethren have been consigned to bondage, or to perish by the sword, or to dwindle in unbelief, and mingle with the Lamanites.[39]

Mormon returns to this theme in a few chapters to treat it in more detail. Internal division (insurrection), theft, squabbling, idol wor-

---

36. Alma 48:1–2.
37. Alma 48:4.
38. Alma 62:43.
39. Alma 50:21–22.

ship, and sexual sin are the causes of their wars (with the Lamanites). So, here is the catalog of Nephite fissionists in the book of Alma:

1. The Amlicites who refused to accept the result of an election and rebelled.[40]

2. The Nephites of Ammonihah, whom we consider religious dissenters, but the angel warns Alma that in addition to religious rebellion, "they do study at this time that they may destroy the liberty of thy people, (for thus saith the Lord) which is contrary to the statutes, and judgments, and commandments which he has given unto his people."[41]

3. The Amalekites and the Amulonites,[42] who (like the Ammonihahite leaders) followed the order of Nehor.[43] After they dissented to become Lamanites because of their "more wicked and murderous disposition," they were appointed captains of the Lamanites.[44]

4. The "Zoramites became Lamanites"[45] after Alma led a failed mission to recover them[46] (these latter two comments in Alma 43 are framed within the context of parts of the Lamanite armies). Although their separat-

40. Alma 2–3.
41. Alma 8:17.
42. Alma 21:2.
43. Alma 21:4.
44. Alma 43:6.
45. Alma 43:4.
46. Alma 31–35. Alma's confrontation with Korihor is the prelude to the Zoramite mission, as Korihor's death under a stampede of Zoramites is the introduction to the Zoramites (Alma 30:59–60), just two verses before the Zoramite news and an artificial chapter break between. Like the people of Ammonihah, the Zoramites exile any of the converts from that mission (Alma 35:3–6), whereupon the renegade Zoramite elites start mixing with the Lamanites and inciting war against the Nephites, expelled Zoramites, and the Anti-Nephi-Lehies who gave shelter to the exiles (Alma 35:10–13).

ist religious sect is not labeled of the party of Nehor, the Rameumpton-style worship is schismatic.

5. Amalickiah, a Nephite, conspires to become king and overthrow the lawfully elected government of judges, but unsuccessfully because Moroni₁ counters him with the title of liberty gambit, whereupon the rebel switches sides to the Lamanites.[47]

6. The king-men try to change the laws to permit a king. When the chief judge refuses to alter legislation to permit monarchy and a plebiscite is called, which they lose, the mutineers continue their insurrection against democratic governance, "to overthrow the free government and to establish a king over the land."[48] The king-men attempt subversion at home to assist the Lamanite army's invasion.

7. Finally, the king-men once again make a resurgence, trying to overthrow chief judge Pahoran on the home front, so Moroni₁ gathers an army on the way to the capital and defeats the king-men one last time.[49]

The sum of these dissensions among the Nephites is that the Lamanite military is reinforced by the multiple and continuing streams of Nephite dissenters. The composition of the hybrid Lamanite group is detailed:

> Among all the people of the Lamanites, who were composed of the Lamanites and the Lemuelites and the Ishmaelites, and all the dissenters of the Nephites, from the reign of Nephi down to the present time. Now these dissenters, having the same instruction and the same information of the Nephites, yea, having been instructed in the same knowledge of the Lord, nevertheless, it

---

47. Alma 46, specifically 46:29.
48. Alma 51:5.
49. Alma 62.

is strange to relate, not long after their dissensions they became more hardened and impenitent, and more wild, wicked and ferocious than the Lamanites—drinking in with the traditions of the Lamanites; giving way to indolence, and all manner of lasciviousness; yea, entirely forgetting the Lord their God.[50]

The book of Alma begins with an insurrection against a legally constituted government after a wicked minority refuses to accept an election loss and resorts to mob violence in an attempt to overthrow the result.[51] Moroni$_1$—the military leader—keeps his focus on insurrection and internal division only since the king-men emerged, but Mormon—the recordkeeper—has the longer vision that includes the stretch from the beginning of the book of Alma (87 BCE) to its end (52 BCE).

Mormon includes (in direct quotation) Moroni$_1$'s letters to Pahoran because Moroni$_1$ expresses the larger meaning Mormon wants also to convey, from beginning to end of the book of Alma but especially through those war chapters: the causal factor that triggered those wars with the Lamanites was Nephite wickedness and division:

> For were it not for the wickedness which first commenced at our head, we could have withstood our enemies that they could have gained no power over us. Yea, had it not been for the war which broke out among ourselves; yea, were it not for these king-men, who caused so much bloodshed among ourselves; yea, at the time we were contending among ourselves, if we had united our strength as we hitherto have done; yea, had it not been for the desire of power and authority which those king-men had over us; had they been true to the cause of our freedom, and united with us, and gone forth against our enemies, instead of taking up their swords against us, which was the cause of so much bloodshed among ourselves; yea, if we had gone forth against them in the strength of the Lord, we should have dispersed our

50. Alma 47:35–36.
51. Alma 2:2–24.

enemies, for it would have been done, according to the fulfilling of his word.[52]

Freemen defend lawfully constituted government and the election results that validate such government, for King Mosiah's political reforms were formulated to command adherence to the voice of the people. Mosiah gives the charge in politics to "choose you by the voice of this people, judges, that ye may be judged according to the laws which have been given you by our fathers, which are correct, and which were given them by the hand of the Lord." Mosiah notes that "the voice of the people" is more reliably righteous than alternatives in selecting political leadership: "Now it is not common that the voice of the people desireth anything contrary to that which is right; but it is common for the lesser part of the people to desire that which is not right; therefore this shall ye observe and make it your law—to do your business by the voice of the people." If a situation arises in which the majority becomes wicked, then the result will be rule by wicked leaders, for "if the time comes that the voice of the people doth choose iniquity, then is the time that the judgments of God will come upon you; yea, then is the time he will visit you with great destruction even as he has hitherto visited this land." This lesson is recalled by Amulek as he preached at Ammonihah as recorded in Alma 10:19: "well did Mosiah say, who was our last king, when he was about to deliver up the kingdom, having no one to confer it upon, causing that this people should be governed by their own voices—yea, well did he say that if the time should come that the voice of this people should choose iniquity, that is, if the time should come that this people should fall into transgression, they would be ripe for destruction." The kingmen are merely the last in a series of rebellions against law and order and against God narrated in the book of Alma, illustrating a pattern the historian Mormon wants his readers to recognize.

---

52. Alma 60:15–16.

King-men attempt through riot and insurrection to overthrow such government and valid elections to gratify their own pride, to cover their sins, to swell up their vain ambitions, and to exercise unrighteous control and dominion.

The civil discord isn't restricted to the book of Alma. Helaman 1 records another instance of regime change, a period of political instability when the risk of insurrection is particularly high. Pahoran$_1$, the chief judge dies, and three of his sons vie to succeed him. King Mosiah set up the political system based upon the assumption of a peaceful transfer of power to the next leader (by valid election and not by violence), and such transitions are particularly vulnerable to bad actors. Three of Pahoran$_1$'s sons contest in whatever succession election was held: Pahoran$_2$, Paanchi, and Pacumeni. Pahoran$_2$ wins because, as Mosiah specifies the valid process, he "was appointed by the voice of the people to be chief judge and governor." Pacumeni, does his moral and patriotic duty and "did unite with the voice of the people." Paanchi is a renegade who leads an insurrection such that "that part of the people that were desirous that he should be their governor, was exceedingly wroth; therefore, he was about to flatter away those people to rise up in rebellion against their brethren." The rebellion is stymied when "he was taken, and was tried according to the voice of the people, and condemned unto death; for he had raised up in rebellion and sought to destroy the liberty of the people." Paanchi's followers "were angry, and behold, they sent forth one Kishkumen, even to the judgment-seat of Pahoran$_2$, and murdered Pahoran$_2$ as he sat upon the judgment-seat." Pacumeni, unlike his brother, yields to the "voice of the people," and becomes the next chief judge. Pacumeni does the moral and patriotic action by conceding to the voice of the people. Paanchi rebels against the voice of the people and spawns the series of the secret combinations that work to overthrow the freedom and righteousness of the Nephites. As with the internal rebellions in the book of Alma, the Lamanites attack and almost conquer "because of so much contention and so much difficulty in the government, that they had not kept sufficient guards in the land of Zarahemla; for they had supposed that the Lamanites durst not come into the heart of their lands to attack that great city Zarahemla." The internal disorder leads to external disarray as enemies take advantage of the political confusion.

Moroni$_1$ summarizes the consequences of such Nephite wickedness for the polity and the church. The internal dissension produces external effects. "For were it not for the wickedness which first commenced at our head, we could have withstood our enemies that they could have gained no power over us." That is Moroni$_1$'s (and Mormon's) concentrated assessment of the root causes of Nephite/Lamanite warfare and the dangers that follow. Nephite wickedness and division results in weakness that external enemies attempt to turn to their own advantage. Mormon provides a case study in leadership contrast, one that starts with internal dissention. This time in the church. After Alma$_2$ dies (or disappears) and Helaman takes over leadership of the church, dissension arises, the people swell with pride and riches. This internal discord in the church quickly transfers to political conflict. Amalickiah is introduced in Alma 46:3 (the two points of comparison are introduced separated by just two chapters: Moroni$_1$ is announced in Alma 43:16). Amalickiah entices the lower judges in the land to support his attempt to reinstate monarchy, with him as king, of course. This is a theological/politico conflict for it started as a church/state clash with those traitorous judges willing to back authoritarian conflict:

> Thus they were led away by Amalickiah to dissensions, notwithstanding the preaching of Helaman and his brethren, yea, notwithstanding their exceedingly great care over the church, for they were high priests over the church. And there were many in the church who believed in the flattering words of Amalickiah, therefore they dissented even from the church; and thus were

the affairs of the people of Nephi exceedingly precarious and dangerous, notwithstanding their great victory which they had had over the Lamanites, and their great rejoicings which they had had because of their deliverance by the hand of the Lord.[53]

Amalickiah did "seek to destroy the church of God, and to destroy the foundation of liberty which God had granted unto them, or which blessing God had sent upon the face of the land for the righteous' sake."[54] Moroni₁ then rallies the righteous Nephites behind his title of liberty to rout the insurrectionists against democratic governance and righteous church practice. Amalickiah recognizes the weakness of his rebellion, so he defects over to the Lamanites.[55]

These two leadership models and motivations (rebellion against God and nation on Amalickiah's part and defense of freedom and religion on Moroni₁'s part) are explicitly contrasted just a few chapters later, after Amalickiah succeeds by *coup d'état*, deception and murder in becoming the Lamanite king. Then King Amalickiah succeeds through lies and propaganda in stirring up the Lamanites to anger which trumps their natural reluctance to start a war, and he prepares them for battle with the Nephites. Mormon summarizes Amalickiah's motives compared to Moroni₁'s: "Now it came to pass that while Amalickiah had thus been obtaining power by fraud and deceit, Moroni, on the other hand, had been preparing the minds of the people to be faithful unto the Lord their God."[56] Moroni₁ also prepared the people temporally by prompting the building of fortifications.

As with their leaders, the Lamanites and Nephites have similar communal motivations. ("And now, as Moroni knew the intention of the Lamanites, that it was their intention to destroy their brethren, or to subject them and bring them into bondage

---

53. Alma 46:6–7.
54. Alma 46:10.
55. Alma 46:29–33.
56. Alma 48:7.

that they might establish a kingdom unto themselves over all the land"[57]). The central Nephite catastrophe during these dark times was a failure to stay unified: the Lamanite desire is to establish a unified kingdom by force over all the descendants of Lehi and the Mulekite group. Not all varieties of unification are equally desirable. The Nephites, on the other hand, merely wanted to defend themselves ("it was the only desire of the Nephites to preserve their lands, and their liberty, and their church"[58]), for their cause wasn't to aggregate power to a single unrighteous leader. Rather,

> The Nephites were inspired by a better cause, for they were not fighting for monarchy nor power but they were fighting for their homes and their liberties, their wives and their children, and their all, yea, for their rites of worship and their church. And they were doing that which they felt was the duty which they owed to their God; for the Lord had said unto them, and also unto their fathers, that: Inasmuch as ye are not guilty of the first offense, neither the second, ye shall not suffer yourselves to be slain by the hands of your enemies.[59]

Contrary to Amalickiah, who was an enemy of the church and of Christian belief in his narcissism and thirst for power, Moroni₁ "was preparing to support their liberty, their lands, their wives, and their children, and their peace, and that they might live unto the Lord their God, and that they might maintain that which was called by their enemies the cause of Christians."[60] Moroni₁ was a leader whose people followed him only in self-defense:

> And Moroni was a strong and a mighty man; he was a man of a perfect understanding; yea, a man that did not delight in bloodshed; a man whose soul did joy in the liberty and the freedom of his country, and his brethren from bondage and slavery; Yea,

---

57. Alma 43:29.
58. Alma 43:30.
59. Alma 43:45–46.
60. Alma 48:10.

> a man whose heart did swell with thanksgiving to his God, for
> the many privileges and blessings which he bestowed upon his
> people; a man who did labor exceedingly for the welfare and
> safety of his people. Yea, and he was a man who was firm in
> the faith of Christ, and he had sworn with an oath to defend
> his people, his rights, and his country, and his religion, even to
> the loss of his blood. Now the Nephites were taught to defend
> themselves against their enemies, even to the shedding of blood
> if it were necessary; yea, and they were also taught never to
> give an offense, yea, and never to raise the sword except it were
> against an enemy, except it were to preserve their lives.[61]

The Nephite rules for just war are articulated in the following
verses. According to those rules, after a third provocation by an
enemy, the Nephites are justified in using violence in self-defense:

> And they were doing that which they felt was the duty which
> they owed to their God; for the Lord had said unto them, and
> also unto their fathers, that: *Inasmuch as ye are not guilty of the
> first offense, neither the second, ye shall not suffer yourselves to be
> slain by the hands of your enemies.* And again, the Lord has said
> that: *Ye shall defend your families even unto bloodshed.* Therefore
> for this cause were the Nephites contending with the Lama-
> nites, to defend themselves, and their families, and their lands,
> their country, and their rights, and their religion.[62]

The phrases I have italicized represent a direct quotation from
the Lord. That would suggest a straightforward denial of a principled prohibition of violence in self-defense. So, once again to
emphasize, a Girardian or English pacifist has a challenging task
to defend the notion that the God of the Book of Mormon opposes
the use of violence in self-defense when the opposite position is
quoted directly from the mouth of God.

---

61. Alma 48:11–14.
62. Alma 43:46–47. Italics added. See Mason and Pulsipher, Proclaim, 163–65 to
read an exegesis of this "Nephite just war" doctrine.

Mormon reserves the highest praise for Moroni$_1$. Although a military man, Moroni$_1$ was also deeply religious, deserving comparison to his contemporaneous leaders of the church, for he believed the Lord would deliver the Nephites from their enemies: "this was the faith of Moroni, and his heart did glory in it; not in the shedding of blood but in doing good, in preserving his people, yea, in keeping the commandments of God, yea, and resisting iniquity."[63] Mormon writes,

> Yea, verily, verily I say unto you, if all men had been, and were, and ever would be, like unto Moroni, behold, the very powers of hell would have been shaken forever; yea, the devil would never have power over the hearts of the children of men. Behold, he was a man like unto Ammon, the son of Mosiah, yea, and even the other sons of Mosiah, yea, and also Alma and his sons, for they were all men of God.[64]

For Mormon and Moroni$_1$, it was enough for the latter to desire peace with the Lamanites but be ready to take up the sword and title of liberty against insurrectionists and external enemies to preserve the liberty, religion, and lives of his people. Mormon is the narrator of both the Nephite just war doctrine and the high praise of Moroni$_1$. Mormon writes no criticism of Moroni$_1$, whether for falling short of Christian ideals of violence minimization or for being insufficiently pacifist. If Moroni$_1$ delusively believes the God of heaven endorses his obligation to violently defend his people, his religion, and his family, then Mormon operates under the same misapprehension.

---

63. Alma 48:16.
64. Alma 48:17–18.

Pacifist

The Anti-Nephi-Lehies present the best case for the renunciation of violence in the Book of Mormon as a kind of global obligation. I have argued that Mormon, in conveying the example to us, limits the applicability of their vow to the group itself, thus restricting any generalization from the case to a larger rule.[65] The people of Ammon aren't deontologists when it comes to violent self-defense. The Doctrine and Covenants does indeed state strongly the obligation to "renounce war and proclaim peace."[66] But in the same section, the modern scripture—like the Book of Mormon does in commanding the people of God to abstain from violence until a third offense—tells the Saints to "bear it patiently and revile not against" an enemy after the first provocation.[67] If it happens a second time, the victim will be blessed by God if attacked again.[68] If it happens a third time, the victim will be manifoldly blessed for a nonviolent response; however, if the perpetrator strikes again, the Lord says, "I have delivered thine enemy into thine hands,"[69] and permits the use of force. So, there is the commandment to defer violence in self-defense, but not the prohibition of it.

The Book of Mormon contains some support for the position that God doesn't endorse violence, according to Mack Stirling. The allegory of the olive tree might assert that God punished the Jaredites for wickedness by destroying them, but the Jaredite narrative itself asserts it was their own human sin and warfare that caused their destruction. The book asserts that punishment comes

---

65. Alma 24.

66. Doctrine and Covenants 98:16.

67. Doctrine and Covenants 98:23.

68. Doctrine and Covenants 98:25.

69. Doctrine and Covenants 98:26, 29. Three times Nephi is either told of Laban or remembers the assertion that "Behold the Lord hath delivered him into thy hands," "Slay him, for the Lord hath delivered him into thy hands," and "I knew that the Lord had delivered Laban into my hands for this cause" (1 Nephi 4:11, 12, 17).

by the wicked, not from God: "Mormon thus puts full responsibility for bloodshed on human beings, though equating such bloodshed with the 'judgments of God on the wicked.'"[70] Girard expresses the thought as it might come from Mormon 4:5: "Jesus doesn't need to finish off all the bad guys. They finish each other off."[71] The maximal Girardian position one can take toward the Book of Mormon is to state that sometimes it moves the reader to eschew violence. Sometimes it endorses violence, in the name of God. As Stirling says about the Bible, a Girardian might say about the Mormon scripture:

> Girard thus sees ancient Israel as a people journeying out of the violent sacred (myth, ritual, useless or harmful prohibitions) toward knowledge and worship of the true God. The journey does not occur in a straight line but rather with delays, reversals, and failures of understanding. Ancient Israelite religion is always a compromise between the violent sacred and true worship, even as revelation struggles to end or transform the violent sacred. Much of ancient Israelite religion, therefore, does not reflect the pure will of God but shows a dynamic interplay among revelation from God, Israel's spiritual sensitivity to the revelation, and vestiges of the violent sacred foundations of their social and cultural milieu.[72]

The Girardian could assert that Book of Mormon passages endorsing violence are failures of those who wrote and lived the experiences to understand and live up to the true message of the scripture. Such a position seems more like an expurgation than an exegesis of the text.

---

70. Stirling, "Violence," 79–80. See also Mormon 4:5 and Doctrine and Covenants 63:33.

71. Mack C. Stirling and Scott Burton, "Scandals, Scapegoats, and the Cross: An Interview with René Girard," *Dialogue: A Journal of Mormon Thought* 43, no. 1 (Spring 2010): 130.

72. Stirling, "Violence," 75.

England draws upon the range of LDS scriptures and statements to support his pacifism: the New Testament, the Doctrine
and Covenants, First Presidency messages, and the statements
of presidents of the church.[73] England also explicitly draws upon
Girard's theory.[74] England, naively in my judgment, asserts a
"straight line" between the great atrocities of the twentieth century: My Lai, the Khmer Rouge, the blitz and bombing of civilians
in Germany and Britain, Pearl Harbor, Hiroshima, and the Cold
War.[75] Few straight lines exist in history, not from a human perspective; one can draw straight lines, but they aren't given to us by
history but by our retrospective reading of the historical evidence
and record. Stirling mentions the lack of straight lines in biblical
history. Any product made from the crooked timber of humanity is not given to straightness, and the moral equivalence in the
assertion that throws all modern resorts to violence into the same
smelting pot, making the end product indistinguishable from all
that went into the pot, is morally offensive.

Like all researchers and writers, England is subject to confirmation bias. The scriptures or historical examples he uses to support his argument are subject to various interpretations or contain
passages in conflict with nonpreferred excerpts. One can find various strategies to minimize or deny the contradictions, but they
are usually ad hoc rationalizations applied to a sometimes willing
and at times recalcitrant text. Selective use of source material sim-
plifies one's argumentative task: just ignore the disagreeable narratives or selections. I have been trying to complexify rather than
simplify because I think the world is chaotic and opaque, such that
the creative task God started on the first day remains unfinished

---

73. Eugene England, "Late Night Thoughts at the End of a War," *Dialogue: A
Journal of Mormon Thought* (Summer 1991): 7–9.
74. Eugene England, "Healing and Making Peace—In the World and the Church,"
Sunstone 15, no. 6 (December 1991): 36–46. See, especially, page 40.
75. Eugene England, "Fasting and Food, Not Weapons: A Mormon Response to
Conflict," *BYU Studies* 25, no. 1 (Winter 1985): 12.

because that is the nature of our life on earth. We are charged with finishing the creative act by exercising dominion. The yet-unorganized portions of the cosmos break out in hurricanes, earthquakes, black holes, colliding galaxies, tsunamis, star nurseries, inexplicable human violence, range fires, stars going supernova, and many other manifestations. Adam and Eve's assignment was to organize the portion of creation assigned to them. We are still engaged in that task. Let me point to some examples of how human violence and warfare are part of that unfinished creation that we need to examine clear-eyed and in all its complexity.

England asserts a universal prohibition on human violence and a renunciation of all violence by God. This was so from before the foundation of the world. In a premortal council in heaven, the Savior presented his plan for this creation. In his essay "The Prince of Peace," England asserts that "His plan, even before his incarnation, was non-violent. We sometimes forget that the main reason Satan's plan would not work was that it was a plan of violence, a plan of force, which claimed it would 'save' everyone through coercion."[76] Yet consider the rest of the analogous situation to which England refers. Immediately following the presentation of the two plans in the council, a war in heaven was fought over which plan would prevail. Presumably, there were no pacifists in these two armies of disembodied spirits clashing before day and night were even instituted. One doesn't know how incorporeal beings engage in combat (although Milton wrote an excessively long poem about the topic), but a war requires combatants, and one side was led by Jehovah and Michael and the other by Lucifer. The Savior's council plan didn't entail violence, but defense of that plan did. On the following page, after comments about the peaceful plan, England invokes "thoughtful people" who might be disturbed by violence

76. Eugene England, *Making Peace: Personal Essays* (Salt Lake City, UT: Signature, 1995), 231.

narrated in the Old Testament. He writes, "But if we look carefully at the Old Testament that idea, that God himself is violent,
can be rejected."[77] But "looking carefully" by "thoughtful people"
won't resolve the interpretive problem that easily, and I think that
thoughtful people who look carefully can disagree on this exegeti-
cal issue. If the God who preexisted the Old Testament was not an
absolutist pacifist who led a successful war in which the defeated
were expelled (exiled, like one-half of the Leviticus 16 scapegoats),
why would the God of the Old Testament be? This is violence and
expulsion from before the foundation of the world.

England frequently invokes the section in the Sermon on the
Mount where Christ urges that his listeners "resist not evil" where
"it is assumed to mean we should be passive in the face of evil":[78]
being a pacifist is not the same as being passive but requires active,
but nonviolent, intervention. England equates "resist not evil" with
being pacifist, but there are many types of evil and many kinds
of resistance, contra England: "In fact, it is the apostle Paul who
makes the requirement, 'resist not evil,' meaningful. He teaches it
this way: 'Be not overcome of evil, but overcome evil with good'
(Rom. 12:21). And of course nonviolent direct action is exactly
that—not ignoring evil, but overcoming it with courageous good."[79]
But an equivocation occurs here: evil is equated with violence and
good equated with nonviolence. Could Paul have defined *good* in
such a way that would sometimes include violence? Might violence and goodness not always be mutually exclusive?

In the same essay collection, the essay "Thou Shalt Not Kill"
also appeals to the Sermon on the Mount injunction to "resist not
evil."[80] Surely Christ has a more expansive concept of resisting evil
than restricting such resistance to using only nonviolent means. If

77. England, *Making*, 232.
78. England, *Making*, 235.
79. England, *Making*, 241.
80. England, *Making*, 159.

a man strikes you on the right cheek, is turning the left cheek also to be struck the only way to "resist not evil"? Could not a blow or two to disable an assailant also qualify? If two teens start a fist-fight on a school campus, might not resisting evil involve a teacher forcefully restraining the instigator before serious injury occurs? If a sexual assault is in progress, would not a bystander be justified in resisting that evil even through the use of force? Resisting evil and not resisting evil don't cover the entire field of possibilities. They might overlap but not completely, and perhaps not even largely. England's reading equates not resisting evil in such contexts with pacifism, but still acting in such a way that the aggressor must recognize the humanity of the victim.

England never mentions another important scriptural passage relevant to the phrase "resist not evil." He cites the passage from the Sermon on the Mount in Matthew[81] and in 3 Nephi's sermon at the temple.[82] He brings Paul in as a witness to the same injunction. But the same language of "resisting evil" or "not resisting evil" is used to opposite effect in the book of Alma. Moroni$_1$ writes a letter to Pahoran, the chief judge, castigating the ruler for not providing sufficient supplies or soldiers to the war effort against the Lamanites. Pahoran responds, summarizing the central government's own travails. He urges Moroni$_1$ to bring troops to put down a rebellion on the home front. Notice the wording: "Therefore, my beloved brother, Moroni, *let us resist evil*, and *whatsoever evil we cannot resist with our words, yea, such as rebellions and dissensions, let us resist them with our swords*, that we may retain our freedom, that we may rejoice in the great privilege of our church, and in the cause of our Redeemer and our God."[83] Pahoran flips the wording of what will become a chief component of the Sermon on the Mount/sermon at the temple. Jesus implores his audience

---

81. Matthew 5:39. England, *Making*, 159.
82. 3 Nephi 12:38–39. England, *Making*, 159.
83. Alma 61:14.

generally to resist not evil. Pahoran—working in very specific circumstances—not only implores Moroni$_1$ to resist evil but, failing the success of doing so peacefully with words, to do it with the sword.[84] He attributes this cause to "our Redeemer and our God." When England uses nonviolent terminology as "an absolute ethic," such absolutism runs against the grain of other scriptural considerations of the applicability of violence and refuses to acknowledge that morally complex world in which we live. Such absolutism as a deontological rule can even be dangerous when situations such as East Timor and World War II arise.

Back in Chapter 12, "So Persecuted They All the Prophets," I noted that even though he was a devoted pacifist, Girard concedes that in some situations he would indulge in violence to protect his family, and he speculated that if France had preemptively invaded disputed territory, the violence of World War II's European theater might have been avoided and the world would have been better for the early intervention. Justifiably, England extols the results of nonviolent direct action in achieving peace: Gandhi, the Marshall Plan, Anwar Sadat's peace overture to Israel, Martin Luther King's civil rights movement. On the next page he admits that in certain circumstances he himself might resort to violence, to protect his wife or children: "But the highest ethic would call me to do everything possible, long before the attack, to avert the threat of attack (including building a less violent and sexist society where attack

---

84. England invokes a useful interpretive principle from Hugh Nibley. Sometimes the scriptures forbidding violence are general rules when those countenancing violence occur in specific contexts as exceptions to the rule. Eugene England, "Can Nations Love Their Enemies? An L.D.S. Theology of Peace," in *Dialogues with Myself: Personal Essays on Mormon Experience*, by Eugene England, 135–52 (Midvale, UT: Orion, 1984), 136. But acknowledging that sometimes exceptions apply ought to blunt the universal assertion that an "absolute ethic" against violence might be the relevant moral concern. England, *Making*, 159. On page 158 of the same source, England asserts that "even in the Old Testament the Lord, whom Mormons understand is Christ, commanded, without qualification, 'Thou shalt not kill.'"

on my wife and children would be less likely), to use a minimum of violence, and to follow up with doing good to the victimizer as well as the intended victim."[85] These are admirable sentiments, and admirable actions when made applicable to life. Even though England refers to the pacifist imperative as an "absolute ethic," even when we are pushed by extreme circumstances to violently defend our loved ones against violence, these foremost value commitments come into conflict with each other and present an ethical paradox for us. We need then to "minimize the violence and dehumanization and to return quickly to our full humanity and its obligation to do only good to others."[86] The impulse to minimize the violence and dehumanization just might follow from an appropriate early application of violence.

---

85. England, *Making,* 173.
86. England, *Making,* 175.

To Say and To Do

> The great texts are deeper, stronger, and larger than our readings; they interpret our theories rather than allow our theories to interpret them.
>
> J. Bottum[1]

As a literary critic and a believer, I am committed to the notion that the Book of Mormon is much more sophisticated than our standard readings of the text. Both critics and believers have woefully underread the scripture, making much less of the text than it should be. We are, however, called to be better readers simply by our acceptance of discipleship. Disciplined discipleship calls for readers to recognize that the scripture's complexity and beauty are part of its substance and prophetic message. I have pointed out that after each stage of the creation, God pauses to call the day's work "good,"[2] and after the final day, He ratchets up the praise: "God saw every thing that he had made, and, behold, it was very good."[3] Not limited to the pragmatic qualities of the new world, the account notes that the trees God planted in the garden, like everything in the synoptic summary, were not only good but also beautiful: "out of

---

1. J. Bottum, "Girard among the Girardians," *First Things* 61 (1996): http://www.firstthings.com/ftissues/ft9603/revessay.html.

2. Genesis 1:4, 19, 12, 18, 21, 25.

3. Genesis 1:31.

the ground made the Lord God to grow every tree that is pleasant to the sight, and good for food."[4] Specifically mentioned are two trees: the tree of life and the tree of knowledge of good and evil. Notice the aesthetic quality of repetition in the text when in the next chapter Eve repeats the divine judgment as the serpent introduces her to the tree of knowledge of good and evil. Eve "saw that the tree was good for food, and that it was pleasant to the eyes, and a tree to be desired to make one wise, she took of the fruit thereof, and did eat, and gave also unto her husband with her; and he did eat."[5] Eve is already cluing in during this interim status to the purpose of life— that humans, made in the image of God, are imitating the divine initiative by loving, and living, and immersing themselves in joy and beauty. She is already, before the fall, beginning to make pragmatic judgments (she "saw the tree was good for food") but also aesthetic distinctions on the order of a critique of judgment ("it was pleasant to the eyes"), and going even a step further as a consequentialist making moral judgments about results (she inferred that it was "a tree desired to make one wise"). Adam is preoccupied with naming creatures and establishing dominion over the animals while Eve is already dividing the world conceptually into useful things, beautiful things, and prudential things; each approach is good and necessary in the human task of establishing dominion over the creation. Nephi[1] instructs his readers to "feast upon the words of Christ; for behold, the words of Christ will tell you all things what ye should do."[6] Feasting requires that we not only recognize the nutritional value of the meal but also the presentation, the color palette, the fragrance, and the other aesthetic qualities of the feast. The creation is to be delighted in, not merely consumed.

Just before God pronounces the creation "very good," a charge is given to the human pair. Having established dominion over the

---

4. Genesis 2:9.
5. Genesis 3:6.
6. 2 Nephi 32:3.

chaos through the creative effort, causing the plants and animals (and humans, apparently) to be pre-loaded with reproductive systems before death and birth are even introduced into the world, because each of the human couple is created in the image of God,[7] God delegates to the humans the responsibility to have dominion over and subdue the natural world around them: "And God blessed them, and God said unto them, Be fruitful, and multiply, and replenish the earth, and subdue it: and have dominion over the fish of the sea, and over the fowl of the air, and over every living thing that moveth upon the earth."[8] As the apex of the created order, the humans are given dominion (power, authority, control) over the plants for food, and the plants are already intended to reproduce for God so states: "Behold, I have given you every herb bearing seed, which is upon the face of all the earth, and every tree, in the which is the fruit of a tree yielding seed; to you it shall be for meat. And to every beast of the earth, and to every fowl of the air, and to every thing that creepeth upon the earth, wherein there is life, I have given every green herb for meat: and it was so."[9] The hitch is that the charge to "Be fruitful, and multiply, and replenish the earth, and subdue it: and have dominion over the fish of the sea, and over the fowl of the air, and over every living thing that moveth upon the earth"[10] can't be accomplished while in their current state of innocence and immortality. They must be separated from the fruit of the tree of life and go through a kind of puberty in order to reproduce.

After Adam and Eve are exiled from the garden, they are still obligated to exert dominion and subdue the earth. Just as God brought order to chaos in the creation, Adam, Eve, and their pos-

---

7. Genesis 1:26–27.
8. Genesis 1:28.
9. Genesis 1:20–30. "Green herb for meat" is just Elizabethan English for "plants for food." Humans are vegetarians until Noah exits the barge after the flood when God expands the human diet to include animal flesh (Genesis 9:1–3).
10. Genesis 1:28.

terity are charged with bringing order to the lone and dreary world outside the garden. This they do through agriculture and animal husbandry, the occupations engaged by their first two sons, Cain and Abel, and by beautifying and tidying up the earth by tending the remains of the garden that fell into the world with them. That is the dominion to which humans are called, to build but also to preserve and conserve their natural inheritance. The harvest won't be as simple as picking fruit from a tree for food; instead, the earth is under a curse: "Thorns also and thistles shall it bring forth to thee; and thou shalt eat the herb of the field; In the sweat of thy face shalt thou eat bread, till thou return unto the ground; for out of it wast thou taken: for dust thou art, and unto dust shalt thou return."[11]

When Noah, a second Adam who, like the first, was the father of all mankind and both gardeners to boot, is given a similar charge to go into what is essentially a brand new world reborn after the sins and violence of the previous creation, the humans are given the same charge: "And God spake unto Noah, saying, Go forth of the ark, thou, and thy wife, and thy sons, and thy sons' wives with thee. Bring forth with thee every living thing that is with thee, of all flesh, both of fowl, and of cattle, and of every creeping thing that creepeth upon the earth; that they may breed abundantly in the earth, and be fruitful, and multiply upon the earth."[12] A new element is introduced to this creation version 2: seasons, planting time, harvest time, day and night rotations.[13] The next chapter begins with a repetition of the reproductive command: "And God blessed Noah and his sons, and said unto them, Be fruitful, and multiply, and replenish the earth."[14] Noah fulfills that command

---

11. Genesis 3:18–19. That curse is, by the way, lifted when Noah exits the ark with the animals (Genesis 8:21).
12. Genesis 8:15–17.
13. Genesis 8:22.
14. Genesis 9:1.

to subdue the earth by becoming a gardener and planting a vine-yard.[15] His sons exercise dominion by spreading over and organizing the earth through farming and pastoral occupations. Chapter 10 of Genesis further elaborates not only on the descendants of Noah's sons, but also specifies what lands they settled,[16] ending the play-by-play with a recap: "These are the families of the sons of Noah, after their generations, in their nations: and by these were the nations divided in the earth after the flood."[17]

The believing reader of the Hebrew Bible, the New Testament, and the Book of Mormon is called in the example provided by Eve to appreciate not only the utilitarian qualities of the creation more generally but also the works of beauty in the Hebraic narrative. She admirably went beyond the practical elements to appreciate the aesthetic qualities of the world. We, all the descendants, are called upon to follow the principle that what happened to the mothers happens to the daughters. We should appreciate and articulate the beauty and complexity of the narratives we inherit from the past and more generally the world around us.

The early Church was reproved by the Lord for not being sufficiently attentive to the Book of Mormon, and I am not sure the condemnation has been lifted: "And they shall remain under this condemnation until they repent and remember the new covenant, even the Book of Mormon and the former commandments which I have given them, not only to say, but to do according to that which I have written."[18] I haven't attempted a complete survey of violence in the Book of Mormon and the cure for that human propensity for mayhem. I have sampled large portions of the scripture to focus the reader's attention on the text's tendencies. I am certain that almost all readers will be surprised at the frequency

---

15. Genesis 9:20.
16. Genesis 10:1–32.
17. Genesis 10:32.
18. Doctrine and Covenants 84:57.

and casualness of the stories about violence in the scripture, and the implication of Deity in that violence. As with the Bible, we tend not to notice the theme or the consistency; we tend also to justify the violence as necessary expedients to meet local conditions, or the human response to the divine command. The book itself asserts a message that it claims transcends the particular circumstances of the writers. Speaking specifically to descendants of Lehi to whom the Book of Mormon would be delivered in some distant future, Mormon also widens the audience by speaking to latter-day gentiles.[19] But more directly to the "remnant of the house of Israel" in the latter days, Mormon urges a renunciation of violence: "Know ye that ye must lay down your weapons of war, and delight no more in the shedding of blood, and take them [weapons] not again, *save it be that God shall command you.*"[20] Even in this valedictory context after Mormon's people have largely been destroyed by violence, the principle of nonviolence is qualified by local and particular concerns.

We have inherited a morally complex world in which we are often badly served by universal prescriptions and proscriptions. Some ethical decisions are easy to make because we don't have conflicting or competitive principles to sort through. "Thou shalt not . . . commit adultery, . . . nor do anything like until it,"[21] is a fairly straightforward choice. "Don't murder" is another prescription that usually doesn't force a hard moral choice (recognizing that *murder* and *killing* are not synonyms). But Girard's universal prohibitions against engaging in violence and warfare seem to present a more paradoxical situation that requires moral negative capability. Girard helps us read both books of scripture better than we did before Girard. His textual approach is an example for us to follow. His readings of violence he generalizes to a too inflexi-

---

19. Mormon 5:9.
20. Mormon 7:1, 4.
21. D&C 59:6.

ble moral conclusion that doesn't match the complexity of the two scriptural texts. Shouldn't Western nations such as Belgium (the former colonial ruler) and the United States (the only country with heavy airlift capabilities sufficient to the task of transporting trucks, armored personnel carriers, and helicopters) when faced with the Rwandan genocide in 1994 have sent troops and military equipment to stop the mass murder of civilians by their own government? A utilitarian calculus might have been the best moral tool to apply rather than a Girardian injunction against engaging in violence or deontological preachments against killing perpetrators. Eight hundred thousand people murdered with clubs and machetes in one hundred days. We are sometimes ill-served when we let universal rules do our moral reasoning for us, even when our conscience and the light of Christ end up confirming those reasoned directives. We often let the victims of violence multiply and fill graves much as the people of Ammon lost 1,005 of their number until the Lord specifically instructed them to flee to the protection of the Nephites.[22] The morally appropriate Nephites

---

22. Alma 27:11–12 has the Lord directing Ammon to remove the Anti-Nephi-Lehies to leave their current home where they are endangered. They have yet to request protection of the Nephites. The Nephite chief judge asks for input via the "voice of the people," the wisdom of crowds, who propose to grant the people of Ammon the land of Jershon. Defensive, but still violent, surrogacy permits the Anti-Nephi-Lehies to live relatively peacefully while still providing material support to the Nephite armies: "And behold, we will set our armies between the land Jershon and the land Nephi, that we may protect our brethren in the land Jershon; and this we do for our brethren, on account of their fear to take up arms against their brethren lest they should commit sin. And now behold, this will we do unto our brethren, that they may inherit the land Jershon; and we will guard them from their enemies with our armies, on condition that they will give us a portion of their substance to assist us that we may maintain our armies" (Alma 27:23–24). The Nephites, moved by compassion, are pragmatic, but the Anti-Nephi-Lehies are admirable in their adherence to their fundamental principles: "they were perfectly honest and upright in all things; and they were firm in the faith of Christ, even unto the end. And they did look upon shedding the blood of their brethren with the greatest abhorrence; and they never could be prevailed upon to take up arms against their brethren; and they never did look upon death with any degree of terror, for their hope and views of Christ and the resurrection"

took up a violent defensive stance to prevent the multiplication of victims. Overemphasis on the noteworthy and praiseworthy pacifism of the Anti-Nephi-Lehies' response to the situation can make us forget that their Nephite defenders also made an appropriate moral choice that was no less brave or laudable. Facing Lamanites, sword in hand, in battle requires no less courage than kneeling down before them unarmed.

Shouldn't the Allies leading up to and during World War II have confronted the Axis powers to prevent even worse misery and death that an Axis victory would have entailed? Aren't there occasions when humanitarian interventions justify violence against aggressors? When Russia invaded Ukraine in 2022 with pretextual arguments about defending Russia's own security and the safety of Russian-speakers on Russia's borders, surely Western countries were morally right to supply weapons, offensive and defensive, to Ukraine, especially considering the crimes against humanity the Russian army and political leadership have perpetrated. When governments bomb, gas, and shoot their own citizens, as has happened for decades in Myanmar, wouldn't outside intervention (sometimes less lethal in the form of sanctions or diplomatic isolation) be a moral cause? Or in Syria? In Haiti or similar persistently failed states, where the aggressors preying on their own citizens are criminal gangs in the absence of any central government? In the latter case, an outside force would be the only option, although all options are bad with low possibilities of redeeming the situation. The Black Hawk Down Incident, Somalia 1993, demonstrates what happens when even a superpower with some additional proxies such as Pakistani troops under UN auspices insert themselves with good intentions but nonexistent local knowledge of complex civil wars in failed states. Another example

---

(Alma 27:27–28). A utilitarian approach has room to recognize and even admire categorical principles. I am not sure the traffic goes both ways.

of U.S. naïveté while carrying out an intervention with humanitarian intentions was the bombing of the Marine barracks at the Beirut airport (October 23, 1983). On a peacekeeping mission where there was no established peace to keep, with no knowledge of the warring parties in the Lebanese civil war, the Marine Corps lost 220 Marines, the Navy eighteen sailors, and the Army three soldiers. In some situations, the only intervention model that should be considered is prayer. Outside intervention is likely to make the situation worse.

A successful interposition model comes from East Timor (if foreign intervention *after* the murders of hundreds of thousands of innocents can be called successful). With the island of Timor divided in half in August 1975, the Indonesian army invaded from West Timor (already recognized as under Indonesian sovereignty) to annex the eastern side of the island, East Timor. Indiscriminately murdering civilians, the genocide was justified by the Indonesian government as an attempt to save the victims from the lingering conditions of Portuguese colonialism and unify the islands in the Indonesian archipelago under one government. The initial campaign killed between 50,000 and 100,000 East Timorese. About 2,300 Indonesian soldiers and related militia casualties resulted from skirmishes or from disease during the resulting violence.[23] The violent occupation of East Timor continued with only isolated cells of resistance. The Indonesian government kept tight control over the territory so little-to-no news escaped to the outside world, conveying the notion that the occupied were entirely happy under Indonesian rule.

In 1999, the UN sponsored a referendum (initially proposed by the Indonesian government because of its complete lack of awareness of East Timorese sentiments and how such a plebiscite would

---

23. "East Timor Genocide," *Wikipedia*, https://en.wikipedia.org/wiki/East_Timor_genocide (Sept. 30, 2023).

turn out if held fairly) on independence. The Indonesian army and government ratcheted up the violence to frighten the population. On the day of the plebiscite, men's heads were decapitated by Indonesian militias and displayed on pikes at voting locations as a warning to the locals. After the vote came in favor of independence (79 percent for autonomy), the violence against civilians increased in an ethnic cleansing campaign that resulted in 80 percent of the housing stock being destroyed, followed by hundreds of thousands of new refugees.[24] Two factors turned the Indonesian oppression and genocide around, making it possible for East Timorese independence under the country name Timor-Leste: (1) international publicity and the resulting pressure from foreign governments, and (2) the implied but not at all subtle threat of violence that accompanied an international peacekeeping force under UN auspices led by Australia. Sometimes (most often) appeals to the humanity and compassion of aggressors are inadequate to get the initiators of genocide to back down; humanitarian appeals and prayers backed by rifles and helicopter gunships are more likely to succeed. To have faith that the Hitlers and Stalins of world history will keep promises made to the Neville Chamberlains of history is beyond naïveté. The Australian government positioned combat aircraft and troops in its far north as a threat against Indonesian escalation. Five other nations provided more aircraft and ships to add more emphasis to the expression of concern. When the international force landed troops in East Timor, the militias rapidly dissipated, retreating back to Indonesia.[25] The threat of force was essential and the morally

---

24. Angel Rabase and Peter Chalk "The East Timor Crisis and Its Consequences." *Indonesia's Transformation and the Stability of Southeast Asia*, Rand Corporation, https://www.jstor.org/stable/10.7249/mr1344af.12. (Accessed Oct. 1, 2023). Mica Barreto Soares, "Timor-Leste, 20 Years On," *The Interpreter*. Lowy Institute, (Aug. 16, 2019). https://www.lowyinstitute.org/the-interpreter/timor-leste-20-years. (Accessed Oct. 1, 2023).
25. "International Force East Timor," *Wikipedia*, https://en.wikipedia.org/wiki/International_Force_East_Timor (Sept. 30, 2023).

correct way to resolve the East Timorese situation. Since its independence in 2002 Timor-Leste has experienced relative prosperity, relative peace, and fragile-but-sustained democracy: probably the best outcome an observer could have hoped for.

When principled pacifism prevents the Timor-Leste-style results by obstructing any action beyond prayers, then that specific commitment to nonviolence has lapsed over into immorality. Not to do what can be done to confront evil and genocidal violence in the territories of East Timor, Rwanda, the Third Reich, and Haiti is timorousness masquerading as peacefulness, quietude impersonating fortitude. These situations in which the moral balance should fall in favor of violent intervention may be less common than those in which nonviolent abstention is the prudential and moral course, but agonizing moral calculation requires balancing consequences and universal principles.

In each of the cases I have cited in the previous paragraphs, prudential considerations would have to be taken into account. What is the likelihood of successful intervention to reduce the bloodshed? Can the necessary resources be marshalled and deployed? Who would lead and participate in the operation? This would likely come down to making a utilitarian calculation regarding human life. Moral outrage would need to be weighed against consequentialist projections regarding success. Perhaps citing the cases of World War II and the Russian invasion of Ukraine are instances of cherry-picking on my part, selecting the easy examples where one has to be devoid of moral awareness to the point of needing a conscience transplant before one could support Nazi-led Germany's attempt to exterminate Ashkenazi Jews, or Putin-led Russia's attempt to reestablish a Czarist empire and lost world prestige by invading Ukraine. But sometimes the hard cases and the easy cases need to be taken into account when handling ethical considerations.

How about less polarizing cases? Lawyers have a saying that hard cases make bad law. Reasoning from extreme positions or circumstances to generate more generally applicable rules that are intended to apply to a broad range of other cases can skew the results. The same may be true of both hard and easy case studies in settling ethical issues. The questions being asked regarding whether resorting to violence might be the morally right and ethically preferred option, among those options available. Here follow some hypothetical case studies that might help clarify:

1. The hostage taken by an armed criminal: a gun-toting criminal in the commission of a robbery takes an innocent bystander hostage. Police officers have the perpetrator cornered, but the repeat offender is getting more agitated and irrational. Once the criminal loses focus and drops the barrel of the handgun toward the ground, a police sniper shoots and kills the perp. The hostage is traumatized but otherwise unhurt.

   a. This case would fall under the category of protection of innocent human life. This isn't murder. I judge it to be an acceptable use of lethal force on utilitarian grounds. It would violate Girard's universal proscription against violence, but even most deontologists (I would think: most of the time I am a deontologist) would approve of the response on the principle that saving innocent (even not so innocent) life is a main priority, and in this case two principles we strongly adhere to ([1] don't kill and [2] protect innocent people) appear mutually exclusive.

2. Infiltration of a terrorist organization for a targeted assassination: Let's say a terrorist group has a history of raiding the farms of locals to steal food and supplies but also occasionally kidnapping girls barely or not

even yet in their teens from boarding schools, taking them deep into the backcountry. Some are taken as wives by the terrorists and impregnated to produce a next generation of marauders. Some few are negotiated for by their families and returned upon payment. The military, embarrassed by its inability to protect its own citizens, resorts to asymmetrical tactics of its own by recruiting and paying an assassin to infiltrate the terrorist organization and assassinate its leader. Pretending to be a recruit and informer working against the government to help the kidnappers, the assassin finds the terrorist group and requests a private audience with the terrorist leader. When alone, the assassin pulls out a hidden knife and disembowels the opponent, then escapes into the jungle to notify the military and lead it against the terrorist camp.

a. Should such subterfuge and murder be viewed as valid, moral, and ethical responses to the violence perpetrated by the terrorists? A utilitarian would likely endorse the action if the prospects of success are high. In fact, the possibility of achieving the government's goals would be the foremost yardstick. A deontologist committed to the principle "deception is always immoral" would likely object to the action as well as to the killing. The relevant principle here, as with the previous case study, would be protection of innocent life, the civilians' and the girls'. I would think most deontologists would come to a similar conclusion based on that principle and approve the mission. Other contradictory principles might mitigate (such as "don't murder"), but the central issue is not the farmers' lost crops or the reluctance to take the terrorists' lives; it is the innocent lives of the girls victimized.

b. This case study is my modern adaptation of a biblical story. The Israelites are serving eighteen years of hard bondage to the Moabites, led by the Moabite King Eglon. Israel cries to the Lord for a deliverer. Ehud, from the tribe of Benjamin (known for its left-handed warriors), straps a dagger to his inner right thigh and enters Eglon's palace. The guards search him for weapons, but don't consider the left-handed possibility. Ehud sends word that he is an Israelite turncoat and has secret information to offer the king. With an audience in the corpulent king's private chambers, Ehud draws near to whisper in the king's ear, whereupon he pulls out the dagger, burying it so deeply in the king's abdomen that he can't pull it out of the corpse. In a very early closed-door murder mystery scene, Ehud apparently escapes the king's protection detail at a well-protected palace through the sewer opening, rallies the Israelites, and defeats the Moabites.[26] The text seems to involve the Lord only marginally. The children of Israel committed sin, so "the Lord strengthened Eglon, the king of Moab against Israel."[27] The Lord has only a bit role in the liberation story itself and isn't mentioned again. The deliverance from bondage isn't explicitly attributed to God but to Ehud's agency and daring. Under a deontological analysis, the ethicist would, I would judge, evaluate which principle is paramount: don't kill, or prioritize the liberation of the girls and

---

26. Judges 3:12–30.
27. Judges 3:12.

prevention of future abductions. That seems a fairly easy decision in favor of infiltration and execution. For a utilitarian, the moral choice comes down to the probability of the mission's success.

3. Considering more localized case studies, what if a university criminology researcher commonly went on ride-alongs with the local police department. After becoming a familiar face to the officers, the researcher is sufficiently trusted that one officer introduces the researcher to a circle of rogue cops who after dark take young alleged offenders to an abandoned warehouse to deal some extra-judicial street justice. Should the researcher report the violence and risk being cut off from research sources? Should the academic risk subjecting the police officers to the violence of a judicial process and a prison possibility?

   a. Concern for the victims should be the paramount issue. The researcher has a moral obligation to report the abuse to trigger an investigation and judicial process against the officers. Deontological considerations ought to override consequentialist concerns, for a duty adheres to report the criminality just as a duty adheres to police officers to obey the law. The researcher is implicated in violence by remaining silent but also by reporting the violence resulting in the forcible removal of the former police officers to a judicial proceeding and prison.

These case studies illustrate that when push comes to shove, even all but the most dedicated pacifists will reluctantly push back against the notion that pacifism should be established as a universal rule. Even some such pacifists would likely admit that general rules need to adapt to localized limits and conditions.

Case studies are used in teaching ethics because one can eliminate or adopt all the messiness of the real world to strip down
to the core issues or pile on ethical complications. Scriptural case
studies serve a similar function. The passages from the Book of
Mormon record attribute the end of the Nephites and Jaredites
to mimetic conflict, both individual and group (at other times
attributing the extinctions to other causes such as the adoption of
secret oaths and conspiracies that lead to the violent struggle over
resources or power, another form of mimetic struggle in zero-sum
systems).[28] The differences and similarities can illuminate slight or
large gradations of ethical or unethical behavior and distinctions.
The Jaredite leaders get caught in a cycle of mimetic rivalry and
anger.[29] These two competitors battle until "the Spirit of the Lord
had ceased striving with them, and Satan had full power over the
hearts of the people; for they were given up unto the hardness of
their hearts, and the blindness of their minds that they might be
destroyed; wherefore they went again to battle."[30] The slaughter
continued as they were "drunken with anger, even as a man who is
drunken with wine."[31] The result is that the Jaredites are all killed
except Coriantumr (whom the prophet predicted would survive
to be buried by a successor people) and Ether (the only Jaredite
noncombatant).

The Nephites suffer a similar fate, and that is the lesson of
repetitions in Hebraic scripture: recurring events repeat because
through their recurrence, an emphatic message is conveyed and
history itself is woven in a pattern of repeating fabric; repetition is
also entwined with the strings of the universe and the threads of

---

28. Ether 8:20–21.
29. Ether 13:27, between Coriantumr and Shared; Ether 14:24–30 and 15:4–6,
between Shiz and Coriantumr, in which anger and vengeance is transmitted to
their subjects.
30. Ether 15:19.
31. Ether 15:22.

human experience.[32] The Lamanites are caught in a swirling whirl-wind of hatred and anger, as are the Nephites. Mormon notes his fears that the Nephites will be eliminated, for the Nephites "do not repent, and Satan stirreth them up continually to anger one with another"; they had given themselves over to anger and revenge, with both Lamanites and Nephites indulging in murder, canni-balism, rape, and torture.[33] The Lamanites are depraved, but the Nephites are worse: "And they have become strong in their per-version; and *they are alike* brutal, sparing none, neither old nor young; and they delight in everything save that which is good; and the suffering of our women and our children upon all the face of this land doth exceed everything; yea, tongue cannot tell, neither can it be written."[34] Even victory in war doesn't ease the resort to cruelty, for after winning the conflict and killing as many Neph-ites as they can, the Lamanites "are at war one with another, and the whole face of this land is one continual round of murder and bloodshed; and no one knoweth the end of the war."[35] Even after surviving longer than he expected and writing more in the record, Moroni₂ notes that the situation hasn't changed: the Lamanite "wars are exceedingly fierce among themselves; and because of their hatred they put to death every Nephite that will not deny the Christ."[36] Not only individuals but entire nations can be caught up in demonic mimeticism. The Nephite destruction is a repetition of the Jaredite extinction, and the antidote is a return to Christ and to repentance: "I know that [the Nephites] must perish except they repent and return unto him. And if they perish it will be *like unto the Jaredites,* because of the wilfulness of their hearts, seeking for blood and revenge."[37] Even in suffering for the wickedness of the

---

32. Genesis 41:32.
33. Moroni 9:3, 5, 7–11.
34. Moroni 9:19.
35. Mormon 8:8.
36. Moroni 1:2.
37. Moroni 9:22–23.

people, Mormon urges the cure to his son: "May Christ lift thee up, and may his sufferings and death, and the showing his body unto our fathers, and his mercy and long-suffering, and the hope of his glory and of eternal life, rest in your mind forever."[38]

Nephites and Jaredites both reject the grace of God and the call to repentance. The remedy for this violent rivalry is to accept the gospel of Christ and the peace it brings. Not to let go of all desire, but to reject human forms of imitation.

Girard believes the Christian revolution is a kind of time-release capsule that has had its impact over centuries in reducing violence. By revealing that victims are innocent, the New Testament has gradually (then more rapidly) expanded the horror we feel at violent scapegoating. But humans still have the need for this kind of catharsis, so having the scapegoating phenomenon revealed as a charade also brings a danger. If we still need the scapegoating function but it no longer works because we realize its falsity, how are we going to provide a pressure valve for society? Girard sees the present as a particularly dangerous period for humanity. We have tremendous weapons of individual and mass destruction with the same human nature in need of scapegoats. The breakdown of the scapegoating function because we are aware of how it works means we have fewer tools to contain outbreaks of violence.

Steven Pinker provides empirical evidence for the same reduction of violence, but he attributes the decline to six social trends: (1) the shift from hunter-gatherer societies to agricultural units with governments; (2) the nation-state system with central authority and the interest in suppressing violence within the state; (3) the Enlightenment with its reasoned reaction against slavery and sadism; (4) the reduction in explicit warfare since WWII; (5) the decline of proxy wars since the Cold War; and (6) organized movements to reduce violence against minorities, women and

---

38. Moroni 9:25.

children. He also identifies five inner demons that are less prominent today than in the past: (1) predatory violence to gain objects
we desire; (2) violence fueled by desires for dominance; (3) systems of justice replacing private revenge; (4) lowering of human
sadism; and (5) a lessening of utopian visions (with proponents
willing to use any means to be achieved). Finally, he notes five
historical forces: (1) centralized states that pull violence from the
hands of individuals and groups in order to maintain a monopoly; (2) world commerce that increases the costs of conflict; (3)
shifts from masculinization to feminization and an accompanying
less frequent resort to violent policies; (4) cosmopolitanism that
helps us see others as much like us; and (5) increasing rationality to calculate the costs of conflict.[39] Pinker's book is detailed in
marshaling evidence to support the claim that we live in the most
peaceful time in human history. For Pinker, modernity is a force
for alleviating violence. By making humans less tribally and locally
oriented, we are much less likely to commit violence against the
other. When we see people suffering from violence in Africa or
the Balkans, in movies or on TV, we are much more likely to think
they are much like us. As a result, "today we may be living in the
most peaceable era in our species' existence."[40] Pinker and Richard Dawkins blame religion for much of the violence humans have
committed throughout history. Girard's position contradicts such
assertions advanced by particular varieties of the Enlightenment
as he argues that humans can and have countered and reduced
violence by the pure power of reason without positing the need for
assistance of gods. "Girard shows that, culturally and historically,
the opposite is closer to the truth,"[41] argues Scott Cowdell. It is

39. Steven Pinker, *The Better Angels of Our Nature: Why Violence Has Declined*
(New York: Penguin, 2011), xxiv–xxvi.
40. Pinker, *Better Angels*, xxi.
41. Scott Cowdell, *René Girard and Secular Modernity* (Notre Dame, IN: University of Notre Dame Press, 2013), 59–60.

the biblical message of love and renunciation of violence that triggered the change of trajectory from medieval to modern in which sympathy for the victim spreads from the gospel message to the Enlightenment, and on to us who live after modernity.

While all religions encourage compassion and actionable empathy, it is not just biblical religions, it is Christianity and Judaism and their Western heritage go beyond compassion. According to Gil Bailie, "The empathy for victims—*as victims*—is specifically Western and quintessentially biblical. The burr under the saddle of 'Western' culture, the source of its moral uneasiness and social restlessness, is precisely this growing empathy for victims. Most of the West's political innovations are linked to it, and our most deeply held social and moral sensibilities are suffused with it."[42] Bailie attributes the West's often quixotic interventions in the world in places such as Somalia or the Balkans in the wake of Yugoslavia's disintegration to this sympathy for the victim modeled after Mother Teresa (Bailie notes a combination of Mother Teresa and John Wayne in these muscular, compassionate interventions). Such sympathy results from the history of the biblical heritage expanding and transforming the West's view of how we should treat others—and a sometimes abandonment of realpolitik, so powerful are the photographic and TV images of the civilian victims of cluster bombs and man-made famine. Bailie writes, "The fact is that the concern for victims has gradually become the principal moral gyroscope in the Western world. Even the most vicious campaigns of victimization—including, astonishingly, even Hitler's—have found it necessary to base their assertion of moral legitimacy on the claim that their goal was the protection or vindication of victims."[43] Select your own examples if you don't remember Hitler's "concern" and "empathy" for the German-speaking res-

---

42. Gil Bailie, *Violence Unveiled: Humanity at the Crossroads* (New York: Crossroad, 1995), 19.
43. Bailie, *Violence*, 20.

idents of the Sudetenland and putative victims of Czechoslovakia, Vladimir Putin's crocodile tears for the Russian-speaking citizens of eastern Ukraine and Crimea, and Tojo's assertion that Japan needed to spread its own moral principles contrary to Western morals in order to save fellow Asians from Western corruption.

Pinker's view of human nature is radically different from Girard's. For Pinker, humans can use their reason to rearrange the institutions of society (media, educational, religious, familial, national, governmental, and commercial) to decrease the incidence of violent behavior. For example, the idea that humans have basic rights is a result of modernity.[44] While Girard is more Freudian when it comes to human nature, Pinker is clearly more Lockean. We are hardwired for violence, says Pinker, but we have countervailing impulses (such as empathy and cost-benefit analysis) that "under the right circumstances—impel us toward peace, like compassion, fairness, self-control, and reason."[45] But it isn't just circumstances but our own rationality that can change our views to rid our societies of "human sacrifice, witch hunts, blood libels, inquisitions, and ethnic scapegoating," as well as "slavery, despotism, torture, religious persecution, cruelty to animals, harshness to children, violence against women, frivolous wars, and the persecution of homosexuals."[46] Pinker, who has few kind comments for religious belief, even notes that some thinkers attribute this decline in so many different measures of violence to divine providence: "I can easily resist the temptation, but agree that the multiplicity of datasets in which violence meanders downward is a puzzle worth pondering."[47] I want to provide an alternative to Girard's explanation of the decline of violence. But note that the two theories aren't necessarily in opposition, as Pinker himself notes. Divine provi-

44. Pinker, *Better Angels*, 475.
45. Pinker, *Better Angels*, 483.
46. Pinker, *Better Angels*, 690–91.
47. Pinker, *Better Angels*, 694.

dence or continuing reverberations from the Christian revelation could be the force behind what Pinker documents, even if Pinker doesn't think much of the hypothesis.

I differ from Girard and England in that they are focused on violence, I on the victims of violence. Both of them pronounce in favor of pacifism, a universal dedication to a refusal of violence (even though both admit to exceptions to that rule). My rule would be more pragmatic: we have an obligation to protect the victims of violence and aggression when it can be done, even if violence is required to do so. Some may object that such a rule establishes Western nations or the United States as the policeman or moral nanny of the world. So be it. Some would correctly observe that the United States or Western European colonial nations have hardly been historical paragons of pacific policy toward other nations and peoples. Lessons from the past can be learned and liberty granted in the future to that gospel time-bomb of peace. My central argument here is that in the difference of emphasis between violence or victims of violence, the crux of moral decision making, could make a vast difference when evaluating the morality of force, sometimes making violent intervention a moral necessity.

I have already referred to Joseph Spencer's idea that the Book of Mormon is intentionally designed to be inconvenient, to upset our expectations and reorient our world.[48] Its purpose is to disorient its reader to reorient differently. A sacred discontent is evident in the Book of Mormon text as much as in the Bible, a discontent with human thoughts, aspirations, and works. Alma says to Korihor that the prophets, the scriptures, "yea, and all things denote there is a God; yea, even the earth, and all things that are upon the face of it" witness the existence of God.[49] But all our human, all too human attempts to domesticate the divine, to harness divinity,

---

48. Joseph M. Spencer, "René Girard and Mormon Scripture," *Dialogue: A Journal of Mormon Thought* 43, no. 3 (Fall 2010): 6.
49. Alma 30:44.

to contain and understand it work only partially as we see and understand partially in this phase of mortality—through a glass, darkly. The Book of Mormon is an abundant event that escapes our attempts to pin it down and put its force behind our own purposes. This reservation is as true of my own readings of the scripture as they are of anyone else's. The text is so bountiful that my readings, too, inevitably show only one aspect or perspective of the abundance and fall short of the glory with which the Book of Mormon is infused.

We encounter the same problem with reading the New Testament and the Hebrew Bible; they can be mistaken for simple narratives that self-interpret and require little work from the reader, but they too are abundant events that overtop our efforts to confine them and pin them down. Peter (the foremost of Christ's disciples), in many ways, prefigures every other follower of Christ.[50] But Peter is himself an ambivalent character. At the end of the gospel of John, Peter should be at his apex. As the leader of a nascent group of followers that will become a great church and expand into the entire globe, Peter will boldly declare the gospel even at the cost of beatings, imprisonment, and death. Instead of immediately going about the work of the church after the resurrection of Christ, Peter decides to "go a fishing," and the disciples with him follow him.[51] Having caught no fish all night, the disciples see Jesus on the shore, not recognizing him. The Lord tells them where to catch fish, and this triggers insight. Peter dives off the boat and swims to greet the Savior. When the disciples come ashore, Jesus already has a fire going with fish and bread ready to eat. The key narrative element is the charcoal fire: "As soon then as they were

---

50. The literary connection between Peter's betrayal of Christ in John 18 and the fishing expedition in John 21 is a commonplace of Johannine scholarship. See Mark A. Matson, "Feed My Sheep: The Pastoral and Ecclesial Conclusion to John's Gospel," *Leaven* 24, no. 2 (2016): 1–6, and P. J. Hartin, "The Role of Peter in the Fourth Gospel," *Neotestamentica* 24, no. 1 (1990): 49–61.
51. John 21:3.

come to land, they saw a fire of coals (ἀνθρακιὰν, *anthrakia*) there, and fish laid thereon, and bread."[52] After dining, Jesus addresses Peter three times: "Simon, son of Jonas, lovest (*agapas*) thou me more than these?"[53] The Greek word *agape* comes from a root that means the highest form of self-sacrificing love exemplified by God when the same gospel asserts that "God so loved (*ēgapēsen*) the world that he gave his only begotten Son."[54] But Peter asserts, "Yea, Lord; thou knowest that I love (*philo*) thee."[55] *Philo* is a different Greek word for love, so there isn't a complete correspondence between the love Jesus is trying to teach Peter and that under-stood by Peter (although I doubt Jesus was teaching Peter a Greek philological lesson). Jesus is trying to teach Peter the kind of love that will be required of his new leadership position in the absence of the Lord. "Feed (*boske*) my lambs" is the Lord's rejoinder.

A second time Jesus poses the question to Peter: "Simon, son of Jonas, lovest (*agapas*) thou me?"[56] Puzzled, no doubt, at the repetition of the question, Peter answers with the same verb he used before: "Yea, Lord; thou knowest that I love (*philo*) thee." The injunction again is to "Feed my sheep"; the verb isn't *boskō*, as it is the first and the third time. Instead, it is *poimainō*, which means something more like "shepherd my sheep." Peter's pride was likely wounded at the third iteration of the question, but the verbs in the question and the answer show that Peter hasn't clued into the point Jesus is making: divine love requires sharing that amity as broadly as possible, not just between teacher and disciple but with as large a circle as can be taught and discipled. "He saith unto him the third time, Simon, son of Jonas, lovest (*phileis*) thou me? Peter was grieved because he said unto him the third time, Lovest

---

52. John 21:9.
53. John 21:15.
54. John 3:16.
55. John 21:15.
56. John 21:16.

(*phileis*) thou me?" Peter's love is affectionate and cherishing of his master, but Jesus wants a higher love from the first disciple, one that serves and sacrifices for the beloved, even if Jesus must adapt the verb to Peter's more constricted notion of love.[57]

What could have been Peter's moment of triumph is instead one of a three-fold rebuke that he needs to be reoriented (Peter still needs conversion, as do we all) to serve more deeply. Jesus drives the point home: "Verily, verily, I say unto thee, When thou wast young, thou girdedst thyself, and walkedst whither thou wouldest: but when thou shalt be old, thou shalt stretch forth thy hands, and another shall gird thee, and carry thee whither thou wouldest not."[58] In God's service to the sheep of the fold, Peter will need to be buoyed up and carried by Deity rather than dressing and directing himself. Peter's will and desires need to be fixed on another cardinal point from their current alignment, a change of magnetic poles that is going to profoundly disorient him yet. Peter feels reproved, and he should. Peter is still becoming rather than having arrived as we all are still in process, still undergoing divinization.

The charcoal fire and the three-fold rebuke on the shores of the Sea of Galilee are the two key elements that allude to another passage in the Gospel of John. The story of Peter in the house of Caiaphas contains those two features and the two passages should be read as interlocking companion narratives. Peter is snuck into the house of the high priest as Jesus is undergoing his trial ritual. In the cold, as a group huddles around a charcoal fire, Peter is questioned about his affiliation with the defendant: "And the servants and officers stood there, who had made a fire of coals (*anthrakia*);

---

57. I am not sure that the Gospel writer expects Peter, this Galilean fisherman, to be a Greek-language philologist, but the writer does seem to expect more expansive emotional sophistication out of his reader. Words are not the lesson here: the concept of love is.

58. John 21:18.

for it was cold: and they warmed themselves: and Peter stood with them, and warmed himself."[59] As they stood there a damsel questioned Peter, "Art not thou also one of this man's disciples? He saith, I am not."[60] A second time Peter is confronted about his relationship to Jesus: "And Simon Peter stood and warmed himself. They said therefore unto him, Art not thou also one of his disciples? He denied it, and said, I am not."[61] A third time the question is posed, "Did not I see thee in the garden with him?"[62] Set around a fire of coals, Peter denies Christ thrice. This is the same Peter who in another gospel asserts he would die first before denying Jesus.[63] On the shores of the Sea of Galilee Peter stood triumphant, the new leader of an *ekklesia* and doctrine he will from this point nurture to envelop the world. But Jesus's three-fold question not only teaches him something about the kind of love that will be required, but also reminds him of his greatest failure, his inability to stand by Jesus in Caiaphus's residence. Without the grace and support of God's power, Peter isn't up to the task for "another shall [yet] gird thee, and carry thee whither thou wouldest not."[64] Our own attempts to shape our futures and destiny are rough-hewn compared to the job divinity can perform on us.

Peter is the first of the disciples to recognize Christ's identity, and Christ calls Peter his rock. Just as Greek, Latin and most modern languages connect the name *Peter* with the word *rock*, the Aramaic word for Peter, *kephas*, means an ordinary stone, which has the same root as the name of the former Jewish high priest—Caiaphas. The Caiaphas principle applies to Peter and the disciples as much as it applies to the high priest in the willingness to

---

59. John 18:18.
60. John 18:16.
61. John 18:25.
62. John 18:26.
63. Mark 14:31.
64. John 21:18.

sacrifice the one so the nation can be saved.[65] That makes Peter, and us, not just the rock through which revelation will continue in the church; Peter is also the stumbling block in addition to being the cornerstone.[66] Peter will be the stone, the foundation, of the church, but he is at that point the stumbling block. Each believer has the potential to be both, even concurrently. The message Peter is called to share is more abundant than Peter's ability or understanding yet unrealized. The message we are called to read and enact is more abundant than our comprehension and reading capability. It overbrims our cups meant to hold and contain the word no matter how large the cups we bring to the communion, and even if we borrow all the vessels we can from our neighbors, the abundance would still fill to the brim and overflow.[67]

René Girard is a useful guide in reading the scriptures; he helps us see aspects of the text that we have not yet understood, to notice moral imperatives that escape our view. Even Girard's astute readings shouldn't be taken as scripture. My default tendency as a reader of scripture is to let scripture correct the reader rather than the other way around. If one permits Girard to correct the Bible or the Book of Mormon, then one can easily see which text is being taken as foundational. "It is also an important implication of Girard's theory itself that religious practitioners, and by extension scholars of religion, could not have penetrated the mysteries that have remained hidden, until he revealed them,"[68] as Trevor L. Jordan writes. For Girard, all religion, even Christian religion, is at base obfuscation and concealment—concealment that Girard seeks to overcome of these deceptions propagated since the foundation of the world. Girard helps us capture a part

---

65. Bailie, *Violence Unveiled*, 273.

66. Bailie, *Violence Unveiled*, 274–75.

67. 2 Kings 4:1–7.

68. Trevor L. Jordan, "Scapegoating Girard: Violence and the Future of Religion," *St. Mark's Review* 202 (2007): 33–34.

of the divine excess we experience in the Bible and the Book of Mormon; he helps us understand our own implication in violence and endorsement of aggression so we can better renounce war and proclaim peace as we embrace and embody the divine initiative and revelation.

Bibliography

Adams, Rebecca. "Narrative Voice and Unimaginability of the Utopian 'Feminine' in Le Guin's *The Left Hand of Darkness* and 'The Ones Who Walk away from Omelas.'" *Utopian Studies* 2, nos. 1–2 (1991): 35–47.

Alexis-Baker, Andy. "Violence, Nonviolence and the Temple Incident in John 2:13–15." *Biblical Interpretation* 20 (2012): 73–96.

Alonso, Luis Enrique and Carlos J. Fernández Rodríguez. "Debt and Sacrifice: The Role of Scapegoats in the Economic Crisis." *Religions* 12 (2021): Available at https://doi.org/10.3390/rel12020128.

Alter, Robert. *The Art of Biblical Narrative.* New York: Basic, 1981.

Alter, Robert. *The World of Biblical Literature.* New York: Basic, 1992.

Amit, Yairah. "The Dual Causality Principle and Its Effects on Biblical Literature." *Vetus Testamentum* 37, no. 4 (1987): 385–400.

St. Augustine. *The City of God.* Translated by Henry Bettenson. New York: Penguin, 1984.

Aus, Roger David. "The Death of One for All in John 11:45–54 in Light of Judaic Traditions." In *Barabbas and Esther and Other Studies in the Judaic Illumination of Earliest Christianity,* by Roger David Aus, 29–63. Atlanta: Scholars, 1992.

Avioz, Michael. "Divine Intervention and Human Error in the Absalom Narrative." *Journal for the Study of the Old Testament* 37, no. 3 (2013): 339–47.

Bailie, Gil. *Violence Unveiled: Humanity at the Crossroads.* New York: Crossroad, 1995.

Bater, B. Robert. "Apocalyptic Religion in Christian Fundamentalism." In *Curing Violence: Essays on René Girard.* Edited by Mark I. Wallace and Theophus H. Smith, 287–304. Sonoma, CA: Polebridge, 1994.

Batty, J. Clair. "The Atonement: Do Traditional Explanations Make Sense?" *Sunstone* 8 (Nov.–Dec. 1983): 11–16.

Beardsworth, Richard. "Logics of Violence: Religion and the Practice of Philosophy." *Cultural Values* 4, no. 2 (2000): 137–66.

Becerra, Daniel. "The Biblical Canon." *The Bible and the Latter-day Saint Tradition*. Edited by Taylor G. Petry, Cory Crawford, and Eric A. Eliason. Salt Lake City, UT: University of Utah Press, 2023. 117–28.

Berlin, Isaiah. *The Hedgehog and the Fox: An Essay on Tolstoy's View of History*. New York: Touchstone, 1986.

Boreas, George. René Girard IX: Origin of Kings. Available at https://www.georgeboreas.com/blog/ren-girard-ix-origin-of-kings.

Bottum, J. "Girard among the Girardians." *First Things* 61 (1996): 42–45. Available at http://www.firstthings.com/ftissues/ft9603/revessay.html.

Boyce, Duane. *Even Unto Bloodshed: An LDS Perspective on War*. Salt Lake City, UT: Greg Kofford Books, 2015.

Boyce, Duane. "Were the Ammonites Pacifists?" *Journal of the Book of Mormon and Other Restoration Scripture* 18, no. 1 (2009): 32–47.

Brooks, Joanna. "Racist Remarks By Popular BYU Religion Professor Sparks Controversy." *Religion Dispatches* (February 29, 2012), available at https://religiondispatches.org/racist-remarks-by-popular-byu-religion-professor-spark-controversy/.

Bushman, Richard. "The Lamanite View of Book of Mormon History." In *By Study and Also By Faith*. Vol. 2. Edited by John M. Lundquist and Stephen D. Ricks, 52–72. Salt Lake City and Provo, UT: Deseret Book and FARMS, 1990.

Butchart, Garnet C. "An Excess of Signification: Or, What Is an Event?" *Semiotica* 187, no. 1–4 (2011): 291–307.

Chilton, Bruce. *Abraham's Curse: Child Sacrifice in the Legacies of the West*. New York: Doubleday, 2008.

Chilton, Bruce. "René Girard, James Williams, and the Genesis of Violence." *Bulletin for Biblical Research* 3 (1993): 17–29.

Church of Jesus Christ of Latter-day Saints. "Race and the Priesthood." Gospel Topics Essays. available at https://www.churchofjesuschrist.org/study/manual/gospel-topics-essays/race-and-the-priesthood.

Cohen, Michael. *Murder Most Fair: The Appeal of Mystery Fiction*. Teaneck, NJ: Fairleigh Dickinson University Press, 2000.

Collins, John J. "The Zeal of Phinehas: The Bible and the Legitimation of Violence." *Journal of Biblical Literature* 122, no. 1 (2003): 3–21.

Collins, Robin. "Girard and Atonement: An Incarnational Theory of Mimetic Participation." In *Violence Renounced: René Girard, Biblical Studies, and Peacemaking*, Studies in Peace and Scriptures. Vol. 4. Edited by Willard M. Swartley, 132–53. Telford, PA: Pandora, 2000.

Cowdell, Scott. *René Girard and Secular Modernity*. Notre Dame, IN: University of Notre Dame Press, 2013.

Daly, Robert J. Foreword to *Must There Be Scapegoats? Violence and Redemption in the Bible*. Raymund Schwager, v–viii. Translated by Maria L. Assad. San Francisco: Harper & Row, 1987.

Daube, David. *The Exodus Pattern in the Bible*. London: Faber and Faber, 1963.

Davies, Douglas. "Gethsemane and Calvary in LDS Soteriology." *Dialogue: A Journal of Mormon Thought* 34, nos. 3–4 (Fall–Winter 2001): 19–25.

Denning, Steve. "The Myth of Moral Equivalence: The Battle for the Soul of America." *Forbes* (Oct. 29, 2018): Available at https://www.forbes.com/sites/stevedenning/2018/10/29/the-myth-of-moral-equivalence-the-battle-for-the-soul-of-america/.

Dionne, E. J., Jr. "Moral Equivalence and Donald Trump." *Washington Post* (Sept. 10, 2016): Available at https://www.washingtonpost.com/blogs/post-partisan/wp/2016/09/10/moral-equivalence-and-donald-trump/.

Dostoevsky, Fyodor. *The Brothers Karamazov*. Translated by David McDuff. New York: Penguin, 1993.

"East Timor Genocide." *Wikipedia*. (Sept. 30, 2023). Available at https://en.wikipedia.org/wiki/East_Timor_genocide.

England, Eugene. "Can Nations Love Their Enemies? An L.D.S. Theology of Peace." In *Dialogues with Myself: Personal Essays on Mormon Experience*. Eugene England, 135–52. Midvale, UT: Orion, 1984.

England, Eugene. "Fasting and Food, Not Weapons: A Mormon Response to Conflict." *BYU Studies* 25, no. 1 (Winter 1985): 1–14.

England, Eugene. "Healing and Making Peace—In the World and the Church." *Sunstone* 15, no. 6 (Dec. 1991): 36–46.

England, Eugene. "Hugh Nibley as Cassandra." *BYU Studies* 30, no. 4 (1990): 104–16.

England, Eugene. "Late Night Thoughts at the End of a War." *Dialogue: A Journal of Mormon Thought* 24, no. 2 (Summer 1991): 7–9. Also available at Eugene England Foundation, eugeneengland.org/wp-content/uploads/sbi/articles/1991_1_001.pdf.

England, Eugene. *Making Peace: Personal Essays.* Salt Lake City, UT: Signature, 1995.

England, Eugene. "Moroni and His Captains: Men of Peace in a Time of War." *Ensign* 7, no. 8 (Aug. 1977): 28–36. Available at https://churchofjesuschrist.org/study/ensign/1977/09/Moroni-and-his-captains-men-of-peace-in-a-time-of-war.

England, Eugene. "My View: Was Chamberlain Right?" *Deseret News* (Sept. 28, 1988): Available at https://www.deseret.com/1988/9/29/18779600/my-view-was-chamberlain-right.

England, Eugene. "On Finding Truth and God." In *Why the Church Is as True as the Gospel: Personal Essays on Mormon Experience.* Eugene England, 109–23. Salt Lake: Bookcraft, 1986.

England, Eugene. "A Second Witness for the *Logos*: The Book of Mormon and Contemporary Literary Criticism." In *By Study and Also By Faith: Nibley Festschrift.* Vol. 2. Ed. by John M. Lundquist and Stephen D. Ricks, 91–125. Salt Lake and Provo, UT: Deseret and FARMS, 1990.

England, Eugene. "The Tragedy of Vietnam and the Responsibility of Mormons." Eugene England Foundation. Available at eugeneengland.org/wp-content/uploads/sbi/articles/1967_e_001.pdf. First published in *Dialogue: A Journal of Mormon Thought* 2, no. 4 (Winter 1967): 65–100 [pages 71–91 for England's contribution to the roundtable].

England, Eugene. "The Weeping God of Mormonism." *Dialogue: A Journal of Mormon Thought* 35, no. 1 (2002): 63–80.

England, Eugene. "Why Nephi Killed Laban: Reflections on the Truth of the Book of Mormon." *Dialogue: A Journal of Mormon Thought* 22, no. 3 (Fall 1989): 32–51.

England, Eugene. *Why The Church Is as True as the Gospel: Personal Essays on Mormon Experience.* Salt Lake City, UT: Bookcraft, 1986.

Evans, Carl D. "Naram-Sin and Jeroboam: The Archetypal *Unheilsherrscher* in Mesopotamian and Biblical Historiography." In *Scripture in Context II: More Essays on the Comparative Method.*

Edited by William W. Hallo, James C. Moyer, and Leo G. Perdue, 97–125. Winona Lake, IN: Eisenbrauns, 1983.

FARMS. "Better That One Man Perish." In *Pressing Forward with the Book of Mormon: FARMS Updates of the 1990s.* Edited by John W. Welch and Melvin J. Thorne, 17–19. Provo: FARMS, 1999, 17–19. This material is also in *Echoes and Evidences of the Book of Mormon.* Edited by Donald W. Parry, Daniel C. Peterson, and John W. Welch, 356–57. Provo: FARMS, 2002

Feldman, Karen S. "On Girard's Biblical Realism." In *Mimesis, Desire, and the Novel: René Girard and Literary Criticism.* Edited by Pierpaolo Antonello and Heather Webb, 55–67. East Lansing: Michigan State University Press, 2015.

Fleming, Chris. *René Girard: Violence and Mimesis.* Malden, MA: Polity, 2004.

Foord, Martin. "The 'Epistle of Straw': Reflections on Luther and the Epistle of James." *Themelios* 45, no. 2 (August 2020): Available at https://www.thegospelcoalition.org/themelios/article/the-epistle-of-straw-reflections-on-luther-and-the-epistle-of-james/.

Fox, E. "Stalking the Younger Brother: Some Models for Understanding a Biblical Motif." *Journal for the Study of the Old Testament* 60 (1993): 45–68.

Frazier, James G. *Folklore in the Old Testament.* Abridged ed. New York: Avenel, 1988 [1923].

Friedman, Richard Elliott. *Who Wrote the Bible?* New York: Summit, 1987.

Girard, René. "Are the Gospels Mythical?" *First Things* 62 (April 1996): 27–31. Available at http://www.firstthings.com/ftissues/ft9604/girard.html.

Girard, René. "The Bible Is Not a Myth." *Literature and Belief* 4 (1984): 7–15.

Girard, René. *Deceit, Desire, and the Novel: Self and Other in Literary Structure.* Translated by Yvonne Freccero. Baltimore: Johns Hopkins University Press, 1965.

Girard, René. "The First Stone." *Renascence* 52, no. 1 (Fall 1999): 5–17.

Girard, René. "The Founding Murder in the Philosophy of Nietzsche." In *Violence and Truth: On the Works of René Girard.* Edited by Paul Dumouchel, 227–46. Stanford: Stanford University Press, 1988.

Girard, René. *I See Satan Fall Like Lightning*. Translated by James G. Williams. Maryknoll, NY: Orbis, 2001.

Girard, René. *Job: The Victim of His People*. Translated by Yvonne Freccero. Stanford: Stanford University Press, 1985.

Girard, René. "Nietzsche versus the Crucified." In *The Girard Reader*. Edited by James G. Williams, 243–61. New York: Crossroad, 1996.

Girard, René. *Notes from the Underground: Feodor Dostoevski*. Edited and translated by James G. Williams. East Lansing: Michigan State University Press, 2012.

Girard, René. *The Scapegoat*. Translated by Yvonne Freccero. Baltimore: Johns Hopkins University Press, 1986.

Girard, René. "The Scapegoat as Historical Referent." In *The Girard Reader*. Edited by James G. Williams, 97–106. New York: Crossroad, 1996.

Girard, René. *A Theater of Envy: William Shakespeare*. New York: Oxford University Press, 1991.

Girard, René. *Things Hidden Since the Foundation of the World*. Translated by Stephen Bann and Michael Metteer. Stanford: Stanford University Press, 1987.

Girard, René. *Violence and the Sacred*. Translated by Patrick Gregory. Baltimore: Johns Hopkins University Press, 1972.

Girard, René. *When These Things Begin: Conversations with Michel Treguer*. Translated by Trevor Cribben Merrill. East Lansing: Michigan State University Press, 2014.

Givens, Terryl. *People of Paradox: A History of Mormon Culture*. New York: Oxford University Press, 2007.

Givens, Terryl. *Stretching the Heavens: The Life of Eugene England and the Crisis of Modern Mormonism*. Chapel Hill, NC: University of North Carolina Press, 2021.

Givens, Terryl and Fiona Givens. *The God Who Weeps: How Mormonism Makes Sense of Life*. Salt Lake City, UT: Ensign Peak, 2012.

Goff, Alan. "Boats, Beginnings, and Repetitions." *Journal of Book of Mormon Studies* 1 (1992): 67–84.

Goff, Alan. "How Then Should We Read? Reading Mormon Scripture after the Fall." *FARMS Review* 21, no. 1 (2009): 137–78.

Goff, Alan. "The Plagiary of the Daughters of the Lamanites." *Interpreter: A Journal of Latter-day Saint Faith and Scholarship* 61 (2024): 57–96.

Available at https://journal.interpreterfoundation.org/the-plagiary-of-the-daughters-of-the-lamanites/.

Goff, Alan. "Types of Repetition and Shadows of History in Hebraic Narrative," *Interpreter: A Journal of Latter-day Saint Faith and Scholarship* 45 (2021): 263–318. Available at https://journal.interpreterfoundation.org/types-of-repetition-and-shadows-of-history-in-hebraic-narrative/.

Goff, Alan. "Uncritical Theory and Thin Description: The Resistance to History." *Review of Books on the Book of Mormon* 7, no. 1 (1995): 170–207.

Golsan, Richard J. *René Girard and Myth: An Introduction.* New York: Garland, 1993.

Goodhart, Sandor. "'al lo-chamas asah' (*although he had done no violence*)': René Girard and the Innocent Victim." In *Violence Renounced: René Girard, Biblical Studies, and Peacemaking.* Studies in Peace and Scriptures. Vol. 4. Edited by Willard M. Swartley, 200–217. Telford, PA: Pandora, 2000.

Goodhart, Sandor. "The End of Sacrifice: Reading René Girard and the Hebrew Bible." *Contagion: Journal of Violence, Mimesis and Culture* 14 (2007): 58–78.

Goodhart, Sandor. "'I Am Joseph': René Girard and the Prophetic Law." In *Violence and Truth: On the Works of René Girard.* Edited by Paul Dumouchel, 53–74. Stanford: Stanford University Press, 1988.

Goodhart, Sandor and Ann W. Astell. "Substitutive Reading: An Introduction to Girardian Thinking, Its Reception in Biblical Studies, and This Volume." In *Sacrifice, Scripture, and Substitution.* Edited by Ann W. Astell and Sandor Goodhart, 1–36. Notre Dame, IN: University of Notre Dame Press, 2011.

Grant. John 11:49f. https://versebyversecommentary.com/2017/11/13/john-1149f/.

Grimsrud, Ted. "Scapegoating No More: Christian Pacifism and New Testament Views of Jesus' Death." In *Violence Renounced: René Girard, Biblical Studies, and Peacemaking.* Studies in Peace and Scriptures. Vol. 4. Edited by Willard M. Swartley, 49–69. Telford, PA: Pandora, 2000.

Greenspahn, Fredrick E. *When Brothers Dwell Together: The Preeminence of Younger Siblings in the Hebrew Bible.* New York: Oxford University Press, 1994.

Grossman, Jonathan. "The Design of the 'Dual Causality' Principle in the Narrative of Absalom's Rebellion." *Biblica* 88, no. 4 (2007): 558–66.

Gruesser, John. "Never Bet the Detective (or His Creator) Your Head: Character Rivalry, Authorial Sleight of Hand, and Generic Fluidity in Detective Fiction." *The Edgar Allan Poe Review* 9, no. 1 (Spring 2008): 5–23.

Gustavson, Mark S. "Scriptural Horror and the Divine Will." *Dialogue: A Journal of Mormon Thought* 21, no. 1 (Spring 1988): 70–83.

Haglund, Kristine L. *Eugene England: A Mormon Liberal*. Urbana, IL: University of Illinois Press, 2021.

Hamerton-Kelly, Robert G. *The Gospel and the Sacred: Poetics of Violence in Mark*. Minneapolis, MN: Fortress, 1994.

Halpern, Baruch. *The First Historians: The Hebrew Bible and History*. San Francisco: Harper and Row, 1988.

Hamerton-Kelly, Robert G. *Sacred Violence: Paul's Hermeneutic of the Cross*. Minneapolis, MN: Fortress, 1992.

Hansen, Lorin K. "The 'Moral' Atonement as a Mormon Interpretation." *Dialogue: A Journal of Mormon Thought* 27, no. 1 (Spring 1994): 195–227.

Hardin, Michael, ed. *Reading the Bible with René Girard: Conversations with Steven E. Berry*. Lancaster, PA: JDL, 2015.

Hardin, Michael. "Sacrificial Language in Hebrews: Reappraising René Girard." In *Violence Renounced: René Girard, Biblical Studies, and Peacemaking*. Studies in Peace and Scriptures. Vol. 4. Edited by Willard M. Swartley, 103–19. Telford, PA: Pandora, 2000.

Hartin, P. J. "The Role of Peter in the Fourth Gospel." *Neotestamentica* 24, no. 1 (1990): 49–61.

"International Force East Timor." *Wikipedia*, https://en.wikipedia.org/wiki/International_Force_East_Timor.

Jenkins, Philip. *Laying Down the Sword: Why We Can't Ignore the Bible's Violent Verses*. New York: HarperCollins, 2011.

Jerryson, Michael and Mark Juergensmeyer, ed. *Buddhist Warfare*. New York: Oxford University Press, 2010.

Johns, Loren L. "'A Better Sacrifice' or 'Better Than Sacrifice'? Response to Michael Hardin's 'Sacrificial Language in Hebrews.'" In *Violence Renounced: René Girard, Biblical Studies, and Peacemaking*. Studies in Peace and Scriptures. Vol. 4. Edited by Willard M. Swartley, 120–31. Telford, PA: Pandora, 2000.

Jordan, Trevor L. "Scapegoating Girard: Violence and the Future of Religion." *St. Mark's Review* 202 (2007): 31–38.

Josephus, Flavius. "Antiquities of the Jews." *The Life and Works of Flavius Josephus*. Translated by William Whiston. Grand Rapids, MI: Baker, 1974 reprint.

Kaplan, Grant. *René Girard, Unlikely Apologist: Mimetic Theory and Fundamental Theology*. Notre Dame, IN: University of Notre Dame Press, 2016.

Kass, Leon R. *The Beginning of Wisdom: Reading Genesis*. New York: Free Press, 2003.

Katzoff, Charlotte. "Divine Causality and Moral Responsibility in the Story of Joseph and His Brothers." *IYYUN: The Jerusalem Philosophical Quarterly* 47 (Jan. 1998): 21–40.

Kearney, Richard. *Anatheism [Returning to God after God]*. New York: Columbia University Press, 2010.

Keats, John. *The Letters of John Keats*. Edited by H. E. Rollins. 2 vols. Cambridge, UK: Cambridge University Press, 1958. Vol. 1. https://books.google.com/books?id=Hx_fFPMTzvIC.

Keijzer, Nico. "A Girardian View of the Criminal Justice System." Available at https://www.girard.nl/texts_online/k/Keijzer_Nico_2.pdf.

Keim, Paul. "Reading Ancient Near Eastern Literature from the Perspective of Girard's Scapegoat Theory." In *Violence Renounced: René Girard, Biblical Studies, and Peacemaking*. Studies in Peace and Scriptures. Vol. 4. Edited by Willard M. Swartley, 157–77. Telford, PA: Pandora, 2000.

Kerr, Fergus. "Revealing the Scapegoat Mechanism: Christianity after Girard." In *Philosophy, Religion and the Spiritual Life*. Royal Institute of Philosophy Supplement 32. Edited by Michael McGhee, 161–75. Cambridge: Cambridge University Press, 1992.

Kierkegaard, Soren. *The Crowd Is Untruth*. Translated by Charles K. Bellinger. Grand Rapids, MI: Christian Classics Ethereal Library, (written in 1847). Available at https://www.ccel.org/ccel/k/kierkegaard/untruth/cache/untruth.pdf.

Kula, Irwin. Obey God or Question God? Abraham's responses to the destruction of Sodom and Gemorrah and to the command to Sacrifice Isaac provide two conflicting models. *My Jewish Learning*. Available at https://www.myjewishlearning.com/article/autonomy-vs-heteronomy-in-the-covenantal-relationship/.

Larsen, Val. "Killing Laban: The Birth of Sovereignty in the Nephite Constitutional Order." *Journal of Book of Mormon Studies* 16, no. 1 (2007): 26–41.

Lasine, Stuart. "Manasseh as Villain and Scapegoat." In *The New Literary Criticism and the Hebrew Bible*. Edited by J. Cheryl Exum and David J. A. Clines, 163–83. Valley Forge, PA: Trinity Press International, 1994.

Lee, Poong-in. "Is an Anti-sacrificial Reading of Hebrews Plausible?" In *Sacrifice, Scripture, and Substitution*. Edited by Ann W. Astell and Sandor Goodhart, 424–44. Notre Dame, IN: University of Notre Dame Press, 2011.

Lefebure, Leo D. *Revelation, the Religions, and Violence*. Maryknoll, NY: Orbis, 2000.

Livingston, Paisley. *Models of Desire: René Girard and the Psychology of Mimesis*. Baltimore: Johns Hopkins University Press, 1992.

Lohr, Joel N. "'So YHWH Established a Sign for Cain': Rethinking Genesis 4,15." *Zeitschrift für die Alttestamentliche Wissenschaft* 121, no. 1 (Mar. 2009): 101–103.

Mabee, Charles. "Un/rivaling the Old Testament: Before the Law." In *Curing Violence: Essays on René Girard*. Edited by Mark I. Wallace and Theophus H. Smith, 100–17. Sonoma, CA: Polebridge, 1994.

Marion, Jean-Luc. *Being Given: Toward a Phenomenology of Givenness*. Translated by Jeffrey L. Kosky. Stanford: Stanford University Press, 2002.

Marion, Jean-Luc. *In Excess: Studies in Saturated Phenomena*. Translated by Robyn Horner and Vincent Berraud. New York: Fordham University Press, 2002.

Mason, Patrick Q. *The Mormon Menace: Violence and Anti-Mormonism in the Postbellum South*. New York: Oxford University Press, 2011.

Mason, Patrick Q. and J. David Pulsipher. *Proclaim Peace: The Restoration's Answer to an Age of Conflict*. Provo, UT: BYU Maxwell Institute/ Deseret, 2021.

Matson, Mark A. "Feed My Sheep: The Pastoral and Ecclesial Conclusion to John's Gospel," *Leaven* 24, no. 2 (2016): 1–6.

McKenna, Andrew J. *Violence and Difference: Girard, Derrida, and Deconstruction*. Urbana: University of Illinois Press, 1992.

McMahon, Edward. "Violence-Religion-Law: A Girardian Analysis." In *Curing Violence: Essays on René Girard*. Edited by Mark I. Wallace and Theophus H. Smith, 182–203. Sonoma, CA: Polebridge, 1994.

McMurrin, Sterling M. *The Theological Foundations of the Mormon Religion*. Salt Lake City, UT: University of Utah Press, 1965.

Meek, Russell L. "Intertextuality, Inner-Biblical Exegesis, and Inner-Biblical Allusion: The Ethics of a Methodology." *Biblica* 95, no. 2 (2014): 280–91.

Meltzer, Françoise. "A Response to René Girard's Reading of Salome." *New Literary History* 15, no. 2 (Winter 1984): 325–32.

Merrill, Byron R. "There Was No Contention." In *The Book of Mormon: Fourth Nephi through Moroni, From Zion to Destruction*. Edited by Monte S. Nyman and Charles D. Tate, Jr., 167–83. Provo, UT: Religious Studies Center, 1995.

Mill, John Stuart. *Utilitarianism*. Edited by Geraint Williams. London: Everyman, 1993 (1861).

Miller, Adam S. "Messianic History: Walter Benjamin and the Book of Mormon." In *Rube Goldberg Machines: Essays in Mormon Theology*. Adam S. Miller, 21–35. Salt Lake City, UT: Kofford Books, 2012.

Miller, Marlin E. "Girardian Perspectives and Christian Atonement." In *Violence Renounced René Girard, Biblical Studies, and Peacemaking*. Studies in Peace and Scriptures Vol. 4. Edited by Willard M. Swartley, 31–48. Telford, PA: Pandora, 2000.

Moberly, R. W. L. "The Mark of Cain—Revealed at Last." *Harvard Theological Review* 100, no.1 (2007): 11–28.

Morgan, Jacob. "The Divine-Infusion Theory: Rethinking the Atonement." *Dialogue: A Journal of Mormon Thought* 39, no. 1 (Spring 2006): 57–81.

Morrill, Susanna. "Finding the Presence in Mormon History: An Interview with Susanna Morrill, Richard Lyman Bushman, and Robert Orsi." *Dialogue: A Journal of Mormon Thought* 44, no. 3 (Fall 2011): 174–87.

Morrison, Stephen D. *Seven Theories of the Atonement Summarized*. Available at https://www.sdmorrison.org/7-theories-of-the-atonement-summarized/.

Morson, Gary Saul. *Hidden in Plain View: Narrative and Creative Potentials in "War and Peace."* Stanford: Stanford University Press, 1987.

The Nation. Caiaphas, Trump, and Moral Bankruptcy. November 27, 2018. https://www.nationthailand.com/lifestyle/30359416.

Nibley, Hugh. "Forever Tentative . . ." In *Since Cumorah*. Second ed., The Collected Works of Hugh Nibley. Volume 7. Hugh Nibley, 213–27. Provo and Salt Lake City, UT: Deseret Book and FARMS, 1988.

North, Robert. "Violence and the Bible: The Girard Connection." *Catholic Biblical Quarterly* 47 (1985): 1–27.

Olsen, Steven L. "The Death of Laban: A Literary Interpretation." *FARMS Review* 21, no. 1 (2009): 179–95.

Orsi, Robert. *Between Heaven and Earth: The Religious Worlds People Make and the Scholars Who Study Them*. Princeton, NJ: Princeton University Press, 2005.

Orsi, Robert A. *History and Presence*. Cambridge, MA: Belknap, 2016.

Ostler, Blake T. "Atonement in Mormon Thought." Personal Website. Available at www.blakeostler.com/docs/AtonementInMormonThought. pdf.

Ostler, Blake T. *Exploring Mormon Thought: The Problems of Theism and the Love of God*. Vol. 2. Salt Lake City: Kofford Books, 2006.

Packer, Boyd K. "The Mediator." *Ensign* (May 1977): 54–55. Available at https://www.lds.org/liahona/2011/04/the-mediator-jesus-Christ, and a video version of this soteriology, called "The Mediator," is available at http://www.lds.org/media-library/video/book-of-mormon-presentations#2007-01-0005-the-mediator.

Panek, LeRoy Lad. *The Origins of the American Detective Story*. Jefferson, NC: McFarland, 2006.

Pinker, Steven. *The Better Angels of Our Nature: Why Violence Has Declined*. New York: Penguin, 2011.

Polzin, Robert. *Samuel and the Deuteronomist: A Literary Study of the Deuteronomic History: 1 Samuel*. San Francisco: Harper & Row, 1989.

Potter, R. Dennis. "Did Christ Pay for Our Sins?" *Dialogue: A Journal of Mormon Thought* 32, no. 4 (Winter 1999): 73–86.

Quinones, Ricardo J. *The Changes of Cain*. Princeton: Princeton University Press, 1991.

Rabase, Angel and Peter Chalk. "The East Timor Crisis and Its Consequences." *Indonesia's Transformation and the Stability of Southeast Asia*. Rand Corporation, Available at https://www.jstor.org/stable/10.7249/mr1344af.12.

Robertson, Stuart D. "Mimesis, Scapegoating, and Philo-Semitism: Reading Feldman and Girard." In *Sacrifice, Scripture, and Substitu-

tion. Edited by Ann W. Astell and Sandor Goodhart, 232–36. Notre Dame, IN: University of Notre Dame Press, 2011.

Sacks, Jonathan. Argument for the Sake of Heaven. *The Rabbi Sacks Legacy*. Available at https://www.chabad.org/parshah/article_cdo/aid/4422484/jewish/Argument-for-the-Sake-of-Heaven.htm.

Schramm, Jan-Melissa. "'Let Us Carve Him as a Feast Fit for the Gods': Girard and Unjust Execution in Nineteenth-Century Narrative." *Mimesis, Desire, and the Novel: Rene Girard and Literary Criticism*. Edited by Pierpaolo Antonello and Heather Webb, 161–74. East Lansing: Michigan State University Press, 2015.

Schwager, Raymund. *Must There Be Scapegoats? Violence and Redemption in the Bible*. Translated by Maria L. Assad. San Francisco: Harper & Row, 1987.

Schwartz, Regina M. *The Curse of Cain: The Violent Legacy of Monotheism*. Chicago: University of Chicago Press, 1997.

Scubla, Lucien. "The Christianity of René Girard and the Nature of Religion." Translated by Mark R. Anspach. In *Violence and Truth: On the Work of René Girard*. Edited by Paul Dumouchel, 160–78. Stanford: Stanford University Press, 1988.

Skinner, Andrew C. "Zion Gained and Lost: Fourth Nephi as the Quintessential Model." In *The Book of Mormon: Fourth Nephi through Moroni, From Zion to Destruction*. Edited by Monte S. Nyman and Charles D. Tate, Jr., 289–302. Provo, UT: Religious Studies Center, 1995.

Snyman, S. D. "Trends in the History of Research on the Problem of Violence in the Old Testament." *Verbum et Ecclesia* 18, no. 1 (1999): 127–45.

Soares, Mica Barreto. "Timor-Leste, 20 Years On." *The Interpreter*. Lowy Institute. Available at https://www.lowyinstitute.org/the-interpreter/timor-leste-20-years.

Sommer, Benjamin D. "Exegesis, Allusion and Intertextuality in the Hebrew Bible: A Response to Lyle Eslinger." *Vetus Testamentum* 46, no. 4 (Oct. 1996): 479–89.

Spencer, Joseph M. *An Other Testament: On Typology*. Salem, OR: Salt, 2012.

Spencer, Joseph M. "René Girard and Mormon Scripture." *Dialogue: A Journal of Mormon Thought* 43, no. 3 (Fall 2010): 6–20.

Stavrakopoulou, Francesca. *God: An Anatomy*. New York: Knopf, 2022.

Stavrakopoulou, Francesca. *King Manasseh and Child Sacrifice: Biblical Distortions of Historical Realities.* Berlin: Walter de Gruyter, 2004.

Stirling, Mack C. "Understanding the Violent Sacred." *Sunstone* 133 (July 2004): 33–35.

Stirling, Mack C. "Violence in the Scriptures: Mormonism and the Cultural Theory of René Girard." *Dialogue: A Journal of Mormon Thought* 43, no. 1 (Spring 2010): 59–105.

Stirling, Mack C. and Scott Burton. "Scandals, Scapegoats, and the Cross: An Interview with René Girard." *Dialogue: A Journal of Mormon Thought* 43, no. 1 (Spring 2010): 107–34.

Sunstein, Cass R. "When Crowds Aren't Wise." *Harvard Business Review* (Sept. 2006): Available at https://hbr.org/2006/09/when-crowds-arent-wise.

Surowiecki, James. *The Wisdom of Crowds: Why the Many Are Smarter Than the Few and How Collective Wisdom Shapes Business, Economies, Societies and Nations.* New York: Anchor, 2004.

Swanson, Tod. "Colonial Violence and Inca Analogies to Christianity." In *Curing Violence: Essays on René Girard.* Edited by Mark I. Wallace and Theophus H. Smith, 121–36. Sonoma, CA: Polebridge, 1994.

Swartley, Willard M. "Discipleship and Imitation of Jesus/Suffering Servant: The Mimesis of New Creation." In *Violence Renounced: René Girard, Biblical Studies, and Peacemaking.* Studies in Peace and Scriptures. Vol. 4, edited by Willard M. Swartley, 218–45. Telford, PA: Pandora, 2000.

Talmage, James E. *Jesus the Christ: A Study of the Messiah and His Mission according to the Holy Scriptures both Ancient and Modern.* Salt Lake City, UT: Deseret, 1976 [1915].

Taysom, Stephen. "Abundant Events or Narrative Abundance: Robert Orsi and the Academic Study of Mormonism." *Dialogue: A Journal of Mormon Thought* 45, no. 2 (Winter 2012): 1–26.

Treisman, Rachel. "5 years after Khashoggi's murder, advocates say the lack of justice is dangerous." *NPR* (Oct. 2, 2023): Available at https://www.npr.org/2023/10/02/1202937036/jamal-khashoggi-mbs-murder-saudi-arabia-human-rights.

Turner, Rodney. "The Lamanite Mark." In *The Book of Mormon: Second Nephi, the Doctrinal Structure.* Edited by Monte S. Nyman and

Charles D. Tate, Jr., 133–57. Provo, UT: BYU Religious Studies Center, 1989.

Tvedtnes, John A. "The Charge of 'Racism' in the Book of Mormon." *FARMS Review* 15, no. 2 (2003): 183–97.

Weaver, J. Denny. *The Nonviolent Atonement*. Second ed. Grand Rapids, MI: Eerdmans, 2011.

Welch, John W. *The Legal Cases in the Book of Mormon*. Provo, UT: BYU Press and Maxwell Institute, 2008.

Welch, John W. "Legal Perspectives on the Slaying of Laban." *Journal of Book of Mormon Studies* 1, no. 1 (1992): 119–41.

Williams, James G. *The Bible, Violence, and the Sacred: Liberation from the Myth of Sanctioned Violence*. San Francisco: Harper, 1991.

Williams, James G. Foreword of *I See Satan Fall Like Lightning*. René Girard, ix–xxiii. Maryknoll, NY: Orbis, 2001.

Williams, James G. "History-Writing as Protest: Kingship and the Beginning of Historical Narrative." *Contagion* 1 (Spring 1994): 91–110.

Williams, James G. "King as Servant, Sacrifice as Service: Gospel Transformations." In *Violence Renounced: René Girard, Biblical Studies, and Peacemaking*. Studies in Peace and Scriptures. Vol. 4. Edited by Willard M. Swartley, 178–99. Telford, PA: Pandora, 2000.

Williams, James G. "Sacrifice, Mimesis, and the Genesis of Violence: A Response to Bruce Chilton." *Bulletin for Biblical Research* 3 (1993): 31–47.

Williams, James G. "'Steadfast Love and Not Sacrifice.'" In *Curing Violence: Essays on René Girard*. Edited by Mark I. Wallace and Theophus H. Smith, 71–99. Sonoma, CA: Polebridge, 1994.

Zakovitch, Yair. *"And You Shall Tell Your Son . . .": The Concept of the Exodus in the Bible*. Jerusalem: Magnes, 1991.

ALAN GOFF earned a bachelor of arts degree with a double major in English and political science from Brigham Young University. He also earned masters' degrees in English and political science (the latter with an emphasis in political philosophy) from BYU. His doctorate was granted by the University at Albany from the Doctor of Arts Program in Humanistic Studies, an interdisciplinary doctoral program with his studies focused on the intersection of philosophy and literary theory. Now retired from the academy, he spent most of his working life as a professor of liberal arts and sciences at DeVry University, teaching humanities, literature, ethics, and composition courses at the Phoenix, Arizona campus.

www.ingramcontent.com/pod-product-compliance
Lightning Source LLC
Chambersburg PA
CBHW061547120626
46550CB00004B/1399